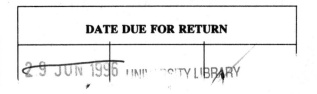

Regulation of Securities
and
Futures Dealing

AUSTRALIA

The Law Book Company
Sydney

CANADA

The Carswell Company
Toronto, Ontario

ISRAEL

Steimatzky's Agency Ltd.
Tel Aviv

PAKISTAN

Pakistan Law House
Karachi

INDIA

N.M. Tripathi (Private) Ltd.
Bombay

Eastern Law House (Private) Ltd.
Calcutta

M.P.P. House
Bangalore

Universal Book Traders
Delhi

Regulation of Securities and Futures Dealing

John R. C. White

*Solicitor and Head of
Conduct of Business,
Securities and Futures Authority*

LONDON
SWEET AND MAXWELL
1992

Published by
Sweet and Maxwell Limited of
South Quay Plaza, 183 Marsh Wall, London E14 9FT;
Computerset by PB Computer Typesetting, Pickering, N. Yorks;
Printed and bound in Great Britain by BPCC Hazell Books,
Aylesbury, Bucks., Member of BPCC Ltd.

**A catalogue for this book is available
from the British Library**

ISBN 0 421 462507 ✓

0186833

Dedication

To

GLENYS and INDIA

Acknowledgment

The Principles and The Financial Supervision Core Rules (Appendices 1 and 2) have been reproduced with the kind permission of the Securities and Investments Board (SIB). The Draft Model Prescribed Disclosure Statement; Non-private Customer Notice; Conduct of Business/Client Money/Safe Custody/Customer Disclosure and Consent Requirements tables and the Model Clauses for Customer Agreements (Appendices 4 to 7 respectively) have all been produced with the kind permission of the Securities and Futures Authority (SFA).

Preface

I should make clear straightaway that this book is my personal commentary on, and interpretation of, the Securities and Futures Authority's (SFA's) "new settlement" rulebook. I have written it in my private capacity, outside my employment with SFA. It is not an SFA sponsored or vetted publication.

Nevertheless, because of my employment within a financial services regulator since 1987 and my close involvement in rule drafting and interpretation during this time, I hope that my comments and thoughts will be helpful, especially in guiding SFA member firms and their advisers with respect to the implementation of, and compliance with, the new rule requirements.

I have tried to provide helpful and comprehensive commentary. A significant part of the book analyses the Securities and Investments Board's (SIB's) Principles and Core Rules, as these form a major part of the new settlement regime applying to SFA firms. My commentary on the Core Rules extends beyond the Core Conduct of Business Rules to include the other directly applicable SIB rules such as those on client money, financial supervision, unsolicited calls, cancellation rights and stabilisation.

This book, therefore, is not limited to Conduct of Business regulation. It also examines authorisation and membership provisions, and complaints, arbitration and enforcement procedures. I have tried to produce a helpful guide on the client money and safe custody regulations; and a synopsis on SFA's new financial supervision rules which will probably be implemented towards the end of 1992. The majority of the chapters, however, are concerned with Conduct of Business and connected issues, including provisions in related legislation, such as the Financial Services Act 1986, the Unfair Contract Terms Act 1977, the Misleading Advertising Directive 1984, the Company Securities (Insider Dealing) Act 1985, the Drug Trafficking Offences Act 1986 and the Prevention of Terrorism Act 1989.

The book is up to date to the time of writing this preface, namely April 30, 1992. I have included amendments which have been proposed but not made at the time of writing, on the assumption that they will be implemented. I hope, as many in the United Kingdom financial services sector, that we can now have a period of stability for several years without any major structural or rule changes. This may be a naive hope bearing in mind the proposals for a new retail self-regulating organisation, the introduction of uncertified shareholdings (TARUS) and rolling settlement, the Law Commission's review of fiduciary duties, and the work still to be done in implementing the European

Community's single market programme with respect to financial services.

This book would not have happened without the encouragement and support of my wife, Glenys, who has typed the manuscript. I have had little time for my family during the last four months whilst writing it. I am also indebted to the editorial team at Sweet and Maxwell for its support and contribution.

John R.C. White
Salisbury
April 30, 1992

Contents

Chapter

Table of Securities and Futures Authority Rules

All references are to paragraph numbers

Table of Securities and Investments Board Rules

All references are to paragraph numbers

Table of Statutes

All references are to paragraph numbers

Table of Statutory Instruments

All references are to paragraph numbers

Table of Cases

All references are to paragraph numbers

EC Directive

All references are to paragraph numbers

Table of Abbreviations

AFBD	Association of Futures Brokers and Dealers
BES	Business Expansion Scheme
CMR	Client Money Regulations
CRR	Counterparty Risk Requirement
FIMBRA	Financial Intermediaries, Managers and Brokers Regulatory Association
FSA 1986	Financial Services Act 1986
GEMM	Gilt Edged Market Makers
IMRO	Investment Management Regulatory Organisation
LAUTRO	Life Assurance and Unit Trust Regulatory Organisation
LIFFE	London International Financial Futures and Options Exchange
NASD	National Association of Securities Dealers
OTC	Over the Counter Market
PEP	Personal Equity Plan
PRA	Position Risk Adjustment
PRR	Position Risk Requirement
RPB	Recognised Professional Body
SAR's	Substantial Acquisition Rules
SEAQ	London Stock Exchange's Automated Quotation System
SEMB	London Stock Exchange Money Brokers
SEO	Senior Executive Officer
SFA	Securities and Futures Authority
SIB	Securities and Investments Board
SRO	Self-Regulating Organisation
TSA	The Securities Association
UCITS	Undertakings for Collective Investment in Transferable Securities

Stop Press

Paragraph 5–003 (Customers of appointed representatives)

It was only intended that a person should be customer in relation to associated business where the firm also carries on, or intends to carry on, with or for him, regulated business. A person should not be a customer where the only activities which concern him are associated business.

At the time of writing, there is much concern about the wide scope of the definition of associated business and the reference in Rule 5–1(1)(c) to business which is held out as being for the purposes of investment. There is a worry that the former definition and the latter phrase bring within the scope of the Conduct of Business Rules activities which would by themselves not be investment business because of the exemption for groups and joint enterprises in paragraph 18 of Schedule 1 to the FSA 1986. As will be seen in paragraphs 4–014 and 4–015, SFA has deliberately made paragraph 18 activities subject to the rules on trade reporting and compliance, but only where the activities would amount to regulated business if they were not exempted by paragraph 18 from the definition of investment business. The Core Rule definition of associated business, however, is relevant in the context of more Conduct of Business Rules (see paragraphs 4–012 *et seq.*) and SFA's extension to the definition of customer (see paragraph 5–002).

In the past under TSA and AFBD rules some firms took considerable comfort from the fact that a fair proportion of the business which they did was not subject to the rules because it was done with or through group companies within the paragraph 18 exemption. This was especially common where an investor was introduced by one company to another group company (which, apart from the paragraph 18(3) exemption, would be a paragraph 13 arranging activity unless the exception in note 6 to paragraph 13 applied). Although it could be argued that the paragraph 18 exemption ought only to have related to the activities between the two group companies themselves, with a customer being protected under the rules in respect of the introduction where the introducer is an authorised person and with respect to any subsequent service provided by the receiving firm if it, also, is authorised under the FSA 1986. (At least, such a solution would be sensible in protecting the investor. If the introduction is to a group company which is not subject to FSA 1986 regulation, then the investor ought to be given the prescribed disclosure warning: see paragraphs 4–020 *et seq.*)

This is an area which, almost certainly, will require further clarification.

Paragraph 7–008 (Guaranteed stops)

Proposed changes will require a warning that there is no independent third party guarantee and that compensation under the Investors Compensation Scheme will not cover the stop limit. In addition, a firm should not provide a guaranteed stop in respect of a discretionary account.

Paragraph 12–014 (Exceptions to contents requirements for specific advertisements)

A firm should not rely on the exception in sub-paragraph (ii) where the advertisement relates to an investment which could readily be purchased or sold by private customers through other firms. A significant number of specific investment advertisements, however, will not trigger many of the disclosures referred to in paragraphs 12–016 and 12–017 as they will be irrelevant.

Nevertheless, note that to comply with the basic fair and not misleading obligation (paragraph 12–009), it may be necessary to give some risk warnings of the kind required for specific investment advertisements. And, where a firm is approving a specific investment for an overseas person which is not directed at private customers (and, therefore, exempt from the detailed contents requirements), the advertisement must contain the prescribed disclosure warning about the loss of FSA 1986 protection if it is calculated to lead, even only indirectly, to the overseas person doing non-regulated business with private customers in the United Kingdom (see paragraph 12–023).

Paragraph 18–003 (Connected customer)

An amendment since Consultative Paper 61 permits connected customers' transactions to be settled by way of the settlement money bank account provided a cheque is received on or prior to trade date.

Another amendment means that the reference in paragraph 18–003 to PEP should now read "qualifying savings plan" which will include PEPs, unit trust and investment trust savings plans.

Chapter 1

New Settlement

Background

From the very beginning when the main provisions of the Financial **1–001**
Services Act 1986 (FSA 1986) came into force on April 29, 1988, there
was a lot of criticism of the rules applied by the Securities and
Investments Board (SIB) and the self-regulating organisations (SROs)
to the investment business firms which they authorised. The criticisms
were that the rules were far too detailed and legalistic, providing too
many intrusive and onerous obligations which went beyond simple
investor protection. The rules were not easy to understand and
implement; and, therefore, firms found themselves having to employ
lawyers, accountants and other professionals within newly formed
Compliance Departments.

There was concern that the new rules would make the United
Kingdom an uncompetitive place in which to do investment business;
there was now too much regulation, and it was regarded as substantially
increasing firm's costs, without any obvious benefit to investors. In fact,
as it turns out, the investors are paying for the regulation: SIB as a
non-governmental body receives most of its income from levies on the
SROs; the SROs in turn receive their income from the membership fees
which they charge the firms they authorise; and, in turn, the firms pay
for the costs of their SRO fees and the costs of their Compliance
Departments from commissions and other profits made from their
business. The complaint was that the costs of implementing the new
regulatory system were increasing the costs for investors in doing
investment business, especially private customers now that they could
no longer benefit from the previous subsidisation of their dealing costs
by non-private customers under the old fixed-commission system
(abolished in 1986 under "Big Bang").

One of the reasons for writing detailed, legalistic rules was the **1–002**
creation of the civil right of action under section 62 of the FSA 1986,
which gave anyone who suffered loss as a result of a contravention of
SIB's or the SROs' rules designed to provide protection to investors, a
right to claim damages in the civil courts. The right was available to
anyone who suffered loss as a result of such a contravention, even if he
did not have a direct customer relationship with the firm responsible for
the rule breach and even if he was another large investment house
rather than an individual.

Another defence which the SROs put forward for their writing
detailed rules was the requirement in Schedule 2 to the FSA 1986 that

1

the SROs' rules afford investors protection at least equivalent to that afforded in respect of the rules made by SIB. There was concern that SIB had interpreted this requirement too tightly, requiring SROs almost to mirror SIB's rules on a line-by-line basis.

The firms which needed authorisation from several SROs also complained about a lack of harmonisation. Each SRO, because of the equivalence requirement, had similar rules dealing with similar issues. Yet, each SRO, as an autonomous body, had adopted different drafting styles and different structures for its rulebooks. Therefore, provisions in common areas were not always the same between one rulebook and another and certainly would not appear in the same place in each of the rulebooks.

1–003   Hence, from the very beginning of the new rulebooks coming into force, there was much pressure for their redrafting. This redrafting was openly encouraged by the Government in the amendments which it made to the FSA 1986 in the Companies Act 1989. The effect of these amendments was to make SIB and the SROs rewrite their rules. Of course, the only problem with rewriting rulebooks three and four years after the original rulebooks have come into force is the new expense and work required from the investment business firms. By the time the new rulebooks come out, firms and their staff are familiar with working with the first rulebooks; they know where to find particular provisions, having resolved many of the interpretational problems, and have set up systems and procedures for implementing and monitoring compliance with the rule provisions. The mere fact of redrafting the rule provisions, even if the main substantive obligations remain unchanged, will initially impose costs on firms. Staff will have to become familiar with the new requirements; learn where they can be found in the rulebooks; assess whether the new drafting throws up different interpretational issues; and implement, as necessary, changes to the firm's systems and procedures for implementing and monitoring compliance with the new rules. The "light at the end of the tunnel" is that, once firms have gone through this pain of implementing the new rulebooks, it should be simpler and easier to do investment business in the long run.

Section 62

1–004   One of the major changes introduced by the Companies Act 1989 was the introduction of a new provision in section 62A restricting the right of action, with a few exceptions, to private investors. This provision came into force on April 1, 1991 (S.I. 1991 No. 489).

The definition of private investor for the purposes of section 62 is discussed in paragraphs 5–038 and 5–039 below in relation to customers. However, it should be noted that the restriction to private investors does not apply in three important cases:

1. The restriction to private investor does not apply where the contravention concerns any rule or similar requirement prohibiting an authorised firm from seeking to exclude or restrict any duty or liability. This provision relates to Core Rule 15 (Securities and Futures Authority (SFA) Rule 5–24) on customers' rights (see discussion in paragraphs 6–006 to 6–008 below).

2. The second case is where the contravention concerns a rule or similar requirement which is designed to ensure that a transaction in an investment is not effected with the benefit of unpublished information which, if made public, would be likely to affect the price of the investment. In other words, any person is still able to sue under section 62 where his loss stems from a breach of a rule preventing insider dealing.

3. Finally, a person who is acting in a fiduciary or representative capacity, for example a trustee, can claim on behalf of the person to whom he owes his fiduciary obligations if that person, in his own right, would qualify as a private investor, even though the representative does not.

In these cases, any person who suffers loss as a result of the rule contravention will be able to sue.

Restricting the right of action under section 62 to private investors automatically enabled the freeing-up of the rulebooks, without the need for the same detail and legalistic drafting. This is because the real concern about section 62 was that it would be used by large non-private investors, and even other authorised investment businesses. These persons, unlike private investors, would be able to afford to mount a civil action under section 62 and would have more reason for contemplating such an action. For example, one investment business might consider suing another for a failure of best execution. The argument might relate to a fraction of a penny in respect of the price, for example, a tick on a bond price. Although this does not sound much, it could be worth a considerable amount to the firms involved because of the sheer size of the order which was transacted at the disputed price.

Even before section 62 was restricted to private investors, however, **1–005** the fears about it had to some extent disappeared since even the large customers and other authorised investment businesses were not suing each other. Of course, it could be argued that this was a result of the legalistic drafting which gave little room for different interpretations; but the drafting was not always that detailed and unambiguous!

Private investors have always been much more likely to seek redress by using the complaints and arbitration procedures offered by SROs; and SFA's Disciplinary Tribunal can, when imposing a penalty on a firm, also make a compensation order in favour of a customer who has suffered a readily determinable loss as a consequence of the disciplined firm's misconduct (Rule 7–31).

Of course, in thinking about restricting section 62, it is important not to forget that someone who is not a private investor may still be able to sue in the civil courts because a particular action by one authorised firm may not merely amount to a breach of a SIB or an SRO rule, but also to a breach of an express or implied contractual term, or may amount to a breach of a duty of care under the law of negligence.

Adequacy

1–006   The Companies Act 1989 amendments have replaced the old equivalence test, which many regarded as the major contributor to the unfriendly, detailed and legalistic approach of the rulebooks. The criticism was that an SRO did not have sufficient autonomy to write rules specifically directed at the types of investment business firms which it was responsible for authorising, in the context of the markets in which these firms operated and the customers with whom they dealt. The idea behind having several SROs was to ensure that financial services regulation was imposed in a way which was relevant to particular markets, with the regulation ultimately being the responsibility of the practitioners within each market. As SIB was staffed mainly by ex-civil servants, rather than practitioners, there was a concern that equivalence was unnecessarily hampering the SROs in devising regulations which were most suitable for their particular areas of responsibility within the overall industry.

1–007   The new test of adequacy requires SROs to have rules which, taken together with SIB's Statements of Principles, designated Core Rules and other codes of practice, are such as to afford an adequate level of protection for investors. The provision goes on to say that, in determining whether an adequate level of protection is afforded, regard must be had to the nature of the investment business carried on by an SRO's members, the kinds of investors involved and the effectiveness of its arrangements for enforcing compliance. In other words, unlike with equivalence, adequacy does not concentrate merely on an SRO's rules, comparing them with those of SIB. It is judged by looking at the markets in which an SRO's firms operate and the types of investors with whom they deal. Therefore, an SRO can properly take account of the fact that the persons with whom its firms deal are themselves sophisticated and knowledgeable about the nature of the business and risks involved. It can also have regard to the fact that its firms are subject to other regulations, such as the rules of an investment exchange, which obviate the need for the SRO to impose similar regulations. Finally, adequacy takes into account the SRO's management and organisation to ensure that not only does it have the right regulations but also effective arrangements for enforcing compliance with those regulations.

Due to concerns about the costs of implementing the SIB and SRO rules introduced in 1988, a new requirement is introduced obliging SROs, in framing rules, to take into account, in relation to those to whom the rules are to apply, the cost of complying with the rules and any other controls to which they are subject. In order words, an SRO is directed to weigh up the cost, in terms of the firm, in providing the protection against the value to investors of the protection provided.

These provisions concerning adequacy and the costs of compliance sounded very good initially to the SROs, but the 1989 amendments were also directed at another problem, namely the harmonisation of rules. This conflicted, to some extent, with giving SROs greater freedom to write rules specifically relevant to the types of firms which they regulated, rather than being subject to the requirement to write rules equivalent to those of SIB.

Principles and Core Rules

To ensure that there was sufficient harmonisation of the main rule **1–008** requirements throughout the whole of the financial services industry, SIB was given power to issue Statements of Principle and to designate rules which could apply across the whole of the industry.

The Principles were intended as universal statements of the standards expected of any type of investment business done with any person. There are 10 of them and they came into force on April 30, 1990. They apply directly to the conduct of investment business and financial standing of all persons authorised under the FSA 1986, whether members of SROs or firms certified to do investment business by a recognised professional body (RPB), such as lawyers, accountants and actuaries.

The Principles can be seen as the Ten Commandments for investment business. They set the basic standards and are intended to be easily intelligible, whether they are being read by an investment business firm or an investor. They are not exhaustive of the standards expected of an investment business firm. On the other hand, compliance with SIB's designated Core Rules and the underlying third tier rules of an SRO, or with the investment business rules of an RPB, does not necessarily amount to conformity with the Principles. For example, there will be lacunae in the coverage provided by the various rules: a firm may find that there are ways of side-stepping some of the rule obligations. In such a situation, the firm, however clever it has tried to be, may find that it is in breach of a basic and overriding obligation enunciated in a Principle. Interestingly, in late 1991, in respect of dealings in London FOX's property index futures contract, five SFA firms were disciplined for a failure to observe high standards of market conduct (Principle 3) rather than for a breach of any other rules. The Principles may also be regarded as setting down a moral, ethical code for all investment business.

One point to note about the Principles is that, unlike the designated Core Rules and the other rules of the SROs and RPBs, they do not give rise to an action for damages under section 62. However, this does not mean that an investor cannot claim compensation in respect of a breach of a Principle, because, as discussed earlier, SFA's Disciplinary Tribunal can order a compensation payment when imposing a disciplinary penalty for a breach of a Principle.

1–009 The Principles are set out in Appendix 1 below. One point to note is that under Principle 3, which is concerned with a firm observing high standards of market conduct, a firm must also comply with any code or standard which is endorsed for the purposes of this Principle. In due course, SFA intends to endorse:

(i) the London Code of Conduct issued by the Bank of England in respect of dealings on the wholesale money markets;

(ii) the City Code on Takeover and Mergers and the Rules Governing Substantial Acquisitions of Shares; and

(iii) the Oil Market Code of Conduct issued by SIB.

Once these Codes are endorsed, firms will be expected to comply with them in the same way as any Principle and will be disciplined for a breach of any provision in one of the Codes in the same way as they can be disciplined for breach of a Principle. In the case of the London Code of Conduct and the Takeover Code, however, SFA would not proceed without first consulting with the Bank of England or the Panel, who would be able themselves to take appropriate action under their own respective powers; but there may be occasions when it is more suitable for SFA to take action, especially in view of the wide range of sanctions available to SFA and the fact that the matter could affect a firm's fitness to do other investment business.

Additionally, although the Principles are expressed by SIB as applying to all authorised persons, SFA has extended their scope by stating that the Principles apply directly to registered persons (Rule 2–24(3)). So individuals employed by SFA member firms who are individually registered with SFA can themselves be disciplined where they breach a Principle or cause their firm to be in breach of one.

Core Rules

1–010 In addition to the power to issue Principles with respect to the conduct and financial standing expected of any authorised person, SIB was given power through the 1989 amendments to designate rules in respect of conduct of business, financial resources, client money and unsolicited calls. These rules are often termed the "Core Rules". Unlike the Principles, however, they do not apply to firms which are certified to do investment business by RPBs. They only apply to members of SROs and, then, only in respect of the investment business for which an SRO member firm is subject to regulation by his SRO. For example, if a firm is a member of an SRO and also a listed money market institution under section 43 of the FSA 1986, the Core Rules would only apply to the firm when it is doing the type of investment business which is subject to regulation by the SRO, rather than when it is carrying on investment business subject to the Bank of England's supervision in respect of the firm's section 43 listing.

Once designated by SIB, the Core Rules apply directly to SRO member firms whether or not an SRO has included them within its rulebook. The first Core Rules to be designated were the five concerned with financial regulation. They came into force on August 1, 1990. They are set out as Appendix 2 below.

The next set of designated rules are the Common Unsolicited Calls   **1–011** Regulations. There are 20 of these and they deal with the permissions available under section 56 of the FSA 1986 setting out the circumstances in which an unsolicited call may be made. These regulations had a phased commencement, partially applied from September 1, 1991 and then applying in full from January 1, 1992. The permissions to make cold calls are explained in Chapter 13 below.

Another set of Core Rules are the new Client Money Regulations which came into force on January 1, 1992 (see Chapter 18 below). Whereas Core Rules do not apply to members of RPBs, the Client Money Regulations have been specifically designated to apply to the members of one RPB, namely members of the Institute of Actuaries who hold certificates to do investment business.

Finally, the remaining Core Rules are those relating to conduct of business. There are 40 Core Conduct of Business Rules and they were made by SIB on January 30, 1991. Although SIB called these Rules "the Core Conduct of Business Rules", when people talk about the Core Rules, they are often only referring to these Core Conduct of Business Rules, rather than the designated rules and regulations described above for financial supervision, unsolicited calls and client money. (Often in this book the term "Core Rules" will be used in the more limited sense of meaning merely SIB's designated rules for conduct of business.)

The Core Conduct of Business Rules do not have a single commencement date in respect of all SRO members. Instead, SIB will bring them into force for the members of each SRO at such time as that SRO is able to bring into force its newly drafted third tier provisions to provide support, under the new adequacy test, to the Principles and Core Rules. The Core Rules were designated for members of the Investment Management Regulatory Organisation (IMRO) with effect from November 30, 1991, the date on which the new IMRO rulebook came into force. They were designated to apply to members of SFA with effect from April 1, 1992, SFA's new rulebook commencement date.

1–012   The Common Unsolicited Calls Regulations and the Client Money Regulations are detailed provisions which are complete in themselves. SFA, however, has provided to a very limited extent some additional provisions in support of both sets of regulations. The Core Financial Supervision Rules and the Core Conduct of Business Rules need further amplification within individual SRO rules. This further amplification is often referred to as "the third tier".

The Core Rules give a little more flesh to the basic obligations contained in the Principles, but are still written in general terms, suitable to apply to all types of investment business done by members of SROs. Therefore, it is necessary for each SRO, at the third tier, to explain, extend or qualify the basic Core Rule obligations in the context of the particular types of investment business which that SRO regulates.

As the Core Rules are part of the exercise of trying to ensure greater consistency and harmonisation within the area of financial services regulation, it is surprising that they do not apply to members of RPBs. The reasons appear to stem from the fact that the RPBs formed a strong lobby when the provisions relating to designated Core Rules were discussed in Parliament. It was argued that the Core Rules were not so relevant in the context of RPB members who undertake investment business as an ancillary activity to their main professional work which is non-investment business, and reliance was placed on the fact that the RPBs had a substantial body of well tested and understood professional regulations already in place to regulate their members. They wanted to avoid the expense required in rewriting their investment business rules to fit in with the new Core Rules settlement. Although the RPBs would not accept Core Rules, however, they were keen to take advantage of the new adequacy test.

Derogation

1–013   The provision dealing with Core Rules states that it may be provided that they have effect, either generally or to such extent as may be specified, subject to the rules of an SRO. In other words, it is possible for an SRO in its third tier to provide qualifications or exceptions to Core Rule obligations: namely to derogate from them. However, an SRO cannot derogate wherever it feels like it. It must have the necessary authority, which will either come from the drafting of the Core Rule itself or in a separate derogation permission from SIB which will be made part of the commencement order bringing the Core Rules into force for the particular SRO's members. Nine of the 40 Core Conduct of Business Rules contain, within their drafting, provisions enabling general qualifications to be made by an SRO. These are rules which contain phrases such as: "Subject to any exceptions contained in the rules of an SRO of which it is a member, a firm must . . .". Apart from these provisions (and four of them only apply to part of the Core

Rule in which they appear), any further qualifications by an SRO must be authorised in a separate instrument issued by SIB.

In fact, it is in determining the extent to which an SRO can derogate from the Core Rules that the conflict is evident between two of the main amendments made to the FSA 1986 by the Companies Act 1989. Adequacy was intended to free up rulebooks, enabling SROs to develop rules specifically relevant to the types of investment business they regulated, without having to draw up provisions equivalent to those of SIB. On the other hand, the idea of introducing Principles and Core Rules was to set common regulatory standards throughout the industry and lead to a degree of harmonisation between the rulebooks of the various financial services regulators. If the Principles and Core Rules are to be accepted as general standards across the industry and lead to a degree of harmonisation, then SIB cannot allow too many qualifications and exceptions to the Core Rules. Naturally, therefore, SIB has taken a fairly restrictive approach to the SROs' qualifications and exceptions.

There are two important points to be noted in the context of **1–014** derogations. Although derogations are permitted under the legislation in respect of Core Rules, they are not available in respect of the Principles. As the introduction to the Principles makes clear, observance of other rule requirements does not necessarily amount to conformity with the Principles. Therefore, a firm could find itself in breach of a Principle where it was following a properly permitted SRO derogation to a Core Rule provision. The second point concerns those Core Rules which, within their own drafting, permit general exceptions. Any exception which an SRO writes will still have to satisfy the adequacy test: so, although a Core Rule which starts with the words "Subject to any exceptions" would suggest that an SRO is free to write any qualifications which it likes, there is a limitation placed by the fact that the SRO's rules must still provide adequate investor protection when taken together with the Principles and Core Rules.

It has come as rather a shock to some SROs to find the extent to which the greater freedom, apparently permitted by the 1989 amendments, to write rules under the adequacy requirement has in practice been constrained by the desire to achieve standardisation in rule requirements through the imposition of Principles and Core Rules. In fact, the old equivalence test had never been as tight a straitjacket as some critics made out. SROs had been able to introduce a number of qualifications and different provisions to those contained within the SIB rules.

SFA's new rulebook

When SIB first set about the task of drafting Principles and Core **1–015** Rules, it was not intended to change any of the existing substantive rule requirements. The purpose was merely to rewrite the existing rules in a simpler, more understandable style. As the exercise progressed, however, the opportunity was taken to examine all of the existing requirements and decide to what extent reform was needed in the sense both of deleting some obligations as not really contributing to investor protection, and of extending the scope of others to cover gaps where the existing regulations were thought not to give effective protection. Therefore, it quickly became clear that SROs could not merely bolt the Principles and Core Rules on to their existing rulebooks, but would have to carry out a major revision exercise in respect of their third tier requirements.

In fact, SFA had always been keen, from the earliest days, to rewrite its rules in a shorter, less detailed fashion and, therefore, it welcomed the opportunities provided by the 1989 changes. Certainly, SFA's new rulebook is considerably shorter than the old ones; and SFA has not provided any additional third tier provisions to 15 of the 40 Core Conduct of Business Rules. In the case of some of the other Core Rules, SFA's third tier is very small and consists of guidance or minor modification to the Core Rule drafting.

SFA used the Core Rule exercise as an opportunity not merely to revise its Conduct of Business Rules, but also the whole of its rulebook. Obviously, revision would have been necessary anyway because of the fact that SFA consists of the merger of two SROs, namely The Securities Association (TSA) and the Association of Futures Brokers and Dealers (AFBD), which occurred on April 1, 1991.

It was hoped that all of SFA's new rulebook could come into force at the same time, namely, April 1, 1992, exactly a year after the merger of TSA and AFBD. This has not been possible, because, as explained above, the new Common Unsolicited Calls Regulations and the new Client Money Regulations came into force on January 1, 1992. Also, it proved more difficult to merge the financial supervision requirements of the two SROs so that the implementation of the Financial Rules has been delayed until later in 1992.

Style

1–016   Readers of the new rulebook should be aware of an important stylistic approach which has been adopted. Any Core Conduct of Business Rule appears in the rulebook in bold type. The same applies to any definition which has been settled by SIB with reference to the Core Rules. As regards SFA's qualifications and exceptions to the Core Rule drafting, sometimes these have been included as insertions within an actual Core Rule paragraph or definition. Such modifications can easily be distinguished because they appear in an ordinary type face, like the rest of SFA's third tier provisions. All words which are italicised mean that they are defined terms for which there is a special meaning within the Definitions Chapter (Chapter 9) or an appropriate cross-reference to the FSA 1986.

The Core Conduct of Business Rules order and numbering system has not been adopted because it was felt that some of the Core Conduct of Business Rules would fit more appropriately in chapters other than the one relating to Conduct of Business Rules. When reading the rulebook, however, any provision which is a Core Rule one has its Core Rule number set out in brackets at the end of the particular provision. Appendix 3 below lists the Core Conduct of Business Rules, identifying the relevant SFA rule numbers.

Chapter 2

Rule Interpretation

The difference has already been explained concerning the legal effect **2–001** between the Principles, Core Rules and SFA's third tier provisions. SFA can take disciplinary action for a breach of any of them and has the power to award compensation, but only a breach of the Core Rules and SFA third tier rules gives rise to an action for damages under section 62 of the FSA 1986.

The Principles, as we already know, provide overriding obligations, written in general terms. Conforming with all of the Core Rules and additional SFA provisions does not guarantee compliance with the Principles. Additionally, SFA has written an interpretation provision to its rules (Rule 1–3) emphasising that all of the rules, which, for the purposes of the SFA definition, include Principles, Core Rules and SFA third tier provisions, must be read in a business-like and practical manner. SFA also emphasises that a firm must have regard to the spirit as well as to the letter of a rule.

In analysing points of interpretation relating to the rules, firms should not try to be clever and look for ways of avoiding specific rule obligations. Firms should ask themselves what is the intention behind a particular rule provision; what types of abuse is it intended to prevent; is it intended to prevent the firm either engaging in the activities contemplated or carrying out those activities in the manner contemplated? In other words, if a particular course of conduct seems wrong from an ethical or moral standpoint, it is likely that it is not permitted, either by the Core Rules and supporting third tier rules or within the scope of the Principles.

Formal guidance (Rule 1–4(1))

It was realised early on, when planning the introduction of new **2–002** rulebooks, that if they were to be written in a shorter, simpler style, with less detailed provisions, investment businesses and their employees would sometimes need guidance as to how to comply with the new general provisions in particular circumstances. Also, both SIB and the SROs saw that there were advantages in dealing with some regulatory issues through guidance rather than rule provisions.

Guidance does not have to have the same legal effect as a rule. Therefore, it can be written in a less precise but sometimes more intelligible style. It can give examples of how to comply with a rule obligation in particular circumstances, without trying to set down comprehensively the steps which must be followed to comply with the rule obligation with respect to every possible permutation in which the relevant business covered by the rule is done.

Guidance under the new settlement rulebooks takes two forms: formal guidance and informal guidance. The effect of formal guidance is that it provides a "safe harbour" to firms in respect of their compliance with the rules. There is a presumption that a firm has complied with a rule where:

(i) it has complied with formal guidance relating to that rule issued by SFA or SIB; and

(ii) in reliance on the standards set in that guidance, the firm believes on reasonable grounds that it is acting in conformity with the relevant rule.

Note that this provision only applies where the firm is relying on formal guidance; and, in respect of SFA firms, it is only guidance which has been issued by SIB or SFA relating to the particular rule. It is not good enough for a firm merely to follow the steps set out in the guidance. The firm must independently come to a decision that, by relying on that guidance, it will be acting in conformity with the relevant rule.

Formal guidance is defined as guidance intended to have continuing effect, which is in writing and which is issued generally or to a class of persons. In SFA terms, formal guidance is the guidance which appears in the actual rulebook. This is the guidance which appears underneath particular rule provisions or underneath particular definitions. It also includes material issued in SFA Board Notices which are specifically headed "guidance", and refer to Rule 1–4(1).

Note that guidance is not a rule in itself. Therefore, a firm does not commit an offence by failing to adhere to a guidance note. But, of course, it is a brave firm which ignores a guidance note and remains confident that it has complied with the relevant rule.

Whilst dealing with the question of formal guidance, it is relevant to note that, as part of the 1989 amendments to the FSA 1986, SIB was given power to issue codes of practice with respect to any matters dealt with by Principles or Core Rules. To date, SIB has not issued any such code, but, if it did so, the code would have a similar effect to formal guidance.

Informal guidance

2–003   Any other guidance, namely that which does not appear in the rulebook or in Board Notices under the specific heading "guidance", will amount to informal guidance. This does not give the same "safe harbour". SFA's rules state that informal guidance given by SFA, whether through its officers, employees or otherwise, may not be taken to be an authoritative statement of the meaning of any of the rules; and that reliance on such informal guidance will not itself discharge the responsibility of the firm to comply with the obligations under the rules.

Informal guidance is made up of any notes and explanations about SFA's rules which are given other than in the rulebook and "Guidance" Board Notices: for example, matters contained in other Board Notices and in newsletters. Informal guidance also includes interpretations given by SFA staff. It makes no difference to its status whether the advice from SFA was sought orally or in writing, and whether SFA gave its views in writing or in a conversation.

Firms will obviously ask whether any reliance can be placed on informal guidance if the rules state that, by relying on it, a firm will not of itself discharge its responsibilities to comply with the rules. Of course, although informal guidance does not contain the same presumption concerning compliance as formal guidance, in practice, firms will be able to take some comfort from it. Obviously, the degree of comfort depends upon the particular circumstances. For example, did SFA, when giving an interpretation, know all of the relevant circumstances concerning the firm's business? Have other factors arisen since SFA's views were first sought which could affect the views originally given? At what level was the interpretation given by SFA? For instance, it may be significant that the interpretation was given after full consideration of all the relevant points by one of the standing committees of SFA's Board.

In practice, a firm will have a close relationship with its inspection team. If a firm has approved a course of conduct with this team, it is most unlikely that the firm would be at future risk: certainly not from disciplinary proceedings, which would normally be dependent upon initial instigation by a firm's inspection team. Even if disciplinary proceedings or a civil action are commenced,it would be a strong mitigating factor, even if not a defence, for a firm to show that it had properly relied on the informal guidance.

Rule waivers (Rule 1–5)

A firm which has problems complying with a particular rule provision can always consider applying for a rule modification or waiver. Where such a modification or waiver is granted, then the rule in its altered form is the relevant rule when determining whether or not the firm is complying with the rules of SFA. Therefore, if it is correctly complying with the altered rule and any conditions imposed at the time when the modification or waiver was granted, the firm will not be subject to any disciplinable offence or be liable for an action for damages under section 62 in connection with non-compliance of the

2–004

rule in its unaltered form. Obviously, in determining whether there is any liability, it will be important to assess the date on which the modification or waiver became effective, whether there was any time limit imposed on the alteration and whether the firm was complying with any applicable conditions.

SFA will only alter the requirements of a rule if it considers that:

(i) compliance with them would be unduly burdensome on the firm having regard to the benefit which compliance would confer on investors; and

(ii) the alteration would not result in any undue risk to investors.

In other words, in granting rule alterations, SFA has to weigh up the costs to the firm in requiring strict compliance with a rule against the risks involved to investors in modifying or waiving that rule requirement.

Under SFA's rules, SFA has the power to alter a rule on its own initiative or on the written application of a firm. Where the alteration is being made as a result of an application by a firm, SFA is not restricted to limiting the scope of the alteration to the applicant firm, but may extend it to all member firms generally or to a particular class or classes of its members.

2–005 There is an important restriction, however, which relates to granting waivers of Core Rules and Principles. In this case, the legislation only allows the alteration to be made in respect of the circumstances or particular kind of business carried on by the applicant. There is no power to extend a waiver of a Principle or Core Rule to other SFA member firms other than the applicant. Obviously, this restriction could prove very tiresome. There may be circumstances where a large number of SFA firms are affected in a similar way and SFA considers that all firms in the same circumstances should have the benefit of the alteration. If the alteration concerns a Principle or Core Rule, then SFA will, effectively, have to encourage all of the affected firms to apply for the necessary alteration. It will then be costly and time consuming on the part of SFA, as well as the member firms, in dealing with all of the applications.

Of course, if the alteration is important to so many firms, it could be the case that the Principle or Core Rule should be amended. However, because the Principles and Core Rules apply so widely and have been set by SIB, they are not easy to amend. Before any amendment of the Core Rules can take place, SIB will obviously need to consult with all of the other SROs. After establishing their views and considering what needs to be done, SIB will need to issue a public consultative paper setting out the proposed amendment and the reasons for it. Once it has received comments, SIB will then implement the necessary rule amendment. Close liaison will need to be maintained with all the other SROs to make sure that they are able to enforce the new Core Rule provision and adjust any conflicting third tier requirements at the same time as the new provision takes effect.

The other alternative to amending a Core Rule is to allow the particular SRO whose members are most affected to write a qualification or exception at the third tier. However, this again will need to be contained within SIB's commencement and derogation instrument relating to the implementation of the Core Rules for that particular SRO, unless the matter concerns one of the nine Core Rule provisions which allow general derogations (subject to the adequacy test) by containing a phrase such as: "Subject to exceptions contained in the rules of an SRO". Again, before SIB can amend the relevant commencement and derogation order, it will need to issue a consultative paper setting out the proposed amendment and reasons for it.

2–006

As both these procedures for amending the Core Rules or the derogation instrument will take considerable time, alterations required in fairly short order will have to be dealt with by all the firms affected, or likely to be affected, individually applying for the necessary alteration to their SRO.

Although this restriction on granting alterations on an individual application basis only applies to the Principles and Core Rules, it may be the case that any rule alteration which an SRO makes of a third tier provision could amount to an unauthorised derogation of a Principle or Core Rule. Therefore, in practice, it may be that SROs will rarely be free to grant alterations of their rules on a general basis to firms other than those which have specifically applied for the alteration.

Force majeure (Rule 1–6)

There may be times when some sort of emergency arises which makes it impractical for a firm to comply with one or some rules. An obvious example would be a systems failure. If such an emergency arises and it is outside of the control of the firm or its associates, the firm will not be regarded as being in breach of the relevant rule or rules as long as the emergency subsists, provided the firm:

2–007

(i)   is expeditiously taking all practical steps available to it to relieve the emergency;

(ii) is trying to comply with the particular rule provision or provisions as best it can despite the emergency; and

(iii) notifies SFA immediately of the emergency and of the steps which it is taking.

This *force majeure* provision applies to both Core Rules and SFA third tier rules, but it cannot apply to the Principles because the legislation empowering the drawing up and issuing of Principles does not permit any derogation or qualification to them, except for an alteration granted by SFA to the particular applicant on the two grounds outlined in the previous section: namely, the costs of compliance are unduly burdensome and there is no undue risk to investors in agreeing to the alteration. Obviously, such a procedure is not relevant in a *force majeure* provision where there would not be time to make the application and where the grounds for granting the application would not necessarily be satisfied. Note that, if the *force majeure* provision cannot apply to the Principles, it also cannot apply to any code which is endorsed by SIB for the purpose of Principle 3 (Market Practice).

Indemnities against contraventions (Rule 1–7)

2–008   SFA has a rule preventing a firm from entering into any insurance-type arrangement under which the firm itself would be absolved from paying any fines or compensation which could be ordered against it for breaching any of the rules. This is a public policy measure to prevent a firm letting itself and its employees be susceptible to committing rule breaches if a cap is placed on their liability through such an arrangement.

This provision should not be read too widely. It does not extend to ordinary policies effected to insure a firm against negligence; for example, in conjunction with liability arising from negligent acts committed by employees and injury resulting from defective premises.

Application of rules to employees

2–009   The rules, at least the Principles, Core Rules and SFA's supporting third tier provisions to the Core Rules, are written in terms of obligations imposed on a firm.

However, SFA has also extended all of the rules to employees of member firms who are individually registered with SFA. In completing an individual registration form, the employee has to agree that he will act within the scope of his authority and duties within the member firm; that he will not commit any act or omission which places his firm in breach of the rules; and that he will be fully bound by and subject to the Enforcement Rules. Further, as already explained in paragraph 1–009 above, SFA specifically provides that the Principles apply directly to a registered person (Rule 2–24(3)).

The Enforcement Rules provide (Rule 7–23) that disciplinary proceedings can be brought against a firm or registered person in respect of an act of misconduct. An act of misconduct includes a breach of the rules; a breach of the FSA 1986 or provisions made under it; a failure to comply with an order of SFA; the provision to SFA of false, misleading or inaccurate information; and a failure to comply with a requirement in the Personal Account Notice which is concerned with personal dealings by an employee. It is also stated, however, that an act of misconduct includes an act or omission by a registered person which causes his firm or another registered person to breach one of SFA's rules, the FSA 1986 or provisions made under it.

A good number of the rules, rather than being strict obligations, look at the firm's belief or the steps which the firm has taken. The requirement is that the firm should believe on reasonable grounds or have taken reasonable steps. When looking at whether an employee has committed an act of misconduct, SFA will ignore the fact that the firm itself believed on reasonable grounds or took reasonable steps. Instead, it will look at the actual steps or belief held by the employee and determine whether the steps he took were reasonable or his belief was based on reasonable grounds. There will be situations where the firm itself has taken reasonable steps in the circumstances, but the individual employee has rejected any supervision, training or orders from the firm and so cannot be regarded as having taken reasonable steps or having formed a belief on reasonable grounds.

Note that the extension of the rules and the disciplinary obligations mentioned above only apply to employees who are registered with SFA as directors, partners, managers, representatives or traders. There is, however, another provision (Rule 1–10) which makes a firm responsible for anything said, done or omitted by:

(i) an employee within the scope of his employment; or

(ii) an agent within the scope of his authority (whether actual or apparent).

Therefore, a firm is responsible for everything done by its employees when acting within the scope of their employment; and an employee can be regarded as acting within the scope of his employment even where he specifically disobeys an instruction issued by his employer.

Burden of proof

As pointed out above, many of the rules are subject to a test of **2–010** reasonableness: either the firm must take reasonable steps or it must have a belief based on reasonable grounds.

Where a firm is charged with breaching a rule containing a reasonableness test, an obligation is imposed on the firm (Rule 7–23(4)) to prove that it took reasonable steps or had reasonable grounds for forming the belief. In other words, the onus of proof will initially be on SFA to show that, if the rule had been an absolute obligation, it was broken. It will then be for the firm to defend that charge by showing that it acted reasonably. The reasonableness test is an objective one in the sense that a tribunal will not be determining whether the firm itself had a reasonable belief, but that there were sufficient grounds upon which an ordinary person would reasonably have formed such a belief as the firm held.

Reliance on others (Rule 5–2)

2–011   There is a provision to the effect that a firm will be regarded as having acted in conformity with a rule which relates to information, to the extent that it reasonably relied on information provided in writing by a third party whom the firm believed on reasonable grounds to be independent and competent to provide the information. This is a provision which is only relevant to conduct of business requirements which concern the giving of investment advice and other information to investors. Sometimes a firm itself will not have the necessary expertise or, perhaps, time to establish the accuracy of all the information it is required to give to a customer; for example, some of the information contained in a detailed investment advertisement. In these circumstances, the firm will be protected where the information was provided in the circumstances outlined above.

The first problem with this requirement is that the information has to be provided in writing. This is extremely onerous. The second is that the information has to be provided by a third party whom the firm reasonably believes to be independent and competent to provide the information. What if the information is provided by another group company? It is suggested that the question of independence and competence goes to the experience and ability of the provider of the information, rather than looking at the third party in terms of a group structure. Also, there is nothing to prevent a firm relying on oral information: it will just not have the same rule protection. This is similar to the distinction between formal and informal guidance discussed above.

Where the firm is dealing with an agent who is acting for a customer, then the firm can rely on the accuracy and sufficiency of information about that customer which is supplied by the agent, provided the firm has no reasonable ground on which to doubt that:

(i)   the agent is reliable and honest and acting within the scope of his authority; and

(ii)   the information which he is supplying is accurate and reliable.

2–012   Another provision on this same theme is that, where a firm is required by the rules to send something to a customer, it complies with that provision where it sends the communication, with the prior instructions of the customer, to a person who is independent of the firm; for example, the customer's agent. Sometimes, a customer will not necessarily appoint someone as his agent, but will require certain documents to be sent to another person: such as requiring his contract notes to be sent to his accountant or tax adviser.

There is nothing in the rules to prevent a customer appointing someone as his agent and the agent may well enter into written agreements on behalf of the customer. In such circumstances, however, the firm is advised to ensure that the agent does have the necessary authority from the customer. Certainly, firms should be aware of unauthorised dealings by agents or people purporting to deal as an agent for a fictitious principal in order to hide their own activities. For a further discussion on agents, see the commentary on indirect customers at paragraphs 5–041 *et seq.* below.

Finally, on this subject, a firm does not itself have to send a communication which is required under the rules where it believes on reasonable grounds that this has been or will be supplied direct by another person. For example, a firm which is acting as a stockbroker in an agency capacity may properly have an arrangement with another firm with which it deals, or with which it has contracted all its settlement responsibilities, to provide contract notes direct to its customers. Additionally, a firm which arranges for a customer to enter into an endowment policy or a unit trust would be able to avoid sending out the relevant product particulars if the firm has the necessary reasonable belief that the life company or unit trust manager will send them direct to the customer.

Chapter 3

Membership

Scope of SFA

SFA can authorise any type of investment business within the meaning 3–001
of Schedule 1 to the FSA 1986, except:

 (i)   acting as trustee to a regulated collective investment scheme; or

 (ii) acting as the operator of a regulated collective investment
       scheme which is not one dedicated to—

   (a) options, futures or contracts for difference;
   (b) land and other property-related assets; or
   (c) warrants to subscribe or purchase securities;

   (whether or not the scheme holds other investments).

The appropriate SRO for regulating investment business within the
two exceptions listed above would be the Investment Management
Regulatory Organisation (IMRO).

Although SFA can authorise nearly all types of investment business,
it is primarily concerned with the activities of dealing, arranging deals
and advising on deals. The primary regulatory body for the activities of
fund management and operating collective investment schemes is
IMRO.

Fund Management

An SFA firm would require separate authorisation from IMRO for 3–002
investment management where that management primarily concerns
securities (rather than futures and options) and is the principal activity
of a separately identified division of the firm. Obviously, if the fund
management activity is being carried on by a separate legal person,
namely a subsidiary or associate, it would in any case need to seek
separate authorisation in its own right, because it would not be covered
by any authorisation granted to the main company.

A firm would not need to seek separate authorisation from IMRO for
fund management where this activity is done in conjunction with other
services authorised by SFA, especially if the fund management activities
are carried out for private customers. Additionally, SFA is willing to
authorise a separate subsidiary or associate which only carries out fund
management activities provided the fund management activities are

carried out in close connection with the activities of the main firm and are also aimed mainly at private customers.

Marketing unit trusts

3-003   SFA is willing to cover the marketing, selling and advising on units in collective investment schemes and life assurance contracts where this activity is not the principal activity of the firm, provided the principal activities are authorised by SFA. Otherwise, such activities would more appropriately be authorised by the Financial Intermediaries, Managers and Brokers Regulatory Association (FIMBRA) or, in respect of the marketing activities of the direct sales forces of life companies and unit trust managers, the Life Assurance and Unit Trust Regulatory Organisation (LAUTRO).

Managing unit trusts

Although the operation of collective investment schemes is primarily an IMRO authorised activity, SFA can authorise such operators where the scheme is dedicated to warrants, options, futures, contracts for difference and land and buildings. This is because these newer types of collective investment scheme, which have been able to become regulated schemes since late 1991, are more likely to be operated by specialist brokers in these markets who will already be members of SFA. It was thought right that they should not have to seek separate authorisation from IMRO. IMRO also has the scope, however, to authorise the operators of these types of scheme.

Corporate finance

Both SFA and IMRO can authorise investment business activities which are done under the general heading "corporate finances". Firms which undertake corporate finance business as a main part of their activities will normally be authorised by SFA, although a number of venture capitalists (because of the fund management activity involved) have been authorised by IMRO.

Clucas Report

At the invitation of SIB, Sir Kenneth Clucas conducted an inquiry to make suggestions concerning the future structure of SROs; in particular, to study the feasibility of setting up a new SRO for the retail sector. In his report dated February 28, 1992, he has suggested the creation of a new SRO to regulate investment business primarily done with or directly for private customers. This would mean merging LAUTRO with the majority of FIMBRA. The new SRO would also be able to authorise firms specialising in fund management for private investors, such as unit trust managers and private customer portfolio managers. Members of exchanges, however, even though they might be providing advisory or discretionary investment services for private investors, would be able to remain members of SFA, the SRO for firms dealing with professional investors. IMRO would remain in a slimmed-down form for firms providing fund management services for professional investors and authorised persons and for trustees of authorised unit trusts.

Scope of member firm's authorisation

An SFA member firm can only carry on investment business which is within the scope of SFA and which is also within the firm's business profile, unless the firm is authorised by another SRO or RPB, or is exempt from the requirement to be authorised under the FSA 1986, in respect of the relevant investment business. It should be noted that, although by being a member of SFA a firm will be an authorised person under the FSA 1986 in respect of any investment business which it undertakes, it will be committing a breach of SFA's rules if it acts, not merely outside the scope of investment business which SFA can authorise, but also outside the kinds of investment business described in the firm's business profile: in other words, it will be civilly liable rather than criminally liable. **3–004**

A firm must maintain at all times a business profile describing the kinds of investment business which it is authorised by SFA to carry on and must not carry on any other investment business outside its approved business profile without specific prior permission from SFA, unless that business is covered by other authorisation or exemption. When a firm submits a business profile, SFA has three options:

(i) It can refuse the firm membership, in which case the firm cannot carry on any investment business unless it obtains authorisation from another SRO or RPB or falls within one of the exemptions to the FSA authorisation requirements.

(ii) It can admit the firm to membership, without imposing any restrictions on the kinds of investment business stated in the business profile: the firm is, then, authorised by SFA to undertake all of the types of business described in the profile.

(iii) It can admit the firm to membership, but impose restrictions or conditions relating to the different kinds of investment business for which authorisation has been sought.

SFA could take the view that a firm is fit and proper generally to be admitted to membership, but is not fit to carry on particular types of investment business for which it has sought authorisation. For example, SFA may decide that the firm does not have the necessary resources, staff, capital and systems to undertake certain business.

In completing a business profile, a firm does not merely have to state the kinds of investments and the types of activities in relation to those investments in which it is going to do business. It also has to give details of the kinds of customers with whom it will be dealing, the percentage of its investment business which will be done in the various investments and activities for which it has sought authorisation, and the percentage of its revenue which will be earned from investment business as opposed to other business.

A firm must keep its business profile up to date. Therefore, if there is any significant change in the volume of business which it carries out in respect of particular investments or investment activities, it must immediately notify SFA; as it must if it wants to enter into a new type of activity or carry out an existing activity in a new kind of investment. A firm must receive prior permission from SFA before it undertakes any new kind of investment business.

Fit and Proper Person Test

3–005   Before any investment business can become a member of SFA or any individual can become a registered person, the firm or the individual has to satisfy SFA's fit and proper person test.

In determining whether a firm or individual is fit and proper, SFA will look at:

1. *Financial integrity and reliability*

Obviously, in the case of a firm, SFA will be concerned that it has the necessary financial resources to satisfy the financial resources requirement of the Financial Rules (see Chapter 19 below). In other words, the firm must be generally sound financially and have sufficient capital to enable it to survive poor trading periods, falls in the market values of investments in which it holds positions and clients defaulting on their settlement obligations.

SFA will look at the sources from which the capital is provided and, if the firm seeking membership is not a new company, its past record.

SFA will be interested to know whether the firm has been bankrupt or has entered into liquidation; has been the subject of a receiving or administration order, or a winding-up petition; or has entered into a deed of arrangement or similar agreement with creditors. Similarly, SFA will inquire whether there has been any failure to satisfy a judgment debt under a court order in the last 10 years.

Similar questions will be asked of any individual seeking registration so that his financial integrity and reliability can be properly assessed.

2. *Absence of Convictions or Civil Liabilities*

Under this heading, SFA will examine whether the applicant (which is defined to include both a firm seeking membership and an individual seeking registration) has been:

(i)   the subject of any criminal proceedings (except those for minor road traffic offences), or penalties for deliberate tax evasion;

(ii)   found civilly liable for fraud, misfeasance or other misconduct;

(iii)   involved in any civil litigation where there has been a finding or settlement against the applicant involving a liability in excess of £5,000;

(iv)   subject to an adverse finding in any civil court proceedings in respect of investment business;

(v)   disqualified at any time from being a director, or from otherwise acting in the management of the affairs of any company; and, finally;

(vi)   concerned with the management of any company which has been the subject of any investigation by inspectors appointed under companies or similar legislation, or required to produce documents to the Department of Trade and Industry or the Serious Fraud Office in connection with any investigation.

3. *Competence*

SFA will look to see whether a firm is competent and experienced to carry on the types of investment business for which it is seeking authorisation. This examination will largely centre upon the qualities of the individuals who will manage the firm and the other individuals who will be individually registered as representatives and traders.

SFA places much emphasis on all key staff being individually registered with it. In the case of staff who will give investment advice, manage investments, deal in investments or procure new business, SFA will want to be assured that they have passed or gained exemption from the relevant examinations, or have sufficient experience to obtain exemptions from such examinations; or, if there are no examination requirements, have suitable experience or training. SFA will also want to be satisfied generally about their suitability for employment in the particular posts which they hold in the firm.

4. *Good reputation and character*

SFA must be generally satisfied about the applicant's reputation and character. Obviously, relevant factors include: whether any previous restrictions or refusals have been made in respect of the applicant's right to carry on any trade, business or profession; whether the applicant has been subject to any investigation into allegations of misconduct or malpractice, or has been the subject of an adverse finding from any professional body; whether the applicant has been disciplined or publicly criticised by any regulatory authority or officially appointed inquiry; and whether the applicant has attracted any material adverse publicity.

5. *Efficiency, honesty and fairness*

SFA will be concerned that the firm or registered person will deal honestly and fairly with customers and other people with whom the firm deals in the course of its investment business. SFA will want to be satisfied that both the firm and the registered person will provide an efficient service. In assessing the applicant's fitness under this heading, SFA will have regard to the cumulative effect of matters which, by themselves, might not be sufficient to warrant a refusal of membership or registration.

In considering these five criteria, SFA will take into account any relevant matter which relates to persons associated with the applicant: for example, in the case of an applicant who is an individual, relevant matters relating to members of his family, fellow directors or partners, persons whom he has employed, and any other person or body with whom he has business interests or close ties. In the case of a company seeking membership, SFA will have regard to relevant factors relating to other companies within the same group structure and directors and controllers of the applicant or any other group companies. The same type of analysis will also be done for partnerships.

Controllers

3–006 Obviously, SFA is interested to know who controls a member firm. In relation to a body corporate, a controller is defined to include any person who, alone or with any associate or associates, is entitled to exercise, or control the exercise of, 15 per cent. or more of the voting power of the body corporate or its holding company. "Associate", in this context, includes a person's wife, husband, minor child or stepchild; any body corporate of which he is a director; any employee or partner of his; and any subsidiary to the body corporate or employee of such subsidiary.

In respect of unincorporated associations, "controller" means any person in accordance with whose directions or instructions (disregarding ordinary professional advice) the officers of the association are accustomed to act; or any person who is entitled to exercise, or control the exercise of, 15 per cent. or more of the voting power at any general meeting.

Conduct and structure

In assessing fitness and properness, SFA will pay particular regard to the previous conduct of the applicant in respect of investment business and financial services regulation. It will also be concerned to ensure that the structure of any applicant firm for membership does not result in any unacceptable conflicts of interest between one part of the firm and another, between separate companies within the same group, and between directors, controllers and other major shareholders.

Continuing requirement

Once admitted to membership in the case of a firm, and to registration in the case of an individual, there is a continuing requirement to remain fit and proper. Any matter which could affect the firm's or individual's fitness must be notified immediately to SFA.

Assessed against each activity

One important aspect of the fit and proper test is that it is applied in relation to the particular types of investment business which the firm or the registered person is going to undertake. For example, a firm may easily be regarded as being competent, with the necessary qualified staff, in respect of one type of investment business, but not in respect of another: fit in agency dealing, but not in market making; fit in dealing in United Kingdom domestic equities, but not traded options. SFA will look at the scale of business undertaken by the firm or registered person in respect of the separate investment business activities. For example, a firm may have the necessary staff and systems to provide a good service to 100 customers, but would not be able to cope if it was servicing 150 customers. Similarly, a firm may have the capacity for settling, say, 1,000 transactions per day, but not 2,000 transactions. The type of customers with whom a firm deals will be important. A firm may be regarded as fit and proper for dealing with non-private customers or with execution-only customers who do not require advice, but not fit to deal with private customers for whom more rule obligations apply or to provide discretionary management services.

29

Notify changes

It is because fitness and properness is assessed in respect of the different kinds of business and the scale of business that a firm is required to notify SFA of any changes to its business profile in relation to either of these two aspects; and a firm cannot enter into any new type of investment business or significantly change the scale of its business activities without prior approval from SFA. Also, remember that SFA has reserved to itself the power to impose any condition which it thinks appropriate in authorising a firm and approving its business profile, or in registering an individual.

Individual Registration

3–007 The best way of ensuring that a firm is fit and proper to conduct the types of investment business for which it has been authorised is by ensuring that its employees are well qualified and reliable, and that the firm is directed and managed by honest and competent individuals. Hence, SFA has an individual registration requirement.

Any person who wishes to act as a director, partner, manager, representative or trader of a member firm has to be individually registered. One important advantage of individual registration is that, where a firm is generally efficient and properly supervises staff, SFA can take disciplinary action against an individual within the firm who acts in some unprofessional manner despite the proper training and supervision given by the firm, without the firm itself being disciplined. If the individual, however, acts in an unprofessional way because of lack of control, supervision or training by the firm, the firm can be disciplined for a failure of its management in respect of the individual and the individual can also be disciplined for his own unprofessional conduct. If, in such circumstances, SFA could only go against the firm, then the individual could more easily move to another firm without his past record following him and restricting the activities which he was permitted to undertake.

1. *Directors*

The following must be registered as directors with SFA:

(i) in the case of SFA firms which are not overseas members, any person occupying the position of director, whatever his title, together with any person under whose directions or instructions (not being advice given in a professional capacity) the directors are accustomed to act; and

(ii)   in the case of an overseas member (namely, a body corporate which is incorporated outside the United Kingdom, or whose principal place of business is outside the United Kingdom), any person who occupies a position appearing to SFA to be analogous to that of a director of a company registered under United Kingdom companies legislation, provided that director has responsibility (either alone or jointly) for the management of any part of the firm's investment business in the United Kingdom.

In the case of (ii) above, therefore, it is possible that only one person in the member firm will be registered as a director. If such a firm has no director who is directly responsible for the firm's United Kingdom investment business, it must nominate one to take this position and register him. Although the other directors of the overseas company are not individually registered, SFA still requires sufficient information about them which is relevant to SFA's assessment about the firm's own fitness and properness to conduct the range of investment business for which it is seeking authorisation.

Note that "directors" includes non-executive directors. They are equally subject to the registration requirements and are responsible in the same way as the executive directors for ensuring that their firm remains fit and proper and complies with the rules in conducting its investment business. The only difference in treatment between executive and non-executive directors occurs with regard to SFA's third tier rules on personal account transactions. Non-executive directors are only subject to these rules in respect of their dealings in the shares of the SFA member firm, other companies within the same group and related investments (see relevant sub-paragraph under paragraph 20–007 below).

2. Partners

Similar provisions relate to the registration of partners. In other words, a firm should register not merely partners, but any persons upon whose directions and instructions the partners are accustomed to act. In the case of partnerships constituted outside the United Kingdom or whose principal place of business is outside the United Kingdom, a similar policy applies, as outlined above in the case of bodies corporate, for not requiring all of them to be individually registered.

3. Managers

Any senior executive, unless he is already registered as a director or partner, must be registered as a manager if he has responsibility (either alone or jointly) for the management, supervision and control of any part of his employer's investment business in the United Kingdom. Examples of the types of person covered include the heads of dealing, sales, customer liaison, research and analysis, settlement and clearing, compliance, and finance.

It should be noted that, if an individual has already been registered as a director or partner, he should not also be registered as a manager, even though he manages a particular part of the firm's investment business. The category of registered manager includes those senior executives who do not have the legal status of director or partner, even though, as a courtesy, they may have the word "director" in their job title.

4. *SEOs, Compliance and Finance Officers*

3–008   Every SFA firm must nominate persons to be registered as:

(i)   Senior Executive Officer;

(ii)   Compliance Officer;

(iii) Finance Officer.

The person nominated to be the Senior Executive Officer (SEO) should be the most senior executive who is ultimately responsible for the management of the firm's investment business in the United Kingdom.

Normally, he will be a registered director or partner, except that, on application, a firm which is constituted outside the United Kingdom, or whose principal place of business is outside the United Kingdom, can nominate to this position the General Manager of its United Kingdom branch, even if he is not a director or partner.

The Compliance Officer is the person nominated by the firm as responsible for all compliance matters, other than compliance with the Financial Rules (Chapter 3 of SFA's rule book and see Chapter 19 below). The Finance Officer is the person nominated by the firm to be responsible for compliance with the Financial Rules.

The Compliance and Finance Officers must be registered as managers, if they are not already registered as directors or partners.

SFA requires firms to nominate individuals to fill these three positions for two reasons. It makes sure that the firm clearly establishes within its own internal organisation who is ultimately responsible for the conduct of the various parts of its investment business in accordance with the rules. It also means that there are clearly designated lines of communication between the firm and SFA with reference to all matters concerning the firm's compliance with SFA's rules.

Ultimately, SFA regards the SEO as responsible for all matters concerning the firm's compliance with the rules and any other matters affecting the firm's fitness and properness to continue doing investment business. Therefore, both the Compliance and Finance Officers should have direct reporting lines to the SEO. Of course, it is open to a firm to appoint the same person to two of these positions, or, in fact, to all three. Obviously, this may be necessary in a smaller firm.

5. *Representatives*

Any person employed by a member firm whose duties include **3–009** managing investments, procuring customers to do investment business with the firm or giving investment advice must be registered as a representative.

The register of representatives is divided into a number of sub-categories. A representative is only able to carry out the activities of a representative outlined above in connection with the kinds of investment and investment business covered by his particular sub-category authorisation.

Note that the individual is registered as a representative of his firm and is not, through his individual registration, a person authorised in his own right to carry on investment business under the FSA 1986. Therefore, there is another restriction. Within his sub-categorisation, he can only carry on his duties of a representative in relation to the kinds of investment business for which his firm has been authorised. For example, if he is a General Representative, he is able to act as a representative in relation to any type of investment business. Nevertheless, if his firm is only authorised to carry on investment business in shares and debentures with non-private customers, then the representative will be subject to the same restriction when carrying out his duties.

The sub-categories are:

(i) *General Representative.* As stated above, he is able to carry out the duties of a representative in relation to any type of investment. To become a General Representative a person has to have passed both the Securities Representative and the Futures and Options Representative examinations, or gained exemptions.

(ii) *Securities Representative.* A Securities Representative can carry out the duties of a representative in relation to any types of investment, other than futures and options (including futures and options on indices; namely, contracts for difference). To be registered, a person must have passed the Securities Representative examination or gained exemption. Note that a Securities Representative can carry on, without additional registration or examination qualifications, the duties of a Corporate Finance Representative or a Money Market Representative.

(iii) *Futures and Options Representative.* A representative admitted to this sub-register can only carry on the duties of a representative in relation to futures and options, including futures and options on indices. So, if he wishes to act as a representative in relation to the underlying products, he would also need to be qualified and registered as a Securities Representative. Admission to the sub-register of Futures and Options Representative is dependent upon passing or gaining exemption from the relevant examination.

(iv) *Corporate Finance Representative*. For those representatives whose duties are going to be limited to investment business which falls within the definition of corporate finance business, this is the appropriate sub-register. However, note that both General Representatives and Securities Representatives can carry on corporate finance business without any additional qualifications or registration.

(v) *Money Market Representative*. Inclusion on this sub-register only allows the individual to act as a representative in relation to money market instruments. These are the investments listed in the FSA 1986, Sched. 5, para. 2(2) which are included in the Bank of England's Grey Paper concerned with "the regulation of wholesale markets and sterling, foreign exchange and bullion".

3–010 This register is only relevant:

(i) for those staff who are employed by an SFA firm which, although carrying on activities in the wholesale money markets, is not supervised in respect of these activities by being included on the Bank of England's list of exempted persons maintained under section 43 of the FSA 1986; or

(ii) to staff who, although employed by section 43 listed institutions, act outside the scope of the section 43 exemption because

(a) they deal below the size limits or with people who are not wholesale counterparties, or
(b) they provide discretionary management or ongoing advisory management in respect of portfolios consisting of wholesale money market instruments.

Note that the section 43 exemption only applies to wholesale transactions and advice given in relation to those transactions. An SFA firm which manages a portfolio, whether on a discretionary basis or on an ongoing advisory basis, which consists of wholesale money market investments will not be acting within the scope of its section 43 exemption and, therefore, the individual responsible for managing that portfolio will need to be a registered representative.

At the present time, there is no examination requirement for entry to the Money Market Representative sub-register. Note also that a representative on the General Representative sub-register or the

Securities Representative sub-register does not need to be separately included on this sub-register before being able to carry on the duties of a representative in relation to money market investments.

(vi) *Oil Market Participants Representative.* An individual who is employed by an oil market participant cannot carry out the duties of a representative in relation to an oil market investment activity unless he is included on this sub-register. Unlike with the specialist sub-registers for corporate finance and money markets, it is only a representative on the General Representative sub-register, rather than one on the Securities Representative sub-register, who can act as an Oil Market Representative without being specifically included on this sub-register. As with the Money Market sub-register, there is no examination requirement for this sub-register.

6. *Traders*

A person employed by an SFA member firm must be registered as a **3–011** trader, unless he is already a registered representative, before he can commit his firm in market dealings or in transactions in any investments.

Again, as with registered representatives, traders have two limitations imposed upon them. Firstly, a trader can only commit his firm in market dealings or in transactions in investments which are within the particular sub-category of the register to which he has been admitted. Secondly, a trader is further restricted in the sense that he can only commit his firm in market dealings or in transactions in investments which are within the scope of his firm's business profile: in other words, he must confine himself to the kinds of investment and scale of investment business activity for which his firm has been authorised to do investment business by SFA.

Note that a registered representative can, within the scope of the investment business covered by his particular sub-category, commit his firm in market dealings and in transactions in investments without having to be separately registered as a trader. A person who is only registered as a trader, however, cannot manage investments, procure customers or give investment advice.

A person who is employed by a firm which only acts as agent will need to be authorised as a trader if his firm becomes a party to the transaction, even if this is only in the sense that the firm bears the settlement risk and will be liable for any default by its principal, who will be its customer. A person, however, would not have to be registered as a trader if he merely passes a customer's order to another firm for execution, where his firm has no involvement in respect of the transaction apart from passing the order. Obviously, if this same person has, before passing the order to another firm for execution, given advice to the customer, he will need to be registered as a representative.

Similarly, he will need to be a representative if his job is to find and procure customers for another firm.

The various sub-categories for traders are:

(i) *United Kingdom domestic securities.* This includes gilt-edged securities, but does not extend to options, futures, and contracts for difference.

(ii) *International traders.* This is similarly restricted as (i), in the sense that it does not cover options, futures and contracts for difference. This sub-register, however, covers trading in non-United Kingdom investments.

(iii) *Inter-dealer brokers.*

(iv) *Money brokers.*

(v) *Money market instruments.*

(vi) *Futures and options.*

Although both registered representatives and registered traders can commit their firms in market dealings, only a registered representative may, with the consent of another SFA which is providing clearing functions for his employer, commit that clearing firm in market dealings or in transactions in investments. Remember, however, that the representative will still need to be acting within the scope of the particular sub-category in which he has been registered and within the scope of his firm's business profile.

Appointed representatives not traders

3–012   Another restriction on registration as a trader concerns appointed representatives. An appointed representative of an SFA firm or an employee of such an appointed representative cannot be registered as a trader because the exemption from authorisation for appointed representatives in section 44 of the FSA 1986 only applies to investment business which consists of: procuring persons to enter into investment agreements; giving advice to persons about entering into investment agreements; or giving advice as to the sale of investments issued by his principal or as to the exercise of rights conferred by any investment. Therefore, if an appointed representative or his employee wanted to do any of the activities for which a person needs to be registered as a trader, the appointed representative would have to be an authorised person in his own right. Similarly, an appointed representative or his employee is not able to manage investments, although this is one of the permitted activities of a registered representative. In other words, an appointed representative or his employee, although requiring registration as a representative, can only procure customers to enter into investment agreements or give investment advice.

Examinations

Apart from sub-category (i), there is no examination requirement and a trader can be registered in all or any combination of the above sub-categories. As regards futures and options, it should be noted that a number of investment exchanges set examinations and other admission requirements for individuals who wish to deal in investments traded on the relevant exchange.

Dual registration

Any individual who is already registered as a director, partner or manager will also need to be registered as a representative or trader before he can carry out any of the duties of a representative or trader for his firm. Although there are examination requirements for most of the registered representatives and for the first sub-category of registered traders, passing or gaining exemption from the necessary examination is not by itself sufficient to enable the person to be registered. The fit and proper test requirement applies to all individuals seeking individual registration in whatever category. Therefore, SFA must be satisfied that, besides showing their competence in respect of the examination requirement, the individuals also satisfy all other requirements of the fit and proper person test. Where there is no examination requirement, the individual will still have to show that he meets the competency expected of a representative or trader to be employed in the particular sub-category.

Limitation on registration

There is sometimes a misunderstanding that any employee of an SFA firm who has contact with customers must be registered as a representative. This is not correct. Representatives are only those who manage investments, procure customers and give investment advice. Therefore, back-office staff who send out contract notes or account and valuation statements, and who deal with inquiries from customers about settlement dates, the balances in their account and non-receipt of documentation do not need to be individually registered. Similarly, those who receive orders from customers, transmit orders received from customers to others in the firm for execution, and report to customers in respect of execution, do not have to be individually registered, provided they do not advise customers.

An employee is only giving investment advice where it is specific to an investment agreement. An employee who only gives a general explanation of what the market is doing, what current prices are; or what the firm's terms of business are does not have to be registered as a representative unless what he is doing actually amounts to procuring investors to enter into investment agreements with his firm.

Obviously, it is important to ensure that any staff who are not individually registered and who have contact with the firm's customers are properly supervised to ensure that they do not act in a capacity which would require individual registration. Also, the Head of Settlement and the Head of Sales would need to be registered as managers, unless they are to be registered as directors or partners. In addition, the Head of Sales would almost certainly need to be registered as a representative because he is likely to be procuring customers and giving investment advice.

Overseas employers

3–013   Chapter 4 below discusses the extent to which an overseas branch of an SFA firm is subject to the rules. On the whole, it is only caught where it is carrying on regulated business. Some of the Conduct of Business Rules, however, have a wider application.

An employee of an overseas branch of an SFA firm only needs to be registered as a representative with SFA where he is performing the functions of a representative in connection with any business carried on by the branch which is subject to any of the Conduct of Business Rules in Chapter 5 of SFA's rulebook. Even then SFA will allow him to avoid individual registration if, when he carries out the duties of a representative in the course of business for which his branch is subject to the rules, he is accompanied by a registered representative from the firm's United Kingdom office. It should be noted that the overseas employee who is not himself registered will not always have to be accompanied by a registered representative when he is in the United Kingdom: it will only be when he is doing business for his branch which is not within the "foreign business carve-out" to the rules. He will not have to be so accompanied where he is meeting United Kingdom customers who were "legitimately" solicited by the branch.

Staff from some unauthorised overseas investment businesses sometimes visit the United Kingdom to renew existing customer contacts or to procure new business. To avoid their firms having to seek authorisation under the FSA 1986, the staff may be temporarily attached to authorised firms. The latter firms take responsibility under the rules for the investment business done by the staff of the overseas business. The overseas staff become, therefore, employees of the United Kingdom firms. "Employee" is defined widely to include an individual employed under a contract for services or any other contract under which he will provide services to the "employer"; and also includes an individual whose services are, under an arrangement between the "employer" and a third party (for example, between the United Kingdom firm and the overseas business) placed at the disposal and under the control of the "employer". Where the overseas staff are carrying out the functions of a representative, they will have to be registered as representatives of the United Kingdom firm.

A fuller discussion on the application of the rules to overseas branches and on the authorisation requirements for overseas businesses is given in Chapter 4 below.

Conditions

In admitting an individual to one of the registers, SFA can impose any conditions which it thinks appropriate. For example, in admitting someone to a particular sub-register of representative or trader, SFA may wish to restrict further, within the scope of the particular sub-category, the types of investment business in which the individual can act as representative or trader. Also, SFA could impose a strict condition concerning the supervision of a particular registered person.

Material changes

Both the firm for whom he works and the registered person are under a duty to notify SFA of any material change which is relevant to the individual's registration. This does not extend to just routine matters, for example where the individual's registration category will need to be amended because of a change in his employment duties. The more important aspect is that the firm and the individual are under a duty to notify SFA of any matter which could affect the individual's continuing fitness and properness. Remember, the fit and proper requirement is not merely one which an individual has to satisfy to be admitted to the register in the first place, but is a continuing requirement. On admission to a register, an individual has to agree in writing with SFA that he will not commit any act or omission which places his firm in breach of the rules. He also has to agree to be bound by and subject to SFA's Enforcement Rules.

Subject to discipline after resignation

Like a firm, a registered person remains subject to the jurisdiction of SFA for a period of one year after the firm's resignation from SFA in respect of acts and omissions before the acceptance of the firm's resignation. In assessing the one-year period, it is not necessary that any enforcement decisions have been completed within the 12 months.

The test is that enforcement proceedings have been commenced within the 12-month period, such as SFA commencing an investigation into a possible rule breach or a customer's complaint.

Where the individual who is disciplined by SFA is no longer a registered person, because at the time of the disciplinary decision he is no longer employed by an SFA firm (or, if still employed, is no longer employed in a capacity requiring registration), the Disciplinary Tribunal, in addition to imposing one of the normal penalties, may determine that the person should not be considered fit and proper to be admitted or readmitted to all or any of the registers. In other words, the tribunal could prevent the person being employed in a registrable capacity by another SFA firm in the future.

Appointed Representatives

3–014   The SFA allows certain persons, called appointed representatives, to carry on investment business without being authorised, provided responsibility for them is accepted by other firms who are authorised. The vast majority of appointed representatives are employed to sell the life products and unit trusts of the large life offices and unit trust managers who are authorised by LAUTRO. Often appointed representatives are self-employed salesmen, but a number are companies which employ their own selling staff. In both cases, however, the appointed representatives are employed to promote and sell the products of the authorised person who has accepted responsibility for them.

Although most appointed representatives act for LAUTRO firms, there is a significant number who act for SFA firms. Before Big Bang, many stockbroking firms employed "half commission men" who were self-employed, but introduced business to one particular firm and were remunerated by receiving a substantial share of the commission charged by this firm on any business transacted for the introduced customers.

As explained when talking about individual registration, appointed representatives are not able themselves to deal. They can only procure customers to enter into deals with other persons and give investment advice.

The only reason they do not have to be authorised is because responsibility for their actions is taken by an authorised firm in the same way that such a firm is responsible for the actions of its employees. Therefore, SFA requires appointed representatives to be registered in a similar way as any authorised firm's employees: in other words, appointed representatives must become Registered Representatives.

Where the appointed representative is itself a company, then the company must be admitted to the special "corporate sub-category" of the Register of Representatives and any of its employees who procure customers or give investment advice will have to be individually registered in one of the appropriate sub-categories of this register for individuals.

Effectively, an authorised firm which has appointed representatives is in the position of a mini-SRO. In other words, it has to satisfy itself that any appointed representative is fit and proper to act in such a capacity. As with the obligation on SFA firms and their individually registered staff, the fit and proper requirement for appointed representatives is a continuing one. A firm, like an SRO, must have adequate resources to monitor and enforce compliance by its appointed representatives with the rules. This is because the firm is made responsible, to the same extent as if it had specifically authorised it, for anything said, done or omitted by its appointed representative, or one of his employees, in carrying on investment business for which the firm has accepted responsibility. This is similar to an employer's vicarious liability for the acts and omissions of his employees.

A firm is not responsible for everything which an appointed representative does, because an appointed representative, unless restricted in the contract with the firm appointing him as its Representative, may act also as a Representative for another firm or engage in non-investment business. Many firms will feel, however, that they can properly monitor the fitness and properness of their appointed representatives only if they are restricted to doing business for which the firm has accepted responsibility. Likewise, although under the FSA 1986 an appointed representative can procure customers to deal with, and give advice about dealing in investments with, other persons besides the firm for which he is acting as an appointed representative, the firm may restrict the appointed representative only to procure customers to deal with itself.

Where the firm allows its appointed representative to carry on other financial business, there is a duty on the firm to ensure that the investment business for which it has accepted responsibility is held out as being clearly distinct from the other financial business, so that people who deal with the appointed representative in respect of the other financial business will not be under any false impression that they are subject to protection under the FSA 1986 owing to the firm's responsibility for the appointed representative's investment business.

In respect of the appointed representative carrying on investment business for which the firm has accepted responsibility, the firm must then ensure that the Representative only carries on investment business which is within the scope of the firm's own authorisation from SFA: in other words, the appointed representative is restricted by the profile of authorised business set out in his principal's business profile.

The rules require that there must be a provision in the contract between the firm and its appointed representative to the effect that the firm's employment of the appointed representative can only be terminated with the authority of SFA. This is imposed in an attempt to put the appointed representative in a similar position to a firm resigning from SFA in respect of the appointed representative ceasing to do business, transferring his business or moving to, in effect, a different regulator by becoming the appointed representative of a different firm.

Termination

Cessation of business

3–015   The structure and ownership of SFA firms may often change. Some firms will go out of business for various reasons: sometimes it will be because they are unprofitable; at other times it may be because those running the business decide to retire. Some firms will be taken over or merge with other firms. In other cases a firm will decide to pull out of a particular type of business and sell or transfer that business to another firm.

The rules require that, at least in the case of private customers, where a firm or its appointed representative decides to withdraw from providing any investment service for which it is authorised by SFA, including any related custodian services, the firm must ensure that any business which is outstanding is properly completed or transferred to another firm authorised under the FSA 1986.

In other words, a firm should not completely leave its private customers in the lurch. It must ensure that any outstanding bargains are properly settled and the necessary contract or confirmation notes are sent out. If the business is not being transferred to another firm, then the customers must be given proper notice that the firm is closing down; any balances in the customers' accounts must be properly returned to them, together with any documents of title relating to investments owned by them; and, if the firm has been holding as nominee customers' investments in safe custody accounts, these investments must be properly reregistered in the customers' names and returned to them (or transferred, with their permission, to another custodian).

If the firm is selling or transferring part of its business relating to private customers to another firm, it must take similar steps, but, rather than return everything to the customer, it must ensure that the new firm has all the necessary information and documents to enable it to pick up exactly where the old firm has left off. It will be important that the new firm obtains all the relevant details about customers' business which is being transferred so that it will be able to comply with the suitability requirement in managing portfolios and giving advice.

Obviously, where a business has been closed down or transferred, it is important that the customers should be given as much notice as possible. In practice, however, it will often be difficult to give notice. Some failures occur very quickly. Also, where a sale of a business has been negotiated, both sides will want to keep quiet about their negotiations until the deal is finally concluded. Once the deal is agreed, the sale or transfer may take effect immediately.

In such circumstances, the disposing firm will not have broken the rule provision if it is willing to co-operate fully with the acquirer in ensuring that all relevant matters connected with its customers' accounts are properly transferred. However, where does the new firm stand in connection with the transferred customers? These customers will not have had an opportunity to consent to the transfer and any agreements which they had would have been with the old firm. Therefore, it is important that all the customers affected should be informed immediately about the arrangements being made for the transfer of their business, and the new firm will not be able to treat them as its own established customers until they have signified in some way that they consent to entering into a customer relationship with it.

This could cause problems because it may take some time before the new firm obtains a response from the transferred customers, yet some of them may have had large, discretionary portfolios which require active management, with important decisions and transactions having to be made to protect their interests before they have had a chance to be informed about, and signified their consent to the new arrangements. In such circumstances, the new firm should act to protect these investors, even if it has not had their consent to the transfer. If the customers later consent, then there should be no problem. If the customers do not consent to the transfer, then, technically, they remain customers of the old firm which will still be under a responsibility to ensure that proper arrangements are made for the transfer or completion of outstanding business. It is likely that the new firm is protected in respect of any action which it may have taken before the investors signified their rejection of the new arrangements, on the basis that the new firm can be regarded as acting as the agent of the old firm in respect of the latter's obligation to ensure that the outstanding business is properly completed or transferred.

Assuming that the customers have no objection to the transfer of **3–016** their business, how should the new firm proceed in obtaining their actual consent? In respect of those types of investment services which a firm can provide under the rules without having to enter into a two-way customer agreement which is signed and returned by a customer, the new firm could merely send a one-way document setting out the arrangements which have been made for the transfer of the business and confirming that it will continue to handle the customer's account unless he notifies the firm to the contrary. This one-way document would also set out the basis on which the new firm would be providing its services to the customer. Until such time that the customer, after receiving the document, objected, the new firm would be able to assume that he was willing to do business on the terms stated. Under the new rulebook, except in the case of business which requires a two-way document, a firm does not have to wait for any period of time between sending out its terms of business letter and beginning to transact business with the customer. As long as the new firm is not intending to do business that requires a two-way customer agreement under the rules, it could proceed on the basis of this one-way document, even if, in respect of the same type of business, the customer had entered into a two-way agreement with the previous firm.

The problem about obtaining the customers' consent to the transfer really arises in those cases where a two-way customer agreement is required, namely in respect of contingent liability transactions for private customers and discretionary business for any customer. The same problem also arises in respect of those individual rule obligations which prevent a firm from doing certain types of business without prior consent from the customer. In such circumstances, the new firm would not be able to regard the transferred customers as its own customers until it had obtained their signature to new documentation. The new firm could send out either completely new customer documentation or a short letter briefly explaining the arrangements made for the transfer and asking the customer to sign and return a copy, signifying his consent to the new firm taking on his business on exactly the same terms as applied under his customer agreement with the old firm (or on those terms subject to any revisions set out in the letter informing him about the transfer). The returned signed letter, with its reference to the old agreement, would satisfy the requirements for the customer's written consent, because all of the necessary requirements for a two-way customer agreement would have been included by the reference to the old agreement in the covering letter explaining the transfer arrangements, to which the customer signifies his consent with his signature.

3–017   Where the rules require a two-way customer agreement, then the new firm should not transact business for the transferred customer until he has signed either a new customer agreement or the covering letter on the transfer which incorporates the old agreement; but, as explained above, where the transferred account is a discretionary one which requires active management, it is right, in the interests of the customer, that the new firm should continue to manage that portfolio properly whilst waiting for the customer to signify his consent to the new arrangements. During this period the new firm may be regarded as acting as the agent for the old firm, because, until the customer has been notified about the transfer and made his own election, the old firm, as already explained, is still under its rule responsibility, despite arranging the sale, to see that all outstanding private customer business is properly completed or transferred.

Under the old rules there was a provision that, where a customer's business was transferred between two companies within the same group as part of a group restructuring, the new company could continue to do business with the customer without the requirement for new customer documentation provided the customers were informed within three months of the details of the restructuring affecting them. This provision no longer applies, so firms which belong to groups may wish to include a provision in their customer documentation to the effect that any of the services to be provided by the firm may also be provided by another group company.

A number of customer agreements, especially those based upon TSA's model documents issued in 1988, contain a variation clause allowing a firm unilaterally to change a term of the agreement on notice. Such a provision, however, would not be sufficient to allow another legal entity which was acquiring a business to turn the customer relationship with the old firm into a customer relationship with it.

Whilst mentioning the arrangements for the transferring of business, it is relevant to note that one of the permissions under the Common Unsolicited Calls Regulations under which a cold call can be made on a private investor is where the call is made by the acquirer of a business and its purpose is to enable the acquirer to invite the person called to establish a customer relationship with him (see Chapter 13 below).

Death or incapacity

In the case of smaller firms or firms providing specialist services, the services provided to customers may be significantly affected by the death or incapacity of an individual within a firm. The rules provide that, where this could be the case, the firm must make arrangements to protect the interests of its customers. The relevant Core Rule provision only applies to private customers, but SFA has extended it to all customers. Obviously, the biggest concern is in the case of a sole trader or two-man partnership. Such firms should make arrangements to provide a proper, continuous service to customers to cover any absences due to sickness, holiday, family bereavement, as well as the untimely death of the sole trader or one of the partners. In fact, SFA requires such firms to keep SFA informed on an up-to-date basis of the details concerning arrangements it has with another authorised firm for protecting its customers.

3–018

Resignation

Normally, a firm cannot resign from SFA's membership without giving three months' written notice. The notice must give reasons for, and the circumstances surrounding, the resignation.

SFA's purpose in requiring three months' notice of the resignation and details of the circumstances concerning the resignation is to enable

3–019

it to ensure that, if the firm is ceasing investment business, proper arrangements are made for the winding-up of that business, the completion of outstanding work for its customers and, if appropriate, the transfer of the customers to another firm. Also, it gives SFA time to inquire and investigate as to whether the real reason for the resignation is that the firm wishes to avoid an investigation or disciplinary action in respect of possible rule breaches or other misbehaviour.

In fact, SFA's Membership Committee can refuse to accept the notice of resignation if it considers that any matter affecting the firm should be investigated, or that it is desirable to enable a prohibition or requirement to be imposed or continued under the Enforcement Rules. Obviously, SFA will want to delay a firm's resignation if it considers that it is necessary to take action against the firm to protect investors. Also, SFA would not want a firm to resign from membership merely to avoid disciplinary action and, thereby, be in a position to seek authorisation from another regulatory body without a finding having been recorded against it which would have to be taken into account by another body responsible for authorising it as fit and proper to do investment business.

In some circumstances, even despite a firm giving three months' notice of resignation, matters affecting a firm's fitness to do investment business may only come to light after it has resigned from membership. Therefore, under SFA's rules, a firm and any of its registered persons continue to be subject to SFA's jurisdiction after the firm's resignation in respect of any acts or omissions committed before its resignation. All that is necessary is that SFA should have begun to take proceedings against the firm or registered person within the 12 months following the firm's resignation. For example, it would be sufficient that SFA has issued a Notice of Investigation against the firm, even though no disciplinary proceedings have been instituted. A firm also remains subject to SFA's complaints and arbitration proceedings, provided the investigation of the complaint has begun within the same period. As long as the investigation or other enforcement steps are started within the 12 months following resignation, then the firm remains subject to SFA's jurisdiction for however long it takes to conclude the relevant enforcement, complaints and arbitration proceedings.

3–020 This extension of the jurisdiction beyond the 12 months following resignation only applies in respect of an investigation which was started within this period. Therefore, if, after the 12 months, whilst an investigation is going on in relation to a matter which arose before, a complaint is made to SFA about a completely unrelated matter, SFA would have no jurisdiction in respect of this latter complaint. On the other hand, if an investigation which had been started in respect of one matter within the 12 months threw up information outside the 12 months concerning other possible rule breaches, the firm could be investigated and disciplined for these other breaches because they all stemmed from the original investigation which was started within the time limit.

It should be remembered that the powers which SFA exerts over its members is based on contract. When a firm applies for membership, it agrees to be bound by the rules of SFA which are in force from time to time. The rule concerning the extension of jurisdiction beyond the resignation operates under the original contractual agreement which the firm entered into in applying for membership, and the fact of the firm's resignation from membership does not terminate the agreement to remain subject to SFA's Enforcement Rules in respect of matters existing whilst it was a member.

In some cases, requiring a firm to give three months' written notice of termination of membership may operate harshly, especially if the reasons for resigning are genuine. For example, a firm may want to transfer to the membership of another SRO because its business has developed in a way which is more appropriate for supervision by that SRO; or the firm may want to cease trading and has properly made provisions for the transfer of its business and customers to another firm. Therefore, SFA has discretion to accept a shorter notice period.

Chapter 4

Application

Background

Firms need to know when they are subject to the rules. Some firms **4–001** will be doing business which is not investment business and other firms will have extensive branch networks, with investment business being done from overseas branches with customers who are not in the United Kingdom. The FSA 1986 was set up to regulate investment business in the United Kingdom and its jurisdiction is limited to what is done in or from the United Kingdom. Therefore, non-investment business and investment business done without a United Kingdom connection will not normally be subject to FSA 1986 regulation.

Basically, a firm which operates from a place of business in the United Kingdom will be subject to FSA 1986 regulation in respect of all of the investment business which it does from that place of business, whether business is done within the United Kingdom or with persons based overseas. A firm which does not have a permanent place of business in the United Kingdom will only be subject to regulation to the extent that it is doing investment business with persons in the United Kingdom. This is the broad approach, but it is subject to a degree of qualification.

As already explained, a firm agrees, as part of its application for membership, to be bound by SFA's rules. This means, that under the contract of membership, SFA could impose rules on and regulate any part of a firm's business, even that which is non-investment business or investment business done from an overseas location. In other words, under the contract of membership, SFA can spread its tentacles into areas which, if they were performed by a separately incorporated business, would not require that business to become an authorised person under the FSA 1986. Having said this, the general thrust of the application of the rules to a firm is that they should only apply to those parts of a firm's business which, if they were done by separately incorporated business, would require that separate business to become an authorised person.

Although SFA does not normally impose specific rules affecting a firm's non-investment business or that part of its investment business which is done from a place of business overseas, the way in which a firm carries on non-investment business or operates from an overseas location will be relevant in terms of the fit and proper test. Even though, in respect of its investment business in the United Kingdom, a firm is in compliance with the rules, SFA could take the view that the firm is no longer fit and proper to be an SFA member because of the way in which it is conducting non-investment business or investment business from an overseas location. The firm's non-directly regulated activities could be damaging in terms of its reputation and could lead to doubts about its financial standing and ability to deal with investors in the United Kingdom in an honest and reliable way. So it would be possible for SFA to impose disciplinary sanctions on a firm for matters unconnected with its United Kingdom investment business.

Membership and registration

4–002   There is no general application rule. To begin with, a firm will have to make its own decision as to whether or not it requires authorisation under the FSA 1986, and, if so, which SRO it should apply to. Once a firm applies for membership to SFA, SFA will determine whether or not the firm's business falls within the scope of investment business for which SFA is the appropriate regulatory body. As already discussed, an applicant firm has to give information about itself as a whole, such as its group structure, controllers and directors, and details about non-investment business or non-SFA authorised investment business which the firm carries on.

It should not be forgotten that, in the case of a firm which is not an overseas member (namely, it is not incorporated outside the United Kingdom or its principal place of business is not outside the United Kingdom), all directors or partners have to be individually registered with SFA, even if some of them have no involvement with the investment business activities of the firm. It is only in the case of overseas members that the individual registration requirements are limited to directors or partners responsible for the management of the firm's United Kingdom investment business.

In the case of registered managers, a firm only has to register individually those senior executives who are responsible for the management, supervision and control of any part of the firm's SFA authorised business. Likewise, a firm only has to individually register as representatives or traders those employees (including appointed representatives) who carry on the duties of a representative or trader in respect of the firm's SFA authorised business.

These are, therefore, the first two qualifications to the application of the rulebook. A distinction is made between the registration requirement for directors and partners as to whether the firm is a United Kingdom member or an overseas member. Then, there is a restriction on the registration requirements for managers, representatives and traders to those persons who are employed in respect of the firm's SFA authorised business.

Once a firm is a member, the application of the rules is then dependent upon the type of investment business being done. The Membership Rules, however, have wide notification requirements, so the firm must keep SFA informed of any matter which is relevant to continuing fitness and properness; and the Enforcement Rules allow SFA to take disciplinary action against a firm in respect of its continuing fitness and properness, as well as in respect of specific rule breaches.

Individually registered staff agree, as part of their contract to be registered with SFA, that they will not commit any act or omission which places their firm in breach of any of the rules and will be fully bound by, and subject to, SFA's Enforcement Rules. SFA could take disciplinary proceedings against a registered person for something not directly connected with investment business on the basis that the matter threw into question his fitness to carry on the duties involved in his registered status.

Apart from the fit and proper requirement, however, the application of the rules is mainly limited to a firm's investment business in the United Kingdom, including matters which by themselves do not amount to investment business, but which are done in connection with or part of a firm's investment business.

The Principles

The introduction to the Principles states that they apply to all FSA **4-003** 1986 authorised persons in respect of their conduct of investment business and financial standing. Obviously, financial standing is a general matter relating to fitness and properness. In respect of business undertaken by the firm, however, the Principles are limited to "investment business." Presumably, this means investment business as defined in the FSA 1986.

The question arises, do the Principles extend to any business which, although technically not investment business, is exempt from the authorisation requirements? For example, a firm, although authorised under the FSA 1986, may carry on business for which it does not require authorisation, such as acting in the wholesale money markets under a section 43 listing with the Bank of England. It is suggested that the Principles only apply to that investment business for which the firm has to be authorised. On this point also, remember that Schedule 1 to the FSA 1986 provides qualifications in Part III to the activities which are described in Part II as being investment business. Therefore, a firm will not be caught by the Principles where it is doing something which, although it may appear to be business for investment purposes, falls within these exemptions.

Authorisable investment business

The FSA 1986 requires authorisation before a person can carry on, or **4-004** purport to carry on, investment business in the United Kingdom. Investment business is described as engaging in one or more of the activities which fall within Schedule 1, Part II: namely, dealing in investments, arranging deals in investments, managing investments, giving investment advice, establishing or operating a collective investment scheme; provided none of the exclusions in Part III apply. Part III has exclusions stating that, although a person may be carrying out one of the activities referred to in Part II, it will not be investment business if it is carried out in the circumstances or capacities described in Part III.

Once the investment business test has been satisfied (namely, the business falls within Part II and is not excluded by Part III), it must then be determined whether or not it is investment business being done in the United Kingdom. There are two basic situations. One is concerned with where a person carries on investment business from a permanent place of business maintained by him in the United Kingdom; the other is where a person carries on investment business in the United Kingdom from an overseas location. Where there is a permanent place of business in the United Kingdom, then any investment business conducted from this location will be subject to the FSA 1986 authorisation requirements even if that business is not done with persons in the United Kingdom, but with persons based overseas. Remember that the Isle of Man, the Channel Islands and the Republic of Ireland are not within the United Kingdom, while Northern Ireland is.

Where a person is not carrying on investment business from a permanent place of business maintained in the United Kingdom, then authorisation is required where he engages in one or more of the activities which fall within Part II and which are not excluded by Part III and, also, Part IV, provided that his entering into one or more of these activities constitutes the carrying on by him of a business in the United Kingdom. The authorisation requirement does not apply merely as a result of entering into one of the activities: the person's entering into the activity in the United Kingdom must be done as part of, or as an attempt to build up, regular business in the United Kingdom, rather than as a one-off transaction.

The exclusions in Part IV only relate to persons who have no permanent place of business in the United Kingdom. The first exclusion (paragraph 26) relates to transactions with or through authorised or exempted persons: namely, the dealing in investments or the arranging of deals in investments is done with or through either an authorised person or a person exempted from authorisation under the FSA 1986 who is acting in the course of business in respect of which he is exempt.

The second exclusion (paragraph 27) applies where there is no other authorised or exempted person with or through whom the overseas person is dealing. An overseas person does not require authorisation if he is doing one of the activities in Part II with or in respect of persons in the United Kingdom as a result of an unsolicited or legitimately solicited approach. In other words, the business being done with a person in the United Kingdom must not have resulted from any approach from the overseas person; or, if it has been solicited by the overseas person, the solicitation must have been done in a way which complies with sections 56 and 57 of the FSA 1986. Section 56 is concerned with cold calling and section 57 with advertising. If the person in the United Kingdom has been solicited by the overseas person, it must have been as a result of a cold call which is within one of the permissions for overseas persons in the Common Unsolicited Calls Regulations or an advertisement which, if issued by the overseas person, has been approved by an authorised person.

Regulated business

The scope of SFA's rules try to follow the requirements for authorisation under the FSA 1986. Therefore, the rules should apply to investment business in relation to which the firm needs to be an authorised person, provided that person is not already subject to regulation by another SRO or RPB in respect of the particular activity. **4–005**

This mirroring of the scope of the rules to the scope of the authorisation requirements under the FSA 1986 is dealt with through the Core Rule definition of regulated business and SFA's definition of SFA authorised business. SFA authorised business means any activity which a firm carries on in the course of regulated business within the firm's SFA business profile. Basically, it is that type of regulated business for which the firm has been certified as fit and proper to carry on by SFA in approving its business profile.

Limb 1

Regulated business includes investment business which is carried on from a permanent place of business maintained by a firm (or its appointed representative) in the United Kingdom. This is similar to the first part of the FSA 1986 authorisation requirements. In other words, it is not limited to investment business done with persons in the United Kingdom, but also includes investment business done with persons overseas where that business is carried on from the firm's United Kingdom offices.

Limb 2

The second limb of the definition catches other business carried on with or for customers in the United Kingdom. In other words, it covers business done in the United Kingdom from a place of business outside the United Kingdom. It is like the second part of the authorisation test under the FSA 1986. Unlike Limb 1, it relates to investment business carried on with or for customers. This is similar to the first exclusion in Part IV, Schedule 1, mentioned above, because persons who are not customers are likely to be other authorised persons or exempted persons under the FSA 1986. Obviously, the Core Rule definition of market counterparty, together with SFA's rule extension to this definition, will be relevant as market counterparties are not customers.

There are two exclusions to this second limb to the definition of regulated business. The first exclusion is the more important and is intended to make sure that firms which carry on investment business in the United Kingdom, but not through a separate subsidiary, are at no disadvantage to those which have separate United Kingdom subsidiaries. The exclusions within Part IV, Schedule 1, to the requirements for authorisation under the FSA 1986 apply to persons without a permanent place of business in the United Kingdom and are, therefore, not available to a firm which has a permanent place of business in the United Kingdom, even if the largest part of its investment business is conducted from offices outside the United Kingdom.

4–006 Under the FSA 1986, it is the firm, the legal entity, which becomes an authorised person, rather than the United Kingdom branch office. When the FSA 1986 was brought into force in 1988, the regulators were concerned that firms which operated on an international basis should not be put to the expense or trouble of having to set up a separate subsidiary in the United Kingdom to do investment business. Because the firm as a whole becomes a member of SFA, rather than its United Kingdom office, the rules would have applied to any investment business conducted by the firm, wherever that business was conducted from and irrespective of the different countries in which its customers were located. It was, therefore, necessary to introduce, through the rulebooks, provisions similar to those contained in Part IV, Schedule 1, so that, now, investment business done by a firm's non-United Kingdom offices is only subject to regulation in the same circumstances in which those overseas offices would have to seek authorisation under the FSA 1986 if they were separate legal entities. The aim is that FSA 1986 regulation should apply to investment business done from an overseas place of business in a consistent manner, irrespective of whether that place of business is a branch office of an authorised firm or a separately incorporated company.

This qualification to the application of the rules for overseas branches is often referred to as "the foreign business carve-out" and is contained in this first exclusion to Limb 2 of the definition of regulated business. Regulated business does not include investment business carried on by a firm from an office outside the United Kingdom which would not be treated as carried on in the United Kingdom if that office were a separate person. In other words, the rules only apply to investment business done from a firm's overseas place of business where it it amounts to engaging with customers in the United Kingdom in one or more of the activities coming within Part II, Schedule 1 (and not being excluded by Parts III and IV), and provided the engaging in such activities constitutes the carrying on of a business in the United Kingdom.

The overseas branch benefits from the Part IV exclusions. If the business is only done with or through other authorised or exempted persons, it is not caught. Likewise, if it is entered into with customers in the United Kingdom as a result of an unsolicited or legitimately solicited approach: either the customer has not been approached by the overseas branch; or, if so approached, the approach does not result from any breaches of the cold calling permissions or the rules on advertising. Any business which would have been within the Part IV exclusions if the branch had been a separate legal body should be disregarded in determining whether any other investment activity amounts to the carrying on of a business in the United Kingdom. A branch, therefore, does not lose the protection of the foreign business carve-out merely because of an isolated breach of the cold calling or advertising restrictions; although it will be subject to SFA disciplinary action for the particular rule breach.

In mentioning cold calling and advertising, remember that the firm as a whole is a member of SFA. Therefore, if the firm, through its United Kingdom office, has an agreement with a private investor which permits cold calls, this agreement will enable the overseas branch to call such an investor unless the permission in the customer agreement has specifically been limited to calls by the United Kingdom office. Similarly, as the firm is an authorised person, any advertisement issued by the overseas office in the United Kingdom will not need approval by another authorised person under section 57 of the FSA 1986 because the overseas branch is part of an authorised person. Such an advertisement, however, will have to contain the "prescribed disclosure", warning investors that, if they deal with the overseas branch, they will not be subject to the protections of the FSA 1986 regulatory structure. **4–007**

The second exclusion to Limb 2 of the definition of regulated business relates to business of a firm's appointed representative which is not carried on in the United Kingdom. This is intended to be a similar qualification for a firm's appointed representative when operating from an overseas office.

SFA authorised business

SFA authorised business is defined to mean any activity in the course of regulated business within the firm's SFA business profile. In other words, it does not include the business which a firm does within the foreign business carve-out or investment business in relation to **4–008** which the firm is an exempted person or authorised by another SRO. The definition, however, is wider than that of regulated business in one respect. The latter definition turns on the definition of investment business, whereas SFA authorised business includes activities which by themselves are not investment business, but which the firm undertakes in the course of carrying on investment business which is regulated business. It, therefore, includes another Core Rule definition, namely that of associated business.

The term SFA authorised business is relevant in determining the scope of the Membership Rules. For example, these rules prevent a firm carrying on other investment business unless it is otherwise authorised or exempt under the FSA 1986 in respect of this business. The definition also sets the scope of the individual registration requirements for managers, representatives and traders. For example, an employee who is carrying out the duties of a representative in respect of business within the foreign business carve-out would not need to be individually registered with SFA. Finally, the definition is used in respect of a firm's obligations concerning cessation of business.

Safe custody and client money

4-009   The application of the Safekeeping Rules is that they apply where a firm has custody of a customer's investments in connection with or with a view to regulated business. They apply whether or nor not the custody responsibility by itself is an investment business activity (see paragraph 17–001 below). The relevant factor is the purpose for which the investments are held.

The Client Money Regulations apply where the investment business carried on by the firm is regulated business. Interestingly, investment business is defined, for the purpose of client money, to include activities which are normally excluded under Parts III and IV, Schedule 1 to the FSA 1986. It is suggested that this extension only applies to the reference to investment business within the main body of the Client Money Regulations rather than to the reference to investment business within the definition of regulated business. Otherwise the effect of the foreign business carve-out would be completely lost because it would not be possible to rely on the exemptions referred to in Part IV: namely, dealing with or through an authorised or exempted person; or with customers who have not been solicited in breach of the section 57(1) advertising provision or the permissions in SIB's Common Unsolicited Calls Regulations.

Once it is determined, however, that a firm is doing regulated business, then the Client Money Regulations govern money belonging to clients which is received or held by the firm and which is not immediately due and payable to it, even if it is received or held in the course of an investment business activity which would not itself be authorisable under the FSA 1986 because it is an activity excluded under Part III or IV, Schedule 1.

Conduct of business

The main relevance of the definition of regulated business is in the **4–010** context of the application of SIB's Core Conduct of Business Rules and SFA's third tier Conduct of Business Rules. In many cases, business done by a firm or its appointed representative which comes within the two exceptions to Limb 2 of the definition of regulated business, namely activities within the "foreign business carve-out," is not subject to these rules. There are, however, some specific extensions which are described below.

Core Rules

In talking about the application of the Conduct of Business Rules, it **4–011** is important to remember that the 40 Core Conduct of Business Rules are designated rules and, as such, apply directly to all members of SROs and those persons directly authorised by SIB. SFA has transferred five of these rules to other chapters in its rulebook, rather than include them in the Conduct of Business Rules Chapter (Chapter 5), because they fitted more appropriately under the General Rules (Chapter 1), the Membership Rules (Chapter 2) and the Complaints Rules (Chapter 6). Core Rule 40 is the rule which deals with their application as Core Rules and forms the basis of SFA's application provision for Chapter 5 (Rule 5–1). As the Core Conduct of Business Rules apply to SFA firms directly, the Core Rule part of Rule 5–1 governs their application, even if SFA's additions and qualifications to Core Rule 40 only apply to the rules in Chapter 5. The result of their inclusion in the other chapters means that their application is sometimes wider for SFA members. For example, the provision concerning reliance on formal guidance (Rule 1–4) now applies to any SFA rule.

Advertising

There is a separate application provision within Core Rule 40 (SFA Rule 5–1(4)) which applies to the advertising rules. This is discussed in Chapter 12 below.

Amended drafting

SFA has altered the drafting of some of the Core Conduct of Business Rules. Some of the alterations amount to permitted derogations, whilst others are extensions of the scope of the relevant

Core Rule. It is also worth noting that SFA has not included within its rulebook those elements within the Core Rules which permit general qualifications and exceptions. These are the rules which use phrases such as: "Subject to any exceptions contained in the rules of an SRO of which it is a member." These phrases would not mean anything directly to SFA members, but are more directed at the SROs. Firms should assume that any qualifications and exceptions written by SFA to the Core Conduct of Business Rules are ones permitted either generally by the drafting of the particular rule or specifically under SIB's commencement order of the rules for SFA members.

Associated business

4–012   As already mentioned, the Conduct of Business Rules (which for the purpose of this discussion includes all 40 Core Conduct of Business Rules as well as the SFA's third tier rules in Chapter 5) generally only apply to investment business which is regulated business. To the extent indicated, however, they also apply to the carrying on of other business which is associated business or business which is held out as being for the purposes of investment (Rule 5–1(1)(c)). Associated business is defined to include business carried on in connection with investment business. Therefore, it would include related custodian and settlement services, and matters relating to the constitution and internal management of a firm, including its general arrangements for compliance.

Rules with wider application

This extension beyond investment business which is regulated business is not applicable to all the Conduct of Business Rules: only to those which, by their drafting, indicate a wider application. For example, the rule on inducements (Rule 5–7) applies "in the course of regulated business or otherwise": namely, if an inducement offered or received in respect of non-regulated business would conflict with duties owed to customers in the course of regulated business. The rules on approving advertisements for overseas persons (Rule 5–12), overseas business for United Kingdom private customers (Rule 5–13), and business conducted from overseas with non-United Kingdom private customers (Rule 5–14), apply to investment business which is not regulated business. These rules require warnings to be given about the lack of FSA 1986 protection. The rule on exclusion clauses (Rule 5–24) prevents a firm excluding or restricting duties or liabilities to customers under the FSA 1986 or the regulatory system (which is defined to include the arrangements for regulating a firm under the FSA 1986, including the Principles, Core Rules and SFA's third tier). The rule on suitability (Rule 5–31) imposes the obligation in respect of regulated business or associated business.

Own account transaction

The rules on dealing ahead of research (Rule 5–36), customer order priority (Rule 5–37), fair allocation (Rule 5–42), and trade reporting (Rule 5–49) include the concept of an own account order or transaction. This is a transaction for the firm's own account, or the own account of an associate, which is effected or arranged by the firm in the course of carrying on either investment business or associated business. This is a wide provision because, as already explained, investment business means the business of engaging in any activity within Part II, Schedule 1 to the FSA 1986, which is not excluded by Part III. It includes an isolated activity and one carried on outside the United Kingdom. It is not limited, like the authorisation requirement or the definition of regulated business, to the carrying on of a business in the United Kingdom.

Insider dealing/stabilisation

The rule on insider dealing (Rule 5–46) applies to own account **4–013** transactions in the United Kingdom or elsewhere, and also requires a firm to ensure that it does not effect, in the course of regulated business or otherwise, a transaction for a customer which is prohibited by the insider dealing legislation. The requirement for a firm to comply with the stabilisation rules applies where a firm is taking action, either in the course of regulated business or otherwise, to stabilise the price of securities (Rule 5–47).

Safekeeping/scope

As already mentioned, the Core Rule on safekeeping (Rule 4–1) applies where a firm has custody of a customer's investments "in connection with or with a view to regulated business". The Core Rule on scope of business refers to investment business carried on in the United Kingdom, rather than just regulated business; but SFA has amended this to the kinds of investment business for which the firm is authorised by SFA. Additionally, the SFA rule states that the firm must not carry on, or hold itself out as carrying on, regulated business which is not within SFA's scope, unless the firm is otherwise authorised or exempt (Rule 2–19).

Compliance/cessation of business

The rule on personal dealings (Rule 5–51) refers to responsibilities under the regulatory system. Whereas the rules on records (Rule 5–4) and complaints (Rule 6–1) refer to compliance with the regulatory system. The rule on Chinese walls (Rule 5–3) mentions withholding information obtained in the course of carrying on business of any kind. The information, however, may only be withheld by one part of the firm from another part to the extent that the business of one of the parts involves investment business or associated business. The Core Rule on cessation of business applies where a firm withdraws from providing any investment or related custodian services to private customers. SFA has written its equivalent provision to apply where the withdrawal concerns SFA authorised business (which means activities in the course of regulated business within the firm's SFA business profile) or related custodian services (Rule 2–21). The rule on appointed representatives mentions investment business in the United Kingdom and any financial business which is not investment business (Rule 2–36). Financial business is defined as business which is, or is held out as being, primarily for the purposes of investment.

Reliance on others/experts

The Core Rules on reliance on others (SFA Rules 1–4(1) and 5–2(1) and (3)) and experts (Rule 5–5) have no special scope but link into the application of the various Core Conduct of Business Rules.

SFA third tier

4–014   As regards SFA's third tier rules in Chapter 5, there are some extensions beyond regulated business. For example, SFA has extended the advertising rules and its third-tier rules in support of the Common Unsolicited Calls Regulations to business within the foreign business carve-out (Rule 5–1(2)). The rules are also applied to certain business done for an overseas office of the firm which has a private customer resident in the United Kingdom, even though the business conducted between the overseas office and the customer is not regulated business (Rule 5–1(3)). The compliance review provision relates to an annual review of the firm's "business" (Rule 5–53). There is another rule which impliedly has a wider extension beyond regulated business. This is the support provision to the United Kingdom Takeover Panel's functions (Rule 5–48).

Paragraph 17 activities

Additionally, SFA has extended the meaning of regulated business. For the purposes of the rules in Chapter 5, regulated business includes investment business activities which would otherwise be excluded under paragraph 17 (dealings as principal), Part III, Schedule 1. So the rules are extended to a firm's dealings as principal for its own account, even where the firm has no contact with customers in respect of such dealings. The reason for this extension is so that SFA can take the firm's own dealings into account when examining whether its customers are being properly protected, especially in respect of the provisions on managing conflicts of interest and the dealing rules. This adopts a similar provision in the old TSA rules.

Paragraph 18 activities

For the same reason, SFA has also extended the meaning of regulated business to include paragraph 18 activities (business with or for group companies), but this extension is only for the purposes of the trade reporting requirement (Rule 5–49), the provisions on personal dealings by staff (Rule 5–51), compliance with statements (Rule 5–52), the compliance review (Rule 5–53) and record keeping (Rule 5–54).

SFA's extension of regulated business to include paragraph 17 activities could have been limited to the same rules as the extension for paragraph 18 activities. The extensions are not to give the firm's principal dealings and inter-group activities customer protections; that is meaningless. It is so that SFA has access to reports and records on such dealings and activities for the purposes of determining whether a firm has been dealing with its customers fairly in accordance with the rules, as opposed to favouring itself and other group companies.

Contrast between SIB and SFA extensions

SIB tried to achieve something similar to SFA's extension of **4–015** regulated business by the reference in some of the dealing Core Rules (including insider dealing) to own account orders or transactions. These latter definitions extend to transactions effected or arranged by a firm in carrying on investment business (rather than regulated business) or associated business for the firm's own account, or for an associate acting on its own account. This suggests that principal dealings for the firm's own account, and dealings between the firm and group companies, are caught. The definition, however, of investment business which is relied upon is that in the FSA 1986, which specifically excludes paragraph 17 and paragraph 18 dealings and activities. For principal or group dealings to be included, therefore, they have to come within the reference to associated business on the basis that they are dealings carried on in connection with investment business.

It is important to note that the paragraph 17 and paragraph 18 extensions by SFA only apply in respect of regulated business, not all investment business. SFA did not want to extend its rules to principal deals and inter group activities within the foreign business carve-out. This could be too restrictive, however, because it may be important to look at some own account dealings (whether of a firm or an associate) executed within the foreign business carve-out because of their relationship with regulated business dealings for customers.

The difference between SFA's extensions limited to regulated business and SIB's attempt to include any own account transactions may be significant in terms of record keeping. SFA's Record Keeping Schedule (Appendix 18) requires the recording of details relating to the execution of any transaction. The scope of this record keeping requirement, however, is limited by the application of the Conduct of Business Rules. In other words, records should not normally be required of any matter which is not regulated business (which, for this purpose, includes the paragraph 17 and 18 extensions). The Core Rule on record keeping (Rule 5–54(1)), however, requires a firm to ensure that sufficient information is recorded and retained about its compliance with the regulatory system. This means that a firm may need to keep records of own account transactions within the foreign business carve-out to satisfy its regulator that it has properly complied with those Core Rules which refer to own account orders or transactions (these terms not being restricted, as SFA's extension relating to paragraphs 17 and 18, to regulated business).

Business conducted from overseas offices (Rule 5–1(2))

4–016   It has already been seen that not all investment business conducted in the United Kingdom from an overseas place of business will be subject to the rules. The definition of regulated business tries to put an overseas branch of an SFA firm in the same position as if it was a separately incorporated body.

In other words, before it becomes subject to the rules, the overseas branch must be doing all of the following:

(i)   it must be carrying on in the United Kingdom one or more of the activities within Part II, Schedule 1 to the FSA 1986, which are not excluded by Part III;

(ii) the activities which it carries on in the United Kingdom must not be done with or through an authorised or exempted person;

(iii) the level of investment business activities carried on in the United Kingdom must be such as to constitute the carrying on of a business in the United Kingdom by the overseas branch; and

(iv) any United Kingdom customers with whom the overseas branch deals must not have been acquired as a result of legitimate solicitation.

Legitimate solicitation means that:
(a)   the customer must not have been solicited by the overseas branch: in other words, he has approached the branch of

his own volition, or as a result of a referral which was not
initiated by the overseas branch;

(b) any solicitation by the branch was not made on the person
whilst he was in the United Kingdom; or

(c) any solicitation on the person whilst in the United
Kingdom complied with the permissions on unsolicited
calls made with respect to section 56 of the FSA 1986, or
with the issuing and approval requirements for investment
advertisements under section 57.

Any business done in the United Kingdom by the overseas branch
which does not satisfy all of the conditions in (i) to (iv) above will be
within the foreign business carve-out. As has already been shown in the
previous section, however, some of the Conduct of Business Rules
extend more widely than the definition of regulated business. In some
cases they extend to investment business carried on by an overseas
branch which would normally be within the foreign business carve-out
to the definition of regulated business.

Owing to the fact that it is quite easy for an overseas branch to solicit   **4–017**
legitimately customers in the United Kingdom, SFA has specifically
provided that six of its rules which deal with solicitation apply to a
firm's overseas office, even where that office is acting within the foreign
business carve-out. These are: the two main advertising rules (Rules
5–9 and 5–12, except that the requirement in Rule 5–9(2) to state on a
specific investment advertisement that the firm is a member of SFA is
not required); two of the rules concerned with giving the prescribed
disclosure warning to a private customer that he is not protected under
the FSA 1986 regulatory system (Rules 5–13 and 5–14); and SFA's
support rules to SIB's Common Unsolicited Calls Regulations (Rules
5–17 and 5–18). In other words, for a branch to take advantage of the
foreign business carve-out, it must always comply with all of the rules
relating to unsolicited calls, as well as the majority of the advertising
rules. For example, in respect of advertisements, the overseas branch
will have to ensure that they are fair and not misleading, and contain,
where applicable, the detailed contents required for any similar
investment advertisement issued by branches or firms subject to the full
application of the Conduct of Business Rules.

SFA is trying to ensure that firms cannot too easily channel business
with United Kingdom customers to overseas branches, thereby
depriving the customers of the majority of the protections under the
FSA 1986 regulatory system. So, these six rules apply all the time to a
firm's overseas branch, even if none of the other rules apply because
the branch is acting within the foreign business carve-out.

Where, in respect of a customer in the United Kingdom, an overseas
branch has breached any of these six requirements on advertising, the
prescribed disclosure and cold calling, then, in respect of that
customer, it must comply with all of the Conduct of Business Rules

which would normally apply if it had been business conducted from a United Kingdom base. It can no longer take protection from the foreign business carve-out.[1] The firm, however, still has the protection of this carve-out in respect of other customers in the United Kingdom who were solicited without any breach of these six rules.

4–018   SFA has also imposed some additional conditions which refer back to these six rules where the overseas branch is dealing with private customers. The foreign business carve-out is lost:

  (i)   in respect of any activity or transaction which contravenes, or results from solicitation which contravenes, any of these rules;

  (ii) if the customer has been given any indication that he is or will be a customer of an office of the firm in the United Kingdom in relation to the particular activity or transaction;

  (iii) if the activity consists of the operation, management or winding up of a collective investment scheme; and

  (iv) if the customer already has a relationship with the overseas branch which, when it was established, would have amounted to solicitation in breach of any of these rules.

In these cases the usual rules for business conducted from a United Kingdom base will apply, but only to the particular activity or transaction for the customer, or, in the case of (iv), to any dealings with the customer. In other words, the overseas branch still has the protection of the foreign business carve-out where none of these conditions apply to the relevant customer, activity or transaction.

Business conducted on behalf of overseas offices (Rule 5–1(3))

4–019   Again, this is another restriction on the foreign business carve-out. This provision is aimed at deliberate evasion of the rules where a United Kingdom office of an SFA firm arranges for business to be done for private customers normally resident in the United Kingdom by its overseas office with the purpose of avoiding the full application of the Conduct of Business Rules.

Basically, the rule provides that, where an overseas office has a private customer normally resident in the United Kingdom, it cannot rely on the foreign business carve-out to the application of the rules in respect of the following transactions for that customer:

  (i)   transactions executed by a United Kingdom office of the firm; or

(ii) any transactions executed with the benefit of advice from such a United Kingdom office.

However, before the foreign business carve-out is lost in respect of these transactions, one of two other conditions must be satisfied:

(i) the United Kingdom office must have initially passed the order to the overseas office, or advised the customer in relation to it; or

(ii) the United Kingdom office must have advised the customer to place that order with, or obtain the relevant advice from, the overseas office.

This rule relates to particular transactions and does not apply where a firm generally refers a customer to its overseas office because that office is in a better position to service the customer. This might be the case where the customer wanted to invest in investments traded on a foreign market in the same locality as the overseas office, or wished generally to do business overseas because of preferential tax treatment.

Prescribed disclosure

Where a firm is doing investment business which is not subject to the **4–020** rules, or introducing a customer to an overseas branch of the firm or another firm where the customer will lose the protection of the rules, it must give sufficient warning to the customer, if he is a private customer, of his loss of protection under the FSA 1986 regulatory system.

It is important to realise that the prescribed disclosure only has to be given to private customers. It is a written statement which must explain that all or most of the protections provided under the United Kingdom regulatory system do not apply. Where the business which will be carried on with the customer is outside the territorial scope of the Investors Compensation Scheme, it must include a statement that compensation under the Scheme will not be available to the investor. The warning does not have to be written completely in negative terms. If, as a result of doing business under a different system of law or regulation, the investor will receive other protections or compensation similar to those provided in the United Kingdom, then it can indicate what these protections and compensation are.

SFA has provided guidance as to what the warning should include. This new warning is more extensive than that required under the old rules, which was merely to the effect that the investor would not be subject to the rules and regulations made under the FSA 1986 for the protection of investors, and, if relevant, would be dealing with a person not authorised under the FSA 1986. SFA's guidance states that, besides including a similar general statement, the warning should specifically explain the loss of protection under the Investors Compensation Scheme and the Client Money Regulations, and the lack of access to SFA's Complaints Bureau and arbitration schemes. It should also point out that: the best execution requirement will not apply; charges will not have to be disclosed in advance; and there will be no obligation to comply with the suitability rule, ensuring that any recommendations are suitable in accordance with the investor's investment objectives and financial resources. As already explained, however, the statement can refer to similar protections available under a foreign scheme.

SFA has produced a model prescribed disclosure statement (Appendix 4 below). It follows the guidance in the rulebook and amounts to formal guidance for the purpose of Rule 1–4.

4–021   The prescribed disclosure is required in the following cases:

1. *Advertisements for overseas persons (Rule 5–12)*. A firm must not issue or approve a specific investment advertisement for an overseas investment business which is likely to lead to private customers in the United Kingdom doing investment business with that person which is not regulated business, unless the advertisement contains the prescribed disclosure. (See further discussion in Chapter 12 below.)

2. *Overseas business for United Kingdom customers (Rule 5–13(1))*. An overseas branch of an SFA firm cannot do investment business with private customers in the United Kingdom which will fall within the foreign business carve-out, unless it has made the prescribed disclosure.

3. *Introductions to overseas persons (Rule 5–13(2))*. A firm must not introduce a United Kingdom private customer to another person who will do investment business with that customer which will not be regulated business, unless:

  (i)   it has made the prescribed disclosure; and

  (ii) it has no reason to doubt that the customer will be dealt with in an honest and reliable way by the other person.

This includes any sort of introduction, such as the mere giving of advice to a customer to enter into an investment business relationship with an overseas person, or the making of specific arrangements for business to be done with the United Kingdom private customer by an overseas person.

Sometimes a firm merely makes an introduction and then drops out of the picture. From then on the customer only looks towards the overseas person. The firm may not entirely end its involvement in the sense that it will receive a share of any commission charged by the overseas person for business done with the introduced customer. However, the mere fact that the introducing firm receives a share of commission does not mean that it has a continuing customer relationship with the investor.

In other cases, the introducing firm may continue to have a relationship. For example, it may give advice to the customer and receive his orders, but is not responsible for execution. The introducing firm's responsibility stops at the point at which he passes on the orders for execution to the overseas person. The customer, therefore, has two separate customer relationships. One with the introducing firm in the United Kingdom for advice, receipt and passing on of orders. The second with the overseas firm for the execution of his orders.

If the overseas firm sends contract notes directly to the customer and if the customer is directly responsible to it for settlement, it is more likely that he is the direct customer of the overseas firm. If there is no direct settlement responsibility or communication between the customer and the overseas firm, it is more likely that there is only one customer relationship, namely with the United Kingdom firm. The United Kingdom firm will then be responsible for employing the overseas firm as its sub-agent. It will not need to give the prescribed disclosure, but will be responsible for ensuring that the overseas firm complies with all of the customer rule protections, including the dealing rules, particularly best execution. (See Rule 5–39 concerning reliance on agents for best execution.)

If the introducing firm continues to have a relationship with the **4–022** United Kingdom private customer, then it is important that, in giving the prescribed disclosure, it makes it clear at what point the loss of protection arises. In other words, the customer should know in respect of which parts of the service he will be treated as a customer of the introducing firm and be protected by the rules, and in respect of which parts he will lose those protections because he becomes a direct customer of the overseas person.

In making any introductions or arrangements with an overseas person, the firm must, besides giving the prescribed disclosure, not have any reason to doubt that the customer will be dealt with in an honest and reliable way. This is written as a negative, rather than a positive requirement. In other words, the firm does not have to search out the credentials of the overseas person. However, if there is anything from his behaviour or public knowledge which throws doubt upon his honesty and reliability, the introduction or arrangements should not be made.

It should be noted that the investor will be a customer for the purposes of the introduction, even if the introducing firm has no further contact or involvement with him. Therefore, in making the introduction, the firm will be subject to the Principles, so that, even if Rule 5–13(2) does not require it to make a positive enquiry into the overseas person's background, it must, nevertheless, observe high standards of integrity and fair dealing, and act with due skill, care and diligence. The fiduciary relationship which arises at law with a customer and the firm's obligations under the Principles may require some enquiry before the introduction is made. In particular, Principle 4 requires the firm to know its customer and Principle 5 requires it to give enough information to its customer to enable him to make a balanced and informed decision.

4–023 *4. Business from overseas with overseas customers (Rule 5–14).* Where an overseas branch or firm is communicating with customers outside the United Kingdom within the foreign business carve-out, then, it should not state that it is a member of SFA, or otherwise indicate that it is an authorised person under the FSA 1986; or, if it does so, it must give with equal prominence the prescribed disclosure.

This provision applies to any communication made (whether oral or written), or any advertisement issued, to a private customer outside the United Kingdom. Obviously, if the communication is made orally, then the details of the prescribed disclosure may be given orally. The rule requires that the prescribed disclosure is given at least the same prominence as the indication that the firm is an authorised person.

The Core Rule requires the disclosure to be made every time the overseas firm or branch indicates that it is, or is part of, an FSA 1986 authorised firm. This would be very difficult in the case of firms or branches based overseas who deal regularly with customers in the United Kingdom: for example, firms or branches located in the Channel Islands, Isle of Man or the Irish Republic. They may do a fair amount of business with customers in the United Kingdom which is not within the foreign business carve-out. For example, some of the customer relations may be longstanding and it is difficult to establish now whether the original relationship arose from legitimate solicitation for the purposes of the definition of regulated business. Many such firms and branches deal on the basis that they are subject to the full rules whenever they are dealing with customers in the United Kingdom. They will have standard stationery which refers to their membership of SFA for simultaneous use with customers in the United Kingdom and overseas. It would be costly for them to introduce systems to differentiate, in respect of every communication, whether or not the foreign business carve-out applied; and, if so, either to remove reference to their membership of SFA or to include the prescribed disclosure.

SFA has, therefore, obtained a derogation to the effect that the prescribed disclosure only has to be issued once. There is also a transitional provision: an overseas firm or branch does not even need to send the prescribed disclosure once to existing overseas customers, if it has already given them the shorter disclosure required under the old rules that the customer is not protected under the FSA 1986 regulatory system. This same transitional also applies to 2 and 3 above.

Restriction to private customers

It is important to note that the prescribed disclosure requirement **4–024** only applies to private customers with whom investment business is being done which is not regulated business. It is only investment business, not associated business.

In some ways it would have been better if the rules had applied where the person was a private investor rather than a private customer. It is often assumed that a customer relationship only arises where the normal Conduct of Business Rules apply, rather than in the four situations above which deal with warnings about the lack of customer protection.

SIB's Core Rule definition of customer is not necessarily comprehensive in the sense that it describes two types of person who are not included, and then describes three types who are, including a potential customer. SFA has then added third-tier to the effect that a customer means any person with or for whom a person carries on, or intends to carry on, any regulated business or associated business. Both these definitions of customer, especially the second, could give the impression that an investor who is dealt with within the foreign business carve-out is not a customer and that, therefore, the rules about the prescribed disclosure would not apply. If this is the case, it is unfortunate because it defeats the purpose of writing these warning provisions.

It should be assumed, therefore, that, for the purpose of the prescribed disclosure provisions, the reference to private customer means someone who would be a private customer if the business which was being done with him would amount to regulated business except for the foreign business carve-out. It would not be safe to rely upon a more restrictive approach based upon SFA's linking of "customer" to regulated or associated business. The Core Rules apply directly to all firms which are authorised by being members of SROs, and all four prescribed disclosure provisions are Core Rules.

Special regimes

Many of the Conduct of Business Rules only apply where a firm is **4–025** dealing with customers. If the firm is dealing with market counterparties, then it is only concerned with the rules on market integrity and compliance arrangements. If it has customers, but they are only non-private customers, then it can safely ignore the large segment of the rules which are limited to providing protections to private customers.

Therefore, the answers to the questions whether or not a firm has customers, and, if so, what type of customers, determine the application of the Conduct of Business Rules. In addition, SFA has provided some special regimes disapplying some rules where a firm is carrying on certain activities.

Oil markets (Rule 1–11)

4–026   The first special regime applies to oil market participants when carrying on an oil market investment activity with persons who are not individuals. In connection with this special regime, the rulebook contains definitions of oil, oil collective investment scheme, oil investment, oil market investment activity and oil market participant.

The special regime for oil market participants appears in Chapter 1 of the rulebook (Rule 1–11), because, unlike the other special regimes described later, this regime is not limited to a special application provision to the Conduct of Business Rules. Although, it is in the area of conduct of business where the limited application of the rules which apply to oil market participants is the greatest.

Basically, apart from Conduct of Business, SFA's rules apply to oil market participants to the extent which they are relevant to the business being carried on. On application by the firm, SFA is prepared to waive the requirement for its non-investment business directors to be individually registered with SFA. The Financial Rules only apply in respect of oil market participants who are members of a recognised or designated investment exchange and who, under the rules of that exchange, are entitled to trade with other members; and, in general, the provisions on client money and safe custody are not applicable.[2]

As regards Conduct of Business supervision, oil market participants are subject to the 10 Principles, plus the Oil Market Code of Conduct issued by SIB. This code amounts to formal guidance for the purpose of satisfying compliance with the rules. The relevant Conduct of Business Rules from Chapter 5 of the rulebook are set out in a table. They are: reliance on others (Rule 5–2); SFA's extension to the definition of market counterparty (Rule 5–4); classifying customers as experts (Rule 5–5); issuing and approving advertisements, including direct offer advertisements (Rules 5–9 and 5–10); fair and not misleading communications (Rule 5–15(1)); exclusion clauses (Rule 5–24); the basic obligation to send out a note confirming the essential details of a transaction, but not the detailed contents requirements (Rule 5–34(1)), but including the provisions about averaging (Rules 5–34(12) to (15)); dealing ahead of research (Rule 5–36); and the basic Core Rule requirement, but not SFA's supporting third-tier, on responsible behaviour by staff in respect of personal dealings (Rule 5–51(1)).

The Conduct of Business application rule (Rule 5–1) is included, so that oil market participants are only subject to the Conduct of Business Rules to the extent that they fall within the scope of this rule. They may, therefore, take advantage of the foreign business carve-out to the definition of regulated business. They benefit from another modification. The Conduct of Business Rules do not apply to an oil market participant in respect of business which would have been excluded from the meaning of investment business by paragraph 17(4), Schedule 1 to the FSA 1986, but for the fact that the firm is an authorised person (Rule 8–4, Schedule 2, paragraph 6B).

Paragraph 17(4)

Paragraph 17 basically says that any transaction which a firm enters into as a principal will not be regarded as investment business unless that person is acting as a market maker, a broker dealer, or regularly soliciting orders from the public. This exclusion applies to dealings as a principal in securities (investments which are not options, futures or contracts for difference), whether or not carried on by an authorised person. In respect of options, futures and contracts for difference, the exclusion only operates where the person is not authorised under the FSA 1986, and is entering into the transaction with or through an authorised person, an exempted person, a person with permission to do investment business under paragraph 23, or an overseas office of a person whose head office is outside the United Kingdom and whose ordinary business includes investment business. This means that, once a person becomes authorised under the FSA 1986, all of his principal dealings in options, futures and contracts for difference are caught by the definition of investment business: they are no longer excluded activities under paragraph 17. Many of the activities of oil market participants involve dealing as a principal in futures and options. As the oil market participant is a member of SFA, these activities would be investment business and subject to the rules to the extent that the dealings were not within the foreign business carve-out. For the time being, however, SFA has provided that, where an oil market participant, as part of an oil market investment activity, is dealing as a principal in options, futures, or contracts for difference, it will be able to rely upon the paragraph 17(4) exemption as if it was not an authorised person.

4–027

This qualification follows a similar provision in the AFBD rules. The intention is that, at least for the time being, oil market participants should be treated in a similar way under the new rulebook to the regime applying to them under the old one.

Market counterparty

On the basis that there should be no change, SFA has amended, but only for oil market participants, the Core Rule definition of market counterparty. A person with whom an oil market participant deals may still be regarded as a market counterparty acting in the course of investment business of the same description if he is doing business which would be investment business but for the exclusions in Part III, Schedule 1 to the FSA 1986 (Rule 8–4, Schedule 2, paragraph 6A). In other words, an oil market participant member of SFA can treat as a market counterparty a person who is not authorised to do investment business because he is only dealing in investments as a principal within the meaning of paragraph 17, Schedule 1.

The reason for this separate regime is that trading in oil market investments is not, in practice, carried out with unsophisticated consumers. Most of the dealing is done by oil producers and traders to hedge the risk of their normal commercial activities. Of course, this argument could be made for other options and futures dealers in the commodity markets. For this reason, SFA plans to review the regime for oil market participants and may, in future, impose a tighter regime, similar to that which applies to the other participants in the derivatives markets relating to commodities.

Corporate Finance

4–028   Corporate finance is not a separate category of investment business, such as establishing or operating a collective investment scheme (paragraph 16, Schedule 1 to the FSA 1986). A number of activities, however, done under the generic term of "corporate finance" amount to investment business and, therefore, most firms which do corporate finance business need to be authorised under the FSA 1986. For example, in carrying out corporate finance activities firms will find themselves giving advice on investments or arranging deals in investments. Rarely will firms be managing investments as part of corporate finance activities; although they may sometimes be dealing in investments, for example if they are making an offer for sale of new investments for a company which wishes to raise further capital.

TSA approach

Due to the fact that a large part of the corporate finance activities do not amount to investment business, and because many corporate finance customers are large institutions or experienced investors, it was thought appropriate, in respect of the original TSA rulebook, to provide a lighter regulatory regime for corporate finance business, at least in terms of the Conduct of Business Rules. There was a concern to see that corporate finance business was not unduly hampered by the application of inappropriate regulation, which could have been the case if it had been made subject to those rules more appropriate to providing investment advisory or management services for ordinary investment customers. It was also appreciated that many of the corporate finance activities which a firm would engage in were subject to other forms of regulation, such as: the London Stock Exchange's "Yellow Book" on listing requirements and "Green Book" on the admission of securities to dealings on the Unlisted Securities Market; the provisions on registered prospectuses in the Companies Act 1985; and the City Code on Takeovers and Mergers and the Rules Governing Substantial Acquisitions of Shares published by the United Kingdom Panel on

Takeovers and Mergers. Also, many firms doing corporate finance business are authorised banking institutions and, therefore, subject to the general supervision of the Bank of England under the Banking Act 1987. The corporate finance market is a very competitive one: firms not providing a good service and treating their customers fairly will quickly lose their reputations and income.

Third party investors

When carrying out corporate finance activities for a customer, it is **4–029** quite likely that a firm will have contact with a large number of potential investors. These investors may be shareholders of a target company subject to a takeover offer, members of the public who are being invited to subscribe for a new issue, or selected wealthy investors (whether companies or individuals) with whom the firm is trying to place significant amounts of newly issued stock. It did not seem right, when drafting the new rules, that such investors should be owed customer obligations by the firm. Certainly, there would be a conflict of interest between the firm's duty to its corporate finance customer and these other investors. The firm's prime responsibility would be to its corporate finance customer; so these other investors could not really expect the firm to be responsible for looking after their individual interests.

TSA Rule 1090

As a result, TSA introduced a separate regime for corporate finance. First of all, where a firm was carrying out corporate finance for a customer, it only had to comply with a limited number of the Conduct of Business Rules. Secondly, where, as a result of carrying on these corporate finance activities, it had contact with other investors, it did not have to regard these investors as its customers if the circumstances were such that they could not reasonably expect the firm to owe them duties of best execution and suitability.

This regime was provided in TSA Rule 1090, which set out, in tabular form, a list of 14 different activities which amounted to corporate finance business. This table was quite long and complex. It also caused confusion in the sense that there was a tendency to assume that, wherever a TSA firm was doing an activity which fell within those described in the table, it was doing corporate finance investment business which was subject to the rules referred to in Rule 1090.01. Whereas, in fact, most of the corporate finance activities carried on by firms did not amount to investment business within the meaning of the FSA 1986, because the firm was not giving advice on, or arranging deals in, investments as set out in Part I, Schedule 1. Therefore, to some extent, the table caused confusion. Some firms assumed that, if they were doing one of the activities in the table, they needed to be authorised under the FSA 1986. They, therefore, joined TSA only to find that they had paid the fees unnecessarily because they were not after all doing investment business.

SFA approach

4–030 When work began on the new SFA rulebook, two propositions were considered. The first was that it was no longer appropriate to provide a special regime for corporate finance. The Core Rules made a much greater distinction between the level of protection offered to non-private customers as opposed to private customers. As most of a firm's corporate finance customers would be non-private customers, it was considered that it would not be unduly onerous to require corporate finance firms to comply with all of the Conduct of Business Rules relevant to such customers, especially as a large number of the non-private customer rules related to dealing obligations. These rules would not be relevant in respect of most corporate finance business, as the firms would not be involved in dealing.

The second proposition was that, even if the separate regime remained, the extensive table defining corporate finance business should be dramatically reduced to fit with the new, shorter rulebooks, written in simpler terms.

Initially, SFA's Board adopted the first approach and decided not to provide a separate corporate finance regime. There were, however, strong objections from corporate finance firms who felt that they were being penalised and that, if they had to comply will all the rules, the costs of compliance would dramatically increase without any obvious benefits to their customers. Therefore, the new rulebook provides a separate regime, but only in respect of the Conduct of Business Rules. All the other parts of the rulebook apply in full. The definition of corporate finance business has been substantially shortened, without trying to lessen its scope. In fact, it is arguable that the new definition is wider than the old TSA table. The new regime, however, is not as favourable as the old in the sense that more of the Conduct of Business Rules now apply to corporate finance business. The qualification of not having to treat third-party investors as customers has been continued through an exception to the definition of customer, which is described in paragraph 5–004 below.

As explained above, the rules only apply where the corporate finance activity amounts to investment business within the meaning of the FSA 1986. The definition is divided into two main parts. The first one is concerned with investment services provided to other people. Investment services is defined to mean any activity which a firm undertakes in the course of carrying on investment business; so it includes associated business or business held out as being for the purposes of investment. The second one relates to regulated or associated business which a firm carries on for its own account.

Part A

The first main part of the definition includes investment services 4–031
provided to persons in the circumstances described in the six limbs
below.

Limb 1

This covers investment services provided to any issuer, holder or
owner of investments with regard to the offer, issue, underwriting,
repurchase, exchange or redemption of, or the variation of the terms of,
the investments, or any related matter. This would include the
provision of investment services relating to placements, other than to
placees (who may be exempt from the definition of customer; see
paragraph 5–004 below).

Limb 2

This is a wide provision and relates to investment services provided
to: ordinary business investors; any other company or partnership
which does not satisfy the size requirements of the ordinary business
investor definition (whether or not it may be treated as a non-private
customer under the expert categorisation test); or any international or
supra-national organisation. The services provided must relate to the
manner in which, or the terms on which, or the persons by whom, any
business, activities or undertakings relating to this customer, or its
associate, are to be financed, structured, managed, controlled, regulated
or reported on. As already explained, many of these activities will not
amount to investment business, such as advising a company on its
structure, management or control. Likewise, much of the advice given
to a company about its financing may have nothing to do with
investments within Part I, Schedule 1 to the FSA 1986. The same
applies to general advice about regulation and reporting.

Asset sales

There is some confusion to the extent to which asset sales amount to
investment business. To the extent that they are investment business,
then they would fall within Limb 2 as corporate finance business.

A debenture (a paragraph 2, Schedule 1, investment) includes any
instrument acknowledging indebtedness. Therefore, a document evidencing a bank loan is probably a debenture. If the amount repayable
was linked to a stock index, then it would be a contract for difference
(a paragraph 9 investment).

Although a bank loan may be an investment, the bank which makes
the loan facility will not be doing investment business. It will not be
dealing (paragraph 12), because a note to this paragraph states that a
person who becomes a creditor party to an instrument acknowledging
indebtedness is not to be regarded as dealing. Also, the bank will not

be arranging deals (paragraph 13), because a note to this paragraph exempts a person who is making arrangements with a view to a transaction to which he will himself be a party as principal. There is also an exclusion where the bank is acting as agent to the creditor or debtor, which would extend to a bank arranging syndication of a loan.

4–032 The problem arises where the loan is transferred. There are three methods of transfer:

(i) *Novation*. The original bank arranges for the loan to be repaid by the transferee, who then creates a new loan upon the same terms as the former loan. In this case, there is in fact no transfer, because the original loan is extinguished. The original bank, in extinguishing or surrendering its rights under the loan, may be carrying on an investment activity. By selling its loan in this way, it could be regarded as "dealing". "Dealing" includes "selling", and under paragraph 28, Schedule 1 to the FSA 1986, "selling" includes any disposal for valuable consideration. A "disposal" includes, in the case of an investment consisting of rights under a contract, the surrendering, assigning or converting of those rights.

Therefore, in a novation situation, the "transferor" will be doing corporate finance business, but the "transferee", who in reality acquires nothing from the transferor, will be creating a new loan, which will not amount to an activity within paragraphs 12 and 13.

(ii) *Assignment*. In this case, both the assignor and the assignee will be dealing, in the sense that one is selling and the other is buying an investment. The original bank's rights under the loan agreement remain and are simply assigned.

(iii) *Sub-participation*. Sub-participation does not amount legally to the transfer of the original loan, but, economically, it tries to achieve the same effect. There is a loan made by the sub-participant to the original bank, whose obligation to repay the sub-participant is conditional upon repayment to itself from the lender. Therefore, there is no investment activity: merely the creation of a new loan.

In conclusion, asset sales only amount to investment business where there is an assignment or novation. In the case of novation, however, it is only the original bank (the transferor) which will be doing investment business.

Limb 3

4–033 This applies to investment services provided to any company, whether or not an ordinary business investor, in connection with a proposed or actual takeover, related operation, merger, demerger, reorganisation or reconstruction involving investments issued by the company, its holding company, subsidiary or any associated company.

Limb 4

This covers investment services provided to any shareholder or prospective shareholder of a company which is established, or is to be established, purely for the purpose of effecting a takeover or related operation.

Limb 5

This relates to investment services provided to any person who is acting on his own account in relation to negotiations or decisions relating to the commercial, financial or strategic intentions or requirements of a business or prospective business. Again, many of these activities may not amount to investment business: for example, where the person is providing ordinary finance to the business, in return for a charge over some of its assets. It should be noted that the reference to a business is not limited to businesses which will be run as companies or partnerships.

This limb also applies where the services are provided to a person, acting as a principal for his own account, who is assisting the interests of any other person with or for whom the firm, another authorised person, or any overseas investment business is undertaking corporate finance business falling within limbs 1 to 4 above. However, the person must not be acting solely in his capacity as an investor; in other words, not solely for private investment purposes. Also he must, by acting on his own account, be undertaking all or part of any transactions involved in the corporate finance business being done for the other person.

This, therefore, covers persons whom the firm arranges to underwrite an issue which the firm is advising on, arranging or offering: provided the person, in accepting the underwriting commitment, is not acting purely for private investment purposes. This would exclude most private investors involved in underwriting. They would be subject to the full protection of the Conduct of Business Rules, except to the extent that they came within the exception to the definition of customer (see paragraph 5–004 below). To rely on this latter exception, a firm will have to make it clear to the prospective underwriters that it is acting for another person (namely, its corporate finance customer) and will not be responsible to the underwriters or sub-underwriters for protecting them under the rules as its customers.

Limb 6

This is to cover the situation where there may be more than one adviser in respect of the same activity or transaction. A firm will be regarded as doing corporate finance business where it provides investment services to another person who is undertaking business with or for any person coming within limbs 1 to 5 above, provided the services relate to activities described in those limbs.

Part B

4–034   The second main part of the definition applies to business carried on by the firm for its own account. Where this business is regulated or associated business, and is done in the course of, or arises out of, activities undertaken in accordance with any corporate finance investment services falling within limbs 1 to 6 of Part A above, then the firm will be regarded as doing corporate finance business in respect of its dealings with other persons. However, there is an important restriction. These dealings must not involve transactions with or for, or advice to, persons who are the firm's private customers. In this connection, the concept of indirect customer may be important. If the firm is buying or selling through an agent who has identified his principals before dealing, these principals become customers of the firm. In determining, however, whether a firm is dealing with private customers, the exceptions to the definitions of customer for corporate finance business still apply (as explained in paragraph 5–004 below).

This inclusion of the firm's own dealings within the corporate finance definition is necessary. For example, where a firm is advising a corporate finance customer on a flotation, it may itself accept underwriting responsibilities in respect of the shares being issued or offered for sale. If the offer for subscription or sale is not successful, the firm will end up having to take the shares itself and then sell them on in the secondary market off its own book. Likewise, a firm which is assisting a corporate finance customer in respect of a takeover bid may initially purchase the stock for its own account. A firm which is the lead manager to a new issue would also be dealing for its own account where it was carrying out permitted stabilising activities (see paragraphs 16–004 *et seq.* below).

Applicable rules

4–035   The Conduct of Business Rules which apply where a firm is undertaking investment business amounting to corporate finance business are set out in a table underneath the relevant application rule provision (Rule 5–1(5)).

As already mentioned, the special regime for corporate finance is not as generous as the old TSA regime. Although the list of rules which apply does not appear particularly long, it should be noted that many of the rules not included are, in fact, irrelevant in respect of corporate finance business. For example, the table does not include any of those rules relating to packaged products, business expansion schemes, the operation of collective investment schemes and soft commission arrangements. Although the setting up of a business expansion scheme to finance a new venture would be corporate finance, the rules on business expansion schemes are concerned with marketing and selling such schemes to investors. Likewise, a soft commission arrangement would not be appropriate in a corporate finance context.

A better way of looking at the separate regime for corporate finance is that, if a firm is doing corporate finance business, it has a quick reference point at the front of the Conduct of Business Rules as to which rules are relevant.

Customers

Interestingly, the table includes the rule whereby a customer can be classified as an expert investor, but not SFA's extension to the definition of market counterparty which extends the categories of persons who are not owed customer protections. Likewise, the table does not contain SFA's rule relating to the definition of indirect customer, under which a firm can agree in writing with the agent not to provide indirect customer protections to the agent's identified principals. This will not normally be significant in a corporate finance context. Its exclusion, however, could be important where a firm is relying on the provision about dealing on its own account (paragraph 4–034 above), in which case the transactions must not involve private customers. Also, a firm would not be able to avoid owing those private customer protection rules listed in the table where it is dealing with an agent who, although a non-private customer himself, has identified his principal, a private customer, before the service is provided.

Dealing

The table does not include any of the dealing rules. In practice, **4–036** much corporate finance business does not involve executing transactions, but rather giving advice or arranging deals. Therefore, these rules would not normally be relevant. They have, however, been specifically excluded because of those occasions where a firm may be dealing. In the case of an offer for subscription or offer for sale, it is clearly inappropriate to try to apply such rules as those concerned with customer order priority, timely execution, and best execution. Even if they did apply, persons subscribing for a new issue would not normally be owed customer obligations because they would fall within the corporate finance exception to the definition of customer.

Where the dealing rules could be more relevant is where the firm is acting for a customer who is trying to increase or sell his stake in a company. The customer will want to ensure that his order is executed at the best possible time in terms of current market conditions and at the best price. The rule on timely execution (Rule 5–38) gives a firm some flexibility as to the time at which it executes an order. For example, a firm may postpone execution where it believes that this is in the best interests of the customer. Also, the rule on best execution (Rule 5–39) requires a firm to ascertain the price which is the best available for the customer in the relevant market at that time for transactions of the kind and size concerned. Therefore, account is taken of the unusual size of the transaction, rather than expecting execution at the best price shown on the London Stock Exchange's quotation system (SEAQ) for a normal market size transaction.

Despite this flexibility in the dealing rules, it was decided not to apply them at all in a corporate finance context. It should be remembered, however, that a firm which is acting as fiduciary must always act in the best interests of its customer, and, therefore, should obtain the best deal in the circumstances. Likewise, the Principles apply to all corporate finance customers. A firm will have to apply the appropriate standard of skill and care and observe high standards of market conduct.

Conflicts/market integrity/compliance

The rules which apply to corporate finance business include those on inducements, reliance on others, operating Chinese walls, managing material interests; and those concerned with market integrity, such as insider dealing, stabilisation and support of the Takeover Panel's functions. Also, the provisions concerning a firm's compliance arrangements and the trade reporting requirement are applied. Although trade reporting applies, there are a number of exceptions under this rule which are relevant to corporate finance business. For example, firms do not need to report issuing market allotments or syndication (including primary market placements), repurchase or reverse repurchase agreements, stock lending arrangements, and asset trading (Rule 5–49(2) and see paragraph 16–008 below).

Private customer protections

4–037   A number of the rules which apply only concern private customers. These are SFA's support provisions to SIB's Common Unsolicited Calls Regulations (Rules 5–17 and 5–18); the rule requiring a private customer to give his written consent before he is committed to an underwriting arrangement (Rule 5–25); and those on customer's understanding and risk warnings (Rule 5–30) and suitability (Rule 5–31). These requirements only apply where the corporate finance customer is a private customer. Many persons with whom a firm has contact as a result of carrying out corporate finance business will not be customers because of the relevant exception in the definition of customer (see paragraph 5–004 below).

As regards the understanding of risk and suitability rules, it is only the Core Rule provisions which apply, not SFA's third-tier extensions.

Therefore, a firm does not have to obtain a customer's signature to the Warrants or Derivatives Risk Warning Notices, or give him the specific warning on non-readily realisable investments. A firm may still wish, however, to comply with these third-tier requirements, where relevant, in order to ensure that it has complied with the basic Core Rule obligation that it has taken reasonable steps to enable the customer to understand the nature of the risks involved in any recommendation made by the firm. Obviously, SFA's third tier to the suitability rule is irrelevant to corporate finance business because this only applies where a firm is acting as an investment manager, with a responsibility to ensure that the customer's portfolio remains suitable.

Although the underwriting written consent rule applies, this is only relevant to private customers and, as already mentioned, it would not apply where a firm is arranging for underwriting commitments to be taken up by third-parties who fall within the exception to the definition of customer.

Of course, it is likely that most corporate finance customers will be non-private customers, because either they are ordinary business investors or the firm can classify them as expert investors. It is interesting to note that, even where the customer is a private customer, not all the private customer protections apply. The usual customer agreements requirements are excluded. Also, a firm does not have to give prior disclosure of the basis of charging; nor does it have to give an explanation about the default remedies which it may exercise. It is not subject to the information rule (Rule 5–16), which requires it to give, in respect of non-corporate finance regulated business, adequate information to private customers about its identity and business address, and the identity and status within the firm of employees advising the customer.

Contract notes

Confirmation of transactions is not required: not even the basic Core Rule requirement (which is applied in respect of oil market investment activities). It is understandable that a firm may find it difficult to comply with all the detailed contents requirements for contract notes, but it is expected that a firm should be able to confirm with its customer the essential details of a corporate finance transaction. In practice, therefore, firms should be able to comply with the Core Rule element (Rule 5–34(1)).

Advertising

One of the main changes from the old TSA regime is that some of the advertising rules now apply to corporate finance business, but only to the extent that the advertisement is within the scope of the general application provision for advertisements (Rule 5–1(4) and see Chapter 12 below which contains a detailed analysis of the investment advertising rules). **4–038**

The basic Core Rule obligation (Rule 5–9(1)) applies. This requires a firm, when issuing or approving an investment advertisement, to apply appropriate expertise and be able to show that it believes on reasonable grounds that the advertisement is fair and not misleading.

If the advertisement is a specific investment advertisement, which identifies and promotes a particular investment or investment service, the firm must identify itself as the issuer or approver and state that it is a member of SFA (Rule 5–9(2)). The prohibition on approving specific investment advertisements for units in unregulated collective investment schemes also applies (Rule 5–9(3)), but this is probably not relevant in the context of corporate finance.

Finally, the provision concerning the restriction on issuing or approving advertisements for overseas investment businesses (Rule 5–12) is included. This has already been explained in respect of the prescribed disclosure provision (paragraph 4–021 above), and is discussed more fully in Chapter 12 below.

The detailed contents requirements for specific investment advertisements issued to private investors do not apply.[3] Also the rule containing the restrictions relevant to direct offer advertising (Rule 5–10) is excluded.

The application of the four advertising provisions described above (Rules 5–9(1), (2), (3) and 5–12) should not, in practice, cause too much concern, because a large number of investment advertisements which a firm issues or approves in respect of corporate finance business will not be caught by the advertising application rule (Rule 5–1(4)) and will, therefore, be exempt from these requirements. These are advertisements which can be issued in the United Kingdom by an unauthorised person without having to be approved by an authorised person; advertisements required or permitted to be published by the rules of a designated investment exchange; advertisements subject to regulation by the United Kingdom Panel on Takeovers and Mergers; and scheme particulars for regulated collective investment schemes.

4–039   The exemptions, however, from the basic advertising obligation, that an advertisement must be fair and not misleading, could count for nothing, because of the application to corporate finance business of Rule 5–15 on fair and clear communications. This rule has a similar test to the advertising rule, namely that a communication must be fair and not misleading. It extends to any communication, whether oral or written, with any person, whether or not a customer, provided the communication is designed to promote the provision of an investment service. Further, the rule provides that, where a firm is making a written communication with a private customer to whom it is providing investment services, it must make sure that the communication is presented fairly and clearly. (See paragraph 6–005 below for a further explanation.)

A good argument can be made that the fair and clear communications rule does not apply to investment advertisements. This is because there is a special application provision for investment advertisements which determines how the rules apply to any communication which is an investment advertisement within the meaning of section 57(2) of the FSA 1986. A communication does not stop being an investment advertisement merely because the advertising application provision disapplies the advertising rules to it. The application of the fair and clear communications rule is determined by the general Conduct of Business application rule (Rule 5–1(1)). It, therefore, applies to communications in the course of regulated business, and, if the above argument is valid, only if these communications are not investment advertisements. In addition, the communication has to be one which, like a specific investment advertisement, promotes an investment service.

Even if the fair and clear communications rule applies to exempt advertisements, this should not be too onerous. It will not assist any firm's reputation to issue a communication which is misleading; and, if it does so, it may find itself in breach of section 47 of the FSA 1986. This makes it a criminal offence to issue knowingly or recklessly a misleading statement with respect to investment business. For a discussion on the nature of the fair and not misleading test, see also paragraph 12–009 below.

Exclusion clauses

Although the requirements on customer agreements (Rule 5–23) do not apply to corporate finance customers, the provision on exclusion clauses does (Rule 5–24). The first and third provisions of this requirement apply to all customers, whereas the second provision is only relevant in respect of private customers. A detailed explanation of this rule is given below in paragraphs 6–006 to 6–008.

Money broking

A special regime in respect of the application of the Conduct of **4–040** Business Rules applies to London Stock Exchange Money Brokers and London Stock Exchange Equity Only Brokers, but only in respect of any regulated and associated business carried on by them which constitutes money broking (Rule 5–1(6)).

Money broking is not defined, but it should be assumed that it applies to any of the activities carried on by these money brokers. This is because the Stock Exchange registered money brokers are only able to carry on money broking activities. If they wish to engage in any other types of investment business, this must be done through separate legal entities.

Money broking refers to the activities carried on by intermediaries with respect to stock lending and borrowing. In terms of the United Kingdom markets, the London Stock Exchange Money Brokers' (SEMBs') prime responsibility is to act as money brokers with respect to gilt-edged securities (namely, British Government and British Government guaranteed stocks denominated in sterling). They help provide liquidity to the United Kingdom Government fixed interest markets, enabling Gilt Edged Market Makers (GEMMs) to borrow and lend stock to cover their short and long positions. SEMBs are subject to supervision by the Bank of England in respect of their activities in the gilt-edged market and must comply with the Bank's financial resourcing and reporting requirements. In addition, as London Stock Exchange members, they must comply with the relevant exchange rules, including the special code of practice for money lending in the gilt-edged market.

The London Stock Exchange Equity Only Money Brokers similarly act as intermediaries, but this time between the London Stock Exchange market makers in equities. They are subject to SFA's Financial Rules. They are also subject to the London Stock Exchange's rules relating to money broking, including the code of practice relating to money broking in the equities markets.

Of course, SEMBs may also carry out money broking in equities, in which case they will have to comply with the same provisions as the Equity Only Money Brokers, except that they will still be subject to financial supervision by the Bank of England, which, for this purpose, remains the lead regulator.

4–041   Due to the substantial control by the Bank of England and the London Stock Exchange, and the fact that they cannot engage in other activities, it was considered appropriate to disapply the majority of the Conduct of Business Rules. As with corporate finance, but even more so, many of these rules would not apply anyway to money broking activities; and money brokers will not be dealing with private customers. The rules which apply are those concerning reliance on others, Chinese walls, inducements, insider dealing, support of the Takeover Panel's functions and the general rules on compliance arrangements.

Similar to corporate finance, the basic advertising obligation has been applied: the requirement to apply appropriate expertise and ensure that the advertisement is fair and not misleading (Rule 5–9(1)); and the requirement to state, in respect of specific investment advertisements, that the firm is the issuer or approver and a member of SFA (Rule 5–9(2)). Unlike corporate finance, however, the provision concerning the issuing or approving of advertisements in respect of overseas investment businesses (Rule 5–12) has not been applied, on the basis that a money broking firm would not be able to issue or approve such advertisements because it would then be doing a non-money broking activity in breach of its London Stock Exchange membership requirements.

Interestingly, the rule on fair and clear communications, which has been applied at SIB's request to corporate finance business, has not been imposed on money broking firms.

This separate regime for money broking only applies in respect of the small number of London Stock Exchange Money Brokers and Equity Only Money Brokers. There is no special regime for all the other SFA firms who engage in stock lending. These firms are subject to the normal Conduct of Business Rules. Obviously, if they are dealing with non-private customers, they will not be concerned with a fair number of the rules. The dealing rules will apply; also the rule on contract notes (Rule 5–34). Where a firm is acting as an intermediary in respect of stock lending, it will normally be dealing as a principal with both the lender and borrower of the stock, purchasing the stock from the lender and then selling it on to the borrower. In this respect it will be entering into two transactions which will require confirmation. The firm must comply with the detailed contents requirements for contract notes (Rule 5–34(2)). If the stock lending is being done for a customer as part of the discretionary management of his portfolio, to earn extra income, then the valuation statement required under Rule 5–35 will need to take account of the stock lending transactions; and the customer must have entered into a two-way customer agreement setting out the scope of the firm's discretion (Rule 5–23).

One of the most important requirements applying to stocklending (which is not a Conduct of Business Rule anyway) is the restriction in respect of safe custody. A firm may not use for stock lending purposes investments which are held in a safe custody account, except with the prior written consent of any private customer and prior written disclosure to any non-private customer.

Scheme management

The last of the special regimes with respect to the application of the **4–042** Conduct of Business Rules applies to operators of collective investment schemes when they are undertaking scheme management activity. Basically, the operator is the person appointed to manage the assets of the scheme. Scheme management activity means the management of the pooled property within the scheme. It does not include advice given to, or transactions executed for, investors in units in the scheme.

There are two separate tables setting out the rules which apply to such management. The first (Rule 5–1(7)) deals with the management of regulated collective investment schemes, whilst the second (Rule 5–1(8)) deals with the management of unregulated schemes. The difference between the two tables is minor.

In the case of unregulated schemes, the suitability rule applies (Rule 5–31). Where a firm is managing pooled funds, however, the suitability test is determined against the stated investment objectives of the fund, rather than against the individual circumstances of investors in the fund. As the operator will be acting as a discretionary investment manager, he will be subject to SFA's extension to the suitability rule, which requires him to monitor the continuing suitability of all investments made for the fund (Rule 5–31(3)).

SFA's suitability rule is not applied in the case of a regulated scheme. In this case, SFA has written a rule (Rule 5–50) which requires the operator to comply with SIB's Regulated Schemes Regulations 1991. These regulations have their own suitability requirement. A manager is required to see that the particular objectives specified in the scheme particulars are achieved (Regulation 7.02). The rule goes on to restrict the operator from acquiring significant influence over any body corporate in which the funds of the scheme are invested. Significant influence means control over the exercise of 20 per cent. or more of the voting rights of the company. The operator should avoid acquiring such an influence. If he does acquire it, then he must reduce it as soon as reasonably practical having regard to the interests of the scheme participants. At any rate, he must reduce the scheme's holding below 20 per cent. within six months after becoming aware of the influence.

4–043   Apart from the difference between these two rules, the rest of the Conduct of Business Rules which are referred to in the tables apply equally, whether it is a regulated or unregulated scheme. Basically, the rules which have been excluded are those concerned with: the categorisation of customers; customer documentation; marketing and selling of packaged products; the restrictions on off-exchange derivatives transactions and off-exchange market making; and the requirement to follow SIB's stabilisation rules. Also disapplied are the rules on advertising, the prescribed disclosure, fair and clear communications and information about the firm.

The reason for these exclusions is that the rules are not relevant to scheme management, rather than the fact that there is any special disapplication. As it is the pooled fund which is the customer rather than the individual investors in the fund, the rules concerned with customer categorisation, customer documentation and communications with private customers are not relevant. These provisions, however, would apply where a firm is advising, or dealing for, investors who wish to purchase or sell units in the fund. Similarly, in carrying out management of the fund's assets the operator will not be involved in advertising. Where he is promoting or marketing the scheme, however, he will not be carrying out scheme management activity. Therefore, he will be subject to all the usual advertising and marketing rules.

---

[1] It is arguable that the drafting has not achieved this and that the firm may only be disciplined for the breach by its overseas branch of one of these six rules, still enjoying the benefit of the foreign business carve-out for that customer, as well as customers solicited without any such breach.

[2] The main regulations are excluded; and the supplementary regulations which deal with settlement and margined money and SFA's supporting third tier, although not specifically excluded (except in relation to mandates over clients' accounts (Rule 4–17) will not, in practice, be generally applicable.

[3] See note 2 at the end of Chapter 12 in respect of approving a specific investment advertisement issued by a customer with whom the firm carries on corporate finance business.

Chapter 5

Customers

In applying the new rules it is important to make two separate **5–001** distinctions. The first is the distinction between those persons who are customers and those who are non-customers. The second is the distinction amongst customers between those who are private customers and those who are non-private customers.

Of the 40 Core Conduct of Business Rules, only nine apply where a firm is not dealing with customers. Of the 31 Core Rules which apply where a firm is dealing with customers, only 15 apply where the customer is a non-private customer. (See Appendix 3 below.)

Hence, in determining the obligations which a firm owes, it is most important to determine whether or not the firm is dealing with a customer and, if so, whether or not that customer is a private customer.

1. Definition of Customer

Basic definition

The Core Rule definition is not a comprehensive one. It merely states **5–002** that customer does not include:

(i) a market counterparty; or

(ii) a trust beneficiary.

However, it goes on to say that it does include:

(i) a potential customer;

(ii) an indirect customer; and

(iii) a customer of the firm's appointed representative.

SFA extension

In contrast, SFA has added to the Core Rule definition to provide a comprehensive definition of the meaning of customer:

A customer is any person with or for whom the firm carries on, or intends to carry on, any regulated or associated business (for the meaning of regulated and associated business, see paragraphs 4–005 and 4–012 above).

This is a wide definition. It includes:

(i) a person with whom the firm is dealing direct;

(ii) a person for whom the firm is acting as agent;

(iii) a person who is dealing with the firm indirectly through the medium of an agent.

A person is also a customer even though the firm has not yet established any relationship with him, but merely intends to. For example, if a firm approaches someone with the intention or desire that he should become a customer, this person will be a customer even if he rejects the firm's approach. In other words, the firm owes him customer obligations in making the approach, even if the person then subsequently decides, following the approach, not to have any business dealings with the firm. This is what is meant by the use of the phrase "intends to carry on" in SFA's extension and the term "potential customer" in the Core Rule definition.

Indirect customers

The position with indirect customers, namely the identified principals of agents who are themselves customers of the firm, is dealt with in paragraphs 5–041 *et seq.* below.

Customers of appointed representatives

5–003   The customer of a firm's appointed representative is also regarded as the customer of the firm to the extent that the representative is dealing with that person in the course of business for which the firm has accepted responsibility. This covers the situation where the representative is carrying on an act which, if the firm knew about it, would not be authorised by the firm, but which, nevertheless, is one which falls within the general course of the appointed representative's business for which the firm is responsible.

Exceptions: Market counterparty and trust beneficiary

The Core Rule definition says that customer does not include a market counterparty or trust beneficiary. A discussion on market counterparty appears in paragraphs 5–006 *et seq.* below. Trust beneficiaries are not customers because, in law, the owner of the assets is the trustee. It is the trustee, therefore, who is treated as the customer. However, a firm cannot ignore the position of the beneficiaries. For example, if it knew, or reasonably ought to have known, that the trustees were acting in breach of the trust deed or against the interests of the beneficiaries, the firm could be in breach of Principle 1 (Integrity) and Principle 2 (Skill, Care and Diligence).

It is interesting to note that, although only the trustee is a customer of the firm, where an agent is dealing with a firm for an identified principal, then, as a result of the Core Rule definition of indirect customer, the firm owes customer obligations to both the agent and the principal.

Other exceptions

Besides these two Core Rule definition exceptions, SFA has provided three other qualifications to the definition of customer. These relate to corporate finance, the management of collective investment schemes and safe custody.

Corporate finance

A firm does not owe customer obligations to all persons with whom it **5–004** may have contact as a result of carrying on corporate finance business for a particular customer or when the firm is carrying on corporate finance business for its own account. The type of business which is regarded as corporate finance is discussed in paragraphs 4–028 *et seq.* above.

Basically, the persons who are excluded from the definition of customer in this respect are those persons with whom it would be unreasonable to expect the firm to have a customer relationship. The exception relates to situations where there would be too much of a conflict between the interests of the firm's corporate finance customer and the interests of the other persons.

Before a firm can take the benefit of this exception, it has to be satisfied that two requirements are met in respect of the person:

Requirement 1

There must be no material difference between the way in which the firm communicates or deals with this person, as opposed to the firm's communications or dealings with other persons in a similar category. In other words, the firm should not appear to be favouring some persons in a particular category, against others. In determining what is the relevant category, this requirement is broken down to include holders or prospective holders of investments of the size or class concerned, or other creditors or contingent creditors of the company concerned.

Therefore, a firm would not have to treat all shareholders of a company in exactly the same way if, for example, it had decided to target only the largest shareholders with holdings above a particular level. However, when dealing with the shareholders with holdings above this level, it would have to communicate or deal with them on an equal footing, without in any way preferring one to another.

This requirement, with its reference to size and class, is significant. It means that a firm can target particular groups of shareholders within the same class without owing them customer obligations. It is not limited to just shares, but refers to investments and would, therefore, include holders of a particular size or class of debenture. It also extends to prospective holders. This is useful in the context of a placement, so that a firm does not have to treat potential placees of the size or class concerned as its customers, provided it treats them similarly in offering the particular investments to be placed.

The requirement refers to members of the public, and also creditors and contingent creditors. In these cases, there is no reference to size or criteria. Therefore, all creditors or contingent creditors would have to be treated similarly: there could be no differentiation based on the respective sizes of outstanding debts owed to the creditors.

There is an important qualification to this first requirement about treating persons of a particular class in the same way. It does not apply where the firm is arranging or seeking to arrange underwriting or sub-underwriting commitments. In arranging a new issue or making an offer for sale, a firm will normally wish to underwrite the issue. It does not have to treat the persons whom it approaches to accept underwriting commitments as its customers, even if it does not approach all potential underwriters in exactly the same way.

There has been some concern that the reference to not treating the relevant persons "materially differently" is too restrictive. For example, in the case of a firm acting for the purchaser of a private company, the vendor shareholders may receive consideration calculated in different ways and some of them may give warranties. In the case of a firm arranging an offer for sale, distinctions may be made between the persons to whom the shares are offered. In the recent privatisations, preferential terms were given to employees and customers.

A sensible approach must be adopted. In some cases, the difference in treatment will not be material. In other situations, it could be argued that the difference in treatment is only between holders or prospective holders of different sizes or classes of shares. In other words, the difference in the treatment of vendor shareholders may relate to a distinction between the size of their holdings. However, it is not really possible to make the same argument for the distinction made in privatisations between employees, customers and the general public. Therefore, SFA may need to make some further modifications to this requirement.

Requirement 2

The firm must clearly indicate to the person that: (a) it is acting for someone else; and (b) it will not be responsible for protecting him as a customer or advising on the suitability of the relevant transaction. This latter obligation (b) is an onerous requirement and means that, in respect of any corporate finance communications going to persons who satisfy Requirement 1, a firm will have to make it clear that it will owe them no customer obligations. SIB thought it was more appropriate to write Requirement 2 in this way, rather than in the more neutral way of the old TSA Rules which was that the circumstances must be such that the person could not reasonably expect the firm to be responsible to him for best execution or suitability.

It is important to note that, to rely on this exception to the definition of customer in respect of corporate finance business, a firm must be able to satisfy both of the above requirements in respect of the relevant persons (except Requirement 1 for potential underwriters and sub-underwriters).

Collective investment schemes

This exception makes it clear that, where a firm is managing the 5–005 assets of a collective investment scheme (whether or not it is a regulated scheme), its customer is the scheme itself, or rather the trustees of the assets, rather than the individual unitholders in the scheme. The unitholders will be customers of the firms which have advised them and arranged for them to buy and sell units within the scheme. Of course, it may be possible that, in respect of some schemes, a firm will be both the operator of the scheme and also advising and arranging for customers to buy units in the scheme. In this case, the unitholders would only be owed customer obligations in respect of the advice on buying and selling units in the scheme and in respect of transactions for the purchase and sale of those units. They would not be customers in respect of the management of the pooled assets which represent the scheme. So a firm which is managing the assets does not have to generate contract notes in respect of every unitholder each time a transaction takes place in relation to the scheme's assets. Contract notes would only be required for the unitholders when they purchased or sold units within the scheme.

Safe custody

Finally, the definition states that, for the purposes of the Safekeeping Rules, the term "customer" includes all of the persons who have just been described as exceptions (namely, market counterparties, trust beneficiaries, third persons in connection with corporate finance business, unitholders in respect of the operators of collective investment schemes), except where any of these persons are authorised under the FSA 1986. Therefore, it is only authorised persons who are not regarded as a customer for the purposes of the safe custody protections.

2. Market Counterparty

Basic definition

5–006   The Core Rule definition states that a market counterparty is a person dealing with the firm:

(i)   as principal or as agent for an unidentified principal; and

(ii)   in the course of investment business of the same description as that in the course of which the firm acts.

The reference to dealing means that this is a transaction by transaction based definition. In other words, you have to establish whether, at the time of dealing, the person satisfies the requirements of (i) and (ii) above. It is possible to think of situations in which, in respect of one transaction, a person will satisfy the test, but then, in respect of a second transaction, he will not, because, for example, although he is acting in the course of investment business of the same description as the firm, he has indicated, before dealing, that he is acting as agent for an identified principal.

This highlights the problems with the definition. Before dealing, a firm has to know exactly the capacity in which the other person is dealing. The biggest problems centre on what is meant by "identified" in relation to principal where the other person is dealing as agent and what is meant by "in the course of investment business of the same description".

Identification

5–007   Is "identified" satisfied merely by the firm knowing before dealing the name of the agent's principal; or is the identification test only satisfied if the agent has given the firm the same information about the principal in respect of the particular transaction as the firm would require if the principal had been its direct customer for that transaction? In other words, if you, as the firm, are giving advice or making a recommendation, is the identification test only satisfied if the agent has given you enough information about the principal's financial circumstances and investment objectives for you, the firm, to be able to satisfy the suitability test in relation to the principal in respect of the advice or recommendation given?

Without any restriction being imposed through SFA guidance (and such a restriction would amount to a derogation from a Core Rule term which would require authorisation by SIB in its commencement order applying the Core Rules to SFA firms), it is better to assume that any sort of identification by the agent of the principal before dealing, even the mere giving of the principal's name, amounts to identification and, therefore, would take the deal outside the definition of market counterparty. Obviously, this is a blow to many firms dealing with fund managers, agency stockbrokers and intermediaries, who regularly give the name (and often address) of their principal, but only so that the particular transaction can more easily be identified by the agent on receipt of the contract note, or so that the firm can send a contract note direct to the principal.

Of course, the meaning of identification is important because, where the agent's principal is identified to a firm, the agent is not a market counterparty, but a customer of the firm, and the agent's principal becomes the firm's indirect customer; see paragraphs 5–041 *et seq.* below.

Investment business of the same description

Even if the firm has satisfied the first test, namely that the person **5–008** with whom it is dealing is a principal or acting as agent for an unidentified principal, the firm has to satisfy the second test before it can treat this person as a market counterparty. This is the test that both the firm and the other person must be acting in the course of investment business of the same description.

This causes problems. Do you look at both the nature of the investments in Part I, Schedule 1 to the FSA 1986, and the types of activities in Part II, Schedule 1? Or do you just look at the nature of the activities in Part II, irrespective of the type of investments in Part I? For example, is a firm which is a dealer in investments (paragraph 12, Part II) acting in the course of investment business of the same description if it normally only deals in shares (a paragraph 1 investment) when it deals with another person who is only a dealer in bonds (a paragraph 2 investment)? It could be argued that shares and bonds are similar investments. Would the same result still apply where the firm is a dealer in options and futures (paragraphs 7 and 8 investments) and the other person is only a dealer in shares and debentures (paragraphs 1 and 2 investments)? They are both dealers (a paragraph 12 activity), but options and futures contracts are very different to non-derivative investments such as shares and debentures.

If the restriction is limited to the types of investments in Part I, is there any further breakdown within each category of investment? For example, are dealers in financial futures dealing in the course of investment business of the same description as dealers in commodity futures? Again, are dealers in United Kingdom equities doing investment business of the same description as dealers in overseas equities?

·If the term "in the course of investment business of the same description" only relates to activity within Part II, is it a concern whether that activity is a major or minor activity in relation to the firm's investment business as a whole. For example, a fund manager member of IMRO is likely to be authorised by IMRO not only for managing investments (paragraph 14), but also for dealing in investments (paragraph 12). Obviously, the fund manager's main activity is to manage funds rather than deal in investments. However, the question arises, if he is authorised for both activities by IMRO, whether, when dealing with an SFA broker, he could be regarded as acting in the course of investment business of the same description: namely as a dealer. There are a number of people who take the view that managing funds is a very different activity from dealing in investments and that, therefore, the two activities cannot be regarded as activities of the same description, even if the fund management activity incidentally involves some dealing.

5–009   It is suggested that, in practice, it is sensible to look at the main activity carried on by the other person with whom the SFA firm is dealing and, perhaps, also his level of experience and knowledge. In other words, if his main activity is fund management, that person should not be regarded as acting in the course of investment business of the same description as a firm whose main business is acting as a broker–dealer. Similarly, a firm which is a broker–dealer in equities and debentures, and which does not have any experience in commodity futures, should not be regarded as acting in the course of investment business of the same description when it enters into a transaction in a commodity future with a specialist broker in this field. It is more difficult to say whether a financial futures broker can be regarded as acting in the course of investment business of the same description as a commodity futures broker. Obviously, both have a good understanding of the way in which a futures contract works, but the financial futures broker may not appreciate the specialist factors which affect the pricing and investment potential of a commodity future. It is easier to regard a dealer in United Kingdom equities as acting in the course of investment business of the same description as a dealer in overseas equities and, even, as a dealer in traded equity options or in futures and options based on an equity index.

In determining whether it is investment business of the same description, regard should be given to the effect of being treated as a market counterparty. A market counterparty loses all of the rule protections owed to customers. The question to be asked is whether it is appropriate that the other person with whom the firm is dealing should not be protected as a customer because of his professional expertise and understanding in respect of the transaction. If in doubt, err on the side of caution and assume that the other person is not a market counterparty.

SFA extension

It is due to this uncertainty with the Core Rule definition, and its **5–010** operation on a transaction-by-transaction basis, that SFA has introduced a third tier extension to the definition which effectively allows certain persons with whom a firm does business to be treated as market counterparties generally, whether or not in respect of some of the transactions these persons either are acting as agents for an identified principal or are not acting in the course of investment business of the same description as the firm. This once-and-for-all classification relies heavily on the old TSA rule on market professionals.

SFA's extension operates in the following way. The Core Rule definition always applies. Therefore, whether or not someone falls within SFA's extension, he will still be a market counterparty in respect of a particular transaction, if he is dealing:

(i) as a principal, or an agent for an unidentified principal; and

(ii) in the course of investment business of the same description.

In addition, the person may be a market counterparty in circumstances where he is acting as agent for an identified principal or where he is acting (whether or not as an agent) other than in the course of investment business of the same description as the SFA firm, provided he is categorised as a market counterparty in accordance with SFA's extension.

This extension (Rule 5–4) states that a firm may treat any persons falling within the list given there as market counterparties either generally or in respect of particular types of investment business. This SFA classification is done at the start of a business relationship and continues throughout that relationship, rather than the Core Rule definition which is dependent upon the capacity in which the parties enter into a particular deal.

Also, unlike the Core Rule definition, it is not limited to the activity of dealing, but includes any investment activity carried on with the other person, such as giving advice and making recommendations. It also includes any discretionary business undertaken with such a person. This is an important amendment to the TSA approach to market professionals. A market professional under TSA's rules was protected as a full customer in respect of any discretionary investment service provided by a TSA firm.

The limbs to SFA's extension to the definition of market counterparty are:

Limb 1: Other SFA firms

5–011   An SFA firm may treat any other SFA firm as a market counterparty in respect of any type of investment business. This is potentially significant as SFA has a large membership of about 1,400 firms, ranging from small investment advisers, brokers, research boutiques and corporate finance advisory firms, up to large, multi-function securities houses and banks.

A significant number of SFA firms have cross-border investment businesses with branch offices in a number of countries. Where a firm has a wide branch network, the firm as a whole will be a member of SFA, even though it is only required to seek authorisation under the FSA 1986 in respect of the investment business which it is doing in the United Kingdom, with this business normally being conducted from a branch based in the United Kingdom. As the firm, rather than its London branch, is a member of SFA, any investment business relationship which another SFA firm has with any part of this SFA firm can be done on a market counterparty basis, even though the business is done with a branch of the firm outside the United Kingdom which is not engaged in United Kingdom investment business. Of course, this is only relevant where the business done between the SFA firms is subject to the application of SFA's Conduct of Business Rules.

Limb 2: Investment exchange members

5–012   An SFA firm can also treat as a market counterparty any non-SFA firm which is a trading member of an investment exchange. No definition of trading member is provided, but it is only intended to include those members who are able to trade or deal direct with other members on the exchange. Therefore, it includes locals on futures exchanges, but not associate members who have no trading rights and members who are only clearing members, responsible for settling and clearing transactions without being able to deal on the exchange. Again, no definition is given for investment exchange, but it would not include an exchange where no contracts or products are traded which fall within the definition of investments in Part I, Schedule 1.

Unlike Limb 1, there is a restriction on the kinds of investment business which can be done under this extension to the market counterparty definition. A non-SFA exchange member can only be treated as a market counterparty to the extent that the SFA firm is dealing with him in investments of the kind traded on the relevant exchange or any related derivatives. This would include, therefore, off-exchange dealings provided the dealings were in the same types of investments as those traded on the exchange. No guidance is given as to whether "kinds of investments" relates back to the separate categories of investments listed in Part I, Schedule 1. It should do so, except that it is more restrictive.

For example, if you were dealing with a trading member of a financial futures exchange, the kinds of investments dealt in on that exchange in accordance with Part I would be options, futures and contracts for difference (paragraphs 7, 8 and 10). However, that exchange does not deal in all types of options and futures contracts; it only deals in contracts based on financial instruments. Therefore, a non-SFA trading member of the exchange should only be a market counterparty in respect of financial options and futures, not commodity options and futures. Nevertheless, he could be treated as a market counterparty in financial options or futures contracts which are either off-exchange contracts, or contracts quoted or dealt in on a different exchange, because they are the same kinds of investments as those traded on the exchange where he is a member.

Limb 2 provides that you can treat a non-SFA trading member of an exchange as a market counterparty in respect of derivatives related to the kinds of investments traded on the exchange. Derivatives is defined to include options, futures and contracts for difference. Therefore, if you were dealing with a member of an exchange which only trades equities, you could treat him as a market counterparty in respect of any options or futures contracts based on equities, or any contracts for difference based on the movement of the price of any index relating to equities, such as the FT–SE 100. Although the term "derivatives" does not include warrants, the non-SFA trading members of an exchange will be a market counterparty in respect of related warrants because they can be regarded as investments of the same kind as those traded on the exchange. The same applies to related depositary receipts and units in related collective investment schemes.

Limb 3: Overseas off-exchange dealers

A firm can treat a non-SFA firm which is an overseas person as a   **5–013**
market counterparty if that person, as part of carrying on a business, regularly deals in investments off-exchange. An overseas person is someone who is conducting investment business, but not from a place of business maintained by him in the United Kingdom, and, therefore, will not normally be subject to the FSA 1986 authorisation requirements. Where such a person is an off-exchange dealer, he may be treated as a market counterparty in respect of investments of the kind in which he deals off-exchange and related derivatives. Note that this limb is only concerned with overseas persons who are off-exchange dealers. To the extent that they are trading members of investment exchanges, they could be treated as market counterparties under Limb 2.

There may be some uncertainty as to the investments covered by this market counterparty categorisation for off-exchange dealers. It does not extend to any off-exchange transaction, but only those in investments of the same kind in which the overseas person regularly deals off-exchange. The classification is not intended to be so narrow that it only relates to the particular stocks or contracts in which the overseas person acts as an off-exchange dealer; it must relate to investments of a similar nature. For example, if the overseas person acts as an off-exchange dealer in some Japanese equities, he could certainly be treated as a market counterparty in respect of any Japanese equities.

However, could he be treated as a market counterparty in respect of any shares whatsoever? This would obviously be the case if "investments of that kind" refers to the types of investments as listed in Part I, Schedule 1. This is the same problem discussed in paragraphs 5–008 and 5–009 above in relation to the meaning of investment business of the same description in the context of the Core Rule definition. As there, it is suggested that the SFA firm should look at the general experience and understanding of the overseas person. In other words, does he know enough generally about all equities, from his dealings in Japanese equities off-exchange, to be correctly classed as a professional (therefore, a market counterparty) when dealing in any sort of equity? In most cases, the answer ought to be "yes".

Of course, based on this approach, you can argue that investments of that kind include other investments besides shares. For example, if the overseas person regularly deals in Japanese equities off-exchange, he can surely be classified as a market counterparty in respect of ordinary warrants and depositary receipts relating to such equities, together with debentures and other loan stock relating to the relevant companies. Similarly to Limb 2, related derivatives are included. As explained earlier, ordinary warrants, where you subscribe for new shares from the issuer, are not derivatives; but it is worth noting that a number of investments which are referred to as "warrants" are in reality options because the right to acquire these investments is granted not by the original issuer, but by another party, and the right relates to investments which are already in issue.

Although an overseas person becomes a market counterparty because he regularly deals off-exchange, he can, of course, be treated as a market counterparty in respect of on-exchange transactions, even if he is not a trading member of an investment exchange. This would be where the on-exchange transactions are in similar investments to those in which he regularly deals off-exchange.

No explanation is given as to what amounts to regular dealing, but a sensible approach requires an assessment of the type of investment or transaction. For example, a person who occasionally deals in equity swaps could be regarded as dealing regularly because of the comparatively few transactions currently done in these contracts and the limited number of dealers in them.

Limb 4: Inter-dealer brokers

5–014   An SFA firm can treat a non-SFA person who is an inter-dealer broker as a market counterparty in respect of activities undertaken by that person as part of its inter-dealer broking activities. The main example of an inter-dealer broker is the specialist firm which deals with market makers and with brokers dealing as principal, arranging for the purchase and sale of stock to cover the market makers' or broker-dealers' long or short positions. The inter-dealer broker should never disclose either the recipient of the stock to the provider or the provider to the recipient. He stands in the middle between the provider and the recipient and deals with each as a principal.

Limb 5: Wholesale money markets

The final category of persons who can be treated as market counterparties under SFA's extension are: **5–015**

(i) countries;

(ii) central banks or other monetary authorities of any country;

(iii) international banking or financial institutions whose members are countries (or their central banks or monetary authorities); and

(iv) listed money market institutions.

These four types of person, however, can only be treated as market counterparties in respect of debt investments or money market investments.[1] It repeats the category 2 market professional in TSA's rules.

A listed money market institution is a firm which is exempt from the requirements to be authorised under the FSA 1986 because it is listed by the Bank of England under section 43 in respect of its dealings or arrangements in the wholesale money markets in the instruments, and subject to the conditions, mentioned in Schedule 5.

Although country is not defined it would include any province or state in a country. Therefore, the central banks or monetary authorities of a state could be treated as market counterparties under this limb, but not public corporations which merely had the financial backing of a state's or country's government.

Market counterparty notice

Before any of the persons within Limbs 1 to 5 above can be treated as a market counterparty under the SFA rule extension to the Core Rule definition, the SFA firm must have sent to the other person (which could be another SFA firm) a written notice informing it that it will be treated as a market counterparty. The notice can be very short: in fact, only one sentence long. It must make it clear, however, that the other person is to be treated as a market counterparty and will **5–016** lose the benefit of the protections afforded to customers under the rules. The notice does not have to point out the restrictions affecting market counterparty status where the recipient is a non-SFA firm: namely, it does not have to state that the SFA firm can only treat the recipient, if it is a trading member of an investment exchange, as a market counterparty in respect of investments of the same kind as those traded on the relevant investment exchange and related derivatives; or, if it is a listed money market institution, in respect of debt and money market investments.

Once it has sent the notice, the SFA firm can treat the other party as a market counterparty either generally, if it is another SFA firm (Limb1), or in respect of the kinds of investments relevant to Limbs 2 to 5, unless the recipient notifies the SFA firm in writing to the contrary. The notification from the recipient can be general: in other words, it does not want to be treated as a market counterparty at all; or the notification can be in respect of particular kinds of investments. Obviously, as soon as the SFA firm has received the recipient's written notice, it must treat it as a customer to the extent required in its notice, unless the recipient, in respect of the particular transaction, falls within the Core Rule definition: namely, it is dealing as a principal or as agent for an unidentified principal in the course of investment business of the same description.

Exceptions to market counterparty notice

1. *Fellow exchange members*

5–017   There is one important exception to the written notice provision. An SFA firm does not have to send a written notice explaining that it will treat the recipient as a market counterparty where the other person is another SFA firm and both are trading members of the same investment exchange, provided their business dealings are restricted to the kinds of investments traded on the relevant exchange or any related derivatives: in other words, the same restriction as in Limb 2 above for a non-SFA trading member of an investment exchange.

2. *Existing TSA market professionals*

There is another exception contained in the Transitional Rules. The notice does not have to be sent to a person whom the firm was already treating as a market professional under TSA's rules, provided that person falls within the new categorisation requirements. Therefore, an SFA firm which, under TSA's rules, was treating another person as a market professional, can continue to treat it as a non-customer, without the need to send a market counterparty notice, provided that person falls within Limbs 1 to 5 above. Remember, however, the qualifications in the new rules: if the other person is not another SFA firm, it can only be treated as a market counterparty in respect of the limited range of investments or business referred to in Limbs 2 to 5. TSA's only restriction related to persons falling within Limb 5: central banks, monetary authorities and listed money market institutions.

Duty on recipient

The rules place a duty on the recipient of a market counterparty **5–018** notice if he is an SFA firm. No SFA firm which itself has private customers should permit itself to be treated as a market counterparty under SFA's market counterparties rule where it believes that it itself does not have the necessary expertise to protect its own customers in accordance with the rules. In other words, an SFA firm which is a recipient of the notice should reject it if it is relying, in providing investment services to its private customers, on the expertise of the sender of the notice. An example would be where the recipient is an agency stockbroker who specialises in giving advice on shares. If it is dealing for a private customer with a dealer in commodity futures, it should not allow itself to be treated as a market counterparty if it has no real knowledge of the commodity futures market and is not itself in a position to determine whether the particular transaction satisfies best execution and is suitable in respect of its customer's investment objectives and circumstances. In fact, in these circumstances, it may well wish to identify its principal before dealing with the futures dealer in order to make its principal an indirect customer of the latter firm.

Although the rules place an obligation on the recipient, where it has private customers, to determine whether it itself can satisfy its obligations to its customers if it is treated as a market counterparty by another firm with whom it is dealing, there may be particular transactions where the recipient, despite refusing to be treated as a market counterparty under this rule, falls within the Core Rule definition. In respect of these transactions, it will be a market counterparty, despite its general election to the contrary. In other words, it is important to remember that the Core Rule definition applies even where, in respect of the relationship as a whole, the recipient of the market counterparty notice has rejected it and requires protection as a customer.

Obviously SFA firms who have private customers, and who receive market counterparty notices, will have to consider carefully whether or not they require customer protections from other SFA firms with whom they are dealing on behalf of their clients. The more prudent firm, as a precaution, will probably always insist on being treated as a customer rather than a market counterparty. There may be some SFA firms, however, who will refuse to deal with other firms on any basis other than as market counterparties.

An argument can be made that the difference between the level of protection for non-customers, namely market counterparties, and non-private customers is very small. The obligations which apply to non-discretionary, non-private customers are limited to the basic dealing rules and the rules on confirmation of transactions. Many firms observe these requirements as a matter of course, whether or not they are dealing with customers. Therefore, it may be immaterial to the firm as to whether or not the person with whom it is dealing falls to be treated as a non-private customer rather than as a market counterparty.

5–019   The problem really occurs where the recipient who rejects the market counterparty is acting as an agent and identifies its principal. In this case, the indirect customer concept comes into play and the first firm could find itself in a position where it owes private customer obligations in respect of the agent's principal, although, if the agent alone was the customer of the firm, the obligations would only be non-private customer ones. Note that where a person is a market counterparty, whether under the Core Rule definition or SFA's rule extension, then no customer obligations are owed to it, even though it is acting as agent with private customer obligations to its principals.

The danger in requiring the sending of a notice, warning a person that it is to be treated as a market counterparty, is that the recipient will always try to opt into the maximum protection available and will, therefore, reject the notice. As a result, there may be constant letters or notices flying from one firm to another, and the actual relationship which eventually applies will be determined by the respective staminas of the two firms. The firm which sends the last notice before the relevant transaction will almost certainly be the one whose terms dictate the nature of the relationship: either the sending of a market counterparty notice or the return of another notice from the recipient rejecting that status.

Another problem is that, when the notice is received by a non-SFA firm which is not in receipt of the SFA rulebook explaining the effect of the market counterparty status, the recipient will raise questions as to what is meant by being treated as a market counterparty. This, in turn, could require a detailed explanation by the sender of the notice, especially in the case of recipients based overseas.

3. Non-Private Customers

5–020   As stated at the beginning of this chapter, there are two important distinctions to be made. We have already made the first: namely, the distinction between customers and non-customers. The prime example of a non-customer is a person whom the firm intends to treat as a market counterparty.

The second main distinction applies to customers and it is distinguishing private customers from non-private customers. A non-private customer is defined as someone who is not a private customer or who has elected to be treated as a non-private customer in accordance with the rules. A private customer is defined as:

(i)   an individual, unless he is acting in the course of carrying on investment business (for example, a sole trader or someone acting in the course of his employment with an investment business); or

(ii) a small business investor (which is defined as a company, partnership or trustee acting for a trust none of which satisfies the size requirements of the ordinary business investor definition).

This definition of private customer, therefore, means that the main category of non-private customer is contained within the Core Rule definition of ordinary business investor, which has been further extended by SFA. The other category is customers who would normally fall to be treated as private customers, but who satisfy an experience and understanding test enabling them to be treated as non-private customers: these are the customers who are commonly referred to as experts.

Ordinary business investor

Essentially, this definition should be viewed as being similar to the old definitions of business customer under TSA's rules and business investor under AFBD's rules.

Reasonable belief

At the beginning of the Core Rule definition, SFA has added the words: "means a customer who is reasonably believed to be". First, SFA is making it clear that ordinary business investor is a category of customer. Secondly, it is not an absolute test as to whether or not a customer falls within the various limbs of the definition. Categorisation depends upon the reasonable belief of the firm. This reasonable belief test is applied to all the definitions of customer. In other words, a firm is protected if it can show that it had reasonable grounds to believe that a customer came within a particular category, even if, as a matter of fact, the customer did not satisfy the necessary criteria.

It is important to note that the reasonable belief test is not merely a defence to a firm who, as a matter of fact, incorrectly categorises a customer. If the firm has categorised the customer wrongly in accordance with fact, but acted in accordance with a reasonable belief, then the protection afforded by the rules to the customer follows the categorisation made under the reasonable belief test. For example, a body corporate which does not in fact satisfy the size requirements for ordinary business investor, but which the firm reasonably believes does so, would only be protected under the rules as a non-private customer rather than a private customer. There would be no compensation available to the customer for breach of a rule provision which only applies to private customers.

Limbs to definition

5–021   The Core Rule definition of ordinary business investor has three limbs to it. SFA has added another two. All five limbs are dealt with below.

Limb 1: Public authorities

This concerns governments, local authorities or public authorities. It covers the United Kingdom Government, any separate government for Northern Ireland, or any government for a country or territory outside the United Kingdom. It also includes any local authority in the United Kingdom or elsewhere; and any international organisation which has amongst its members either the United Kingdom or another country. (Of course, some Governments and public authorities may satisfy Limb 5 of the SFA market counterparty rule in respect of debt and money market investments.)

Limb 2: Non-individual legal persona

This limb deals with legal persona who are not individuals. Therefore, it covers bodies corporate, partnerships and unincorporated associations. The test is determined by a size requirement and is not dependent upon the understanding and experience of the person. The size criteria vary between, on the one hand, bodies corporate and, on the other, partnerships and unincorporated associations.

A. *Bodies corporate.* When dealing with a body corporate, look at the number of members to begin with. Does it have more than 20 members? If so, then it will be an ordinary business investor if it has a called up share capital or net assets of £500,000 or more. If the assessment is made on net assets, the aggregate of liabilities must be deducted from the aggregate of assets, disregarding any called up share capital and undistributed reserves.

If the body corporate has only 20 members or less, then, before it can be treated as an ordinary business investor, it must have a called up share capital or net assets of £5 million or more.

If the body corporate does not itself satisfy these size criteria, it will be an ordinary business investor if:

(i) it is the subsidiary of a company with 21 or more members and either it, any of its subsidiaries or its holding company has a called-up share capital or net assets of at least £500,000; or

(ii) any of its subsidiaries or its holding company has a called-up share capital or net assets of £5 million or more.

For the purposes of the rules, holding company and subsidiary have the meaning given in section 736 of the Companies Act 1985 (as amended by section 144 of the Companies Act 1989).

B. *Partnerships and unincorporated associations.* If the person is not a body corporate, but a partnership or unincorporated association, it must have net assets of £5 million or more to satisfy the ordinary business investor test, In determining net assets, liabilities in respect of partners' or proprietors' capital and current accounts should be disregarded.

SFA has added into Limb 2 a two-year window. Therefore, a person can be treated as an ordinary business investor where it has satisfied any of these size requirements at any time during the previous two years. This provision is obviously important to firms who are relying upon published annual reports and accounts in categorising their customers. The current report and accounts may well contain information which is out of date in relation to the customer's size at the time when the firm deals with it. Obviously, in this respect, firms can also take comfort from the reasonable belief test discussed above.

Limb 3: Trusts

As stated under the definition of customer, a trust beneficiary is not a customer. The customer is the trustee. The trustee can be treated as an ordinary business investor where he is trustee of a trust which satisfies a size requirement. As with Limb 2, it is the size of the assets which is important, rather than the experience and understanding of the trustee. The size requirement relates to the aggregate value of the cash and investments which form part of the trust's assets. This aggregate value must be £10 million or more and, in arriving at the value, no account is taken of any liabilities of the trust. As with Limb 2, there is a two-year window. Therefore, if the trust has satisfied this size requirement at any time within the previous two years, it can be treated as an ordinary business investor, even if the value of the assets is now below £10 million.

If the trust has assets below £10 million, then it may only be treated as a non-private customer if the trustees are themselves classified by the firm as experts. (See paragraphs 5–026 *et seq.* below.)

5–022

It is important to note in respect of both Limbs 2 and 3 that the size criteria are on-going requirements, rather than requirements which only have to be satisfied on initial categorisation of the customer. The two-year window means that, once the firm has categorised a customer as falling within the ordinary business investor category, it can continue to treat him as such for two years after he ceases to satisfy the size criteria. Thereafter, a firm would have to treat the customer as a private customer unless:

(i) it can rely on the reasonable belief test: in other words, the firm has reasonable grounds for believing that the customer continues to satisfy these size requirements, even if in fact he no longer does so; or

(ii) it can classify the customer as a non-private customer under the test for experts on the basis that he has sufficient experience and understanding to waive the protections owed to private customers.

It is likely that a customer who has been treated as an ordinary business investor, but who no longer satisfies the size requirements, can properly be treated as an expert investor. The only problem here is that written documentation will be required.

Limb 4: Investment businesses

5–023   SFA takes the view that no authorised person, listed money market institution or overseas investment business should be treated as a private customer. Some of these bodies will satisfy the size requirements of Limb 2, but a large number of them will not. Therefore, SFA has added this fourth limb to the Core Rule definition to make sure that all such persons are treated as ordinary business investors.

Note that authorised persons include not only persons who are authorised as a result of being SRO members, but also firms which have certificates to do investment business from a recognised professional body (RPB). Typical RPB members are solicitors and accountants. Many of them carry out investment business to a minor extent. Any investment business which they transact is often done as an integral part of carrying on their main professional work which is non-investment based. Their own professional bodies grant them certificates to do investment business provided the relevant RPB is satisfied that its member is fit and competent to do the investment business for which it is authorised by the certificate.

Obviously, many RPB firms will not have the same experience and understanding as firms which are authorised by SROs. For these latter firms, their investment business will normally be a major, if not the only aspect, of their business. SFA takes the view, however, that any firm which is authorised to do investment business, whether by an SRO or RPB, can properly be treated as a non-private customer. If the firm requires extra protection, then it should arrange for that protection through a contractual agreement with the SFA firm with whom it deals. Note, however, that if it does obtain private customer protection through contract, the firm will still fall within the category of an ordinary business investor for the purposes of the application of the SFA rules and any breach of those rules. If the SFA firm failed to provide a private customer protection which it had agreed to provide under the contract, then the other firm's only remedy would be one in the ordinary civil courts for damages for breach of contract.

Listed money market institutions and, to a lesser extent, overseas investment businesses have been explained in respect of Limbs 5 and 3 under SFA's rule extension (Rule 5-4) to the definition of market counterparty (paragraphs 5-015 and 5-013 above). An overseas investment business is referred to in the rules as an overseas person, but means any person who carries on investment business from a permanent place of business maintained by him outside the United Kingdom. It includes anybody who carries on investment business outside the United Kingdom, however small that business may be and irrespective of the fact that the investment business may be done as a small part of another business which is not investment business.

Although an SFA firm can happily treat all of these people as non-private customers, there is an important note of caution to be sounded. **5-024** This relates to the definition of indirect customer which is explained further in paragraphs 5-041 *et seq.* below. Many of the other authorised persons and overseas investment businesses with whom an SFA firm deals may themselves be acting as agents. If they are, are they acting as agents for identified principals? If they identify their principals before dealing with the SFA firm, then the SFA firm will have to treat those principals as its indirect customers; which, in effect, means treating them in a similar way to the SFA firm's own direct customers. Although the agent, as an authorised person or overseas investment business, will be treated as an ordinary business investor, his identified principal may well fall to be treated as a private customer. Therefore, when dealing for the agent, the SFA firm will, in fact, have to comply with the private customer rule obligations because these are the obligations which it will have in respect of the identified principals. It will only be when the principals are not identified that the SFA firm can disregard the private customer protections when dealing with other authorised persons and overseas investment businesses.

Many solicitors and accountants act as trustees. When they are dealing with an SFA firm in their capacity of trustee, they will not be within Limb 4 because they will not be acting in their capacity of partner or employee of an authorised person, namely their legal or accountancy firm. If they are acting as trustees, they will not be agents, so that the trust beneficiaries, even if identified, would not be regarded as indirect customers. Anyway, as already explained, trust beneficiaries are exempted from the definition of customer.

Note that there is no two-year window under Limb 4 as there is with Limbs 2 and 3. Therefore, if a person is not at the time an authorised person, listed money market institution or overseas investment business (although it previously was within the last two years), it cannot be treated as an ordinary business investor. SFA firms, however, can still rely on the reasonable belief test. This may be helpful, especially where a firm is dealing with an overseas person which the firm reasonably believes is doing investment business. Further, it should be possible to treat a person who used to do investment business as an expert, since he will have sufficient experience and understanding to waive the private customer protections.

An SFA firm will not satisfy the reasonable belief test that the person with whom it is dealing is an authorised person just because that person is a member of a professional body which is also an RPB. Note that not all RPB members will have been granted a certificate to do investment business. Therefore, an SFA firm should not rely, in categorising a firm of solicitors or accountants as an ordinary business investor, merely on the fact that the firm is regulated in respect of its professional legal or accounting activities by the relevant RPB. The SFA firm should make further enquiry to establish whether or not the firm of solicitors or accountants has obtained the necessary certificate to conduct investment business. Provided it has, the SFA firm does not have to make further enquiry as to any limitations which may have been imposed by the RPB, when granting the certificate, in respect of the type of investment business which its member is authorised to undertake.

Limb 5: Trade customers

5–025   This limb picks up a particular type of customer who is categorised as a non-private customer because of his experience and understanding. The reason for including it as a fifth limb under the definition of ordinary business investor is that it is similar to the fourth and last category of business investor under AFBD's rules. The AFBD categorisation stated that a person was a business investor in relation to a transaction in an investment where that person was carrying on a main business which was not investment business and entered into the transaction as an integral part of that main business. The AFBD test was not dependent upon the investor's understanding and experience; merely that the transaction was entered into as an integral part of the investor's business, which itself could not be investment business. AFBD issued a practice note to the effect that, to be regarded as integral, the transaction had to be entered into for the purpose of, or in connection with, and be closely related to, the main business of the investor in question. Also, to come within this sub-category of business investor, the investor could not be an individual, but had to be a company, partnership or unincorporated association.

The type of firm which would have satisfied this test was a producer of a commodity, where that commodity was the subject of a futures contract traded on an investment exchange. In other words, the producer of the commodity could be regarded as a business investor, even if he did not satisfy the usual size requirements in Limb 2 above, where he was entering into a futures contract for hedging purposes. If he was entering into a futures contract which was traded on standard terms on an investment exchange, there would be a presumption that the contract was entered into for investment purposes. He might be entering into the contract, however, because of his knowledge of the commodity which he was producing and to hedge against adverse production conditions. In such circumstances, it was felt right that he should be treated as a business rather than private investor.

When the SFA rules were drafted, however, it was determined that this category of investor (commonly referred to as a trade customer) should only be treated as an ordinary business investor where he had sufficient experience and understanding not to require the usual private customer protections. Hence, such persons are treated as non-private customers under the expert categorisation rule (Rule 5-5). The additional inclusion of them under Limb 5 to the definition of ordinary business investor is really as a cross-reference for ex-AFBD members who are wondering where this particular provision is now to be found. Remember, experts and ordinary business investors are the two sub-categories to the definition of non-private customer.

It should be noted that this inclusion of trade customers under ordinary business investor does not apply in respect of the Common Unsolicited Calls Regulations. In respect of these regulations, an SFA firm should not treat a person who is categorised as an ordinary business investor only under Limb 5 as a non-private investor. This is an important qualification because the restrictions on making un-solicited calls do not apply to non-private investors or customers. (However, see the comment at the end of paragraph 5-040 below.)

Experts

Both TSA's and AFBD's rules allowed for certain persons who would, prima facie, fall within the category of private customer to be treated as non-private customers. Under TSA's rules they were known as experts and AFBD's rules as experienced investors. The new rules contain a similar provision (Rule 5-5). **5-026**

An SFA firm may treat a customer who would otherwise be a private customer as a non-private customer if three conditions are satisfied:

Condition 1

This states that the firm must be able to show that it believes on reasonable grounds that the customer has sufficient experience and understanding to waive the protections provided for private customers. The onus of proof is on the firm to show that it had the reasonable belief. It is an objective test in the sense that the firm must have sufficient grounds on which to base its judgment.

The rule talks about having sufficient experience and understanding to waive the protections provided for private customers. The old TSA and AFBD rules related the experience and understanding to the nature and subject-matter of the transaction entered into with the customer. In fact, TSA's test was based on whether the customer was capable of forming an adequate assessment of the merits and suitability for him of any recommendation made by the firm, as well as understanding the risks involved. It was possible under the wording of the TSA and AFBD definitions to be regarded as an expert in respect of some transactions, but not others.

The Core Rule wording, which SFA has followed, is not linked to an understanding of the risks of particular transactions and an ability by the customer to assess himself the suitability of any recommendation made to him. Instead, it relates to the customer's experience and understanding being sufficient for him to waive the usual protections provided for private customers. It is suggested that, in practice, the two tests are the same. The rules on customers' understanding (Rule 5–30) and suitability (Rule 5–31) are both private customer protections (except that the suitability test has been extended by SFA to apply to discretionary non-private customers).

5–027 The uncertainty comes from whether the test is applied and operates on a once-and-for-all basis in respect of any type of investment business which an SFA firm may do with a customer, or whether a firm can classify a customer as an expert in respect of some business, but not all, as under the old TSA and AFBD rules.

The advantage to a customer of being treated as a non-private customer is that he may be able to negotiate lower dealing and other service charges if the firm owes him less obligations: especially, if it is not concerned with warning him about risks and determining whether its recommendations are suitable in respect of his individual investment objectives and financial circumstances. To make sure that the necessary risk warnings are given and to assess suitability, a firm obviously has to take more time and care in handling a customer. More explanations will be needed and, to assess suitability properly, the firm will regularly have to up-date its information on the customer.

The advantage to the firm is that it can provide a more simplified, streamlined service for its customers if it can treat them all as non-private, whether they are large corporations or individual investors.

It would seem unduly harsh to suggest that a customer who has sufficient experience and understanding in shares and debentures, but not the same knowledge of futures and options, could not be treated as an expert in respect of the former types of investments, merely because there will be occasions when he deals through the firm in futures and options. The other result of an all or nothing test is that the investor, who was categorised as an expert because of his understanding of shares and debentures, could not deal as a private customer in other investments through the same firm. In other words, he would have to deal with one firm as an expert in shares and debentures and with another firm as a private customer in futures and options.

It is suggested that Condition 1 should be read as requiring the assessment to be made in respect of each of the various types of investment business and investment transactions undertaken with the investor. Therefore, it would be possible for a firm, as under the old TSA and AFBD rules, to categorise an investor as an expert in respect of some parts of its business with him, but as a private customer in respect of others. This is the approach suggested by SFA in paragraph 1 of its guidance to this rule which states that the assessment about the customer's experience and understanding must be made in the context of the kind of investments and investment services in which the firm will conduct business with or for the customer.

In determining whether the person has the necessary expertise, the same factors as were discussed in relation to Limbs 2 and 3 under the SFA rule extension to the definition of market counterparty (Rule 5–4) apply (paragraphs 5–012 and 5–013 above). It may not be appropriate to treat a customer who has long-standing experience in the shares of United Kingdom registered companies quoted on the London Stock Exchange as an expert in Japanese equities. Again, just because someone is regarded as an expert in shares and debentures it does not mean that he should, without more ado, be treated as an expert in warrants and options relating to securities in the same companies in which he holds or has held stock. Although a person may be an expert in financial futures and options, he should not, without more, be regarded as an expert in commodity futures and options. Although the nature of the futures and options contracts in the commodities market will be familiar to the investor, he will not necessarily appreciate the risks and suitability of such investments because they are based on commodities, which are very different in nature from those instruments upon which financial futures and options are based.

5–028

Although the old TSA and AFBD rules no longer apply, the details set out in those rules may help with the categorisation of experts. Under TSA rules, if a person was an expert in investments of kind A, then he could also be regarded as an expert in those of kind B, provided his experience in investments of kind A, when supplemented by an explanation about investments of kind B, could lead the firm reasonably to believe that he would be able to understand the risks involved in the kind B investments and be able to make his own assessment of the suitability of the kind B investment recommendations made to him. The TSA rules stated that, if you were an expert in one kind of derivatives, then you could be regarded as an expert in any investment, other than derivatives of a different kind; whilst AFBD rules stated that, if you were an expert in derivatives traded on an exchange, you could be presumed to be an expert in respect of any contracts traded off exchange similar to the ones in which you were an expert when traded on exchange.

5–029   SFA has issued guidance as to the matters which should be taken into account by a firm in determining whether a customer has the necessary experience and understanding to waive the private customer protections. Obviously, the main point, as already discussed, is whether the customer understands the nature and risks of the relevant markets, investments and investment services. In assessing whether he does, a firm can pay attention to the frequency and capacity of previous dealings. Frequency of dealing, however, does not by itself suggest understanding. Therefore, another criterion is the size and nature of the previous transactions; but this is only one guide. Large sized transactions suggest that the customer has a better knowledge of the relevant market and a good understanding of the risks, but this cannot be presumed always. Finally, SFA suggests that the customer's financial standing should be examined. An investor who cannot easily absorb losses must tread more cautiously and, therefore, is less likely to be capable of waiving the private customer protections. On the other hand, just because an investor has large financial resources should not be seen as a sign that he automatically falls to be treated as an expert investor. All of the relevant factors have to be weighed up together. Remember that the onus is on the firm to show that it had reasonable grounds for making the categorisation; and the Record Keeping Schedule (Appendix 18) requires a firm to keep information supporting its categorisation of customers.

Condition 2

5–030   As well as making the assessment about the customer's experience and understanding, the firm must give the customer a clear written warning of the protections under the regulatory system which he will lose. Note that this warning has to be given in writing. SFA has issued guidance stating that the warning should point out the main protections afforded by the Conduct of Business Rules applicable exclusively to private customers which will not apply. The statement does not have to list all of those 16 Core Rules and supporting SFA third tier provisions which apply exclusively to private customers: this would not really mean anything to the recipient. Instead, the statement should be a simple description, explaining in plain language the main protections which will be lost, such as: the provision of risk warnings; ensuring that any recommendations are suitable; prior disclosure of all relevant charges; entering into customer agreements; and the polarisation and other protections provided in respect of the recommending and selling of packaged products. The warning should also explain that the customer will lose his right to sue for damages for breach of any private customer protections which have been removed as a result of his classification as a non-private customer. It should also point out that he will not have access to SFA's Consumer Arbitration Scheme, the scheme under which a private customer can compel a firm to submit to arbitration where the customer's claim does not exceed £25,000. No costs can be awarded against the customer in such an arbitration.

The warning does not have to make any reference to the Investors Compensation Scheme because an expert is still an eligible investor within the scheme despite being classified under the rules as a non-private customer. The definition of eligible investor includes any investor who is not a business or professional investor. Business and professional investors for this purpose are basically market counter-parties or persons falling within Limbs 1 to 4 inclusive of the definition of ordinary business investor under the new rules.

SFA has produced a suggested model warning notice (see Appendix 5 below) which can be sent to persons whom a firm wishes to treat as experts. The SFA model amounts to formal guidance, so that a firm which issues a written warning in the terms of the SFA model will be presumed to have complied with Condition 2.

The SFA model warning contains two paragraphs concerning client **5–031** money. Under the Client Money Regulations, a firm does not have to provide client money protection to a person who is being treated as a non-private customer under the expert categorisation providing the firm has given a clear written warning to that person that his money will not be protected under the Regulations and that, as a consequence, his money will not be segregated from the money of the firm.

Where a firm wishes to treat a person as an expert, namely a non-private customer, it may, in practice, be prepared to honour some of the private customer protections when dealing with this person: for example, the firm may be willing always to give prior disclosure of its charges and to satisfy the suitability obligation in respect of any recommendations which it makes. However, even though the firm is willing to provide some of these private customer protections, it must still, in the warning which it sends, explain that the customer will not be owed these obligations under the rules if he agrees to be treated as a non-private customer. Once a person is classified as an expert investor, the firm is only obliged under the rulebook to comply with those rules which relate to non-private customers. Therefore, even if the firm had told the customer that it would provide him with prior disclosure of charges and satisfy the suitability obligation, the firm could not be disciplined by SFA or sued under section 62 by the investor in respect of a breach of either of these two provisions because there would be no rule breaches in the circumstances. The only remedy which the investor would have would be for breach of contract on the basis that, despite the obligations not being owed to him under the rules, the firm had agreed as part of its contractual relationship with the investor to give prior disclosure of charges and to ensure that any recommendations made to him were suitable in accordance with his investment objectives and financial circumstances.

Condition 3

5–032   Finally, the customer must have given his written consent to be treated as a non-private customer after having had a proper opportunity to consider the written warning required under Condition 2. No explanation is given as to what amounts to a proper opportunity to consider. However, a firm cannot exert any pressure upon a customer to sign the warning. The customer should be given time to read it through carefully, consider its implications, and, if he so requires, raise further questions and seek additional advice either from the firm or from another adviser, such as his solicitor or accountant. The rule does not prevent the warning notice being signed in the firm's offices, but, where the warning is given to the customer and signed by him at the same meeting, it will then be much harder for the firm to show that the customer has had a proper opportunity to consider its implications. The concept of a customer being given a proper opportunity to consider the document before signing is repeated in the rule requiring two-way customer agreements (Rule 5–23(2)).

The Client Money Regulations similarly require an expert to sign after having had a proper opportunity to consider the warning about the loss of client money protection. As explained earlier, this warning has been included in the SFA model notice which requires two separate signatures. The first is a signature giving the customer's consent to be treated as a non-private customer and relates to the loss of protection under the Conduct of Business Rules. The second is his signature signifying his agreement to the removal of the client money protection. In other words, the client money warning can be included in the same document, but the customer is expected to signify his consent to the removal of this protection by a second signature.

5–033   *Exception 1:* Written consent to the warning is not required where the customer is ordinarily resident outside the United Kingdom and the firm believes on reasonable grounds that he does not wish to consent in writing; and it is suggested that he does not even have to be sent the written warning. This exception is continued by and large throughout the Conduct of Business Rules where there is a documentary requirement with a customer. Some overseas customers refuse, for various reasons (including religious grounds and local legal restrictions), to sign any sort of documentation with the United Kingdom firms with whom they deal. Some of the business generated by these customers is substantial and it is appreciated that it is much harder for firms to require them to enter into documentation if the customers cannot be visited easily.

This is not, however, a general exception in relation to all overseas customers. The firm has to form a belief on reasonable grounds. When challenged, it will be for the firm to show that it had grounds for forming its belief. The Record Keeping Schedule (Appendix 18) specifically requires evidence to be maintained supporting a firm's belief that an overseas customer does not require or will not sign any written communications which have to be sent or signed under the Conduct of Business Rules.

It should be noted that this exception only relates to the Conduct of Business Rules. A firm must provide client money protection to an overseas customer whom it is treating as an expert investor unless that customer has signed a document to the effect that he does not require such protection (Regulation 2.02(2), Client Money Regulations 1991). Similarly, there is no exception in respect of overseas customers under the Safekeeping Rules.

Exception 2: There is another exception. Conditions 2 and 3 do not **5–034** apply in the case of employees of SFA firms who are effecting transactions for their own personal account through their firm, provided that their firm has informed them (orally or in writing) that they will not be treated as private customers. A number of firms, as part of their staff dealing rules, require all employees to deal through the firm. In this case, the firm can treat the employees as non-private customers, without sending the written warning required by Condition 2 and obtaining the employee's written consent in accordance with Condition 3; provided the employees can be properly classified as experts under Condition 1, because they have the necessary experience and understanding to waive the protections for private customers. In other words, a firm is unlikely to be able to treat all employees as experts, because some of them will not have the necessary experience and understanding. Further, note that this exception only applies where the employee is dealing through his own firm: it does not extend to employees dealing through other group companies.

Although all employees could not be classified as experts, a firm could decide to treat all employees as execution-only customers. In this case, as long as no advice is given, the firm will not be responsible for complying with the suitability rule (5–31) and understanding of risk requirement (5–30) (except the Derivatives and Warrants Risk Warning Notices which extend to execution-only business; and, note, a two-way customer agreement is required for contingent liability transactions with private customers).

Exception 3: The need to obtain the customer's written consent does **5–035** not apply in the case of trade customers. It should be noted that, like experts, trade customers is not defined. "Expert" is a sub-heading to the main part of Rule 5–5, which repeats the enabling provisions of Core Rule 39 which is concerned with the classification of customers who would otherwise be private as non-private. "Trade customer" appears as the heading to the provision which was largely intended to reflect the fourth category with AFBD's definition of business investor, already described in connection with Limb 5 to the definition of ordinary business investor (paragraph 5–025 above).

Those persons who previously could be treated as business investors under the final category of AFBD's definition of business investor, because they were entering into an investment transaction as an integral part of their main business which was not investment business, can now be classified as non-private customers if Conditions 1 and 2 of the new expert classification test are satisfied. Note that the old AFBD test was merely concerned that the customer was entering into the transaction as an integral part of his main business, which was non-investment business. The new expert investor test, however, requires that, in addition, the customer must have sufficient experience and understanding to waive the protections provided for private customers (Condition 1). Also, the firm must have sent the customer the written warning about the loss of private customer protections (Condition 2).

Unlike Exceptions 1 and 2, it is only Condition 3, the requirement for the customer to sign the warning showing that he consents to be treated as a non-private customer, which is waived in respect of trade customers. However, because the trade customer does not have to sign the written warning, the rule requires that the warning itself must contain a statement informing the customer that he has the right to request to be treated as a private customer. Once the firm has sent the warning, with this statement, to the customer, it can treat him as a non-private customer until the customer informs the firm that he wishes to be treated as a private customer either generally or in respect of the relevant transaction. Note that the request from the customer can be oral or in writing, unlike the request to be treated as a customer by the recipient of a market counterparty notice (which latter request is only operative when it is in writing).

It is important to appreciate that a trade customer is just another variant of the expert investor, the only difference being that a trade customer does not have to give his written consent to be treated as a non-private customer. Note that individuals cannot be trade customers: in other words, this exception to Condition 3 for trade customers only applies to bodies corporate, partnerships and unincorporated associations. An individual who is entering into an investment transaction as an integral part of any non-investment business which he carries on can only be treated as an expert investor if he has signed the written warning.

5–036   *Exception 4:* There is a transitional provision to the effect that a firm does not have to send the written warning (Condition 2) and obtain the customer's written consent (Condition 3) in respect of any customer whom the firm was treating on April 1, 1992, as either an expert investor under TSA's rules, an experienced investor under AFBD's rules, or a business investor (trade customer) under the fourth category of that definition in AFBD's rules. This transitional provision only waives the requirement to send the written warning and obtain the customer's written consent. The firm must still carry out the assessment required by Condition 1 about the customer's experience and understanding. Although it is likely that a firm will be able to satisfy this test in most of these cases, a firm should be aware that the new rule places the onus on the firm to show that it believes on reasonable grounds that the investor has this experience and understanding.

Implications of section 62 with respect to experts

It has already been pointed out that, if, after categorising a person as an expert investor, a firm agrees to provide to him rule protections which are only applicable to private customers, a firm will be committing, not a rule breach, but only a breach of its contractual agreement with the customer if it fails to provide any of these private customer obligations. It is also important to consider the position of experts in respect to the restriction of the right of action under section 62 to private investors. The definition of private investor in relation to section 62 does not automatically exclude all persons who are categorised as experts under the rules.

The restriction for section 62, which came into force on April 1, 1991 (S.I. 1991 No. 489), defines private investor as:

> "An investor whose cause of action arises as a result of anything he has done or suffered—
>
> (a) in the case of an individual, otherwise than in the course of carrying on investment business; and
>
> (b) in the case of any other person, otherwise than in the course of carrying on business of any kind. ... "

This definition is wide enough to include persons who could be treated as expert investors because either they are individuals who are not acting in the course of investment business or they are other persons who are not acting in the course of carrying on any other business. If they are classified, however, as non-private customers under SFA's rules, they will only be able to bring a civil action for damages in respect of a breach of any of those rules applying to them as non-private customers. They would not be able to bring an action for breach of any of those rules which apply only to private customers, unless the firm had not properly classified them as non-private customers in accordance with Rule 5–5. Of course, if the firm had incorrectly classified someone as an expert, then that person would be

5–037

able to bring an action under section 62 for any loss arising from that incorrect classification, including the firm's failure to provide all of the private customer protections owed under the rules, such as suitability (Rule 5–31) and the risk warning requirements (Rule 5–30).

4. Private Customers

Individuals

5–038   Any individual will be a private customer unless:

    (i)   he is acting in the course of carrying on investment business; or

    (ii)   he qualifies to be treated as an expert investor under Rule 5–5.

Of course, an individual who is running his own investment business would need to become an authorised person under the SFA and, as such, would fall to be treated as an ordinary business investor under Limb 4 of that definition.

As already explained, individuals, other than those acting in the course of carrying on investment business, will also be private investors for the purposes of bringing an action under section 62. In this case, experts are not excluded from the definition, although, as already discussed, experts would only be able to sue for a breach of any of those rules which provide obligations in respect of non-private customers.

The Common Unsolicited Calls Regulations distinguish between private and non-private investors. For this purpose, private investor only includes individuals, other than those carrying on investment business; but it, therefore, includes individuals who are classified as experts (non-private customers). Where an unsolicited call is made by a firm which is not an unauthorised overseas investment business, then no restrictions apply if it is made on a non-private investor. The position with overseas persons is slightly different, as described in paragraph 5–040 below.

Non-individuals

5–039   The definition of private customer also includes small business investors. A small business investor is any company, partnership, unincorporated association or trustees acting for a trust which does not satisfy the size requirements in Limbs 2 and 3 of the definition of ordinary business investor (paragraphs 5–021 and 5–022 above). SFA has also provided an extension to the definition to make it clear that it does not include a business which, although not satisfying these size requirements, is acting in the course of carrying on investment business. In this case, the business should fall within Limb 4 of the ordinary business investor definition: it will be an authorised person, a listed money market institution or an overseas person, as defined.

Not all small business investors will be private investors in respect of the right of action under section 62. For the purposes of section 62, non-individuals are only treated as private investors where they are acting otherwise than in the course of carrying on business of any kind. Note that this restriction applies to carrying on any business, rather than just business which is investment business, whereas individuals are only excluded where they are carrying on investment business.

When is something done otherwise than in the course of carrying on business of any kind? The best way of trying to explain this is to look at someone who runs a small shop. If he runs the business in his own name, as an individual, he will be a private investor because he will not be acting in the course of carrying on investment business. On the other hand, he may be running the shop in partnership with someone else or under the guise of a limited company. In either case, he will only be a private investor for the purposes of section 62 if he is acting otherwise than in the course of carrying on business of any kind. This means that, where he enters into any investment transaction or receives any investment service in connection with his business of running the shop, he will not be protected as a private investor, albeit that he will still be a private customer under the Conduct of Business Rules (because he does not fall to be classified as an ordinary business investor or as an expert). He would be acting in the course of carrying on his business if, for example, he was investing profits generated by his business with a view to turning them into increased capital available for reinvestment in the business later on. He could still be regarded as acting in the course of his business if he was investing the profits to provide him with a pension when he retires, unless the investment for pension purposes can be regarded as a purely private matter, not done as part of his business, even though the contributions are funded from his share of the income which he has been able to take out of the business.

Ideally, the definition of private investor for the purposes of restricting section 62 should have been used as the same definition of private customer for the Conduct of Business Rules, private investor for the Common Unsolicited Call Regulations, and eligible investor under the Investor Compensation Scheme. SIB, however, thought the definition devised for restricting section 62 was too narrow for the purpose of defining private customer in relation to the Conduct of Business Rules and considered that small businesses (namely those not satisfying the size requirements of Limbs 2 and 3 of the ordinary business investor definition) should be protected in the same way as individuals, unless they could properly be classified as expert investors or were carrying on business which amounted to investment business. Although there was this concern to extend the scope of the definition for defining private customers for the Conduct of Business Rules, the definition has been restricted for the purposes of the unsolicited calls permissions so that it only catches individuals who are not carrying on investment business; therefore, not including other persons when not acting in the course of any business. The concept of eligible investor under the Investors Compensation Scheme is currently wider than the definition of private customer under the Conduct of Business Rules. "Eligible investor" includes experts, but not market counterparties and ordinary business investors (except that trade customers, Limb 5 of ordinary business investor in SFA rulebook, are eligible investors).

5–040   In fact, there is another complication with the Common Unsolicited Calls Regulations. The regulations make a distinction between calls made by non-overseas persons and overseas persons. An overseas person is defined as a person who carries on investment business, but who does not do so from a permanent place of business maintained in the United Kingdom. Where the call is made by a United Kingdom person, the restrictions are completely lifted to the extent that the call involves a non-private investor (namely, a non-individual or an individual acting in the course of carrying on investment business). However, where the call is made by an overseas person, the permission to cold call applies where the call is made to a non-private customer, rather than a non-private investor.

This is a significant difference. An individual is still treated as a private investor even if the United Kingdom person has classified him as an expert and, therefore, a non-private customer. Whereas the definition of private customer excludes experts. Therefore, an overseas person can cold call an expert, even if that expert is an individual who is not carrying on investment business, provided he is a customer. Whilst a United Kingdom person cannot generally cold call an individual whom it could classify as an expert, whether or not the latter is a customer. This distinction, however, is probably not significant because, in the majority of cases, before a person can be treated as an expert customer, a firm (whether a United Kingdom person or an overseas person) will have had to have obtained his consent to the written warning about the loss of protections and such a warning will often be issued together with or as part of a customer agreement which will include a term giving the firm permission to make unsolicited calls.[2]

It is worth noting that governments, local and public authorities are treated in respect of the Conduct of Business Rules, the Unsolicited Calls Regulations and the restriction to section 62 as being non-private customers and non-private investors; and as non-eligible investors in respect of the Investors Compensation Scheme. Also, the Client Money Regulations and the Safekeeping Rules use the Conduct of Business Rule definitions of private customer and non-private customer.

As pointed out at the end of paragraph 5–025 above, an exception to the Common Unsolicited Calls Regulations has been inserted in Limb 5 of the definition of ordinary business investor. This is irrelevant, however, because experts (including trade customers) are included within the definition of non-private customer for the purposes of these regulations; and trade customers, not being individuals, cannot qualify as private investors.

5. Indirect Customers

The definition of customer includes indirect customers. In other words, **5–041** wherever there is an obligation owed to customers within the rules, it is owed to a firm's indirect customers in the same way as it applies to a firm's direct customers, unless the particular rule itself contains any qualification relating to indirect customers.

An indirect customer means, where a customer is known to be acting as agent, an identified principal who would be a customer if he were dealt with direct. This Core Rule definition means that, in respect of one type of business, a firm will have two customers: namely the agent as its direct customer, and the identified principal as its indirect customer.

Agent as customer

The definition does not operate in all cases where a firm is dealing with an agent. The agent himself must be a customer and he must be acting on behalf of an identified principal who would be a customer if the firm were dealing with him directly. Therefore, the firm is not concerned with identified principals being indirect customers where it is dealing with an agent whom it is treating as a market counterparty, either under the Core Rule definition or under SFA's third tier extension (Rule 5–4).

Identified principal

Even if the agent is not a market counterparty, but a customer, the concept of indirect customer does not operate unless the agent identifies his principal before receiving the investment service. Where the principal is identified beforehand, he must be in the position of someone who would be a customer if he were dealt with direct by the firm: this, therefore, excludes trust beneficiaries, persons coming within the corporate finance exemption to the definition of customer, and persons whom the firm could treat as market counterparties. In respect of market counterparties, it certainly excludes a principal who would fall within the Core Rule definition. In respect of SFA's third tier extension, it would be safe to assume that it only excludes a principal whom the firm could treat as a market counterparty without the need to send the market counterparty notice (namely, any person whom the firm was already treating as a market professional at April 1, 1992, under TSA's rules, or another SFA firm which is a member of the same investment exchange and the dealings are to be limited to investments of the kind traded on the exchange or related derivatives).

Identification

5–042   Of course, there is uncertainty as to what is meant by "identified." This problem has already been discussed in paragraph 5–007 above on market counterparty. There, it was suggested that any sort of identification of the principal beforehand, including the mere giving of his name, would amount to identification. The extent, however, of the identification must go some way to establishing what obligations the firm owes to the principal. For example, if the agent has only disclosed the principal's name, it may be that it is an execution-only transaction. Therefore, the firm is not required to satisfy the suitability obligation in respect of the principal and only has to follow the ordinary dealing obligations, which would be owed anyway to the agent if he is a customer (even if only a non-private customer) and which may often be followed by a firm in practice, whether it is dealing with a customer or a market counterparty.

If the firm is expected to give advice, then it would be right to look at the circumstances in which the advice is requested. Even though the principal has been identified by the agent, is the understanding between the agent and the firm that the advice is for the agent rather than for the agent's principal? Although a firm would owe indirect customer obligations to the principal in respect of the advice if it knew, or ought reasonably to have known, that the agent would rely on the firm's advice to him in framing his (the agent's) advice to his principal.

All this confusion about "identification" means that a firm must be careful when dealing with an agent for an identified principal. If the firm has any doubt as to whether or not it owes obligations to the principal as an indirect customer, the firm must ensure that it receives the same detailed information from the agent concerning his principal as the firm would require if the principal had been a direct customer of the firm.

As already explained, prima facie any rule obligation which is owed to customers applies to a firm's indirect customers. Obviously, if the indirect customer is only a non-private customer, then he is not entitled to private customer protections. In such a case, however, a firm would need to obtain sufficient information from the agent about the principal for the firm to be satisfied that the principal falls within the ordinary business investor definition; or that the necessary requirements have been satisfied under Rule 5–5 enabling the principal to be treated as an expert customer (which means that the warning about the loss of private customer protections has to be signed by the indirect customer himself).

Modifications

There are three modifications to the Conduct of Business Rules in respect of indirect customers. The first relates to two-way customer agreements. Such an agreement is required where a firm is providing investment services to a private customer involving contingent liability transactions or providing discretionary management in respect of any customer; but there is a specific exception for indirect customers in both of these cases. The rule does not even say that the firm has to enter into a two-way customer agreement with the agent acting on behalf of the indirect customer. Of course, as the agent is himself a customer, a firm will require a two-way customer agreement with him in respect of any discretionary management which it is providing for the indirect customer; as it will in respect of contingent liability transactions if the agent falls within the definition of a private customer (even if the indirect customer is a non-private customer).

5–043

The second modification relates to the written risk warning requirements. Written risk warnings are required to be signed by a private customer in respect of recommendations, transactions and discretionary management concerning derivatives (namely, options, futures and contracts for difference) and also in respect of warrants (except in respect of realisations of warrants already held by the customer or in respect of the purchase or sale of warrants attached to another security). There is, however, a qualification in respect of an indirect customer: a firm merely has to have sent the risk warning to the agent and received confirmation from him that the indirect customer has signed it.

The third modification relates to a firm's disclosure of its charges. Before providing any investment services to a private customer, a firm must have disclosed the basis or amount of its charges, unless that customer is an indirect customer. This means that, where the agent is himself a private customer, charges must have been disclosed beforehand, but not where the agent is a non-private customer (even though he is acting for an indirect customer who falls to be treated as a private customer).

Agent's authority

Of course, it can be argued that these modifications are not necessary. Any customer can appoint an agent to act on his behalf and give the agent authority to sign documents for him, enter into transactions for him and receive documents and other communications on his behalf. Therefore, a validly appointed agent would be able to sign agreements on behalf of his principal. In fact, the modification mentioned above in respect of written risk warnings effectively operates as a restriction on the authority granted to an agent in the sense that the risk warning has to be signed by the principal himself, even if he has given the agent authority to sign the document on his behalf. (Contrast this with Rule 5–5 on classifying customers as experts where there is no such special provision.)

This is not the place to discuss the intricacies of Agency Law, but it should be noted that an agent can legally bind his principal when dealing on his behalf with another person, even though in respect of the particular business the agent did not have actual authority from his principal. The principal will be bound if the terms of any document concerning the appointment of the agent gave him the power to enter into that business, even though the principal had, outside the terms of that document, specifically prevented the particular transaction. The same result applies where the agent does not have specific authority under the terms of his appointment, but where there is a recognised practice that a person acting as an agent in the circumstances in which the particular agent is acting has the necessary authority.

Overseas' customers

5–044   As a person can appoint anybody to act as an agent on his behalf, it could be argued that there is no need for the overseas customer exception in relation to those rules which require documents to be sent to and signed by customers. An overseas customer who could not sign himself could always appoint an agent in the United Kingdom to act on his behalf in respect of any investment business conducted with SFA firms.

Independent agents

Certainly, the Core Rules contemplate customers appointing agents in the sense that there is a provision to the effect that any communication required to be sent to a customer may be sent to the order of a customer, so long as the recipient is independent of the firm (Rule 5–2(3)). In other words, the agent should not be an employee (which under the rules is defined to include directors, partners, independent contractors and appointed representatives) of the firm or another group company, or any associate of such an employee unless the associate can be regarded as independent of the firm, which is unlikely. On this point, it is worth noting that under the rule provisions concerning contract notes and valuations, a firm may retain contract notes and valuations for an overseas customer with his prior consent (which can be oral), so long as the contract notes and valuations are retained by the firm's Compliance Officer or an employee designated by him who is not personally involved in handling the customer's portfolio or account.

Two customers

The definition of indirect customer is odd in the sense that it talks about there being two customers, namely the agent as a direct customer and his identified principal as an indirect customer. In reality, where a person is dealing through an agent, there is only one customer relationship. The customer is the principal, albeit that all of the firm's dealings may only be with his agent. The investment service which the firm is providing to the agent is for the benefit of his principal. Therefore, the firm should be concerned about the characteristics of the principal rather than his agent. It is irrelevant whether the agent would fall to be treated as a private or non-private customer. What should concern the firm is whether the principal qualifies as a private or non-private customer. A number of SFA firms who deal with customers through the medium of agents appointed by these customers have entered into customer agreements which have been signed directly by the principals and which go on to empower the firm thereafter to deal with the principals only through their agents. There is nothing to stop a firm continuing with these arrangements. It is suggested that such an arrangement is irrelevant in the context of the indirect customer definition. In these situations, the principal will be a direct customer of the firm and his agent will not be a customer in his own right.

Intermediaries

Indirect customer is more relevant in the context of agents who used to fall within TSA's rules on intermediaries. It was appreciated that a number of agents felt that they would lose their special relationship with their principals if the latter entered into direct agreements with TSA firms. TSA's rules stated that an intermediary relationship was created with an agent where the agent requested the firm to deal for a particular client, or to give investment advice suitable in relation to the circumstances of a particular client, if: **5–045**

(i) it was clear from the circumstances that the agent was expecting the firm to be responsible to the agent's principal in a similar way as if the principal had been a direct customer of the firm; and

(ii) that expectation was consistent with the terms of any customer agreement between the firm and the agent (although it was not necessary to have a written agreement).

The rules said that it was immaterial whether the firm knew the identity of the agent's principal; and also stated that, although the agent was the firm's customer, the firm had to treat the agent's principal as if he had been the firm's direct private customer, except to the extent that there was an agreement to the contrary between the firm and the agent. They also provided a protection to the firm in the sense that it could rely on the information provided by the agent about the principal and could satisfy those rule requirements requiring disclosure to, or consent from, the customer by making the disclosure to, or obtaining the consent from, the agent.

TSA's rules on intermediaries, however, were limited to agents who were, basically, banks, building societies, lawyers, accountants and actuaries. The indirect customer concept is similar in the sense that a firm does not have to enter into a direct customer agreement with an agent's principal: but, unlike TSA's Intermediaries Rules, there is no restriction on the types of agents who can take advantage of this facility under the rules to pass on the duty of protecting the principal to the SFA firm. Although there is now a restriction in the sense that the principal has to be identified before the service is provided by the firm.

Reliance on agent

The new rules also do not contain the same extensive protection to firms in being able to rely upon the agent. The three provisions which are now relevant in this context are:

(i) Rule 5–2(1) (a Core Rule provision) which provides that a person is taken to act in conformity with any of the Conduct of Business Rules as to information to the extent that he can show that he reasonably relied on information provided in writing by a third party whom he believed on reasonable grounds to be independent and competent to provide the information;

(ii) Rule 5–2(2) (SFA's third tier) to the effect that a firm may rely on the accuracy and sufficiency of information concerning a customer which is supplied by his agent provided the firm has no reasonable ground on which to doubt the authority, honesty and reliability of either the agent or the information supplied; and

(iii) Rule 5–2(3) (another Core Rule provision already discussed) enabling a firm to send to the order of a customer any communication required to be sent to him under the Conduct of Business Rules, so long as the recipient is independent of the firm.

Professionals as agents

In devising its third tier rules, SFA wanted to limit the concept of **5–046** indirect customer to agents who were not authorised persons, listed money market institutions or overseas investment businesses. Certainly, in the case of authorised persons, SFA took the view that it should be the nearest authorised person to the customer (whether or not acting in an agency capacity) who should have prime responsibility for servicing that customer. If this person was an agent, he should not be able to avoid his obligations merely by identifying his principal before dealing on the latter's behalf with another authorised person. If the agent did not himself have the necessary ability, experience, procedures and systems to protect his principal under the rules, he should either pass on that customer to another firm which did have them, or contractually agree with this other firm that it should owe the necessary obligations either to the agent or direct to his principal, in which case the obligations would only be owed under contract, rather than under the rules. The agent himself would be a customer, but, because he was an authorised person, he would fall to be treated as a non-private customer (Limb 4 of the definition of ordinary business investor; see paragraphs 5–023 and 5–024 above). If an authorised person acting as agent failed to protect his principal properly, then it would be for the regulator responsible for authorising him to take appropriate enforcement action.

The members of other SROs and RPBs who deal as agents with SFA firms were happy to take advantage of the indirect customer concept to pass on to SFA firms the obligations owed under their own regulator's rules to their principals. The best solution which SFA could achieve was that the concept of indirect customer should not operate where there is an agreement in writing between the agent and the firm to this effect.

It should be noted that the definition of indirect customer makes it possible for one SFA firm to owe customer obligations to the principal of another SFA firm where the latter is acting as an agent. This would be the case where the SFA firm acting as agent is not a market counterparty. If he is a market counterparty, then the concept of indirect customer does not apply: to apply, the agent himself has to be a customer. Where a firm is acting as agent for an identified principal, then that firm cannot be a market counterparty under the Core Rule definition: so it could only be treated as a market counterparty under SFA's third tier extension (Rule 5–4). Before one SFA firm can treat another SFA firm as a market counterparty under this rule extension, normally it must have sent a market counterparty notice; and, under Rule 5–4(4), an SFA firm which has private customers should not allow itself to be treated as a market counterparty unless it believes that it will be able to protect its customers properly under the rules.

Double protection

5–047   Where the agent is an authorised person, the principal effectively receives double protection. The agent must protect him under the rules of its own SRO or RPB. In addition, the other firm with whom the agent deals must treat the agent's principal as its own customer. It was owing to this double protection that SFA considered it was appropriate, at least, to waive the concept of indirect customer where the agent was another authorised person.

Exclusion by agreement

As already stated, however, the only way of avoiding the indirect customer protections is to have an agreement in writing between the agent and the firm. The agreement in writing can be a one-way document sent by the firm to the agent, the terms of which become agreed if the agent then continues to deal on behalf of identified principals with the firm without objecting to those terms. This must be the case because there is a separate definition in the Core Rules of a two-way customer agreement, which is described as a document signed by the customer after having had a proper opportunity to consider its terms.

Half-way position

At SIB's request, SFA has introduced a "half-way house". A firm can agree with the agent that it will owe the agent's identified principals some, but not all, of the customer obligations. In this situation, the principals will only be the firm's indirect customers to the extent specified in the agreement. In all other respects, the principals will be customers just of the agent.

One customer

SFA has tried to remove the anomaly in the Core Rule definition of regarding both the agent and the indirect customer as customers at the same time. SFA's rules state that, to the extent that the identified principal is an indirect customer, then the principal, rather than his agent, is the customer of the firm. In all other respects, it is the agent which is the customer of the firm, not his principal.

Single agreement

As with the old TSA rules on intermediaries, SFA thinks that a firm should be able to enter into a single agreement with an agent which covers a number of indirect customers. SFA does not want to impose upon the agent a requirement to sign a separate customer document on behalf of each of his identified principals. This provision is useful, for example, in the case of the Public Trustee and other agents who act for a large number of principals. It means that where the rules require disclosure to, or consent from, a customer, the firm can have a single document sent to, or signed by, the agent which is expressed to cover all or some of his identified principals. SFA, however, requires that separate risk warnings, contract notes and portfolio valuation statements should be generated for each individual indirect customer. These do not have to be sent directly to the indirect customer, only to the agent. It is then up to the agent to pass them on.

Note that the qualification which SFA has written to the indirect customer definition, allowing a firm to avoid indirect customer obligations where there is an agreement in writing, applies, at the moment, in respect of any agent, not merely those which are authorised persons, listed money market institutions or overseas investment businesses. (Although it is possible that this qualification will be restricted to such agents, namely those coming within Limb 4 of the ordinary business investor definition.) Even if there is an agreement in writing with the agent that indirect customer obligations are not to be owed to the agent's identified principals, the firm will still owe customer obligations to the agent, and the extent of those obligations will depend upon whether the agent falls to be classified as a private or non-private customer.

Confirmation to RPB members

Although the agreement in writing between the firm and the agent is **5–048** only necessary where the firm wishes to avoid indirect customer obligations, many agents will want written confirmation from the SFA firms with whom they deal that the firms will provide indirect customer obligations to the agents' identified principals. Such confirmation will be required by solicitors and accountants who wish to rely upon the permitted third party exception in their RPB rules. This exemption enables the agent to avoid some customer obligations if he has written confirmation from the SFA firm that it will owe them instead direct to his principals.

FIMBRA

Also, certain members of FIMBRA are prevented from doing particular kinds of securities business with SFA firms unless there is a direct agreement between the FIMBRA firm's principal and the SFA firm. These are the Category 3 members. Such a member must not deal as a principal with his client. As regards deals in shares, debentures, government or public securities, warrants and certificates representing such securities, the Category 3 member must arrange the deal through a regulated dealer, and then only if the security is readily realisable (unless he has written authority from FIMBRA to deal in non-readily realisable investments). He must not himself be a party to the contract for the purchase or sale of the security. The contract must be direct between the regulated dealer and the FIMBRA member's client. A regulated dealer is a person who is authorised by SIB or an SRO to provide dealing and settlement services.

A Category 2 FIMBRA member is subject to similar restrictions, except that he may be a party to the contract with the regulated dealer for the purchase or sale of a security. In this case he must have a written agreement with the dealer (signed by both him and the dealer) specifying which of them is to accept responsibility for settlement if the client defaults. There are no such restrictions on a Category 1 member, who can carry on any investment business regulated by FIMBRA.

Settlement responsibility

A number of agents do not wish to take on settlement liability and expect their principals to be directly responsible for settlement to the firm with whom the agent is dealing on their behalf, even where the principal is not identified. In 1988, TSA issued a Board Notice to the effect that a firm did not have a customer relationship for the purposes of the Conduct of Business Rules with an agent's principal merely because it entered into a separate agreement with him concerning the settlement of any business undertaken with the agent on his behalf. Of course, now that the concept of indirect customer operates where the agent's principal is identified, a firm which wishes to find out who the principal is for settlement purposes will find itself owing full customer obligations to the principal unless there is the agreement in writing between the agent and the firm to the effect that indirect customer obligations are not to be owed, even if the agent is not accepting any settlement risk on behalf of his principal.

6. Execution Only Customers

5–049   There is no separate definition of an execution-only customer under the new rules. An execution-only customer will still be either a private or non-private customer. Because he is not requiring advice, he will not be owed those obligations which apply only where a firm is making a recommendation or exercising discretion, such as the warnings about risk (Rule 5–30) and suitability (Rule 5–31); but the usual dealing obligations (Rules 5–36 to 5–42 and 5–44 to 5–45) will apply.

7. Discretionary Customers

Similarly there is no separate category of discretionary customers. They will either be protected as private or non-private customers, rather than, as under TSA's rules, all receiving the same protection. Note, however, that SFA has extended the Core Rules on two-way customer agreements (Rule 5–23(2)) and suitability (Rule 5–31) to discretionary business for non-private customers.

5–050

[1] Money market investment is not defined, but it is intended to include any investment falling within paragraph 2(2), Schedule 5 to the FSA 1986, or any other investment which is principally related to such an investment including a collective fund invested in such investments. Debt investment is similarly not defined, but it would cover investments within paragraphs 2 and 3, Schedule 1, and investments within paragraphs 4, 5, 7, 8, 9 and 11, Schedule 1, which are principally related to paragraph 2 or 3 investments. It would also include units in a collective investment scheme which held a substantial majority of its assets in any of the investments referred to in the previous sentence.

[2] Another interesting point arises from the use of the term customer rather than investor for overseas persons' calls. On the face of it, the permission for overseas persons is more restrictive because the use of the term customer would suggest that there has to be an established customer relationship between the person called and the overseas person. However, it is suggested that, in practice, there is no difference between the use of the term "investor" and that of "customer" because the definition of customer includes a person with or for whom a firm intends to carry on investment business. Most unsolicited calls will be made with the intention that some investment business should be carried on with the person called. Therefore, the permission for overseas persons could be wider as non-private customer includes experts, unlike non-private investor; but it is unlikely that SIB's draftsmen intended this result. (See also Chapter 13 below.)

Chapter 6

Customer Agreements

Background

When the SIB and SRO rulebooks first came into force, there were **6–001** extensive provisions on customer agreements. This was because introducing a requirement which obliged a firm to set out in writing the nature of its relationship with the customer was seen as essential in terms of investor protection: a customer would know on exactly what basis a firm was providing investment services to him, including both the firm's duties to the customer and any obligations on the part of the customer to the firm.

The requirements, however, for customer documentation quickly resulted in one of the main criticisms of the new FSA 1986 regulatory system. The rules required new documentation to be completed with firms' existing customers as well as new customers. In some cases, customers had relationships with firms going back many years. Also, in drawing up a customer agreement, firms often included many matters which were not strictly required under the rules, but which the firm wished to include to protect itself. Hence, some of the agreements were very long and detailed, containing wide ranging clauses excluding liability on the part of firms and provisions which were not necessarily easily comprehensible to ordinary investors.

One of the ironies of customer agreements was that, in the case of firms dealing for private customers, the customers really had no option but to accept unamended all of the firm's terms of business as set out in the customer document. Such customers lacked the commercial bargaining power of institutions; and for firms to amend their terms to suit individual cases would be much more costly than providing their services on the same basis to all private customers.

The customers who were more likely to obtain variations of the firm's terms of business were the large non-private customers, due to the amount of business which they generated with the firm. Hence, in respect of terms of business letters between firms and their non-private customers, sometimes the actual terms on which a firm was dealing with its customer were never agreed. A firm would send out its standard terms of business letter, which would be returned with suggested amendments by the customer. The firm would then either send out another unaltered terms of business letter or make a few alterations, without accepting all the suggestions made by the customer. The customer would then review the second letter and probably return it stating that he still could not agree to the terms. Terms of business letters were going backwards and forwards without being agreed, but yet a firm would still be dealing with the customer. If there was any dispute, it would probably be difficult to determine which terms applied. It would depend upon the stamina of the respective negotiators employed by the firm and the customer. In other words, the one that had last replied before the transaction in dispute was executed would probably be the one whose terms were regarded as applying to the deal on the basis that the other party must have accepted those terms by continuing to deal.

The new rules have tried to deal with some of these problems whilst acknowledging the value to a customer of knowing exactly where he stands when dealing with an investment business firm.

Approach of the new rules

6–002   SIB still sees a value in requiring customer agreements, as long as they can be drafted in terms which are more friendly to the customer. On the other hand, SFA questions their value in some respects. Once there is a requirement for a written customer agreement, there is always a danger that it will become quite a comprehensive, legally drafted document. As one starts to put down in writing some aspects of the customer relationship, there is a temptation to include all aspects.

As explained earlier, private customers are not in practice able to negotiate any variations from a firm's standard terms. Also, it is questionable to what extent a customer reads and assimilates the agreement before signing it. If he is keen to do some form of investment business with a firm, a customer will complete any preliminary matters, such as signing a customer agreement, as quickly as possible without reading all the detail; in the same way that a person buying consumer goods on credit may sign the agreement without properly reading it, his main concern being to know what his monthly payments will be. Additionally, relationships with investment firms may continue over several years, so that, unless the customer is regularly sent a new agreement, he will forget over a period of time much of the detail contained in his agreement. Not many customers will keep their agreement close to hand at all times when dealing with their brokers. Therefore, the customer agreement is not necessarily the best medium to give risk warnings and explain all of the potential future liabilities of a customer.

SFA saw value in not requiring formal customer agreements in too many cases, but, instead, requiring specific disclosures to be made to, or consents obtained from, customers before certain types of business could be done with them. The advantage of this approach is that the customer is put on notice about the important factors relating to a new type of business at the point at which it specifically affects him, rather than reading the details months or years before in a standard document when the warnings or disclosures are not relevant to the type of business which he is then involved in with the firm. Also, by restricting the cases in which a formal customer agreement is required, the regulators could avoid criticisms that it is their own rules which have been responsible for long, legalistic documentation. The piecemeal approach to documentation means that firms can more easily tailor the agreement to the type of customer and kind of business being done with him, and that the terms of the agreement can be built up with the extra warnings and consents over a period of time as the relationship develops.

Two-way written agreements (Rule 5–23(2))

The Core Conduct of Business Rules only require two-way customer agreements for private customers; and then only where the investment services being provided involve: **6–003**

   (i)   contingent liability transactions; or

   (ii) discretionary management.

A two-way customer agreement is defined as an agreement in writing to which the customer has signified his assent in writing in circumstances where the firm is satisfied that the customer has had a proper opportunity to consider its terms. In other words, the customer has to sign and return the agreement to the firm after having a proper opportunity to consider it. As long as the customer is given this opportunity to consider the terms, it does not matter that he signs it on the firm's premises rather than receiving it by post and considering it at his leisure at home. Obviously, where a customer signs an agreement on his first visit to a firm, it may be more difficult for the firm to argue that he had a proper opportunity to consider its terms, especially if the agreement is long and complicated. On the other hand, there may be advantages in the customer signing the document on the firm's premises if an employee is available to answer any questions that customer may have arising from his reading of the agreement and to give an explanation of the most significant clauses. It would be better if this employee were someone who was not responsible for handling the customer's account; otherwise he might be under pressure to sign the person up as a new customer of the firm. Note that the agreement must be signed before the relevant service can be provided.

Contingent liability transaction

A contingent liability transaction is defined as a transaction in an option, future or contract for difference (collectively referred to as derivatives), but only if the customer may be liable to make further payments when the transaction falls to be completed or upon the earlier closing out of his position. Obviously, not all transactions in derivations are caught; but it is not entirely clear which are exempted. Therefore, a cautious approach suggests that two-way customer agreements should be used wherever a firm is providing investment services (including an execution-only dealing service) relating to any derivatives for private customers. Certainly, any futures contract must be a contingent liability one because, unless the position is closed out earlier, there is an obligation to complete the underlying transaction on the due date; and even if the investor intends that the contract should be closed out early, he could be subject to a further liability. The fact, however, that initial and variation margins are required on futures contracts does not itself make them contingent liability within this definition.

Is an options contract caught? In the case of the purchase of such a contract, the buyer's loss is limited to the premium he has paid for the contract. He is under no obligation to exercise the option and, obviously, will only do so if it is to his favour. It is, therefore, suggested that the purchase of such a contract is not a contingent liability transaction. The seller (writer), however, of such a contract is in a different position. If he is writing an uncovered call option or a put option, he will clearly be subject to a further liability if the option is exercised against him. The position is, however, slightly different in the case of writing a covered call option because any loss which the writer will suffer as a result of the exercise of the option will be a paper loss, namely the difference in the exercise price and the current market value of the stock: as the writer already holds the stock, he will not be subject to any further real cost because he will not have to buy the stock at a higher price than that at which he can sell it. It is suggested that the purchase of an option and the writing of a covered call option should not have to be regarded as contingent liability transactions; but firms may feel more comfortable in having a two-way customer agreement anyway when acting for private customers in these instruments.

Discretionary management

No definition is provided in respect of discretionary management, but it is clear that the requirement applies to cases where a firm has some sort of discretion over the management of a customer's assets. The requirement for a customer agreement here could cause problems in the cases of customers who are normally advisory, rather than discretionary, but who give the firm discretion during a temporary period because of a holiday or business trip. Prima facie a customer agreement would be required, unless the discretion given by the customer amounts, in effect, to a contingent order: in other words, the firm is only empowered to buy or sell the portfolio, or individual stocks within the portfolio, when the market generally or prices in the particular stocks move above or below predetermined points. In this case, the firm can be regarded as not exercising discretion, but acting on specific instructions from the customer. The situation would be different if the firm was, after selling any of the stock at the predetermined limits, free to reinvest the proceeds in such other stock as it considered most appropriate.

A two-way agreement is required wherever a firm exercises discretion. Therefore, an agreement is still necessary, even where the only investments managed for the customer are units in regulated collective investment schemes within a PEP (personal equity plan).

Unlike the old TSA rules, which treated all customers, whether private or non-private, and even market professionals, on the same basis in respect of discretionary management, SIB's Core Rules continue into the area of discretionary management the distinction between the level of protection offered by the rules to private and non-private customers. Hence, the Core Rule only requires a two-way customer agreement for private discretionary customers. SFA has, however, extended the requirement to all discretionary customers, so that SFA firms will have to enter into two-way written agreements with non-private customers where they are providing discretionary management. There is, however, one significant change from the old TSA rules. Under the new rules, a market counterparty, which equates in many ways to the TSA definition of market professional, is not regarded as a customer at all. Therefore, a two-way agreement will not be required in respect of any discretionary management provided to a person whom the firm is treating as a market counterparty under SFA's extension (Rule 5–4) to the Core Rule definition of market counterparty.

Overseas customers

There is one important exception to the two-way customer agreement requirements. This relates to overseas customers, but it does not extend to all overseas customers: only to those where the firm has a belief on reasonable grounds that they do not wish a two-way customer agreement to be used. A similar qualification applies throughout the Conduct of Business Rules (but not the Client Money Regulations and Safekeeping Rules) wherever there is a requirement to obtain a customer's written consent (except those rules concerned with credit, margin, underwriting and default: Rules 5–25 to 5–28). It was included because of the difficulties which some firms have in obtaining such customers' signatures. The business transacted with some of these customers is quite lucrative and it was decided, therefore, that an unnecessarily strict customer agreement provision should not be imposed which might have the result of such customers preferring to do business with investment firms in other countries. The reference to the customer not wishing a two-way agreement to be used suggests that a firm does not need to send the agreement for information if it believes that, besides not wishing to sign it, the customer does not even want to receive it.

The only danger in providing such an exception is that it is easy for an unscrupulous firm or employee to set up fictitious accounts to conceal trading done for the firm, the employee or other persons. The rules place the onus on the firm to show that it has a reasonable belief that the overseas customer does not wish to sign. In addition, the Record Keeping Schedule (Appendix 18) requires a firm to keep evidence to support its belief that the customer does not require or will not sign any written communication required to be sent or signed under the Conduct of Business Rules. Obviously, if the customer does not want to sign documents, it is unlikely that a firm will obtain a written notice signed by him informing the firm that he will not sign any other documentation. Therefore, the only evidence which a firm may be able to retain in its records to support its reasonable belief may be a memorandum confirming a telephone conversation with the customer or a notification from an agent appointed by him.

However, the relaxation for customer documentation in respect of overseas customers in the Conduct of Business Rules has been largely negated by the fact that a similar provision is not contained in the Client Money Regulations and the Safekeeping Rules.

Indirect customers

Two-way agreements are not required for indirect customers. However, the firm should still have a two-way agreement with the agent to cover his principal. A separate agreement is not required with the agent for each of his principals. Rule 5–6(5) permits a firm to have a single agreement with the agent which is expressed to cover a number of indirect customers. The agreement could either list the indirect customers in an appendix to it or contain a general provision to the effect that it includes such principals as the agent identifies from time to time as being covered by its terms. However, despite having a single customer agreement with the agent covering all his identified principals, the firm must generate separate Warrants and Derivatives Risk Warning Notices (Rule 5–31(2)), confirmation and similar notes (Rule 5–34), and valuation statements (Rule 5–35) for each indirect customer, even though they are sent to the agent. (See also paragraph 5–043 above.)

Other written agreements (Rule 5–23(1))

6–004   Although the Core Conduct of Business Rules only require two-way customer agreements for private customers in the two cases cited above, they contain a requirement that, wherever a firm provides investment services to a private customer on written terms, the agreement must set out in adequate detail the basis on which those services are provided. Therefore, although two-way written agreements are only required in limited circumstances, wherever a firm has set down any contractual term in writing with a private customer, in practice it must provide a full agreement because of this provision which requires adequate written detail of the basis on which the firm is to provide its services. The agreement can, however, be tailored to the particular type of service to be provided for that customer, rather than having to be a standard agreement which includes details concerning the bases on which the firm provides services to any of its customers.

The fact that this provision mentions "written contractual terms" and "agreement", without using the term "two-way customer agreement", suggests that it applies wherever the firm sends a one-way notice to a customer which contains contractual provisions, even if the customer is not required to signify his consent to the terms by signing and returning a written copy. It follows the initiative on customer agreements made in 1989 when the rules were relaxed to allow one-way, rather than two-way, agreements to be used for private customers provided the service was an uncomplicated one and related to advice and dealing in readily realisable shares, gilts and bonds, plus shares in investment trusts and units in regulated collective investment schemes.

However, this provision runs contrary to the approach that SFA has tried to adopt by restricting the circumstances in which full customer agreements are required and relying much more upon disclosures and consents being provided as the services undertaken by a firm with a customer develop and increase. The Core Rule provision means that, as soon as a firm starts to provide any service in a way which requires a written disclosure, it must draw up a customer agreement even if it is only a one-way document.

Control of unfriendly documentation

Although SIB requires customer agreements for many private customers, it still wants to prevent the unfriendly, legalistic agreements of the past, which had wide exclusion clauses. Therefore, in preparing customer documents, firms must be aware of two other rules which have an important effect upon style and contents.

Fair and clear communications (Rule 5–15)

The first part of this rule applies to any communication, whether oral or in writing, to any person, whether a private or non-private customer or a market counterparty. The test is that a firm should only make communications which are designed to promote the provision of investment services if it can show that it believes on reasonable grounds

6–005

that the communication is fair and not misleading. As with other requirements, there is a reasonable belief test, but the obligation is clearly on the firm to prove, if challenged, that it had the belief and that it was reasonable to hold such a belief in the circumstances.

This is a basic obligation, applied widely. It duplicates some other provisions. For example, it is similar to the obligation in the advertising rule, which requires advertisements to be fair and not misleading.

In applying this provision, it is relevant to consider the nature of the audience to whom the communication is addressed. Therefore, although it applies when a dealer in one SFA firm is communicating with a dealer in another firm on a market counterparty basis, it will be acceptable in such a situation to use market jargon, reliance being placed upon the degree of expertise and knowledge which the other person has.

This rule has a second part which relates specifically to private investors. A firm must take reasonable steps to ensure that any agreement, written communication, notification or information which it gives or sends to a private customer to whom it provides investment services is presented fairly and clearly. The word agreement is not defined, but it is suggested that this provision only relates to written communications, with the word "agreement" signifying something in writing and the word "written" before "communication" also qualifying "notification or information."[1] Of course, this provision, although limited to something which is in writing, would not be restricted to communications on paper, but would include communications disseminated through a screen based information system. Perhaps, it is because the second part of the rule only relates to written documentation that the obligation on the firm is to take reasonable steps, rather than hold a reasonable belief.

Having established that the second part of the rule has a more limited application, it is difficult to know what the difference between the two tests is in relation to the clarity of the communication. The first test is that the communication is fair and not misleading, whilst the second is that the information is presented fairly and clearly. The difference is between "not misleading" and "clearly". "Clearly", perhaps, indicates that the communication must be presented in a way which is readily understandable to the investor, whereas "misleading" means that the communication should not contain anything which is false or which could give an incorrect impression. Obviously, the distinction is quite a fine one and, in practice, there may be no real difference.

Certainly, the second test is not dependent upon the ability of individual recipients to understand the communication, but "clearly" may indicate that a firm should have regard to the expected level of understanding of the particular group of persons to whom the communication is addressed.

Even if the exact difference between the two is not entirely clear, both provisions will certainly be used by regulators in ensuring that customer documentation with private customers is readily understandable, especially in respect of any exclusions of a firm's liability and any explanation of the obligations of the customer to the firm.

Exclusion clauses (Rule 5–24)

One of the biggest concerns about customer agreements was the **6–006** extent to which firms used them to exclude liabilities which they owed under the rules, the FSA 1986, contract and the law of negligence. Hence, SIB was concerned to bring in a Core Rule on this subject and, as has been explained in paragraph 1–004 above, the restriction of section 62 to private investors does not apply in respect of a breach of this rule.

Rules of construction

The courts have always taken a strict approach to the interpretation of exclusion clauses. Basically, a clause which tried to exclude liability for fraud, deliberate breach of a duty owed or wilful default, such as gross recklessness, would be held invalid. Also, exclusion clauses have been interpreted *contra proferentem*. In other words, where there has been any doubt as to their scope or meaning, the courts have interpreted the clauses against the interests of those relying upon them. The courts have been less willing to uphold wide, extensive clauses. In addition, they have taken into account the status of the parties to the agreement, being less willing to enforce exclusion clauses where there is unequal bargaining power. The courts have concentrated on the substance of a relationship, rather than its form; and have decided that, despite the written words used in an agreement, the real relationship between the parties was a different one, and, therefore, wider obligations were owed by one party to the other than appeared to be the case from the face of the agreement.

Unfair Contract Terms Act 1977

This Act introduced provisions which supported the approach taken by the courts in construing exclusion clauses. Under the Act, a person cannot exclude or restrict his liability for negligence, except in so far as the relevant contractual term or notice satisfies the requirement of reasonableness (section 2(2)). The mere fact that a person has agreed to, or is aware of the exclusion, is not of itself to be taken as indicating his voluntary acceptance of any risk (section 2(3)).

Where one of the contracting parties deals as a consumer, or on the other's written standard terms of business, the other party to the contract may not:

    (i)   when himself in breach of contract, exclude or restrict any liability of his in respect of the breach; or

    (ii) claim to be entitled to render a contractual performance substantially different than that which was reasonably expected of him (or render no performance at all),

except in so far as (in respect of both (i) and (ii) above) the contract term satisfies the requirement of reasonableness (section 3).

In determining whether the exclusion is reasonable, the courts will examine whether the term was a fair and reasonable one to have included, having regard to the circumstances which were, or ought reasonably to have been, known to or in the contemplation of the parties when the contract was made (section 11(1)). If the exclusion was contained in a notice which was not part of the contract, then it will only be upheld if it is fair and reasonable to allow reliance on it, having regard to all the circumstances obtaining when the liability arose (section 11(3)). As with the *contra proferentem* rule, the burden of proving the requirement of reasonableness is on the person relying upon the exclusion clause (section 11(5)).

A person is regarded as dealing as a consumer for the purpose of section 3 if, in relation to the other party, he neither enters into the contract in the course of a business, nor holds himself out as doing so. The onus is also on the party relying on the exclusion clause to show that the other party did not deal as a consumer.

In determining whether an exclusion clause does satisfy the statutory reasonableness test, the courts will still take into account the old Common Law rules on construction and matters such as: the clarity of the clause; the relative bargaining strengths of the contracting parties; whether the person who deals as a consumer had any realistic possibility of being able to obtain variations of any of the standard terms offered by the other party; the inducements offered, such as reduced dealing charges, for dealing on terms offering less protection; the acceptability of such terms within the market; and the nature and extent of the liability being excluded.

Restriction to securities dealing

6–007   Sections 2 and 3 of the Unfair Contract Terms Act 1977 do not apply so far as the contract relates to the creation or transfer of securities, or any right or interest in securities (Schedule 1, paragraph 1(*e*)). "Securities" is not defined, but, as the Act was drafted before the futures and options markets really took off and developed in the United Kingdom in the 1980s, it could be argued that this exclusion relates to all investments, rather than the definition of securities within the new rules, which excludes derivatives.

The fact that the exception is limited to a "contract relating to the creation or transfer of securities" suggests that it is limited to the dealing function, namely entering into transactions in securities, rather than other investment services provided by a firm, such as giving investment advice and carrying on discretionary management. Therefore, although there is a restriction in the Act in the way it applies to investment business, it should not be assumed that it never applies to any contract or relationship which a firm enters into with respect to investment business.

Sections 2 and 3 also do not extend to any contract of insurance (Schedule 1, paragraph 1(a)). In this case, there is no reference, as in the case of securities, to the contract relating to the creation or transfer of a policy. But, it is suggested again, that the exception may not extend to the giving of advice in respect of life policies.

Core Rule

Owing to the exclusion of the Unfair Contract Terms Act to securities dealing, it was thought appropriate to introduce a Core Rule specifically dealing with the validity and acceptability of exclusion clauses in investment agreements. The rule is divided into three parts.

Provision 1. The first rule deals with any written communication or **6–008** agreement and prevents a firm from seeking to exclude or restrict any duty or liability to a customer which it has under the FSA 1986 or the rules of its regulator (including the Principles and Core Rules). Note that this provision applies to all customers, but only where the exclusion is contained in a written communication.

When the provision talks about a firm not being able to exclude or restrict any duty or liability under the rules of its regulator, account should be taken of the fact that some rules are written in absolute terms, whereas others contain mechanisms by which their provisions can be modified. For example, the best execution obligation is absolute in terms of private customers, but can be modified in respect of the execution of orders for non-private customers with the customer's consent. Therefore, a firm would not be in breach of this first provision where it includes within a written agreement with a non-private customer an exclusion that it will not provide best execution; whereas it would commit a rule breach in respect of such a clause in a written agreement with a private customer: even though all of the transactions for the customer satisfy the best execution test.

Provision 2. The rule then goes on to say that in respect of any written communication or agreement with a private customer, a firm cannot, unless it is reasonable to do so in the circumstances, seek to exclude or restrict:

    (i)   any duty to act with skill, care and diligence; or

(ii) any liability for failing to exercise the degree of skill, care and diligence which may reasonably be expected of the firm in the circumstances.

This second provision is effectively applying the reasonable test of sections 2 and 3 of the Unfair Contract Terms Act 1977. It is questionable, however, whether this second provision is really necessary in view of the scope of the first.

The first states that it is not possible to exclude or restrict any duty or liability under your regulator's rules. The rules include the Principles; and Principle 2 states that a firm should act with due skill, care and diligence. It is probably helpful, however, to have this specific provision, especially if someone decides to argue that Principle 2 is limited to a duty to act with skill, care and diligence in complying with individual rule provisions, rather than generally. Where a firm has a fiduciary relationship with a customer, it may owe other duties to a customer besides those specifically set out in the rules. This provision will prevent the firm from unreasonably excluding or restricting either its duty to exercise skill, care and diligence in the context of the general law; or its liability for failing to exercise such skill, care and diligence. In connection with liability, the rule refers to skill, care and diligence which may reasonably be expected in the circumstances. Surely, this must be limited to the firm's liability for obligations arising (even if only impliedly) at law due to the contractual or fiduciary relationship which the firm has with the customer?

These two provisions on exclusion clauses do not make any agreement void which contains a clause in breach of the rule, but the firm would not be able to rely upon such a clause and could be disciplined for a rule breach. It is unlikely that an investor will be able to claim compensation for such a breach, because his loss will not stem from this breach alone, but rather from the firm's failure to comply with another rule or to exercise its duty to act with skill, care and diligence as required under Principle 2.

Provision 3. Finally, this rule contains a third provision which relates back to the other two: namely, a firm which has included a valid exclusion or restriction clause cannot seek unreasonably to rely upon it. In other words, a firm may have validly included the clause, but, if in all the circumstances it is unreasonable to do so, it should not rely on it to exclude or restrict its duty or liability. This is clearly picking up on the reasonable test of the Unfair Contract Terms Act 1977. It will often be difficult to enforce such a provision because views vary so much as to what circumstances would make it unreasonable to rely upon a properly included exclusion clause. The Common Law construction rules on exclusion clauses and the cases since 1977 on the interpretation of the reasonableness test in the Unfair Contract Terms Act will be relevant in this context.

This third provision is not specifically restricted to private customers or, even, any customer; nor is it restricted to written agreements. So, it could be argued that it applies to any exclusion clause in relation to any person; but, because it refers to "any such duty or liability", it is suggested that its application is limited to the scope of the first two provisions, namely written communications or agreements with customers (first provision) and private customers (second provision).

It is interesting that the first two provisions are limited to written material. A fair amount of business can be done under SFA's rules, not just with non-private customers, but also with private customers, without the need for any written documentation. Obviously, there will still be a contractual relationship between the firm and the customer, and, as part of the terms of that relationship, the firm could try to exclude or restrict its liability orally. In practice, however, it will be difficult for a firm to prove that the exclusion clause was properly made a term of the contractual relationship, unless it is the type of clause which is regularly understood by custom as applying within the relevant market in that type of relationship. This is more likely to be the case where a firm is dealing with a large non-private customer which, although not another market counterparty, is a professional participant in the market.

Information about the firm

Having mentioned the fair and clear communication test and before dealing with the contents requirements for customer agreements, this is an appropriate place to talk about the basic information which a firm must give about its identity to private customers (Rule 5–16). Where a firm is providing investment services to a private customer, it must take reasonable steps to ensure that the customer is given adequate information about the firm's identity, business address, its regulation by SFA, and the identity and status with the firm of its employees and other agents who have contact with the customer.

6–009

This is a one-off provision, unlike the similar provision in the old rules which required a firm's name, address and regulator to be shown on every publication. Also, the information does not have to be given in writing. There was a provision in the old TSA rules that the name of the firm's regulator did not have to be included on business cards, which was important for some firms whose employees travel between a number of countries. If their card contained a reference to the firm's membership of SFA when they were working in a country to which the rules did not apply, it would have to have included a disclosure that the regulatory protections under the FSA 1986 did not apply. Under this new rule, it is still possible to leave off a reference to the firm's membership of SFA, on the basis that, when the employee hands over his card to a private customer, he gives an explanation that his firm is regulated by SFA. It is also because this rule only requires a one-off disclosure of the firm's address that the requirement to state the address on every contract note has been deleted.

There has been some confusion concerning the rule's reference to the identity and status of the firm's employees and other agents. Potentially, the provision is very wide and could mean that every employee or agent who has contact with a private customer with respect to any investment service which is being provided by the firm must give his identity and status. This would include telephonists, clerks and secretaries who have no responsibility for advising customers or managing their investments. It is suggested that firms should apply this provision in a pragmatic manner, and that identity and status only have to be given in respect of employees and agents who carry out the functions of procuring customers, advising them on investments and managing investments for them: namely, registered representatives.

The reference to status means the position of the individual within the firm, rather than his status as a registered representative. The reason for the disclosure is that the customer knows something about the position and responsibilities of the person dealing with him. A mere disclosure that he is an SFA registered representative may not mean much to a private customer, although it would not be wrong for firms also to include this status on employees' business cards.

The reference to agents includes appointed representatives of the firm. In this case, the person would need to point out that he is an appointed representative of an SFA firm, giving the name and address of the firm, together with a reference to the firm's membership of SFA.

Contents of customer agreements

6–010   As explained above, a two-way customer agreement is only required in two cases:

(i)   contingent liability transactions for private customers; and

(ii)   discretionary management for any customer.

Where the firm is providing any discretionary service, then the agreement must include any limitations on the firm's discretion, such as restrictions on the type of investments which can be purchased.

SFA's rules require a two-way customer agreement to include matters set out in two tables. The first table consists of compulsory requirements for every two-way agreement, whilst the second table sets out requirements which should be included if applicable to the type of service being provided by the firm. These two tables are part of the rules, so a failure to include a relevant provision from the table will mean that the firm is committing a rule breach. Although, instead of providing all the details in the one document, it will be sufficient if the agreement refers to other documents which contain the missing details. The reference should make it clear that the details referred to are incorporated as terms of the customer agreement. Firms will find it useful to incorporate by reference terms which are likely to be amended frequently, such as charges, as this will obviate the need for formal written amendment to the signed agreement.

Two-way agreements have to include details of a customer's investment objectives. Again, this could be complied with by reference to a questionnaire completed by the customer. Investment objectives include the basis of risk which can be undertaken and whether the customer wishes income or capital growth. Two-way agreements are required for execution-only business in contingent liability transactions for private customers: in this case, the requirement to obtain a customer's investment objectives is clearly inappropriate. It should be emphasised that the contents requirements in the tables are only required in those cases where the rules require a two-way customer agreement, rather than in every case where a customer signs an agreement with the firm.

Apart from the detailed contents requirements for two-way customer agreements, a firm is free to design its own customer agreements and terms of business letters. In other words, a firm needs to determine the level of services which it is providing to its customer and then look at the relevant rules to see whether, before providing any of these services, it must obtain the customer's written consent or make a written disclosure. It is only where the service to be provided by the firm relates to one of these written consent or disclosure requirements that it will have to produce any sort of written customer agreement or terms of business letter. Note the requirement discussed in paragraph 6–004 above that, wherever a firm provides services to a private customer on written contractual terms, it must draw up an agreement (albeit a one-way terms of business letter) which sets out in adequate detail the basis on which its services are to be provided.

SFA has produced a breakdown of those rules which require disclosure to or consent from customers in three tables: Table I is for private advisory customers; Table II is for all discretionary customers; and Table III is for non-private advisory customers. These tables appear as Appendix 6 below.

Model agreements/clauses

The firm is free to construct its customer agreements and terms of business letters in any way it wishes. Obviously, if a two-way customer agreement is required, then the necessary contents must be included as set out in the two tables referred to above. In all cases, however, a firm is free to use its own drafting style, provide its own order for the clauses which are required in the agreement and include matters besides **6–011** those which have to be included under the rules. The two controls discussed above should not be forgotten, however, namely the fair and clear communications test and the provisions on exclusion clauses.

SFA has produced a series of model clauses (reproduced as Appendix 7 below) which firms may use in drawing up customer agreements. The use of these clauses is not obligatory, but the clauses are given the status of formal guidance. In other words, a firm which uses one of the model clauses will prima facie be regarded as having made the type of disclosure required by the rule to which the clause relates.

The model clauses document is divided into two parts. Part I contains those clauses which may be used in either a one-way or a two-way customer document. The extent to which the clauses have to be included will depend upon the nature of the services which the firm is providing. The clauses in Part II are only relevant to a two-way customer agreement because they relate to rules where the firm cannot act without obtaining the customer's prior consent. Again, however, a firm only needs to include those clauses from Part II which relate to the services being undertaken for the customer.

The document makes it clear that a firm may wish to include other clauses which, although not relating to specific rule disclosure and consent requirements, may be relevant in terms of a firm complying with the overriding test relating to written documents with private customers: namely, the requirement to set out in adequate detail the basis on which the firm's services are provided (paragraph 6–004 above).

Although there is no model clause relating to the amendment of a customer agreement, a firm may wish to provide such a clause. There is nothing to stop a firm including a variation clause under which it can unilaterally vary, on notice, a provision in a two-way customer agreement. The important point is that any variation should not become effective until it is notified to the other party, thereby giving the other party the option of refusing to accept the variation and, if necessary, withdrawing from the agreement.

Revision of agreements made under old rules

With the coming into force of the new SFA rules, it is important that firms should review all of their existing customer documentation. For example, a firm could find that the old rules required it to contain in the customer agreement details about a rule provision which has no longer survived under the new rulebook. If the firm does not amend its agreements to remove this provision, it could then find that it owes under contract (because of the reference in the customer agreement) an obligation to the customer which it no longer has to provide, or which it can provide in a different form, under the new rules.

In practice, this is not really a problem because the main substantive obligations between the old rules and the new rules are the same: it is merely that there has been a slight shift of emphasis. For example, there is no longer a specific rule requirement to give an explanation of stabilisation to private customers, yet it may be necessary for a firm to give such an explanation or warning to comply with the understanding of risk rule (Rule 5–30).

Similarly, the old rules prevented a firm from entering into a transaction in a non-readily realisable investment for an advisory private customer or for any discretionary customer unless the customer had been given a written summary of the firm's obligations to obtain a fair and reasonable price. The new rules do not contain such a written warning requirement, although any private advisory or discretionary customer (but not a non-private discretionary customer) must have been given an oral warning of the difficulties in establishing a proper market price, and if relevant, arranging a subsequent sale (see paragraphs 7–004 and 7–005 below).

In reviewing existing customer documentation, a firm may find that it does not need to draw up a completely new agreement to remove some provisions contained in the old one. If the old agreement contained a variation clause allowing a firm to vary terms on notice, then the firm could rely on such a clause in amending the old agreement to fit in with the requirements under the new rules.

Transferring a customer's business

In fact, a completely new agreement is not even necessary where **6–012** customers from one firm are transferred to those of another firm as a result of an inter-group reorganisation, a sale of part of a business or the closing down of a firm. The new firm could decide that it is happy to continue to do business with the transferred customers on the basis of the terms under which the old firm operated, or on those terms subject to a few modifications.

In such a case, the new firm should send a letter to the customer informing him of the change of ownership, give the customer details of the new firm and explain that the new firm is willing to service the customer on the same terms as the old firm, or on those terms subject to any modification set down in this letter. If the services to be undertaken by the new firm are ones which can be provided under the new rules without the need for a two-way customer agreement or any other signed consent by the customer, then this letter would be sufficient to satisfy the requirement for private customers that the agreement must set out in adequate detail the basis on which the services are to be provided. Although full details would not be given in the covering letter, the agreement with the customer will consist of both the covering letter and the old agreement to which the letter refers. This is so even if the old agreement had been signed by the customer. If, on the other hand, the services which the new firm wishes to provide are ones which can only be provided under a two-way customer agreement, then the new firm would have to require the customer to sign and return a copy of the letter informing him about the change of ownership. If the customer then returns the signed copy, he will have entered into a two-way customer agreement with the new firm as a result of the letter's incorporation of the terms of the old agreement. (See also paragraphs 3–015 *et seq.* above.)

No transitional provision

SFA has not provided a transitional provision in respect of customer agreements. In other words, if the firm relies on its old agreements, it must be careful to determine that these agreements will comply with the new rules, and it should also assess to what extent it may owe contractual obligations where there are no relevant new rule provisions. As explained above, it may be quite easy for many firms to amend unilaterally their original agreements because they contain empowering provisions providing for future variations by the firm.

---

[1] In fact, SFA has put the word "written" before "agreement" in reproducing this Core Rule in its rulebook (Rule 5–15(2)).

Chapter 7

Understanding Risk

Basic obligation

The Core Rule obligation on a customer's understanding only applies **7–001** where a firm is dealing with private customers; and then, only when it is either recommending a transaction or acting as a discretionary manager (Rule 5–30(1)). It does not apply to investment advice of a general nature: only to specific advice which amounts to the recommendation of a transaction, whether a purchase or sale. The restriction to "recommending a transaction" suggests that it does not apply to a recommendation not to enter into a transaction: such as a recommendation to keep an investment rather than sell it, or a recommendation not to purchase an investment.

The obligation is that a firm must take reasonable steps to enable the customer to understand the nature of the risks involved. There is a subjective element to this. In other words, a firm should take into account the current understanding and previous course of dealing of the investor. For example, to comply with the rule it may be necessary to inform a new investor that the value of his investments could go down, even if he is only buying blue-chip stocks or units in well-managed, non-volatile regulated collective investment schemes. For established customers such a warning would be unnecessary. In this case, the warning should relate to any new type of risk to which the investor has not been subject previously.

Written warnings: warrants and derivatives

In support of this Core Rule obligation, SFA requires (Rule 5–30(2)) **7–002** written risk warnings to be sent to private customers in respect of warrants or derivatives (options, futures and contracts for difference). As with the Core Rule, this requirement is restricted to private customers (unlike the old AFBD and TSA provisions). However, it extends further than the Core Rule in the sense that it applies before a firm arranges or executes any transaction in a warrant or derivative for a private customer, even if the customer is not receiving advice, but dealing on an execution-only basis. (Remember, in the case of an execution-only transaction in a contingent liability transaction, a two-way customer agreement is also required.)

The customer must have signed the relevant warning after being given a proper opportunity to consider its terms before the firm can recommend, arrange or execute any such transaction. This is similar to the two-way customer agreement requirement.

7–003   There are, however, some important qualifications:

1. The Warrants Risk Warning Notice (Appendix 14) does not have to be signed by a private customer where he is realising warrants which he already holds, or where he is buying or selling warrants attached to another security. A security is defined as any investment, other than a derivative or a life policy.

2. In the case of overseas customers, the warnings do not have to be signed by any customer whom the firm believes on reasonable grounds does not wish to consent in writing. In fact, the warnings do not even need to be sent to such a customer if the firm believes that he does not wish to receive them.

3. In relation to indirect customers, the firm has to have received confirmation (which may be oral) from the agent that the indirect customer has signed the relevant warning. This provision mirrors a similar provision under the old TSA rules, but in that case the provision was more relevant because there were occasions where the intermediary would not want to disclose the identity of his principal. However, the indirect customer concept only works where the identity of the principal is known to the firm.

4. The new style Derivatives Risk Warning Notice (Appendix 15) does not have to be sent to a private customer who has already received an old style derivatives risk disclosure statement under TSA or AFBD rules. Note, however, that the old rules did not require any written risk warning for warrants. Therefore, the Warrants Risk Warning Notice will have to be signed by existing customers before a firm can recommend, arrange or execute transactions in warrants or act as a discretionary manager of a portfolio containing warrants, unless the qualification in 1. above applies.

In respect of the two written warnings required by SFA, the Warrants Notice (Appendix 14) should not be amended in any way. The Derivatives Notice (Appendix 15), however, can be amended to a limited extent.

The Derivatives Notice attempts to explain, in a general way, the separate risks attaching to the various types of derivatives contracts. Therefore, if a firm will only be dealing for a customer in some of the contracts referred to in the Notice, it can leave out those paragraphs which solely relate to the special risks attaching to other types of contract. For example, a firm which does not deal in futures, contracts for difference, traditional options, the writing of options and off-exchange transactions could leave out the paragraphs under these headings. Similarly, a firm which is not dealing on foreign markets or in margined instruments, or otherwise requiring collateral, could leave out the paragraphs under these headings. There are certain paragraphs, however, which must be included. These are those under the headings: commissions; suspensions of trading; clearing house protections; and insolvency.

The note at the end of the Notice also states that a firm may include descriptions of the types of investments covered by the Notice, provided such descriptions do not lessen the effect of the risks explained in the SFA model.

A firm may combine both the Warrants and Derivatives Notices, and they can be incorporated into a two-way customer agreement, except that the customer must sign separately the warning notice part. His signature at the end of the agreement will not be regarded as sufficient to show that he has properly read and understood the warnings.

Oral warnings: non-readily realisable investments

SFA also requires (Rule 5–30(5)) that a firm recommending to a private customer a transaction in a non-readily realisable investment must: **7–004**

(i) warn him about the difficulties in establishing a proper market price;

(ii) if the recommendation concerns a purchase, warn him about the difficulties in finding a market if he subsequently wishes to sell; and

(iii) disclose any position knowingly held by the firm or an associate in the investment or a related investment.

A non-readily realisable investment is one which is *not* a life policy, a unit in a regulated collective investment scheme, a foreign exchange transaction, or an investment (including a warrant or derivative) which is traded frequently on or under the rules of a recognised or designated investment exchange. Recognised investment exchanges are those recognised by SIB under the FSA 1986, whereas designated investment exchanges are those overseas exchanges which SIB has designated as affording investors comparable protections to those of a recognised investment exchange. No explanation is given as to what is meant by traded frequently, but some comparison has to be made between the frequency of trading in similar stock. "On or under the rules" of the exchange means that the investment does not actually have to be traded on the exchange, provided the deal is subject, in some way, to regulation by the exchange. The requirement is not linked to whether or not the stock is listed; so it would include stock on the London Stock Exchange's Unlisted Securities Market and even stock traded under that exchange's Rule 535.2, provided that, in both cases, trading in the stock was frequent.

The warning may be oral, given at the time of making the recommendation, or it may be included in a written customer agreement. A suitable clause has been included in SFA's model clauses for customer documents (Appendix 7 below). Such a clause, however, in a customer agreement would not be sufficient to satisfy requirement (iii) above: namely, the position held by the firm or an associate in the investment or a related investment. The rule requires the fact of the holding of the position to be disclosed, rather than a general warning beforehand that a firm or its associate may or may not have material positions relating to subsequent recommendations made to the customer. "Associate" includes: other undertakings in the same group as the firm; appointed representatives of such an undertaking or the firm; and any person whose business or personal relationship with any of the above could reasonably be expected to give rise to a community of interest between them which may involve a conflict of interest in dealings with third parties. A related investment would include warrants, options or futures based on the first investment, or debt investments in the same company where the first investment was an equity.

7–005   The warning requirement does not apply to discretionary business. In this case, a firm should only be entering into a transaction in a non-readily realisable investment for a private customer if it considers it suitable in terms of the customer's financial standing, investment objectives and any restrictions placed upon the firm's discretion. It also does not apply where a firm is dealing on an execution-only basis.

SFA no longer provides a support rule to the London Stock Exchange in respect of any investments suspended from listing or subject to other dealing restrictions imposed by the Exchange. Under the old TSA rules, a firm could not deal in such investments without the prior permission of TSA. Under the new rulebook, a firm is free to deal for customers in such investments, provided, if it is an Exchange member, it has permission from the Exchange. Such investments, however, would clearly be non-readily realisable. Therefore, if the firm recommends any transaction in them, rather than just carrying out an execution-only order, it will have to comply with the warning requirement for non-readily realisable investments (Rule 5–30(5)).

Additional warnings

7–006   In guidance at the end of Rule 5–30, SFA has emphasised that, in order to comply with the Core Rule requirement of ensuring that the customer understands the nature of the risks involved, it may be necessary to give additional warnings or explanations to those specifically required by SFA's third tier rules for warrants, derivatives and non-readily realisable investments.

As indicated earlier, there is a subjective element to the Core Rule requirement. The firm must take steps to enable the individual customer to understand the nature of the risks involved; but this is tempered by an objective assessment in the sense that the steps taken by the firm must be reasonable in the circumstances. If the firm has taken such reasonable steps, it does not matter that the customer did not actually understand all of the risks.

In the majority of cases, the sending of the written warning notices for warrants and derivatives and the giving of the basic oral warning required for non-readily realisable investments should mean that the firm has taken reasonable steps to enable the customer to understand the risks involved. However, a firm should not always assume that, because it has given the specific warnings required by SFA's third tier rules, it has always satisfied the Core Rule obligation.

An example of where a firm might need to take further steps is where **7–007** it issued the Derivatives Risk Warning Notice at the beginning of a customer relationship, and then, for the first months, or year or two, of dealing for the customer, the firm did not enter into any derivatives transactions, or, if so, only in a limited range of the types of contracts covered by the Notice. Once the firm begins to enter into other derivatives transactions for the customer some time after he has signed the Notice, it may be necessary, in order to comply with the Core Rule, specifically to draw his attention to paragraphs within the Notice as containing warnings which are particularly relevant now to the new contracts.

This may be very important for firms relying on the old style derivatives risk disclosure statements sent out in 1988 under TSA's and AFBD's rules, especially as the new Derivatives Notice is intended to be written in a more friendly, simple and understandable style, whilst also being shorter than the old warning statements.

Again, a firm may need to explain more to a customer in respect of a non-readily realisable investment than is required under SFA's third tier rule, especially if there are additional risks attaching. For example, it is a deal executed off-exchange, or in a foreign country which does not have a mature, effective regulatory system; or there are no recognised dealers in the investment. The firm may need to explain adverse market reports or rumours about the issuer of the investment; the risk of adverse foreign exchange movements; matters affecting the reliability of any intermediaries or custodians involved; and any unusual or excessive transaction costs.

As part of its guidance, SFA has said that additional warnings and **7–008** explanations may be necessary in relation to: unregulated collective investment schemes; investments which are subject to stabilisation; and guaranteed stops in respect of derivatives transactions. In such circumstances, the firm should be warning the customer: about the general fact that an unregulated collective investment scheme does not comply with SIB's detailed regulations and approval scheme for regulated schemes; that the affect of stabilisation can make the market price of a new issue temporarily higher than it would otherwise be; and that a customer will be paying higher transaction charges for the benefit of a guaranteed stop: in other words, the premium which the customer pays for the restriction offered by the firm in respect of his loss.

SFA has included paragraphs on stabilisation in its model customer documentation (see Appendix 7 below), but it may still be necessary to give an oral warning at the time of dealing to ensure that the customer properly understands the risk. The warning is pertinent to purchases of investments affected by stabilisation because, once the stabilising activities end, the value of the investments may fall, even though they are still readily realisable investments. Remember that the warning should extend to the purchase of related investments whose price could be affected by the stabilisation.

Chapter 8

Credit, Margin and Default

Credit (Rule 5–27)

A firm must not lend money or extend credit to a private customer in connection with regulated business, nor must it arrange for another person to do so, unless certain requirements have been complied with. This provision is only a private customer rule and only applies where the firm acts with knowledge. The reference to knowledge becomes important in terms of the Chinese walls rule (Rule 5–3) explained in paragraph 15–014 below. Basically, the brokering side of the firm would not be in breach of this requirement if it itself does not extend credit to the customer, but another part of the firm which acts as an authorised banking institution does so and the brokering side is unaware of the provision of credit by the banking side. The rule, however, catches a firm which itself does not provide the credit if it arranges for a loan to be provided to the customer by another person. So the brokering side would be caught where it acts with knowledge in the sense that it arranges for someone else, such as another group company which is an authorised banking institution, to arrange credit facilities for its customers.

The rule does not prevent the offering of credit to customers for investment purposes. Instead, it aims at ensuring that any credit arrangements which are provided are operated on a sensible basis in the interests of, and with the full knowledge of, the customer. Therefore, before a firm extends credit, it must have made an assessment about the financial standing of its customer, and, based on that assessment, it must be satisfied that the arrangements are suitable in respect of the likely investment transactions to be entered into by the customer. In other words, the firm must be satisfied that the credit arrangements are suitable in terms of the risks which the customer can afford to bear, his obligations to repay and the types of investment transactions for which he is going to use the credit offered.

The rule states that this assessment should be based on the information disclosed by the customer. Obviously, if the customer refuses to disclose any information, a firm will not be able to argue that the provision of credit is suitable. Anyway, it would be an unwise firm which extended credit without properly assessing the customer's ability to repay. The requirement, however, is not quite the same as the ordinary suitability rule in the sense that the assessment does not have

8–001

8–002

to be made against other information about the customer of the firm is, or should be, aware; it only has to be based on the actual information disclosed by the customer.

In assessing whether the credit arrangements are suitable, the firm should look at all of the relevant arrangements, including applicable interest charges, penalties for late payment and any security which the customer has to provide for the loan. For example, it would be difficult for a firm to argue that it is suitable to offer credit to a private customer for the purposes of making investments where the loan is to be secured by a substantial charge over the customer's house, unless the investments are directly related to the purchase of the house or involve annuities for old age, pension plans, school fees payment plans and other similar arrangements.

Once the firm has satisfied this suitability obligation, it must enter into a written agreement with the private customer under which he gives his written consent to the arrangements. This agreement must specify the maximum amount which the firm, or the lender (where the firm is arranging the provision of credit through a third party), may lend to the customer, together with details of the amount or basis of any charges which are to be levied in connection with the loan. It would be acceptable, in respect of charges, for the written agreement to refer to another document setting out the charges: for example, a reference to the firm's interest charges, as stated on its current rate card or some similar document. If there is such a reference, however, the actual amount or basis of the charges must be disclosed before they are incurred (Rule 5–33(2)). Also, the system for amending the charges should be based on some standard criteria, such as changes in current bank interest rates, rather than allowing any sort of arbitrary change which the firm desires. Otherwise, the firm could be in breach of the unreasonable charging requirement (Rule 5–33(1)), or Principle 1 (Integrity) which requires a firm to observe high standards of integrity and fair dealing. In this connection, note Principle 5 (Information for Customers) which requires a firm to take reasonable steps to give a customer it advises, in a comprehensible and timely way, any information needed to enable the customer to make a balanced and informed decision.

To sum up, before credit can be extended to private customers, a firm must have satisfied a suitability test, and entered into a written agreement which sets a maximum credit limit and discloses details about the charges relating to the credit.[1]

8–003 There is an exception to all of these requirements. This is where a firm settles a securities transaction in the event of default or late payment by the customer, or pays an amount to cover a margin call made on a customer, provided, in this latter case, that the firm does not itself cover the margin call for a period longer than five business days. There may often be genuine reasons why a customer is late with making a settlement payment or satisfying a margin call. For example, he may be unaware of the requirement due to temporary incapacity, such as illness, or absence on holiday or business. Similarly, the customer may have remitted the funds, but they are not immediately available because of standard delays in the banking clearing system. Problems with late payments may become more frequent once the London Stock Exchange introduces rolling settlement.

Margin (Rule 5–28)

SFA has provided some fairly extensive arrangements relating to the payment of margin. Where a firm effects a contingent liability transaction for any customer, not just a private customer, which may involve the customer in paying margin, whether at the outset or subsequently, then the firm must:

8–004

(i) make sure that the customer provides any margin which is payable; and

(ii) is aware of the consequences of not paying the margin: in other words, having the position closed out against him to his financial loss.

The firm must also monitor daily the amount of margin which must be paid by the customer and ensure that the aggregate amount of any margin required from him is covered by cash, equity balances or acceptable collateral. If there is a shortfall, then the firm must fund the difference until the shortfall is eliminated.

A contingent liability transaction is defined as a transaction in a derivative under which the customer may be liable to make further payments when the transaction falls to be completed or upon the earlier closing out of his position. It should be assumed that it includes any derivatives transaction secured by margin (see the discussion in paragraph 6–003 above).

The rule goes on to say that a firm should not effect a contingent liability for any customer unless it can show that it believes on reasonable grounds that the customer understands all the aspects relating to margin. These are: the circumstances in which he may be required to provide margin; the particular forms in which margin may be provided; the particular steps which the firm may be entitled to take if he fails to provide the required margin; and any other circumstances (besides the failure to provide margin) which may lead to a customer's position being closed out without prior reference to him. The firm must also point out that if he fails to meet a margin call by a time limit specified by the firm, his position may be closed out.

As two-way customer agreements are required for any private customer entering into a contingent liability transaction, the firm is required by the margin rule to give the above explanations in this agreement, unless it is an overseas customer who does not want a two-way agreement to be used. In this case, the explanation can be set out in a separate document. This document, however, must be signed by the customer: there is no exception similar to that for two-way customer agreements, experts and risk warnings. With respect to non-private customers, the margin explanation does not have to be given in writing; but this will obviously be the easiest way of a firm satisfying the requirement that it can show on reasonable grounds that the customer had the necessary understanding.

8–005   Where the firm is entering into an on-exchange contingency liability transaction for a customer, then the amount of margin which it requires the customer to provide must be of an amount or value at least equal to the margin requirements of the relevant exchange or clearing house. Firms cannot normally enter into contingent liability transactions for private customers off-exchange (Rule 5–44 and see paragraphs 11–025 and 11–026 below).

Normally, the firm must close out a customer's open position where he fails to meet a margin call after a period of five business days. This matches the reference to credit already referred to where it was stated that a firm can extend credit to a private customer, without satisfying the requirements on suitability and a written agreement in Rule 5–27, to cover a margin call, provided it is done for a period no longer than five business days.

8–006   The only circumstances in which a firm can keep a customer's position open after five business days[2] where he has failed to meet a margin call are:

(i)   Where it makes an unsecured loan to a customer provided the loan is granted subject to an adequate credit management policy. Such a policy has to be approved in writing by SFA and satisfy a number of criteria. Subject to (iii) below, it is only where a firm has such an approved policy that it can offer unsecured loans for the purposes of covering margin for longer than five days. A firm is not required to have an approved adequate credit management policy, but, where it does so, obviously it needs to cover this unsecured credit in terms of the financial resources required under the Financial Rules; although the Counterparty Risk Requirement is less than it would otherwise be where the unsecured lending is provided under such an approved policy.

(ii)   A firm can make a secured loan for the purposes of covering margin beyond five days if:

(a)   an adequate credit assessment is made of the customer by an employee of the firm who is individually registered by SFA, provided he is independent of the trading or marketing functions of the firm; and

(b)   the maximum amount of the credit has previously been set out in writing, which, in the case of a non-private customer, can be in a one-way document, but which in the case of a private customer has to be in a two-way customer agreement (or, in the case of an overseas customer who does not want a two-way agreement to be used, in a separately signed document).

(iii)   The firm can keep the customer's position open beyond five days if the customer has been contacted and agreed to provide the relevant margin, and the firm is satisfied that the failure to supply the margin by the relevant date is due to temporary circumstances beyond the customer's control and that the margin is being made available.[3]

Where a firm has kept the position open (in one of the circumstances listed above) beyond five days by making either a secured or unsecured loan, it must, as soon as reasonably practical, inform the customer, if applicable, of the extent to which his previously agreed credit limit has been exceeded.

Of course, there is nothing to stop a firm closing out a customer's **8–007** position before the five days, provided that it has made it clear to the customer that his position will be closed out at an earlier date if he fails to meet a margin call. In this case, the firm can then close out the position where the margin remains outstanding beyond this earlier specified date.

Owing to the loss which a customer can suffer if his position is closed out early where he has failed to meet a margin call, firms are encouraged to make appropriate arrangements with their customers to cover margin calls in cases where a customer may not be easily contactable.

As the margin rule only applies to derivatives transactions involving a contingent liability transaction, a firm is not subject to the five-day closing out requirement where it covers further calls on securities which are partly paid. Neither would the firm have to satisfy the suitability or written agreement requirements of the credit rule (Rule 5–27), because the firm would only be covering a default or late payment by the customer.

Underwriting

In connection with the discussion on these rules warning a customer **8–008** about additional financial liabilities to which he may be subject, it is appropriate to consider SFA's requirements concerning underwriting. A firm must not execute transactions for a private customer, or effect or arrange a discretionary transaction for any customer, under which the customer will incur obligations as an underwriter or sub-underwriter without his prior written consent. This requirement relates to underwriting or sub-underwriting in connection with any form of issue of investments, including any offer for subscription, offer for sale or placing of investments, or any takeover offer where the consideration does or may consist of investments.

The customer's consent may be general or related to a specific issue of investments. The rule does not state that the customer must be specifically warned about the risk which he has taken on in respect of an underwriting transaction, but such a warning would be necessary in prespect of private customers if the firm is to comply with the understanding of risk requirement (Rule 5–30(1)).

Default

8–009   A restriction is placed upon the extent to which a firm can realise other assets of the customer in respect of a default. Where a customer has given an order to purchase investments and then fails to pay by the settlement date, the firm can try to recoup its loss by selling these investments. Likewise, if a customer fails to satisfy a margin payment, a firm may close out the customer's position and, as we have already seen, is normally required to do so where the call remains unmet after five business days.

The selling, however, of the actual investments which the customer has failed to pay for, or the closing out of the customer's position, may not fully compensate the firm for the investor's default. The firm may wish to realise other assets which it holds on the customer's behalf or set off against its claim any cash which it is holding for the customer. The firm will normally have a lien against the customer's other assets, including cash.

8–010   SFA's third tier rules, however, state that a firm may not realise other assets of a customer in satisfaction of a default unless:

(i)   it is legally entitled to do so; and

(ii)   (a)   prior to any default, it gave the customer written notice of the default remedies which it might exercise; or

(b)   if it gave no such notice prior to the default, it has explained to the customer the remedies which it may exercise at least three business days before it tries to exercise these remedies.

The explanation under (ii) (b) above may be given orally. This restriction on exercising default remedies by giving notice only applies in the case of private customers. In other cases, the firm will be able to exercise any remedies which it properly has under law.

Overseas customers

Notice that in respect of all the requirements described above, there **8–011** is no exception for overseas customers as there is with respect to the other Conduct of Business provisions on customer agreements and other documentation.

[1] At the time of writing, the suitability requirement has not been included in the rule; only the requirement to obtain the customer's written consent to the credit arrangements has been included. SFA, however, intends to impose a suitability obligation in Rule 5–27 in the terms described in paragraph 8–002; and anyway, it is good practice to carry out such an assessment before providing credit.

[2] Of course, where the loan is made to a private customer, Rule 5–27 will also apply as discussed in paragraphs 8–001 *et seq.* above.

[3] At the time of writing this is only a proposed amendment.

Chapter 9

Suitability

This Chapter discusses those rules relevant to the suitability obligation: **9–001** namely, the "know your customer" requirement (Principle 4—Information about Customers): the suitability rule (Rule 5–31); the prohibition on churning (Rule 5–43); and the rule on charges (Rule 5–33).

Know your customer

There is no longer a specific Core Rule or third-tier rule which requires a firm to obtain details about a customer's investment objectives and financial circumstances. It is necessary, however, for a firm to obtain such information if it is to comply with the suitability requirement.

In fact, the reason why there is no specific rule requiring a firm to know its customer is due to the fact that Principle 4 deals with this issue, and also the suitability test is judged against information disclosed by the customer and other information of which the firm ought reasonably to be aware.

Principle 4 states that a firm should seek from customers whom it advises, or for whom it exercises discretion, any information about their circumstances and investment objectives which might reasonably be expected to be relevant in enabling the firm to fulfil its responsibilities to them. This Principle applies to all customers, not merely those customers who are owed the suitability obligation: namely, private advisory customers and discretionary customers.

The firm's obligation is to seek the information, rather than to obtain it. Therefore, a firm can still act for a customer even if he refuses to disclose information which the firm has requested. In these circumstances, the firm would have to comply with the suitability rule based on whatever information the customer has disclosed, however deficient, and any other information about him of which the firm should reasonably have been aware.

Principle 4 is not specifically linked to the suitability requirement: instead, it talks about a firm obtaining information relevant in enabling it to fulfil its responsibilities to its customer. Suitability, however, is the main rule which turns upon the individual circumstances and investment objectives of a customer. Other rules where the obtaining of information from the customer will be relevant are those dealing with: the classification of customers as expert investors; the understanding of risk requirement; and any of those rules which require prior consent from the customer before the firm can take a particular course of action. So, although the Principle applies to non-private customers, it is really only in the area of private advisory customers and discretionary customers where it really bites.

If a firm has an indirect customer, then it must obtain information from the agent about his principal. The firm can rely upon the accuracy and sufficiency of the information provided by the agent as long as it has no reason to doubt the authority, honesty and reliability of either the agent or the information supplied (Rule 5–2(2)). The amount of information required will depend whether the indirect customer falls to be treated as a private or non-private customer and the nature of the service to be provided, whether execution-only, advisory or discretionary.

Suitability

9–002   The suitability rule (Rule 5–31) is one of those requirements subject to a reasonable steps provision. It also has a wider application than most of the other rules because it applies where a firm is acting in the course of associated business, as well as regulated business. In other words, the foreign business carve-out will be available to negate the requirement in relation to business done by a firm's overseas branches, but the suitability test applies to any business done in connection with investment business which is not "foreign business", even if that business by itself does not amount to investment business.

Suitability applies to personal recommendations to a private customer or discretionary transactions for any customer. The rule says that the recommendation or transaction must be suitable for the customer having regard to facts disclosed by that customer and any other relevant facts about him of which the firm is, or reasonably should be, aware.[1]

9–003   As regards recommendations, the rule only applies to private customers. It has to be a personal recommendation. Therefore, recommendations given in brokers' newsletters and other research material is not caught because such recommendations cannot be regarded as being of a personal nature. They are general recommendations which are made available to all of a firm's customers, or a particular class of them.[2] If a broker, however, turns his standard newsletter into a personally styled letter through his word-processing system, any recommendations contained in that document would be caught because they then become personal for the particular customer. Certainly, the customer will feel he has received a personal recommendation.

The recommendation has to concern a specific investment or investment agreement. Therefore, recommendations about the market generally would not be caught. "Investment agreement" is defined in section 44(9) of the FSA 1986 to mean any agreement, the making or performance of which by one of the parties constitutes an activity which falls within Part II, Schedule 1, ignoring the exclusions in Parts III and IV. In other words, the agreement is entered into as part of the firm's activities of dealing or arranging deals in, managing, or advising on the types of investments referred to in Part I; or as a result of establishing, operating or winding up a collective investment scheme. The reference to the activities in Part II means that, for example, the suitability requirement applies equally to a recommendation to enter into a discretionary management agreement or into an agreement concerning advisory or dealing services, as to a recommendation relating to a specific transaction.

The rule also applies to the effecting or arranging of a discretionary **9–004** transaction. Discretionary transaction is not defined, but clearly applies to any transaction which the firm enters into without prior reference or specific instructions from the customer. It is important to make a distinction between discretionary transactions and conditional orders placed by a customer where he requires a firm to buy or sell an investment if the price goes below or above a predetermined figure. The execution of the latter order does not amount to discretionary business. On the other hand, if the instruction is to sell or buy an investment at a price and time which the broker considers right, it is suggested that this is a discretionary transaction; and, before a firm can enter into a discretionary transaction, it will require a two-way customer agreement (Rule 5–23(2)). Such agreements are required where the investment services provided to the customer involve discretionary management of his assets. It is suggested that as soon as there is any sort of discretionary management, even if it only relates to one transaction, then the two-way agreement requirement comes into play (see paragraph 6–003 above).

The recommendation or discretionary transaction must be suitable. There has, in the past, been some debate as to what amounts to suitability. Does the investment or transaction have to be the one which is the most suitable for the customer in the circumstances; or is the requirement that it must not be an unsuitable recommendation or transaction? It is suggested that the right approach is somewhere in the middle. At the very least, the recommendation or transaction must not be unsuitable. The problem is that sometimes there are a number of possibilities which are equally suitable; or, if there are any differences, they are very minor.

Suitability has to be judged on what information is available at the time of the recommendation or transaction, rather than by assessing the recommendation or transaction later in time, looking at how the investment has since performed. Also, judging suitability is rather a subjective test. There are clear cases where all competent advisers or managers will take a similar view on the unsuitability of a recommendation or transaction. But there will be many other recommendations or transactions where the views of competent managers and advisers differ substantially. This is why the test cannot be the most suitable investment of a range of investments, because it is never possible to determine objectively exactly what the most suitable investment is.

9–005 In determining suitability, it is not merely comparing like with like. For example, an investment adviser may have recommended a suitable share in terms of looking at equities generally, but, it may not be suitable for the investor to invest directly in shares because of the small amount of resources he has available to invest and his desire to minimise risk. It may be more suitable for such an investor to invest in units in a collective investment scheme. In other words, suitability is not dependent upon choosing the best performing investment of a particular category of investment, but requires a survey of the whole market to determine, first, what type of investment is suitable, and, then, within a particular type, which particular investment the customer should hold. In fact, although it may not always be easy to decide which particular investment within the same category is the most suitable, it will be easier to determine which category, amongst a number of different categories, is.

The suitability test applies wherever a firm is making a recommendation or exercising discretion. It applies equally to a one-off transaction with an investor who is unlikely to become a regular customer of a firm, as it does to an established customer, with a long-standing relationship with the firm. The rule is triggered where a firm makes a recommendation or exercises discretion.

9–006 This is important because it clearly does not apply where a firm is dealing on an execution-only basis. Therefore, it is not applicable to those brokers who only hold themselves out as providing execution-only dealing services; or to deals done for a firm's existing advisory or discretionary customers in respect of which no recommendation is given[3] or no discretion is exercised. This is a very different emphasis from the old TSA rule where a firm had to warn an existing customer about the unsuitability of any order which he placed, even though the firm had not been asked to give advice, unless there was a provision in the customer agreement enabling the firm to deal with the customer on some occasions on an execution-only basis. A firm can now deal for established advisory and discretionary customers on an execution-only basis without being subject to an obligation to warn the customer about the obvious unsuitability of the transaction. Certainly, this is the case under the rule, even if it is questionable whether such an obligation is implied at law through the fiduciary relationship which a firm has with its customer. Also, it could be argued that, if the order from the customer is clearly unsuitable, a firm should point this out if it is to comply with Principle 1 (Integrity) and Principle 2 (Skill, Care and Diligence). Principle 1 requires a firm to observe high standards of integrity and fair dealing, whilst Principle 2 requires a firm to act with due skill, care and diligence.

The concept of execution-only dealing or execution-only customer is not specifically referred to in the rules; but suitability only applies where a firm has made a personal recommendation about a specific investment or investment agreement, or effected or arranged a discretionary transaction. It is very difficult for a firm not to give any comment when it is operating an execution-only dealing service. For example, many investors, without access to screen-based information, will want some indication from a firm before placing orders as to how the market has been performing. It is suggested that, if a dealer is giving general comment on the market and likely trends, he is not changing his status from an execution-only dealer. This would only happen where his comments become more specific in nature and amount to a recommendation. In other words, he would have to be giving advice relevant to the types of investments listed in Part I, Schedule 1 to the FSA 1986. It would only be when his advice took on this specific quality that he would be caught by the suitability rule and would also need to be registered with SFA as a registered representative; where he was merely acting as a dealer, not giving specific investment advice, he would only have to be registered as a trader.

Where a firm has an established customer relationship, it will need to **9–007** keep up-to-date the information which it has about the customer's circumstances and investment objectives to ensure that it continues to give suitable advice. There is a very easy temptation for a firm to send out a financial questionnaire at the beginning of a customer relationship, receive this back completed by the customer and then file it away, without making any attempt to keep it up to date. It is important to keep the information up to date and this is backed up by a requirement in the Record Keeping Schedule (Appendix 18). This requires that in respect of all private advisory customers and all discretionary customers, a firm must maintain a record of the details which it has obtained about the customer's circumstances and investment objectives, including the date on which the information was last up-dated or checked. It is no good a firm saying that the particular account executive who deals with a customer keeps up to date as a result of telephone conversations with that customer. The firm must have some way of recording any changes in the customer's circumstances either on a computer file or a hard copy file. The obligation concerning cessation of business should not be forgotten. A firm must make arrangements to protect the interests of customers where they would be significantly affected by the death or incapacity of an individual within a firm (Rule 2–21(2)). A firm would be in breach of this requirement if the information about a customer was only stored in the mind of one particular account executive. If something happened to him, how could the firm continue to service the customer properly in accordance with the suitability requirement?

In recording information about a customer's investment objectives, a firm needs to be fairly precise. It is no good only requiring a customer to sign boxes to show that he wants low, medium or high risk. If a customer has ticked to show that he wants low risk, it is unclear whether he is indicating that he wants his portfolio as a whole managed on a low risk basis, even if some of the individual investments held within it are medium or high risk investments; or whether he is intending that every single investment transaction or decision should be carried out on a low risk basis. Therefore, where firms require customers to indicate the level of risk which they are prepared to accept, they should make it clear that this is in relation to the overall management of the portfolio or in respect of particular percentages of the total assets held in the portfolio.

Investment manager

9–008   SFA has extended the suitability requirement where a firm acts as an investment manager. Investment manager is a Core Rule definition which is relevant in the context of the Core Rule on portfolio valuations and accounts (Rule 5–34) and those on polarisation and packaged products (Rules 5–19 to 5–22).

Investment manager is defined as a firm which either:

(i)   manages an account or portfolio in the exercise of discretion; or

(ii) has accepted responsibility on a continuing basis for advising on the composition of the account or portfolio.

Confusion arises as to the scope of the definition where a firm does not have discretion (Limb (ii) above). Many securities brokers hold themselves out as being investment managers, but would not necessarily regard themselves as having accepted responsibility on a continuing basis for advising on the composition of an account or portfolio. It is suggested that, before a firm falls within the Core Rule definition of an investment manager, there has to be a clearly identifiable body of assets belonging to the customer over which the firm has control in some way and for which it is accepted by both the firm and customer that the firm has an on-going responsibility to advise on its composition. It is easier to argue that a firm has control over the customer's assets where those assets are held in the name of a nominee company controlled by the firm or an associate, or in a safe custody account held or arranged by the firm even if registered in the customer's name. If the firm does not have this form of direct control over the assets, it will be more difficult to assume that it has accepted responsibility on an ongoing basis for advising on the composition of the account or portfolio. For instance, it will have no control over whether or not the customer deals in respect of some of his assets through other dealers.

Even if the firm has control for safe custody purposes, this does not necessarily signify that it has accepted responsibility on a continuing basis to advise on its composition. A firm will not have accepted this responsibility merely because it occasionally telephones a customer with investment suggestions. For many firms, with customers who do not have large sized investments, it would not be economic for either the firm or the customer to offer this ongoing advisory responsibility. However, the regular provision of a valuation statement may suggest that a firm has accepted the responsibility of investment manager.

The easiest way of dealing with any uncertainty caused by this **9–009** second limb to the definition of investment manager is for a firm to write to its advisory customers informing them that, although it will be prepared to give advice at the customer's request or sometimes on the firm's own initiative, and even provide occasional valuations, the firm is not accepting responsibility to keep the customer's portfolio under regular review and advise on a continuous basis on its composition.

Of course, it is accepted that firms may not find it acceptable to write directly to customers saying that they will not act as an investment manager. One way around the problem is to write to the customer saying that the firm is acting as their investment adviser, but does not have management responsibility. Another way of dealing with trying to distinguish whether a customer is a simple advisory one, or an investment management advisory one, is for a firm to draw up a list setting out the criteria it will use in analysing whether customers are to be treated as pure advisory or investment management advisory customers. If the firm then follows these criteria, it will be hard to argue that a customer, which has been classified by the firm as falling on one side of the divide, should really be classified as falling on the other side.

The danger with cutting down too much the scope of investment manager for the suitability and valuation rules is that the carve-out to polarisation is reduced. The provisions on polarisation, and the strict requirements on advising about in-house or other group products where a firm is not polarised, do not apply where a firm is acting as a customer's investment manager (see Chapter 14 below).

Where a firm is acting within the definition of investment manager, **9–010** then, under SFA's third tier extension to the Core Rule on suitability, it has a responsibility to ensure that all discretionary portfolios for any customer and all advisory portfolios for private customers remain suitable in terms of the customer's circumstances and investment objectives. In other words, a firm is under an obligation to keep the customer's account or portfolio under continuous review in terms of its suitability wherever it is acting as an investment manager, unless the investment management services are advisory (rather than discretionary) for non-private customers.

It seems right that, where a firm has accepted an ongoing responsibility to advise on a customer's portfolio (Limb (ii) of the investment manager definition), it should be under an obligation to keep the portfolio under regular review as to its continuing suitability. The two requirements go hand in hand. Therefore, it could be argued that, if a firm has not accepted a responsibility for keeping a customer's portfolio under regular review as to suitability, it is not an investment manager.

The extent to which a firm has to keep a portfolio under review as to its continuing suitability will depend upon the nature of the portfolio, including its size and make-up. For example, if it is a small portfolio, containing blue-chip stocks, it does not require such active management as a larger portfolio containing much more volatile investments. In the case of the first portfolio, it is not in the customer's interest to have more active management due to the fees involved in such management and the fact that frequent changes in the investments in the portfolio will reduce long-term profits because of the transaction costs.

Pooled funds

9–011   Where a firm has pooled, with his agreement, a customer's funds with those of other customers with a view to taking common management decisions, then the firm complies with the suitability requirement by taking reasonable steps to ensure that any transactions are suitable for the fund, having regard to the stated investment objectives of the fund. This modification of the suitability requirement applies whatever the arrangement for pooling is, whether it is a regulated or unregulated collective investment scheme. Of course, if it is a regulated collective investment scheme, then the trustees will be under a duty to ensure that the managers of the scheme operate it properly in accordance with the scheme's stated investment objectives.

This modification only operates where the customer's funds are pooled with those of others. It does not apply merely because common management decisions are made in respect of a number of separate discretionary customer accounts. In this case, the decision must be suitable in respect of each of the individual accounts.

Churning

9–012   Suitability looks at the particular recommendation or transaction; although, in respect of an investment manager, SFA has imposed a requirement to keep the portfolio or account under regular review. A firm which churns a customer's account is not necessarily in breach of the suitability rule, unless it is caught by the extension for investment managers, because the individual recommendations and transactions by themselves may be suitable. Therefore, there is a separate provision stating that a firm must not make personal recommendations to private customers, or deal or arrange deals in the exercise of discretion for any customer, if the dealing would reasonably be regarded as too frequent in the circumstances (Rule 5–43). Obviously, the reason for churning accounts is to generate further commissions.

What amounts to dealing which will be regarded as too frequent? An earlier draft of the Core Rule had the criteria judged by the reasonable investment manager or adviser. Would he regard the dealing as too frequent, and, therefore, contrary to the interests of the investor? Although the specific reference to such a person has been dropped, in trying to prove a breach of this rule SFA is likely to call such a person to give evidence as to his view on the course of dealing in question.

Switching

The rule then has a second provision which deals with switching within a packaged product or between packaged products. A packaged product is defined as a life policy, a unit in a regulated collective investment scheme or an investment trust saving scheme. This provision is designed to prevent salesmen increasing their commissions by encouraging investors to surrender unnecessarily one policy or unit trust holding in return for taking out another. This is particularly important in respect of life policies because of the penalties incurred on early surrender and the fact that, in the early years of a new policy, a large element of the premiums paid are taken up in initial costs, including the commissions paid to the salesmen, rather than in investment for the long-term growth of the policy. The rule deals with switching within packaged products as well as from one product to another. Sometimes, surrender fees and commission are paid where an investor switches from one fund to another under the umbrella of the same life policy. This rule will also be relevant in terms of the management of broker funds (see paragraphs 14–019 *et seq.* below).

Charges

The rule on charging (Rule 5–33) only applies to private customers. **9–013** Therefore, unlike suitability, it does not apply to discretionary business for non-private customers. Although the rule only applies to private customers, a firm may need to consider prior disclosure of charges in connection with non-private customers if it has a fiduciary relationship with them, because otherwise it may fall foul of the non-profit obligation. Also, a non-disclosable commission is a material interest which is subject to Rule 5–29. This is because the definition of material interest specifically excludes disclosable commissions under the regulatory system, suggesting that a commission which is not required to be disclosed under the rules is a material interest.

A firm must not charge unreasonably in the circumstances. Charges are defined as including any charge made in connection with investment services, including, where a firm is dealing as a principal, any mark-up or mark-down from the price at which best execution would be achieved. In other words, it does not relate to the whole of a mark-up or principal's turn, but only to that element which, in respect of a sale, is above the best execution price, or, in respect of a purchase, is below the best execution price. Investment services are defined as activities undertaken in the course of carrying on investment business.

It is an interesting question as to what amounts to unreasonable in the circumstances. For example, some firms charge a comparatively high minimum commission charge in order to discourage too many orders from investors in small amounts. To date, regulators have not taken action against such firms for unreasonable charging.

In respect of most firms which charge high minimum commissions, at least their charges will be public and properly disclosed to the customer. The concern arises in respect of hidden charges, such as excessive mark-ups or high charges imposed for non-dealing services. Some firms impose a substantial "compliance charge" on top of their published commission charge: the firm arguing that the "compliance charge" covers the costs involved in complying with the FSA 1986 regulatory requirements. There is nothing wrong with a firm breaking down its charges on a contract note to show separately a commission charge and a compliance charge, as long as the total charges are not unreasonable and unjustifiable. Any charge above the normal dealing fee should represent a true cost or added value.

9–014   The unreasonable charging provision is supported by the disclosure requirement. A firm has to disclose to a private customer the basis or amount of its charges for the provision of its investment services; and also the nature or amount of any other remuneration receivable by the firm (or, to its knowledge, by its associate) and which is attributable to the investment services being provided. The disclosure must be made prior to the service. It can, however, be made orally, rather than in writing. This, therefore, enables a firm to charge for a particular transaction or service a rate higher than that in its published rate card, as long as the customer is alerted to the higher charge before the particular service is provided. Prior disclosure leaves the customer free to decide whether or not he wishes the firm to provide the service at that charging rate.

The rule does not require the actual charges to be shown. A firm can show merely the basis on which it will levy charges: for example, showing commission in terms of varying percentages based on the size or value of the transaction. Note that all charges must be disclosed, not merely transaction commission charges. If a firm wants to charge for valuations, written advice, research, telephone calls and copying, it must have properly disclosed the rate on which its charges will be based before providing the relevant service.

As already explained, mark-up for the purpose of the rules is not the true mark-up or principal's turn, but rather the difference between the transaction price for the investor and the best execution price. Where a firm has fiduciary obligations, it is required to account for the full amount of its profit, namely the full difference between the price at which the firm purchased the stock and that at which it sells it on to the customer, unless it has the customer's consent to receive that profit. It is debatable as to whether or not the type of disclosure required by this rule is sufficient for the firm to assume, in respect of the general law, that it has the customer's consent to keep the profit.

The rule requires a firm also to disclose beforehand the nature or amount of any other remuneration receivable by it or, to its knowledge, by its associate. This does not require a disclosure of the actual remuneration received or receivable: only a statement of the general nature of this other remuneration, not even the basis. In other words, a statement that a firm will be receiving other remuneration, besides the fee charged to the customer, is sufficient. **9–015**

This disclosure stems from a firm's fiduciary obligations. A firm which is a fiduciary cannot make a secret profit. Does a general disclosure, however, in a customer agreement that a firm may, in respect of some transactions, receive commissions from other parties amount to sufficient disclosure for the purposes of the general law? (See paragraphs 15–007 *et seq.* below.) Hopefully, the Law Commission, which is currently reviewing the relationship between regulatory rules and fiduciary duties, will be able to clarify this dilemma a little better after considering the responses to its consultative paper issued in 1992. Also, the nature or amount of the remuneration received by the firm will be relevant in determining whether or not there has been a breach of the rule on inducements (Rule 5–7), which is discussed in paragraphs 15–021 and 15–022 below.

The remuneration which a firm needs to disclose would be where it is acting as an agent and obtains a rebate on the commission charged or profit made by the dealer through whom the order is placed. Likewise, a firm should disclose that it is receiving remuneration because of introducing a customer to another firm who will provide a service direct to the customer.

SFA has provided a specific exemption from the requirement to give prior disclosure of other remuneration received by a firm where that remuneration amounts to commission received in respect of a simultaneous matching transaction or agency cross. Such a transaction is where a firm matches the sale order of one customer with the purchase order of another customer and, in effect, arranges just one transaction, but charges two commissions. In other words, the firm charges its normal commission to each customer, but, because it has **9–016** been able to cross both of their orders, it only needs to effect one transaction. The details of the commission earned on the other side of the cross, however, must be given on the contract note after the transaction has been executed (see paragraph 10–005 below).

Note that the prior disclosure requirement also extends to any remuneration receivable, to the firm's knowledge, by an associate. Where one firm puts the deal through another group company, then any remuneration receivable by the other company from the transaction should be disclosed; at least the nature of that remuneration.

The disclosure of commissions in respect of the sale of packaged products is something which consumer bodies and the Government have been concerned about for some time and it has been the subject of inquiry as part of the Retail Review being carried on by SIB. It is in this area where those providing the services are more likely to be disclosing only the basis or nature, rather than the actual amount, of the charges or remuneration received. In its Consultative Paper 60, dates March 1992, SIB, however, has not proposed any changes to the existing regime for commission dislosure in respect of packaged products.

[1] See the proposed rule amendments in SIB's Consultative Paper 60, dated March 1992, discussed in paragraph 14–007 below.

[2] However, brokers' newsletters and research would be investment advertisements subject to the advertising rules (see Chapter 12 below).

[3] Where the firm's recommendation is not accepted by the customer, the firm should then treat the customer's order as execution-only. To protect itself, the firm should record on the order or dealing slip that its advice was rejected.

Chapter 10

Confirmations and Valuations

Confirmations

The Core Rule on confirmations (Rule 5–34(1)) requires a firm which **10–001** effects a sale or purchase of an investment with or for a customer to ensure that he is sent with due despatch a note containing the essential details of the transaction.

The use of "effects" and the reference to "with or for" a customer makes it clear that the provision applies equally where a firm is arranging a deal as agent, as well as where it is dealing as a principal. It also covers the situation where the firm does not necessarily have a direct customer relationship (such as a market maker), but is executing a transaction for a customer. However, it is not necessary that the two firms which could be involved in the arrangement and execution of a transaction (namely the agency broker and the market maker) both have to send confirmations, because of the provision in Rule 5–2(3) that there is no need for a firm to send a communication itself where it believes on reasonable grounds that this has been or will be supplied direct by another person.

The confirmation note is required for the sale or purchase of any investment, other than a life policy. However, SFA has provided exceptions. A confirmation note is not required in respect of transactions in a personal equity plan (PEP), if the firm or its associate is the plan manager, as long as the customer is sent a regular valuation in accordance with the valuation rules (see paragraphs 10–012 *et seq.* below). It is also not required for non-private customers who have stated, whether orally or in writing, that they do not want one in the following cases:

    (i)   currency, interest rate, equity or commodity swaps;

    (ii) asset trading;

    (iii) stock lending or borrowing transactions; and

    (iv) repurchase or reverse repurchase agreements.

Under the old rules, the confirmation note had to be sent out by the end of the following day after the transaction. Under the new rules, it has to be sent out with "due despatch". It is suggested that a firm complies with the due despatch requirement by sending out a confirmation note at the latest on the day following the transaction, unless it delays for genuine reasons such as awaiting confirmation from a sub-agent which it has used to execute the transaction on an oversea market. However, due to the instant communication methods now available to firms, it should only be in rare cases where a firm is not able to receive confirmation from the sub-agent promptly and send out the necessary confirmation note within a day of the transaction.

10–002   In fact, there is a specific provision (Rule 5–34(7)) to deal with the position where a firm does not have all the information necessary at the time when it is preparing the note. A firm is not required to state those details which are dependent upon information provided by other persons if the information is not available to the firm at the time when the note is prepared, provided the fact that the information is not available is stated to the customer and a supplementary note containing the missing information is sent with due despatch once the details become known to the firm.

The rule on confirmation notes only applies to customers, rather than market counterparties. There is no exception for non-private customers, even with their consent. However, the details which are required may be provided electronically, rather than on a hard copy. Where a firm provides the information electronically, it should be aware of the record keeping requirement (Appendix 18) that firms must keep copy confirmation notes for three years from the date on which they are sent. The record can be maintained on a computer, provided the details originally contained on the note can be produced in hard printed form in English promptly if required by SFA.

Notes may only be retained by a firm for overseas customers. The customer's oral or written consent is required. Retention must be by the Compliance Officer or an employee designated by him who is not personally involved in handling the customer's account.

10–003   An oil market participant does not have to comply with the detailed contents requirements for contract and confirmation notes in respect of a transaction which he enters into as a result of carrying on an oil market investment activity, but he will have to comply with the Core Rule requirement: namely, provide a note confirming the essential details of the transaction.

The Core Rule requires the confirmation note to contain the essential details of the transaction. SFA has spelt out what these details are with respect to the different types of transactions. For example, there is a list of requirements for confirmation notes with respect to transactions in securities. Such notes are commonly referred to as contract notes. A security is any share, debenture, government or public security, warrant, depositary or other certificate representing securities, or unit in a collective investment scheme. It is defined by reference to the headings to the first six paragraphs in Part I, Schedule 1 to the FSA 1986. Therefore, "debenture" includes any form of loan stock, bond, or other instrument creating or acknowledging indebtedness (unless included within the definition of government and public securities).

Contract notes

On a contract note, a firm must give its name and make it clear that **10–004** it is a member of SFA. Confirmations are only required in respect of regulated business. Therefore, if a firm is issuing a contract note which is outside the scope of the rules because of the foreign business carve-out, it should make sure that it does not include a reference to its membership of SFA; otherwise it may fall into the trap of having to give the prescribed disclosure (Rule 5–14). This is required where a firm makes a communication to a private customer outside the United Kingdom in connection with investment business which is not regulated business and indicates that it is an FSA 1986 authorised person.

The customer's name does not have to be stated, as long as there is some identifiable reference to him, such as his account number. The date of the transaction must be given, but not necessarily the time, as long as there is a statement to the effect that the customer will be notified of the time on request.

The note must show the security concerned and the amount bought or sold. Also it must make it clear whether the transaction was a sale or purchase.

The unit price at which the transaction was executed must be shown, together with the total consideration due from or to the customer, which will include any commission or mark-up. If the firm has had to carry out a number of transactions to execute one order and it has decided to show an averaged unit price, the note must make it clear that it is an averaged price. The settlement date is required. This will be the usual settlement date in the relevant market, unless special settlement terms have been agreed between the parties.

The note must show the firm's actual charges to the customer in connection with the particular transaction; in other words, any commission, charge, or mark-up or mark-down upon the best execution price. If there is no transaction charge and the firm is remunerated by a periodic management fee, no charge needs to be shown on the contract note.

It is the firm's own charges which have to be stated, rather than charges raised by other persons involved in the execution chain. However, such charges would have to be included if they are not levied by the other person directly against the customer, but are to be paid by the firm out of its charges.

There is an exception to the requirement to identify separately a **10–005** firm's charges. Where a non-private customer so requests (whether orally or in writing), a firm may provide a note showing a "net price": in other words, a single price combining both the transaction price and any charges, such as commission or mark-up.

The note must also identify the amount or basis of any remuneration which the firm has or will receive from another person in connection with the transaction. As with the rule on prior disclosure of charges (Rule 5–33(2)), it is not the actual amount of the charges which has to be shown; but that rule mentioned disclosing the nature of the other remuneration received, whilst this requires at least the basis of payment to be recorded. Other remuneration receivable by the firm may be commission rebates or shares of charges imposed by any other firm involved in the execution chain. It will also include any commission which the firm charges another party in respect of an agency cross. Notice that the receipt of double commissions on a simultaneous matching transaction has to be shown on the contract note, even though prior disclosure before dealing is not required (Rule 5–33(3)).

If the firm is sharing any of its charges levied on the customer with another person, it must show the amount or basis of the shared charges; unless the charges are only being shared or reallocated amongst associates, such as other group companies which may be dealing on the firm's behalf.

Instead of stating the amount or basis of other remuneration received by the firm, or of charges shared with non-associates, the contract note can merely contain a statement that such information will be made available to the customer on request. Alternatively, the firm may make a general written disclosure to this effect. The disclosure should be made before dealing and could be in a customer agreement. A suitable model clause is included in SFA's guidance for customer documentation (Appendix 7 below).

10–006 If the transaction involves the purchase of a unit in a collective investment scheme, then the contract note must show the amount of any front-end loading. This is defined as deductions for charges and expenses which are not made uniformly throughout the life of the investment, but are loaded disproportionately onto the early years; and, therefore, in respect of a unit trust, include the manager's initial charges, rather than the annual management fee which will be disclosed anyway in the product particulars.

Where the firm executes the transaction as a principal, it must state this fact. Likewise, it must also state if the transaction has been executed with or through an associate. These disclosures, like the ones already described on receipt of remuneration and the sharing of commission, are relevant in respect of a firm's fiduciary obligations to its customer. The problem is that the rules only require the disclosures to be made after the event and only require fairly general disclosures. See the further discussion in paragraphs 15–007 *et seq.* below.

A firm must state on the contract note, where it is relevant, that any dividend, bonus or other right which as been declared in respect of the security, but which has not yet been paid, allotted or otherwise become effective, will not pass to the purchaser under the transaction. In other words, the contract note should make it clear that the security has been purchased "ex-dividend" if it is bought during the period after which the dividend has been declared, but not yet paid.

Some firms have system difficulties in providing this information. If this is the case, there is a qualification in the Transitional Rules that, until further notice, a firm does not have to give this information: but only where the relevant declaration is made on the day of execution or the preceding business day. This transitional provision will be removed in due course because SFA feels that it is important that this information should be supplied to all customers.

Where any interest which has accrued on the security is accounted for separately from the transaction price (which may be the case in respect of transactions in bonds), the amount of the interest which the purchaser will subsequently receive, or the number of days interest for which he will be credited, must be stated on the contract note.

The firm must separately identify any cost, including transaction taxes, which are incidental to the transaction and which will not be paid by the firm out of its own charges. This would include any stamp duty liability, withholding tax or levy such as the Panel on Takeovers and Mergers Levy. However, a firm is only expected to record those costs and taxes which are standard and which it knows will be deducted. It is not required to record any private tax obligations which the customer may have as a result of the transaction.

Finally, the contract must record details of any foreign currency **10–007** exchange which is involved in the transaction. In other words, if a foreign security has been bought in a foreign market, the details of the relevant exchange rate, or a statement that the rate will be supplied when the currency has been purchased, must be given on the contract note. As a number of firms generate separate foreign exchange confirmations, the rule states that this information does not have to be included on the contract note where it is set out on a separate statement provided to the customer. However, this separate statement would have to be sent with due despatch after the relevant currency transaction.

Confirmation notes

There is a separate contents table for confirmation notes relating to **10–008** purchases or sales involving derivatives (options, futures and contracts for difference). The table is similar to that for contract notes, except that, where the firm is stating the unit price for an option contract, it must also include a reference to the last exercise date and the strike price of the option. Instead of the requirement to state the settlement date, the firm must give the maturity, delivery or expiry date of the derivative.

Because the derivatives markets work on a principal-to-principal, back-to-back basis, there is no need for a firm to state that it has dealt as principal. Likewise, the question of stating front-end loading charges is irrelevant: any pooled fund involving futures and options transactions would be a collective investment scheme, with purchases and sales of units in the fund being subject to the contents requirements for securities contract notes. Similarly, the provisions on stating that the security is ex-dividend and the provisions on accrued interest do not apply to confirmation notes.

Difference accounts

10–009   Where a firm enters into a futures transaction which closes out an open position, then the firm must produce a difference account. This must set out all the details required under the confirmation notes contents schedule in respect of each contract comprised in the open position and of each contract by which it is closed out. The difference account note should also show the profit or loss to the customer arising out of the closing out of his position. It should be noted that a difference account is only required where there is an actual closing out; and not where two opposing contracts are kept open until maturity.

Exercise notices

10–010   Where an option is exercised by or against a customer, the firm must provide an exercise notice. This must include the usual details about the firm's identity, customer's identity, the firm's charges and any costs, including transaction taxes incidental to the exercise and which will not be paid out of the firm's charges. The notice must also state the date of exercise, and either the time of exercise or include a statement that the customer will be notified of the time on request. It must show the option concerned, the size involved and whether the exercise creates a sale or purchase in the underlying asset. The strike price of the option must be given and, where applicable, the total consideration due from or to the customer. If the exercise involves the purchase of one currency with another, the rate of exchange involved must be shown, or a statement given that the rate will be supplied once the currency has been purchased. As with contract and confirmation notes, this information may be provided on a separate statement. Note that for a currency option, the rate of exchange will be the same as the strike price.

Averaging

10–011   Sometimes, a firm needs to execute a series of transactions to achieve one investment decision or objective, or to meet orders from customers which it has aggregated. If it has to do so, then it may delay sending out the contract or confirmation note for 24 hours in the case of private customers or five business days in the case of non-private customers. When it sends out the note, it may show a weighted average price in respect of all of the transactions carried out in the relevant 24-hour or five-day period. The note must be sent out with due despatch, in the case of private customers, after the end of each 24-hour period and, in the case of non-private customers, at the end of each five-day period, even if the firm has to make further transactions to satisfy the investment objective, decision or customer's order.

Although the firm may show a weighted average price on the contract or confirmation note, it must treat each of the underlying transactions as a separate transaction for the purposes of complying with the record keeping requirement (Appendix 18). In other words, the firm's records must give the details of each of the transactions involved and the times and prices at which they were executed. As regards trade reporting, the firm must make a separate report for each customer, but may report in the same way as the contract note, showing the underlying transactions for each customer in the relevant period as a single transaction at the weighted average price.

Valuations

The valuation requirement follows the definition of investment manager **10–012** already described in respect of the suitability requirement (see paragraphs 9–008 *et seq.* above). The Core Rule (Rule 5–35(1)) states that a firm which acts as an investment manager for a customer must ensure that he is sent at suitable intervals a report stating the value of the portfolio or account at the beginning and end of the period and its composition at the end. It then goes on to say that, in the case of a discretionary portfolio or account, it must also show charges in its composition between the beginning and end of the relevant period.

This rule applies to all customers for whom the firm acts as an investment manager, not merely private customers. Also, unlike the old rules, it extends beyond discretionary customers to customers for whom a firm has accepted an ongoing responsibility to advise on the composition of their portfolio or account.

SFA has provided two important qualifications to the Core Rule obligation. First, a firm does not need to state the opening value of the portfolio or account at the beginning of the valuation period. Most firms provide this in practice, but a strong argument was made to SFA that some firms' systems (especially those relying on computer bureaux) cannot easily provide this information and that the cost of the necessary systems' developments would be too much in relation to the corresponding benefit to customers, who already have the opening value in the sense that it was the closing value on the last valuation.

Secondly, a firm does not have to send a valuation report to a non-private customer where it is acting as an investment manager in relation to securities on a non-discretionary basis: in other words, it is only acting as an ongoing advisory manager. However, a valuation is required for a derivatives account managed for a non-private customer on an ongoing advisory basis.

The basic rules are that valuation reports must be sent at intervals which are not less frequent than six-monthly in respect of securities or securities related cash balances, and at intervals which are not less frequent than monthly in respect of any derivatives or derivatives related cash balances.[1]

The monthly requirement for derivatives also extends to any pooled account or unregulated collective investment scheme in which the customer has an interest where that account or scheme invests in derivatives. The firm may send to the customer either a valuation of the whole of the pooled account or scheme, which also records the customer's holding in percentage terms, or a separate valuation based upon the value of the customer's individual holding in the account or scheme.

10–013   To sum up, valuations are required:

    (i)   in respect of securities, at six-monthly intervals to all discretionary customers (whether private or non-private), and to all private customers where the firm has accepted an ongoing responsibility to advise on the composition of the portfolio;

    (ii)   in respect of derivatives, monthly to all investment management customers, whether private or non-private, and whether discretionary or ongoing advisory.

The frequency at which valuation statements must be prepared, namely six-monthly for securities and monthly for derivatives, may be extended where the customer has informed the firm in writing that he wishes to receive them at longer intervals. This would be appropriate where the customer has a small, fairly inactive portfolio and does not want to be subject to the costs of having his valuation as frequently as the rules require.

The valuation report must be sent promptly following the end of each valuation period. This test has replaced the old requirement which said that the statement had to be sent out within 25 business days from the end of the valuation period. Obviously, especially where the statements are quite complicated, firms need a little time to prepare them following the end of the relevant period. Therefore, it is suggested that firms should be regarded as acting promptly if they send out the statements within one month of the end of the period: at least, in respect of securities. Firms should aim for a shorter period for derivatives accounts as valuations are required monthly: the longer the time lag, the less useful the valuation because of the greater volatility of such markets.

As with contract notes, a firm may retain valuations for customers not ordinarily resident in the United Kingdom, provided the customer has given his prior consent. They can only be retained by the firm's Compliance Officer or an employee designated by him who is not personally involved in handling the customer's portfolio or account. Of course, the customer's consent does not have to be in writing, because, as explained in paragraph 6–003 with respect to the exception for customer agreements, some overseas customers are not prepared to enter into written documentation. However, the firm would need to have a record available for inspection which confirms this arrangement with the customer.

Advisory—securities

Valuations for investment management ongoing advisory private **10–014** customers in securities only have to show the composition of the portfolio at the valuation date (namely, the end of the valuation period) and its overall value. (Remember, there is no requirement to send any valuation to ongoing advisory non-private customers in securities.) Ideally, firms will show a value for each individual holding. The valuation basis should be shown (namely, mid-market or bid prices), unless this has previously been stated to the customer: for example, in a customer agreement. Note that management charges and cash balances do not have to be shown, but prior disclosure of a firm's charges is required for all private customers (Rule 5–33(2)).

Detailed contents requirements

In respect of the other type of managed portfolios and accounts, **10–015** namely ongoing advisory customers in derivatives and all discretionary customers (whether in securities or derivatives), SFA has provided detailed contents requirements. There are two separate contents tables. One for discretionary portfolios containing securities and the other for any managed accounts holding derivatives (whether discretionary or ongoing advisory). The reason for the different use of the terms "portfolio" and "account" is not significant. It stems from the fact that securities brokers normally talk about portfolios whereas futures brokers often refer to accounts: but, in practice, they mean the same.

It should be noted that, for the purpose of the valuation requirements, warrants are not treated in the same way as derivatives (options, futures and contracts for difference). (In this connection, the writer is only referring to warrants within paragraph 4, Schedule 1, rather than to instruments which are in reality options although they have warrant in their name.) Warrants are put on a par with derivatives as regards the understanding of risk requirement (Rule 5–30) and the rule on direct offer advertisements (Rule 5–10); but, with respect to portfolio valuations, they are treated as securities.

Discretionary—securities

10–016   In respect of discretionary securities portfolios, the valuation statement must include the number, description and value of each security held in the portfolio at the end of the valuation period, together with the amount of cash balances standing at this date to the credit or debit of the customer in respect of the portfolio, and the aggregate amount of the portfolio's value. No guidance is given as to the basis of valuation which should be used, but firms should either show bid prices or mid-market values. In fact, the statement must show the basis on which each security has been valued, and, if relevant, a statement that the basis for valuing a specified security has changed since the previous statement. However, the basis for valuation does not have to be stated if it was included as part of the terms of the two-way customer agreement. There is a requirement under the contents table for two-way customer agreements that a firm must state the valuation dates to which valuations will be prepared: in other words, a statement that they will be prepared monthly or six-monthly following a specified date.

As regards the requirement to state closing cash balances, this information may be shown on a separate statement. This should help firms which regularly prepare for their customers separate cash flow statements. However, if these are prepared on different dates to the valuation statements, the firm must record the current cash balance at the valuation date on the valuation statement.

To comply with the Core Rule obligation, a firm must give particulars of each transaction entered into for the portfolio during the valuation period.[2] SFA also requires particulars of each payment made to the customer and each amount received from the customer dur-ing this period, including, in respect of any currency transactions involved, the descriptions and amounts of such currencies and the relevant rates of exchange. Where full details of payments made to or received from the customer have already been set out in earlier contract notes or cash statements, then the valuation only has to include the aggregate amount of these payments and receipts. Any firm which cannot comply with this requirement will need to apply for a waiver on the basis that the costs of implementing the necessary systems change to provide the information substantially outweighs any corresponding investor benefit.

10–017   The valuation statement should also show the aggregate of any securities or money transferred by the customer, or on his instructions, into or out of the portfolio during the period. In other words, it should record any securities or cash which the customer has handed over to the firm during the valuation period for inclusion in his discretionary managed portfolio.

The aggregate of interest payments, dividends, and other benefits received into the portfolio during the period should be stated, unless these have been disclosed previously upon separate statements, such as earlier contract notes. A firm only has to record the actual dividends and interest payments received into the portfolio. It does not have to account for dividends and interest payments made direct to the customer which do not pass through the firm's hands. Also, no calculation has to be made for interest accrued on a gilt or bond; it is only when the interest is paid that it has to be included.

To give the customer a complete picture, SFA thinks that the valuation statement should include the aggregate of charges and taxes (as known by the firm) deducted in respect of any purchases, sales or management of the securities within the portfolio. However, there is an important qualification here. This information does not have to be disclosed separately on the valuation statement if it has already been given, whether in aggregated or unaggregated form, in earlier contract notes or statements, provided that there is a reference on the valuation statement to where this information has previously been set out. In other words, the firm could state merely that its charges are any management fee set out at the bottom of the statement, plus commission charged in respect of individual transactions as already notified on earlier contract notes.

The valuation should also show any remuneration received by the firm from a third party (except where it relates to an agency cross or other simultaneous matching transaction). But again, SFA enables a firm merely to make a reference to the fact that the basis or amount of this remuneration has been separately disclosed in writing to the customer, such as in a general statement in his two-way customer agreement.

Finally, the valuation must include the particulars of any securities which, at the end of the valuation period, are the subject of a loan to a third party arranged by the firm, or which have been charged by the firm to secure borrowings made on behalf of the portfolio. The aggregate of any interest payments paid out during the valuation period in respect of such loans or borrowings must also be given. It is important to note that this requirement only relates to loans and charges over the customer's securities which have been arranged by the firm. The firm is not responsible for recording details of any loans or borrowings, including securities subject to a charge, arranged by the customer without the involvement of the firm.

Derivatives accounts

The table of contents requirements for derivatives valuations apply to **10–018** any case in which the firm is acting as an investment manager, whether for a private or non-private customer, and whether the firm has discretion or is only an ongoing advisory manager.

The valuation for derivatives has to include each payment received or made by the firm in respect of the account during the relevant month. In respect of each transaction effected during the period to close out a customer's position, it must show the resulting profit to the customer, after deducting the relevant commission, or the resulting loss to the customer, after adding the relevant commission.

The statement must then show the aggregate of each of the following items which relate to the customer's account at the close of business on the last day of the valuation period (the valuation date):

   (i)   cash;

   (ii)   collateral value;

   (iii)   unrealised profits attributable to open positions;

   (iv)   unrealised losses attributable to open positions; and

   (v)   any management fees.

In determining unrealised profits or losses attributable to open positions at the valuation date, the firm does not have to deduct in the case of profit, or add in the case of loss, the relevant commission which would be payable if the position was closed out. Management fees refer to the ongoing fee levied by the firm, and do not include commissions which have been separately shown on earlier confirmation notes. On the other hand, firms are encouraged, as a matter of good practice, to record for the customer the aggregate of all charges, including transaction costs, levied in connection with the general management of the account during the relevant period.

---

[1] At the time of writing it had been proposed within SFA that only six-monthly (rather than monthly) statements should be required where the derivatives are merely open option contracts held to hedge positions in securities within the portfolio.

[2] These details, however, do not have to be included on the six-monthly valuation if they have previously been included on monthly transaction statements or statements set out at the end of each London Stock Exchange account.

Chapter 11

Dealing

Front Running Research (Rule 5–36)

Core Rule

This Core Rule is about treating customers fairly and reflects a firm's **11–001** fiduciary obligations to its customers. It applies where a firm or its associate intends to publish to customers a recommendation, or a piece of research or analysis. Where it is intended to publish, the firm must not knowingly effect an own account transaction in the investment concerned or any related investment until the customers for whom the publication was principally intended have had, or are likely to have had, a reasonable opportunity to react to it.

Notice that the rule also applies where the research is to be published by an associate. An associate is any other group company; any appointed representative of the firm or another group company; and any person whose business or domestic relationship with the firm, another group company, or an appointed representative of either, might reasonably be expected to give rise to a community of interest which could involve a conflict of interest in dealings with third parties. Therefore research published by non-group companies which have such a community of interest with the firm will be caught. This might be where two firms are retained as joint advisers to a customer and one of the firms intends to publish on a matter which is relevant to the project.

The rule applies where there is an intention to publish. The old TSA rule was limited to an intention to publish within the next five business days, but there is no such limitation in the new rule. Neither is there any guidance as to how specific the intention must be, which is a problem because some research projects are in a gestation period for a long time.

The rule does not just apply to recommendations, but also to pieces of research or analysis. Again, this is wider than the old rule which was limited to research recommendations.

SFA understands that the use of the word "publish" means that the rule is limited to written recommendations, research or analysis. Therefore, as clarification, SFA has inserted the word "written" before "recommendation" which is intended to qualify also "piece of research or analysis".

The recommendation, research or analysis must relate to a specific **11–002** investment or investments, because the rule is limited to a firm effecting an own account transaction in the investment concerned or any related investment. A related investment is not defined, but it includes any type of investment whose price could be related in some way to that of the first investment. In other words, related investments would be shares of different classes in the same company; debentures and warrants relating to the company; depositary receipts representing securities in the company; possibly units in a collective investment scheme where the scheme had a substantial investment in the company's securities; and options and futures contracts based on the company's securities.

Unfortunately, the rule gives no guidance as to how specific the recommendation, research or analysis has to be about an investment before a firm is subject to the restriction on dealing in the investment concerned or any related investment. The reference to "research or analysis" suggests that publications which do not amount to specific recommendations about investments are caught if the substance of the research or analysis is likely to have an influence on how readers will regard any investments or related investments concerned.

The rule relates to own account transactions by the firm, irrespective of whether the transaction is the same way as the recommendation. An own account transaction is any transaction effected or arranged by the firm, in the course of carrying on investment business or associated business, for the firm's own account or for the account of an associate acting on its own account. In other words, the transaction is not being done for an unconnected customer of either the firm or its associate. Owing to the wide definition of associate, "own account order" includes orders from a firm's (or its associate's) employees and their close relatives.

11–003 The restriction is that a firm must not knowingly effect an own account transaction. The reference to "effect" covers the situation where the firm is not dealing itself, but arranging the deal through another person. Knowingly means that the restriction does not apply where the employees of the firm who make the decision to deal, who arrange the deal or who execute the deal are unaware of the intention to publish the recommendation, research or analysis. The rule on Chinese walls contains a specific provision that a firm is not to be taken to act with knowledge if none of the relevant individuals involved on behalf of the firm acts with knowledge (Rule 5–3(3)). Although this provision is contained under a rule headed "Chinese walls", it is suggested that it applies whether or not a firm has a Chinese wall arrangement if, in practice, the relevant individuals do not have the necessary knowledge: even if they are employed in positions where it is likely that they ought to have acquired the information. If the relevant employees have the knowledge, then the restriction is that they cannot deal until the customers for whom the publication was principally intended have had a reasonable opportunity to react to it. In other words, the firm does not have to wait until all the customers who have received it have had an opportunity to react, only until those for whom it was principally intended have had such an opportunity. This suggests that firms can properly prefer certain customers with respect to their research.

What amounts to a reasonable opportunity to react? It depends upon the circumstances. If the research is faxed or sent through another instant communication means to the customers for whom it was principally intended, it may be reasonable for the firm to effect an own account transaction within 30 or 60 minutes of sending the information. This would be the case even if the research was sent to other, less favoured customers by post, because the firm would only be dealing for its own account after the customers for whom the information was principally intended have had an opportunity to react to it. Note that these customers do not, in fact, have to have had the opportunity: it merely has to be likely that they had such an opportunity.

Exceptions

Many of the uncertainties in the Core Rule drafting are dispelled **11–004** because of the significant exceptions at SFA's third tier. The rule does not apply where the publication could not reasonably be expected materially to affect the price of the investment concerned or any related investment. In other words, if the firm is merely producing ordinary research and analysis or general recommendations, it does not have to be concerned about the restriction on making own account transactions unless it considers that some aspect of the publication will have a significant affect upon the relevant investments' prices.

To deal with the situation of integrated houses, a firm which is a market maker in the relevant investment is not subject to this rule where it is acting in good faith in the normal course of market making. A market maker is described as someone who holds himself out as able and willing to enter into transactions for the sale and purchase of the relevant investment, determining prices generally and continuously, rather than in respect of each particular transaction. It clearly catches registered market makers on the London Stock Exchange's Automated Quotation System (SEAQ, including SEAQ International). However, it also covers any other dealers who are willing to make continuous bid and offer prices, whether or not their quotations are shown on a screen-based information system. Trading members of floor-based investment exchanges who regularly buy and sell for their own account to maintain market liquidity, whether or not they have specific customer orders to complete, would be market makers.

The rule does not apply where the firm is dealing in order to fill an unsolicited customer's order. In other words, it is a riskless principal transaction: the firm deals as a principal in the market in order to deal the other way as a principal to satisfy the unsolicited customer's order.

The firm can also deal ahead of the publication where it believes on reasonable grounds that this is necessary to fulfil customers' orders which it is expecting to receive as a result of the publication. However, in so doing, the firm must not cause the price of the investment which is the subject of the recommendation, research or analysis to move against its customers' interest by a material amount. Note that this exception is only concerned with the movement in the price of any investment which is the subject of the recommendation, rather than any related investment.

Finally, there is an exception where the firm discloses on the face of the publication that it has effected or may effect own account transactions in the relevant investments. It is suggested that such a disclosure is necessary anyway if a firm wishes to avoid the strict consequences of its fiduciary obligations to its customers. The rule only requires a fairly general disclosure. Something more specific about the firm's own dealing may be required if the firm is to be properly protected in terms of fiduciary law. However, this requirement is tighter than the old rules which permitted a one-off disclosure about dealing ahead of research in a customer agreement, rather than being repeated on each published recommendation.

Front Running Customers' Orders (Rule 5–37)

11–005 The old rules generally prevented a firm from executing own account orders before customers' orders, even if the customers' orders were received after the firm had made the decision to deal for itself. This requirement has now been amended in the sense that the rule, which is called "customer order priority", states that a firm must deal with customer and own account orders fairly and in due turn.

Therefore the firm can deal with orders according to the priority in which they are received, whether the orders relate to deals for the firm's or an associate's own account or for unconnected customers. The use of the word "fairly" suggests that the firm must be satisfied that, by dealing with orders according to the priority in which they are received, it is treating its customers equitably. "Fairness" is judged against the dealing for both customers' and own account orders, rather than being a requirement which only applies to unconnected customers.

It is suggested that the concept of fairness overrides the requirement to deal in due turn. Therefore, fairness may require a later order to be executed first. For example, it may be appropriate to deal with a larger own account order before an earlier customer order because of the effect which the larger order will have on the market, especially if any movement in price would benefit the unconnected customer's order.

This is another one of those cases where the rules appear to modify the obligations which a firm has under fiduciary law to its customers. Therefore, firms may wish to protect themselves by having a specific clause in the customer agreement that they are free to execute orders for their own account and that of an associate before orders for the customer.

Timely Execution (Rule 5–38)

This rule states that a firm must effect or arrange the execution of a **11–006** customer's order as soon as reasonably practical in the circumstances. Obviously, what is practicable in the circumstances will depend upon the particular market and market conditions.

The rule applies where a firm has agreed or decided in its discretion to effect or arrange a current customer order. A current customer order is defined to include both an order for immediate execution and a conditional order for which the condition has been fulfilled. Therefore, if a customer places an order subject to a limit, this is a conditional order until the limit is satisfied, at which time it becomes a current order which must be executed as soon as reasonably practicable in the circumstances.

This concept of current customer order enables a firm to comply still with this rule where it operates a delayed execution service. If the customer, in placing his order, knows and accepts that it will not be executed until a particular time or that it will be executed at any time up until the close of business on a particular day, it does not become a current customer order until the relevant time is reached or just before the close of business on the specified day.

In fact, the Core Rule goes on to permit a firm to postpone the execution of an order where it believes on reasonable grounds that this is in the best interests of a customer. The firm may consider that, if the market is beginning to move upwards, it may be better to delay execution of a sale order so that a higher price may be obtained for the customer. Likewise, it may decide to delay execution so that it can aggregate the customer's order with orders expected from other customers on the basis that a keener price will be achieved for all the customers by putting through a larger-sized transaction. Even if the transaction price is not better, the firm may be benefiting the customer by being able to charge him lower transaction costs as the costs can be spread between all of the customers whose orders have been aggregated.

Best Execution (Rule 5–39)

Coverage

The best execution rule applies whenever a firm deals with a private **11–007** customer. It also applies where a firm fulfils an order from a non-private customer, unless the customer has waived the requirement.

Waived—Non-private customers

11–008   The waiver for a non-private customer may be oral or in writing. It may relate to a particular deal or apply to all business transacted with the customer.

It is suggested that, if a firm sends a one-way terms of business letter to a non-private customer in which it says that it will not provide best execution and the customer continues to deal with the firm without making any specific request for best execution, this will be sufficient for a firm to avoid its best execution obligations. This should be the case even though the warning about not providing best execution was contained in a terms of business letter sent out under the old rules. For example, TSA rules stated that best execution was not required for business customers where there was such a warning in the written terms of business sent to him. Also, TSA rules allowed a firm to avoid best execution without having anything in writing if it was clear from the terms of the customer's order or other relevant circumstances that the firm was not to owe this obligation. Other relevant circumstances were said to include the previous course of dealing between the firm and the customer, the fact that the firm was charging a commission and the services which the firm held itself out as providing. This latter TSA provision no longer applies. Best execution can only be avoided for non-private customers if there is something more specific to show that the customer has waived the requirement, such as failing to object after the receipt of a written warning.

Order

11–009   Even if there is no such waiver, best execution for a non-private customer only applies where a firm is fulfilling an order; whereas it is required for all deals with or for a private customer. The restriction to "order" suggests a less extensive requirement for non-private customers. However, as the definition of order is very wide, in practice there may be no real difference between "executing orders" and generally "dealing" (although see the comment in paragraph 11–016 below).

"Order" includes an order from a customer to effect a transaction as agent; and a decision by a firm in the exercise of discretion for a discretionary customer. It also includes any other order from the customer to effect a transaction in circumstances giving rise to similar duties to those arising on an order to effect a transaction as agent. This latter provision was included to deal with the newer types of options and futures markets on which members deal with each other as principals, even though their transactions may be riskless in the sense that, for example, a firm is dealing so that it can sell the contract on as principal to a customer from whom it has received a purchase order. In other words, the definition of order applies to situations where a firm is acting as a fiduciary and, as explained in paragraph 15–001 below, a firm may owe fiduciary obligations to non-private customers, as well as to private customers.

It is not easy to know in practice, however, whether the circumstances give rise to similar duties as those arising on an order to effect a transaction as agent. It is because of this uncertainty that it was important for SFA to negotiate the qualification to the Core Rule obligation described above, so that best execution does not have to be provided to non-private customers who waive the requirement.

Fiduciary law

Owing to the fact that a firm may owe fiduciary obligations to a customer even where it is dealing with him as a principal rather than as an agent, it is important for a firm which wishes to protect itself sufficiently under fiduciary law where it is not giving best execution to make a sufficiently detailed and explicit disclosure so that it will be regarded as having obtained the customer's informed consent. The disclosure in terms of fiduciary law may have to be more stringent than that required by the rule. **11–010**

Sub-agent

Where the firm is acting as an agent, then it may rely upon another person who executes the transaction to provide best execution, provided the firm believes on reasonable grounds that this person will do so. Where a sub-agent is used the Core Rule definition of indirect customer may be relevant. Where a firm is acting as an agent and identifies its principal, then its principal is owed customer obligations by the other firm with which the agent deals, unless there is an agreement in writing between the agent and the firm which cancels out these obligations in respect of the indirect customer (Rule 5–6 and see paragraphs 5–041 *et seq.* above). Also, remember the provision in the extension to the definition of market counterparty. A firm should not allow itself to be treated as a market counterparty under SFA's extension if it has private customers unless it believes that it can properly protect its own customers in terms of the rules (Rule 5–4(4) and see paragraphs 5–018 and 5–019 above). **11–011**

Best execution and best price

What is best execution? Basically, it is a best price obligation. A firm provides best execution if it takes reasonable care to ascertain the price which is the best available in the relevant market and then deals for the customer at a price which is no less advantageous to him. In other words, the firm can deal with the customer as a principal as long as it is not dealing at a price which is less advantageous than that which it could have arranged in the market as an agent. Also, the firm is not **11–012** restricted to dealing with a customer on exchange, even if the transaction is one which is normally executed on exchange. All the firm is required to do is to deal at a price which is not worse than the best price which it has determined is available in the relevant market at the time of dealing. This is lighter than the London Stock Exchange former rule that a broker could only deal as principal with a customer at a better price than that which he could have obtained as agent.

Relevant market

11–013   What is the relevant market? The test in the TSA rule was limited to the "appropriate market". This was defined as meaning the investment exchange or market on which it was reasonable for the firm to execute the transaction, or, if there was more than one, that which was selected by the firm. It is suggested that a similar test should be applied to defining "relevant market". In other words, a firm does not have to survey the price available in all possible markets in which the particular transaction may be executed. It only has to survey that which is the normal one in which the firm deals, or the one in which it normally deals for the type of customer involved. For example, if a firm is acting for a United Kingdom customer and normally deals for its United Kingdom customers on the London Stock Exchange, it does not have to survey prices in other markets, especially overseas markets. Likewise, if the customer's order has been received after the London market has closed, then the firm should be able to wait until the London market next opens, rather than executing the order in an overseas market which is open at the time at which the customer's order is received, even though the firm may be dealing for its own account or other customers in such overseas markets. In fact, it is probably not in the interests of a private customer to have his order executed on an overseas market where it can easily be executed on the London market as soon as it opens again. The cost of executing the transaction overseas may be greater and the customer may be subject to different settlement obligations which are not as convenient for him as those applying on the London market, even if the overseas deal would be at a better price.

Reasonable steps

11–014   The firm is required to take reasonable steps to ascertain the best price, and this best price obligation is restricted to the size and kind of transaction with which the firm is concerned. Where the relevant market is the London Stock Exchange and the transaction is one within the normal market size for which fixed quotations are available from competing market makers on SEAQ, the best price will be the best bid or offer price for that security recorded on the screen.[1] However, what steps does the firm have to take where the transaction is outside the normal market size or does not relate to an investment for which any fixed bid and offer prices are shown, such as the bond market? Effectively, firms will have to use their own judgment as to whether or not it is appropriate to telephone several market makers or dealers for their prices. The mere fact of telephoning for a price for a particular sized transaction may operate to the disadvantage of the customer, especially if calls are made to several dealers. Word will soon get around the market and the prices which the dealers quote may not be particularly keen as they will be more confident of receiving the particular instruction. Also, how many dealers should be contacted? The mere fact of telephoning around causes a delay in execution, and terms quoted in the first telephone call may not be available when the broker goes back having made another two or three telephone calls to other dealers.

No order

In fact, it is significant how dealings take place on the bond market. **11–015** Normally, a broker or a non-private customer will approach a bond dealer and merely ask for a price. If he likes the price quoted, he will then deal. It is suggested that in these circumstances the bond dealer is not executing an order; not even within the third limb of the definition of order described above where a person is dealing as a principal but with obligations similar to those of an agent.

Conventions of market

SFA has written some guidance on what amounts to reasonable care **11–016** to ascertain the price which is the best available for the customer. This says that SFA will have regard to the conventions of the relevant market. In other words, in assessing what steps the firm has taken and whether the price was the best available, SFA will have regard to market practices. If it is not usual to make several telephone calls in the bond market before dealing for a customer, SFA will not expect it in a particular case. Likewise, if an order for a customer is executed on an exchange, the presumption is that the firm will have satisfied SFA's best execution rule if it has complied with any similar obligations imposed by the relevant exchange.

Qualification

The rule says that the firm must deal for the customer at a price **11–017** which is no less advantageous than the best price ascertained by the firm. There is a qualification. This requirement does not apply if the circumstances require the firm to do otherwise in the interests of the customer. An obvious example would be where the firm is required by the customer to execute the order at a particular fixed price, or at a loss, which could be the case where a customer wishes to minimise a tax obligation. (Remember tax avoidance is acceptable, but not tax evasion.)

Charges

11–018   In determining whether a firm has obtained best execution, no account is taken of any charges disclosed to the customer which are levied by the firm or its agent. "Charges" is defined as any charges made to a customer in connection with investment services, including, in respect of transactions for which the firm owes best execution, any mark-up or mark-down from the price at which best execution would be achieved. Note that this exclusion of charges only applies to those charges which have been disclosed. So, if a firm has not separately identified its mark-up or mark-down, it is the whole price which is subject to the best execution test.

This limitation is significant in relation to non-private customers. Rule 5–34(8) allows a firm to provide to such a customer, with his permission, a "net" contract note showing a single price incorporating the charges within the transaction price. In this case it is that single "net" price which will be subject to the best execution obligation.

Exception

11–019   A general exception to best execution is provided where a firm is purchasing from the operator units in a regulated collective investment scheme or is purchasing a life policy. The firm must still comply with other rules concerning fairness with customers, and, if a recommendation is made, the suitability obligation. This exception merely reflects the difficulties in knowing what is best execution when purchasing a life policy or unit trusts. For instance, many unit trusts are only valued once a day, with the managers pricing on either a historic or forward basis.

Timely Allocation (Rule 5–40)

11–020   A firm must ensure that any transaction which it executes is promptly allocated. The allocation must be to the account of the customer on whose instructions the transaction is executed. If the firm is executing the transaction for discretionary accounts, then it may only allocate direct to those accounts if, before dealing, it had made a decision to deal in principle for its discretionary accounts and had recorded that decision. Note that the requirement is not to have decided exactly what discretionary accounts will be involved and how much stock will be allocated to each account.

In all other cases, the transaction must be allocated to the firm's own account. If the firm then wishes to sub-allocate to other customer accounts, it must regard this later allocation as another transaction. This would be the case where the firm wished to allocate to discretionary accounts after dealing, but had not made and recorded a decision before dealing that it would execute the transaction on behalf of its discretionary customers.

Aggregation (Rule 5–41)

The rule on timely execution states that a firm may postpone execution **11–021** of an order where it believes on reasonable grounds that this is in the best interests of the customer (Rule 5–38(2)). Under Rule 5–41 SFA specifically permits a firm to aggregate a customer's order with other customers' orders or with own account orders. Remember, an own account order is one for the firm's own account or for the own account of an associate.

SFA's rule permits aggregation without any prior disclosure to, or consent from, the customer, provided the aggregation is unlikely to operate to the disadvantage of any of the customers' orders which have been aggregated. It does not matter that the aggregation may inadvertently operate to the disadvantage of one or more of the customers whose orders have been aggregated. The test is that at the time of aggregating it was unlikely to have this effect.

Of course, the reason for aggregating in the first place is normally to benefit customers, because the firm is putting through an order in a larger size and, therefore, is likely to obtain a keener transaction price. At any rate, by bulking orders the firm should be able to reduce its charges to customers. Whether or not the transaction operates to the disadvantage of a customer should be judged not merely against the transaction price, but against all the other costs involved. Therefore, even if a customer has received a slightly poorer price for the transaction, he may have benefited overall because the dealing costs are reduced. For example, as a result of delaying the execution of a sale whilst the firm was awaiting further sell orders from other customers which it wanted to aggregate, the price of the investment may have dropped. The first customer has been disadvantaged in terms of the transaction price; but, as a result of aggregating his order, the firm may have offered him a cheaper dealing service. In these circumstances, he has still benefited from the aggregation if his saving on the reduced dealing charges outweighs the fall in value of the investment.

If the firm is concerned that aggregation may disadvantage one or more of the customers whose orders are involved, then it may protect itself by disclosing to the relevant customers that their orders may be aggregated and that the effect of aggregation may operate on some occasions to their disadvantage. This disclosure can be given orally at the time of dealing or as a general disclosure at the start of a customer relationship in the customer agreement. A standard clause for this purpose is included in SFA's model customer documentation (see Appendix 7 below).

Although it is accepted that aggregation can sometimes operate to the disadvantage of an individual customer, firms should only aggregate because they believe that this is in the overall best interests of their customers. SFA has included guidance to this effect under the rule.

Fair Allocation (Rule 5–42)

11–022 Where a firm aggregates orders, it may find that it is unable to satisfy all the orders which it has aggregated. For example, the volume of the aggregated order may be so great that a firm cannot find a market maker which is prepared to deal with it in such a large size because of the exposure to the market maker in taking a substantial long or short position. Also, a large order could affect materially the price in the investment so that, if the aggregated order has to be split into a number of transactions to put through the market, the later transactions may be executed at a poorer price than the earlier transactions.

The rule on fair allocation is based on a firm's fiduciary obligations to its customers and states that where a firm has aggregated one customer's order with another customer's, then, in the subsequent allocation, it must not give unfair preference to any of those customers whose orders have been aggregated. In other words, a firm must treat all customers fairly as regards each other. It is suggested that it would be a breach of this rule, and certainly a firm's fiduciary obligations, if it favoured one customer merely because his order was larger than another customer's, or because his overall business was worth more to the firm. The only exception would be if there had been properly informed consent by the less favoured customer.

Where a firm has aggregated a customer's order with an own account order, then, in the subsequent allocation, it must not give unfair preference to itself; and, if all the orders cannot be satisfied, it must give priority to satisfying unconnected customers' orders. However, there is qualification. The firm does not have to give priority to unconnected customers' orders if it believes on reasonable grounds that, without its own participation, it would not have been able to effect the customers' orders either on such favourable terms or at all. This would apply where the largest part of the aggregated order is represented by the firm's own account order and, without the firm's participation, either the transaction could not have been completed or it would have been completed at an inferior price.

Firms should be careful of this rule qualification which allows a firm **11–023** to put itself on an equal footing to its unconnected customers, or even give itself preference. A firm would be in breach of a fiduciary obligation unless it has sufficiently discussed the fact and obtained the relevant customers' consents. As discussed in paragraph 15–007 *et seq.* below, a general disclosure in a customer agreement may not be sufficient to modify the firm's fiduciary obligations in such a case.

For the purposes of this rule only, the definition of "own account order" has been slightly modified. A firm does not have to subordinate a transaction undertaken on behalf of the own account of an associate where the associate:

(i)   is acting as trustee of a trust or collective investment scheme, the beneficial owners of which are not associates of the firm; or

(ii) is a regulated life office acting in the transaction solely for the account of its life funds.

In other words, the beneficiaries of the transaction are unconnected with the firm and, therefore, it is right that they should not be treated differently from other unconnected customers.

On-Exchange Transactions (Rule 5–44)

Basically, where a firm is dealing with private customers with respect to **11–024** derivatives, it must not effect, arrange or recommend an off-exchange transaction. The rule is limited to contingent liability transactions, but, as already explained in paragraph 6–003 above, the definition does not always make it clear which derivatives transactions are contingent liability ones. Certainly, this provision applies to futures transactions and the uncovered writing of options.

When is a transaction "off-exchange"? The answer is when it it not "on-exchange." "On-exchange" is defined to mean any transaction effected on or under the rules of a recognised or designated investment exchange. Recognised investment exchanges are mainly authorised exchanges in the United Kingdom, whilst designated investment exchanges are overseas exchanges which have been designated by SIB as providing a similar degree of regulation and protection as recognised investment exchanges. A designated exchange is not directly subject to the United Kingdom FSA 1986 regulatory system.

Note that the definition of "on-exchange" extends to transactions which are strictly not on an exchange, provided they are done under the rules of the exchange. This would cover traditional options arranged by London Stock Exchange members.

"On-exchange" also includes transactions which are both matched and identified as matched with a transaction effected on or under the rules of a recognised or designated investment exchange, unless the transaction is one which is specifically prohibited by the rules of the exchange. This extension is necessary to deal with the options and futures markets where a riskless principal transaction entered into between a firm and its customer may be off-exchange, although it is dependent upon an on-exchange transaction between the firm and another exchange member. However, it does not include certain transactions which, although regarded as matched with an on-exchange one, are not guaranteed in any way by the exchange and which the exchange's own rules prevent being done on exchange.

11–025 There is an important qualification to this restriction on off-exchange transactions. A firm can deal in a contingent liability transaction for a private customer off-exchange where it believes on reasonable grounds that the purpose of the transaction is to hedge against currency risk involved in a position which the customer holds. However, there is no longer an exception, as in the AFBD rules, for limited liability transactions, which were defined as transactions where there was a ceiling on the customer's liability.

Off-Exchange Market Makers (Rule 5–45)

11–026 Whilst the last rule dealt with restrictions on off-exchange transactions in derivatives, this rule is concerned with the sale to private customers of securities which are not quoted on a recognised or designated investment exchange. The rule relates to securities, rather than derivatives, and, therefore, does not apply to a derivative which is not regarded as a contingent liability transaction, even though such a transaction is not caught by the previous rule (Rule 5–44).

The provision does not apply where the securities are "quoted" on the exchange. "Quoted" is not defined, but it is wider than "listed". In other words, it should include any investment for which prices are quoted or available on the relevant exchange, including investments (whether listed or not) for which only indicative prices are shown on SEAQ.

The rule applies where a firm is selling to a private customer whilst giving him the impression that it is a market maker in the security concerned. The requirements are that the firm must give notice (which may be oral rather than written) to the customer, at the time of making the sale, that it is required to ensure that a reasonable price for the repurchase of the security is available to the customer for a specified period. This specified period must be for a period of not less than three months after the date on which the firm gives this notice. The firm is then under an obligation to make available to the customer (whether itself or through another firm) such a price for the specified period.

To sum up, a firm which is making a market off-exchange in the non-quoted security, or at least giving that impression, is under an obligation to repurchase (or arrange for another person to repurchase) from a private customer at a reasonable price for three months after the sale that quantity of the security which it has sold him; and the customer must be informed of this repurchase obligation at the time at which the firm makes the sale.

[1] In practice a significant number of normal market sized transactions are executed within the best price shown on SEAQ, but it is unlikely that a firm could be successfully prosecuted for a failure to take reasonable steps to ascertain the best price where it dealt at the best price available at the relevant time on SEAQ.

Chapter 12

Advertising

Section 57

Under section 57(1) of the FSA 1986, no person other than an auth-   **12–001**
orised person may issue, or cause to be issued, an investment advertisement in the United Kingdom unless its contents have been approved by
an authorised person. In other words, no investment advertisement can
be issued in the United Kingdom unless either it is issued by an
authorised person, or, if it is issued by someone else, it has been
approved by an authorised person.

The section refers to "issue or cause to be issued". "Cause to be
issued" covers the situation where a person, although not physically
issuing the advertisement himself, has initiated its issue. For example,
he has given it to another person who will be responsible for publishing
it. The publisher is merely the means used by him in arranging for his
advertisement to be issued. A person cannot argue that he has not
issued an advertisement merely because he has arranged for someone
else to do it on his behalf. On the other hand, because there is no
qualification on the word "issue", a publisher of someone else's
advertisement will be caught. Therefore, if he is an unauthorised
person, he must ensure that the advertisement has been approved by an
authorised person if the draftsman is not himself authorised.

There is a territorial limit in the sense that the requirement for the
advertisement to be issued or approved by an authorised person only
applies to advertisements issued in the United Kingdom. It is suggested
that it only applies to advertisements issued to recipients physically
present in the United Kingdom, rather than to advertisements which,
although prepared, printed and distributed from a United Kingdom
base, are sent to recipients outside the United Kingdom. It is important
to remember that the United Kingdom does not include the Channel
Islands, the Isle of Man and the Republic of Ireland.

Of course, as you look at whether the recipients are in the United
Kingdom, the requirement also covers advertisements which are
prepared and distributed from an overseas base, but sent to recipients
in the United Kingdom.

Section 57(2) defines "investment advertisement" to mean any
advertisement inviting persons to enter, or offer to enter, into an
investment agreement; or to exercise any rights conferred by an
investment to acquire, dispose of, underwrite or convert an investment
(for example, exercising a warrant or option); or containing information

calculated to lead directly or indirectly to persons doing any of the above. "Advertisement" is then defined (section 207(2)) to include every form of advertising: whether in a publication, or by a display of notices, signs, labels, or show cards; whether by means of circulars, catalogues, price lists or other documents; whether by an exhibition of pictures, or by photographic or cinematographic films; whether by sound broadcasting or television, or by the distribution of recordings; or in any other manner. In other words, an investment advertisement is anything which, however indirectly, could lead the person who sees or hears it to enter into an investment agreement, or to make any other decision with respect to an investment. It does not include, however, personal one-off letters or personal oral communications: the latter are subject to the Unsolicited Calls Regulations (see Chapter 13 below). The definition is wide enough to cover an oral speech, whether or not made through the media described above, and whether or not accompanied by any publication, display or exhibition of the type referred to above. "Investments" are the instruments described in Part I Schedule 1 to the FSA 1986; whilst investment agreement means any agreement, the making or performance of which by either party constitutes an activity falling within Part II, Schedule 1, or which would do so apart from the exclusions in Parts III and IV. In other words, one of the parties to the agreement is dealing in, arranging deals in, managing, advising on, or operating a collective investment scheme relating to, investments.

Any person who issues an investment advertisement in breach of section 57(1) is guilty of a criminal offence. He will not be able to enforce against the other party any investment agreement entered into as a result of such an advertisement; and the other party may repudiate the agreement and receive compensation for any loss suffered.

Exceptions

12–002   Having described investment advertisement in very wide terms, the FSA 1986 then provides substantial exceptions (section 58) from the issuing and approval requirements of section 57(1).

A. *Section 58*

The exceptions are detailed and complicated, but the main ones are highlighted below:

1. Advertisements issued, and relating to investments issued, by governments, local authorities, central banks, or international organisations of which the United Kingdom or another EC member state is a member.

2. Advertisements issued by persons who are exempt from the authorisation requirements under the FSA 1986, provided the advertisements relate to matters in respect of which the persons are exempt.

3. Advertisements issued by nationals of an EC member state (other than the United Kingdom) in the course of investment business lawfully carried on by them in such a state, provided any applicable investment advertising rules made by SIB are complied with.

4. Advertisements issued in connection with listing applications which have been approved by the competent listing authority in the United Kingdom, which is the London Stock Exchange.

5. Any documents which are required or permitted to be published by the listing rules made under Part IV, FSA 1986, or by an approved exchange under Part V.

6. Advertisements issued in accordance with the rules and regulations made under Part V, FSA 1986, in connection with offers of unlisted securities.

7. Prospectuses which are registered under the Companies Act 1985 in connection with offers of unlisted shares or debentures: this is a transitional provision until Part V is brought into force.

8. Advertisements issued in circumstances specified in any of the exemption orders relating to section 57 made by the Secretary of State for Trade and Industry under his delegated powers in section 58(3).[1]

B. *Section 58(3) Orders*

Under his delegated powers, the Secretary of State has exempted the following types of advertisement: **12–003**

S.I. 1988 No. 316

1. Advertisements issued by a body corporate to the creditors or members of it or another group company, or to the holders of its or any group company's shares, debentures or warrants. (Amended by S.I. 1992 No. 274.)

2. Advertisements issued in connection with employee share schemes to people covered by the schemes.

3. Advertisements issued between companies in the same group.

4. Advertisements issued between participators in a joint enterprise.

5. Advertisements issued by suppliers to customers who are not individuals in relation to the financing of goods or services which are not themselves investments.

6. Advertisements issued by a person not carrying on investment business in the United Kingdom if the recipients have had dealings with the person within the past 12 months when they were not resident in the United Kingdom.

7. Advertisements issued to persons sufficiently expert to understand the risks involved. These are advertisements issued to:

    (i)   authorised persons;

(ii) exempted persons in respect of activities for which they are exempt from the FSA 1986 authorisation requirements;

(iii) persons working for the media who are responsible for disseminating investment advertisements received from persons who wish to use the media to publish their advertisements;

(iv) governments, local authorities or public authorities;

(v) bodies corporate, partnerships and unincorporated associations satisfying the size criteria of Limb 2 of the definition of ordinary business investor (see paragraph 5–021 above);

(vi) persons holding a permission to do investment business from SIB under paragraph 23, Schedule 1 to the FSA 1986—but only where the advertisements relate to matters within the terms of the permission;

(vii) employees of any persons listed in (i) to (vi) above whose responsibilities involve them in engaging in investment business activities within Part II, Schedule 1 to the FSA 1986, or which would do so apart from the exclusions in Part III—provided the advertisements were issued to them in connection with their investment business responsibilities; or

(viii) trusts which satisfy the size criteria of Limb 3 of the definition of ordinary business investor (see paragraph 5–022 above)—this was added by S.I. 1992 No. 274.

8. Advertisements concerning shares or debentures in a private company issued to persons who have an existing and common interest with each other and with the company in relation to the affairs of the company.

9. Advertisements issued by trustees or personal representatives to each other or beneficiaries under the relevant trust, will or intestacy.

10. Advertisements issued by operators of overseas collective investment schemes which are recognised under sections 87 and 88 of the FSA 1986, provided the advertisements are issued to persons who are already participants in any scheme recognised under sections 87 or 88 which are operated by the issuer of the advertisement.

S.I. 1988 No. 716

12–004   11. Advertisements issued by a body corporate which has no direct or indirect pecuniary interest in the subject-matter and which are issued for the purpose of promoting or encouraging industrial or commercial activity or enterprise relating to shares in, or debentures of, a private company.

12. Certain investment advertisements issued in connection with the takeover of a private company which has not been subject to any marketing in respect of its shares within the previous 10 years.

13. Advertisements relating to the sale of large blocks of shares in a company in circumstances where the activities in connection with that sale do not amount to investment business because of the exemption in paragraph 21, Schedule 1 to the FSA 1986.

14. Advertisements issued by persons granted a permission to do investment business under paragraph 23, Schedule 1, provided they only relate to matters done in accordance with the terms and conditions of the permission.

15. Advertisements contained in a publication which is sent to other advertisers in that publication or which are sent to an advertising agency responsible for arranging the placement of advertisements.

16. Advertisements required or authorised under legislation other than the FSA 1986.

S.I. 1992 No. 274

17. Ordinary publications issued or caused to be issued by a body **12–005** corporate about its performance where either the company's (or its holding company's) securities are traded or dealt in on an approved market, or the publication forms part of the company's annual report and accounts, provided that, in either case, there is no direct soliciting of dealings in the company's investments and the publications will not lead, even indirectly, to recipients making investment decisions about derivatives.

18. Advertisements issued by a body corporate to persons entitled to bearer securities in it or another group company. This matches the exemption in 1. above (S.I. 1988 No. 316: paragraph 12–003 above) for creditors, members and holders of registered securities.

19. Advertisements encouraging people to purchase, subscribe to, or view media publications and programmes which themselves may give investment advice. The exemption relates to the advertising of the actual publication or programme, rather than to what is said in the publication or programme. However, the advice given in the publication or programme will not amount to investment business, provided, in the case of a publication, its principal purpose is not to lead persons to invest in any particular investment (paragraphs 25 and 25A, Schedule 1 to the FSA 1986).

20. Investment advertisements which merely contain information relating to facilities provided by approved or specified investment exchanges.

21. Advertisements relating to shares in a private company established to manage the fabric or common parts of residential property, or to supply services to such property.

S.I. 1992 No. 813

22. Advertisements directed at informing or influencing persons whose ordinary business involves investment business, including governments, local and public authorities.

23. Advertisements required or permitted to be published by the rules of a relevant EC exchange or other specified exchange which relate to securities traded or dealt in on the relevant exchange.

24. Advertisements which are issued or caused to be issued by a relevant EC exchange or other specified exchange which identify a particular derivative as one which can be traded or dealt in on the exchange.

Relationship between section 57 and SFA rules

12–006   Section 57 only lays down a requirement that an investment advertisement must be issued or approved by an authorised person. It does not prescribe the steps which must be followed before an authorised person can issue or approve an investment advertisement. These are applied through the rules of the FSA 1986 regulators.

Section 57 only applies to investment advertisements issued in the United Kingdom, whereas the normal Conduct of Business Rules apply wherever a firm is undertaking regulated business. A firm which has a permanent place of business in the United Kingdom is normally subject to the rules in respect of any investment business which it does from that place of business, whether it is transacted with investors in the United Kingdom or overseas. As a result, it is not appropriate to apply the general application rule, with its reference to regulated business, to the rules on advertising, because they would then have a wider scope than the issue and approval provisions of section 57(1). Therefore, there is a separate application rule for advertising which largely restricts the basic advertising rules to investment advertisements issued in the United Kingdom (Rule 5–1(4)).

As we have seen, there are a number of exceptions to the section 57(1) requirement. The section 58 exemptions mainly relate to: advertisements which are already subject to regulation imposed by bodies other than the SROs and RPBs; advertisements which are only incidentally investment advertisements, principally aimed at advertising non-investment services; and advertisements directed at people other than private investors. The relevant application rules for the Core Rules and SFA's supporting rules on advertising follow this general approach, by not subjecting to detailed regulation advertisements going to non-private investors, and by not imposing further regulation on advertisements which are already well regulated.

Application Rule (Rule 5–1(4))

This rule states that, except to the extent indicated, the rules **12–007**
concerning the issue or approval of an investment advertisement govern
issue of an investment advertisement in the United Kingdom and
approval of an investment advertisement for issue in the United
Kingdom. This is similar to the scope of section 57(1): the rules only
apply to advertisements issued in the United Kingdom. There is an
extra-territorial aspect in the sense that the rules govern approval
carried out overseas of an advertisement to be issued in the United
Kingdom. The restriction in the old TSA rules that the advertising
rules only applied where the advertisement was likely to be received by
more than 20 private or expert investors has been removed.

The reference to "except to the extent indicated" means that there
are cases in which the rules do not even apply to advertisements issued
in the United Kingdom. Also, in two cases the advertising rules apply
to advertisements issued to investors outside the United Kingdom. Rule
5–14 (already described in paragraph 4–023 above) requires a firm
which issues an advertisement to a private customer outside the United
Kingdom, in connection with investment business which is not
regulated business, to include the prescribed disclosure on the
advertisement if reference is made to the firm's status as an authorised
person under the FSA 1986. Whilst Rule 5–9(5) (explained in
paragraph 12–010 below) applies to advertisements about a firm issued
by another person, whether in the United Kingdom or elsewhere.

The advertising application rule then provides a series of exemptions,
similar to, but wider than, section 58. The advertising rules do not
apply to:

(i)   The issue by an authorised person of an advertisement which
      can be issued in the United Kingdom by an unauthorised
      person without approval by an authorised person. In other
      words, this exception applies to advertisements within the
      section 58 exemptions.

(ii) The issue or approval of a DIE advertisement. A DIE
      advertisement is defined as one issued by a designated
      investment exchange, or one which is required or permitted to
      be published by the rules of such an exchange. DIE exchanges
      are overseas exchanges which have been approved by SIB as
      offering similar protections to United Kingdom recognised
      investment exchanges.

      Why is there no similar exemption for advertisements issued
      by, or required or permitted to be published by the rules of, a
      recognised investment exchange? The reason is that "RIE
      advertisements" are effectively already exempt advertisements
      under section 58 and the Orders made thereunder (see A. 4, 5

and 7 under paragraph 12–002 above, and B. 20, 23 and 24 under paragraph 12–005 above; although notice the restrictions relating to derivatives in 23 and 24).

(iii) The issue or approval of a takeover advertisement. A takeover advertisement is defined as any advertisement to which the United Kingdom Takeover Code applies, or would apply but for any exemption granted by the United Kingdom Takeover Panel. This exemption only applies to the United Kingdom Takeover Panel: it does not include similar advertisements subject to appropriate overseas regimes. "Takeover Code" includes the City Code on Takeovers and Mergers and the Rules Governing Substantial Acquisitions of Shares published by the Panel on Takeovers and Mergers.

(iv) The issue or approval of scheme particulars unless they constitute a direct offer advertisement. "Scheme particulars" is the document containing information about a regulated collective investment scheme. Its contents are subject to the requirements made by SIB under the FSA 1986 or, in the case of a scheme recognised under section 86, by the certifying EC Member State. However, scheme particulars which amount to direct offer advertisements are not exempted and must comply with the rule requirements for this latter type of advertisement (see paragraphs 12–018 *et seq.* below).

(v) the reissue of an investment advertisement which has been prepared and issued by another person, provided the firm believes on reasonable grounds:
   (a) it is an advertisement falling within exceptions (i), (ii), (iii) or (iv) above; or
   (b) it has already been issued or approved by an authorised person and is being issued by the firm to a market for which it was intended at the time of its original issue or approval.

12–008 There is no definition of reissue, but presumably it refers to distributing the advertisement in an unamended form, whether sending out further copies as originally produced, or putting the contents of the advertisement into the firm's own house style, with its name and address, but without any other material amendment. Unlike the other exemptions, this is one qualified by a reasonable belief test: the firm may rely upon it if satisfied on reasonable grounds that (a) or (b) apply.

Under (v)(a), if the advertisement falls within one of the exemptions in (i) to (iv) above, then there are no restrictions on the market to which the firm may issue it, provided, by issuing it to a wider market than that for which it was originally intended, the firm is not removing the advertisement from the scope of one of these exemptions. Otherwise, under (v)(b), provided the advertisement has already been issued or approved by an authorised person, its reissue must be limited to the type of market for which it was originally intended. Apparently, the firm does not have to assess whether the information in the advertisement is still correct and relevant in terms of the market for which it was originally intended. However, before ignoring the fair and not misleading obligation of the advertising rules, the rule on fair and clear communications (Rule 5–15, already described in paragraph 6–005 above) should be noted. This rule applies a similar test to the basic advertising rule to any communication with any person which is designed to promote the provision of investment services. It is not entirely clear as to whether this rule is limited to communications which are not investment advertisements (see additional comments in paragraph 12–011 below).

Basic Obligation (Rule 5–9(1))

Where a firm is issuing or approving an investment advertisement **12–009** which is not within the exemptions (i) to (v) above, it must:

(i)   apply appropriate expertise; and

(ii)   be able to show that it believes on reasonable grounds that the advertisement is fair and not misleading.

So, the advertisement must be fair and not misleading. If it is misleading, then the firm could be liable for committing a criminal offence under section 47(1) of the FSA 1986. This test, although objective in the sense that the firm is not concerned with the understanding of individual recipients, is probably higher than merely stating matters which are not untrue in themselves. The advertisement should present an overall fair picture which is not likely to mislead investors, rather than merely being correct in respect of each individual aspect mentioned.

If challenged about the fairness of its advertisement, then the obligation is upon the firm to prove that it believed on reasonable grounds that the advertisement was fair. This burden of proof is supported generally by Rule 7–23(4) which states that, where a firm is required by a rule to take reasonable steps or similar measures, the onus will be on the firm to show that it has taken those steps or measures. To prove that it has taken reasonable steps, a firm will need to retain some evidence to show what steps were followed and factors taken into account in preparing or approving the advertisement. This is not specifically required under the Record Keeping Schedule (Appendix 18), which only requires a firm to keep copies of specific investment advertisements which it has issued and copies of any investment advertisement which it has approved. However, the relevant Core Rule on record keeping (Rule 5–54(1)) requires a firm to ensure that sufficient information is recorded and retained about its regulated business and compliance with the regulatory system.

A firm is required to apply appropriate expertise. Even if this was not specifically required under the rule, it is implicit in the obligation on the firm to show that it has reasonable grounds for believing that the advertisement is fair and not misleading. In preparing an investment advertisement, a firm, or its employee who is primarily responsible for it, will not necessarily be an expert, able to verify all of its contents and all of the matters which have been taken into account in preparing any recommendation which is included. Therefore, it is important that persons with the necessary expertise are relied upon in the preparation or approval process. Again, owing to the burden of proof on the firm, it may wish to document the expertise which it has relied upon.

Examples of applying appropriate expertise would be where the firm is relying upon: financial information checked or produced by accountants; information about investors' tax positions calculated by tax consultants; and research produced by analysts with special knowledge of the companies whose investments are referred to.

Where a firm is approving an advertisement for an unauthorised person, then, if it is to satisfy the appropriate expertise test, it must either itself have knowledge about the subject-matter of the advertisement, or bring in another person who has such knowledge to verify the information given. In other words, an agency broker who specialises in United Kingdom equities would not himself necessarily have appropriate expertise to approve advertisements relating to non-United Kingdom equities traded on overseas markets. It is even more unlikely that he would have the necessary expertise with respect to derivatives, especially if they were based upon commodities.

In the context of applying appropriate expertise, it is important to note the reliance on others provision (Rule 5–2(1) and see paragraph 2–011 above). This states that, in discharging his rule obligations, a person can rely, to the extent that he can show that it was reasonable to do so, upon information provided to him in writing by a third party whom he believed on reasonable grounds to be independent and competent to provide the information. This does not mean a firm cannot rely upon oral information. However, relying on written information provides a "safe harbour" in a similar way to formal guidance (Rule 1–4). Therefore a firm may wish to ensure that any expertise applied in respect of the issuing or approval of advertisements is confirmed by the expert in writing.

There is no longer a requirement, like that in the old TSA rules, that the firm must believe that the advertisement will continue to satisfy the fair and not misleading test during a reasonable period after its issue, but this is clearly good practice.

Extension

12–010   Although this basic advertising obligation only applies to advertisements which are not within the exemptions in (i) to (v) above (paragraph 12–007), there are two important extensions.

The first applies where the firm states that it is a member of SFA on an exempt advertisement which it has issued or approved (Rule 5–9(4)). SFA was concerned that, by stating on such an advertisement that it was a member of SFA, the firm could give the impression to recipients that the advertisement was subject to regulation by SFA. Therefore the basic advertising obligation described above applies, but none of the detailed contents requirements described below.

This extension only applies to exempt advertisements which come within exemption (i) above (paragraph 12–007): in other words, advertisements which are exempt under section 58 from the requirement in section 57(1) to be issued or approved by an authorised person. It does not affect advertisements not exempt within the terms of section 58, but which are otherwise DIE advertisements, takeover advertisements and scheme particulars. The failure to apply the extension to these other advertisements was probably a slip-up, rather than a deliberate policy decision. It leads to a degree of inconsistency. Also it should be noted that this extension does not apply in respect of investment advertisements issued in connection with corporate finance business or money broking. Therefore, a firm which states that it is a member of SFA on an exempt advertisement which is issued as part of corporate finance business will not have to comply with the basic advertising obligation.

The second extension applies where the firm is not itself issuing or approving an advertisement, but knows, or ought reasonably to know, that another person is issuing one which advertises, even indirectly, the firm's services (Rule 5–9(5)). This extension applies whether the advertisement is issued in the United Kingdom or overseas. If the firm knows, or ought reasonably to know, about the advertisement, it must take reasonable steps to ensure that it, or at least that part referring to the firm, is fair and not misleading. If any investors who enter into investment agreements as a result of the advertisement will not be protected under the FSA 1986 regulatory system, then the firm must also ensure that the advertisement includes the prescribed disclosure.

This second extension was imposed because some overseas businesses, as part of advertising their own services, mention the fact that they will be executing business for their customers through United Kingdom FSA 1986 authorised firms. There is a danger that their customers might, in these circumstances, consider that they will be able to benefit from the protections under the FSA 1986. However, this will not be the case unless the overseas business is acting as an agent and has identified its principals before dealing with the United Kingdom firm, in which case the United Kingdom firm will owe the identified principals indirect customer obligations (unless there is an agreement in writing between the firm and the agent to the contrary—see Rule 5–6 and paragraph 5–047 above).

Whilst mentioning extensions, it is worth remembering the position of overseas branches of an SFA firm, as discussed in paragraph 4–006 above. The overseas branch will be part of an authorised person. Therefore it does not need approval from its United Kingdom branch for any investment advertisement which it issues in the United Kingdom. However, it will not be able to take advantage of the foreign business carve-out unless it complies with all SFA's advertising provisions in Rule 5–9, including the detailed contents requirements for specific investment advertisements (see Rule 5–1(2) and paragraph 4–017 above). Although this provision (extending the advertising rules to a firm's overseas branch) appears before the main advertising application rule (Rule 5–1(4)), it is suggested that exemptions (i) to (v) above (paragraph 12–007) continue to apply.

Fair and clear communications (Rule 5–15)

12–011 As already explained in paragraphs 6–005 and 12–008 above, this provision applies to any communication (whether oral or written) with any person (whether or not a customer) which is designed to promote the provision of investment services. The requirement is that the firm must show that it believes on reasonable grounds that the communication is fair and not misleading. It could be argued that this provision applies to any investment advertisement which promotes an investment service, including all those exempt from the advertising rules.

However, it is suggested that this approach is wrong. Where the communication amounts to an investment advertisement as defined in section 57(2), it should only be subject to the advertising rules in accordance with the advertising application rule described above. Therefore, if it is not caught by this application rule or by the extensions described above, then it is not subject to the fair and clear communications rule.

On the other hand, if the communication being considered does not amount to an investment advertisement, it will be subject to the general application rule for the Conduct of Business Rules (Rule 5–1(1)), rather than the advertising application rule. This means that Rule 5–15 only applies to communications issued as part of a firm's regulated business, because there is no wider extension in the drafting of the rule to associated business or business held out as being for the purpose of investment (see paragraph 4–012 above).

Even if Rule 5–15 applies to investment advertisements, it will not apply to all of those which are exempt from the advertising rules. This is not only because of the restriction of its scope to regulated business, but also because the rule only applies to those communications which are designed to promote the provision of investment services. The concept of promotion is discussed below in connection with specific investment advertisements (paragraph 12–013).

Misleading Advertising Directive (EC Council Directive 84/450)

Whilst discussing the scope of the basic advertising obligation, the **12–012** exemptions to the advertising rules and the scope of the fair and clear communications rule, it is relevant to consider this Directive. Its purpose is to protect against misleading advertising consumers, persons carrying on a trade or business, or persons practising a craft or profession. Therefore, it extends to non-private customers, even market counterparties.

Advertising is defined to mean the making of a representation in any form in connection with a trade, business, craft or profession in order to promote the supply of goods or services. Misleading advertising means advertising which in any way deceives or is likely to deceive the persons to whom it is addressed or whom it reaches. These definitions are very wide and extend to advertisements within the exemptions (i) to (v) above (paragraph 12–007). Therefore it could be argued that, under this Directive, the basic fair and not misleading obligation (Rule 5–9(1)) should apply to any type of investment advertisement.

The Directive requires that an EC member state's courts or administrative authorities which have responsibility for enforcing the prohibition on misleading advertising should be able to require the advertiser to furnish evidence as to the accuracy of factual claims made in his advertising. It is for this reason that both the advertising rule and the fair and clear communications rule require a firm to show that it believes on reasonable grounds that the advertisement or communication is fair and not misleading.

The Control of Misleading Advertising Regulations (S.I. 1988 No. 915) came into force on June 20, 1988. They were made to implement in the United Kingdom the provisions of the Directive. These regulations describe a misleading advertisement as one which in any way, including its presentation, deceives or is likely to deceive the audience which it reaches. Powers to initiate court proceedings were granted to the Director General of Fair Trading. However, these regulations do not apply to investment advertisements issued or caused to be issued by or on behalf of an authorised person or appointed representative. There is one important qualification. They still apply where an authorised person is issuing an advertisement in relation to a matter for which he is exempt from the FSA 1986 authorisation requirements, unless he is acting as an appointed representative.

Specific Investment Advertisements

More detailed provisions apply, besides the basic obligation of fair **12–013** and not misleading, where a firm is issuing or approving a specific investment advertisement. This is defined as an advertisement which identifies and promotes a particular investment or particular investment service. The restriction is really in the word "promotes". Before an advertisement becomes a specific one, it has to put forward in a positive sense the investment or investment service which is the subject of the advertisement. In other words, it is suggested that a bald statement about an investment or a negative recommendation does not amount to "promotion". There has to be some sort of positive recommendation which helps, initiates or assists decisions to acquire an investment or use an investment service.

The basic Core Rule obligation is that, where a firm issues or approves such an advertisement, it must identify itself as the issuer or approver, and also identify itself as a member of SFA (Rule 5–9(2)).

SFA then requires a firm to take reasonable steps to ensure that the advertisement contains, where applicable, the information set out in three tables: the first referring to general contents requirements; the second to specific contents requirements; and the third to risk warnings. However, these detailed contents requirements are not required in four cases.

Exceptions to contents requirements for specific advertisements

12–014   The detailed contents requirements are not required where[2]:

(i)   The advertisement is issued by the firm, or approved by the firm for issue, to persons who are not private customers. This is picking up on an exemption in one of the orders made under section 58 (B. 7 above: paragraph 12–003). However, it is wider, because, unlike that exemption, it extends to advertisements sent to experts. Under SFA's rules, persons who are classified as expert investors (Rule 5–5) are non-private customers.

It should be noted that the definition of customer includes any person with whom the firm carries on, or intends to carry on, any regulated business or associated business (SFA's third tier), also a potential customer (part of SIB's Core Rule definition). So the exception applies even if the recipient is not already an established customer, but is someone whom the firm hopes will become a customer. It, therefore, covers advertisements sent to ordinary business investors, but not potential expert investors because they only become non-private customers after the firm has complied with the categorisation and written warning requirements of Rule 5–5 (see paragraphs 5–026 *et seq.* above).

(ii)   The advertisement clearly states that the investment or investment service which it promotes is not available to private customers. Not only must the advertisement contain this statement, but the firm should, at least if it is issuing the advertisement, ensure that the investment or investment service is not available to private customers. This is because of Rule 5–52 which deals with compliance with statements, and provides that, where a firm is required under the rules to state that it has done or will do something, then it must ensure that it acts in the way stated.

(iii) The advertisement is contained in a newspaper, journal, magazine or other periodical publication published and circulating principally outside the United Kingdom and which is directed to persons outside the United Kingdom. Although the advertisement must be directed to persons receiving it outside the United Kingdom, a firm would not be in breach of this requirement merely because of the fact that some copies of the publication are incidentally on sale in the United Kingdom or are brought back by persons who have received it outside the United Kingdom. Obviously, as more copies are made available for sale in the United Kingdom, it will be harder to conclude that the publication is circulating principally outside the United Kingdom and that anything contained in it is directed to persons outside the United Kingdom.

(iv) It is a short form advertisement. Most short form advertisements will not be specific investment advertisements. They will merely be statements of fact which cannot be regarded as promoting an investment or investment service. However, to the extent that they are specific investment advertisements, they are not subject to the detailed contents requirements: if they were, they could clearly not be short advertisements.

A short form advertisement is defined as one which contains no matters **12–015** other than the following:

    (a)   the identity of, or a symbol or logo representing, the issuer or approver;

    (b)   a reference to the issuer's or approver's membership of SFA;

    (c)   the issuer's address and telephone number;

    (d)   a description of the issuer's business;

    (e)   the fees charged by the issuer;

    (f)   names of investments; prices indicative of those at which the issuer may buy or sell, or arrange transactions in, these investments; how these prices differ from, or relate to, previous prices for, and income and yields from, these investments; or

    (g)   a statement that the issuer has arranged the issue of an investment or transaction, provided it does not imply that an offer to enter into an investment agreement is being made.

It should be noted that short form advertisements only relate to details about the issuer, not associates of the issuer. Therefore, an advertisement (to the extent that it is a specific investment advertisement) giving information in (g) above may only refer to deals arranged or entered into by the issuer, not another group company: otherwise, it will be subject to the usual contents requirements for specific investment advertisements. Of course, a FSA 1986 authorised person may approve a short form advertisement issued or caused to be issued by an unauthorised associate.

General contents requirements (Table 5–9(7))

12–016   These contents requirements apply to all specific investment advertisements. They are concerned with: the clarity and accuracy of statements, promises and forecasts; prohibiting false indications; and requiring that any statements or risk warnings required by the rules are given due prominence.

Specific contents requirements (Table 5–9(8))

There should be no reference to a guarantee, unless it is a legally enforceable arrangement with a third party; in which case sufficient details must be given about the guarantor and guarantee to enable the investor to make a fair assessment about the guarantee's value.

Any commendations which are quoted must be complete, accurate at the time of issue, and relevant to the investment or investment service which is being promoted. The author must have given his consent to the use of the commendation, and the advertisement must disclose whether he is connected with the firm.

Comparisons must be given fairly. Where the advertisement contains details about past performance, the record on past performance must be complete. It must not be selected so as to exaggerate success or disguise failure. Also, the information must be based upon actual past performance, rather than simulated figures. Where information is given about the past performance of a regulated collective investment scheme, the information must relate to the previous five years or, if less, the period from the start of the scheme as a regulated one: no figures should be given which relate to any period during which it was operated as an unregulated scheme. Where the actual return is stated, or comparison is made with another form of investment, the past performance information must be made on an "offer to bid" basis.

Where a firm knows that it, or its associate, may have a position or holding in the investment which is promoted, or any related investment, it must include a general statement to this effect. Specific details about the holding are not required: merely a statement, for example, that the firm is a market maker in the relevant investment. Likewise, if the firm knows that it, or its associate, has provided, within the previous 12 months, significant advice or investment services in relation to the investment concerned, or a related investment, the advertisement must say so. The qualification introduced by the word "significant" applies to both advice and other investment services. It would include advice given in a corporate finance context to the issuer of the investments referred to, but not ordinary advice given to the firm's advisory customers. Again, the statement does not have to specify the nature of the advice or service provided. No disclosure of the material interest is required where the employees responsible for the advertisement did not know about the interest (see Rule 5–3(3) and paragraph 15–014 below).

If the advertisement contains any reference to the impact of taxation, then there are detailed requirements which must be followed. Advertisements for packaged products must state whether or not any cancellation right applies and give details of the period in which the right may be exercised (see Chapter 14 below). Where a regulated collective investment scheme is promoted which has more than 35 per cent. of its assets consisting of government or public securities issued by one issuer, this fact and the issuer's name must be disclosed.

Risk warnings (Table 5–9(9))

A general statement is required that investments can fluctuate in price, with prices falling or rising against the investor's interests. If the investment relates to any geared futures and options fund, warrant fund, or any other fund which invests in such funds, it must explain the risk of sudden and large falls in value and the possibility of a large loss on realisation which could be equal to the amount invested. Where the investment is described as likely to yield income, then warnings must be given, if relevant, that the income may fluctuate and that part of the investor's capital may be used to pay income. **12–017**

Warnings are required if the investment could be affected by changes in rates of foreign exchange. Similarly, where details on past performance are given, a warning must be included that past performance is not a guide to future performance. Likewise, references to the impact of taxation must explain that levels and bases of taxation may change.

Warnings must be given where the investment being promoted is non-readily realisable; and a special warning is required where there is only one market maker. Explanations must be given about an investor's liability for further calls in respect of contingent liability investments, and about the non-guaranteed nature of with-profits life policies.

Where front-end loading is involved, a warning is required that the deductions for charges and expenses are not made uniformly through the life of the investment, but loaded disproportionately onto the early years. Where cancellation rights apply, the advertisement must make it clear that the investor if he exercises those rights, may not obtain a full refund of the amount invested because of the drop in value of the investment before he exercises his cancellation rights. Where it is a property fund which is being advertised, the warning must point out the degree of illiquidity relating to investments in land and building.

Direct Offer Advertisements (Rule 5–10)

12–018 This rule is concerned with the issuing or approval of a direct offer advertisement for the sale of investments or the provision of investment services to a private customer. A firm must take reasonable steps to ensure that it does not issue or approve such an advertisement unless it contains information about the investments or investment services, the terms of the offer, and the risks involved, which is adequate and fair having regard to the regulatory protections (whether United Kingdom or overseas) which apply and the market to which the advertisement is directed.

A direct offer advertisement means the type of advertisement which was previously referred to as "off-the-page" or "off-the-screen". Basically, it is the sort of advertisement where an investor completes a tear-off application form and returns it with his money or credit card details. He has no further contact with the issuer and is committed to selling his investments or accepting the provision of the investment service. Off-the-screen referred to screen-based offers which a customer could accept by keying in his payment details and sending them electronically with his acceptance.

The new term "direct offer advertisement" probably suggests more clearly the nature of this type of advertisement. A direct offer advertisement is defined as a specific investment advertisement (including a preprinted or off-the-screen advertisement) which:

    (i)   contains:
        (a)   an offer by the firm or another offeror to enter into an investment agreement with anyone who responds to the advertisement; or
        (b)   an invitation to anyone to respond to the advertisement by making an offer to the firm or another offeror to enter into an investment agreement; and
    (ii) specifies the manner or indicates a form in which any response is to be made (for example, by providing a tear-off slip).

(i)(a) refers to an offer and (i)(b) refers to an invitation to treat. In respect of (i)(a), there is a binding contract once the investor has made his response in the form required. In the case of an invitation to treat, the investor responds by making an offer in the form required, which is then accepted by the firm or a third party. The contract only becomes binding in the second case after acceptance of the investor's offer by the other party. However, in both cases the investor is effectively bound to the contract once he has completed the response form in the manner required.

It should be noted that this rule does not apply in every case where an investor completes a preprinted form. The form itself has to be part of a specific investment advertisement and it must be a situation where it is not intended that there should be any personal contact between the firm and the investor before he responds in the manner required on the form.

Although the provision specifically refers to the sale of investments, it also includes the purchase of investments. This is caught by the reference to "the provision of investment services". This is only a private customer rule and it is subject to the general restrictions on the scope of the advertising rules. Therefore it does not apply to exempt advertisements, DIE advertisements or takeover advertisements. It does apply, however, to scheme particulars, because where scheme particulars amount to a direct offer advertisement there is no exception to the application of the advertising rules.

As a direct offer advertisement is a specific investment advertisement, **12–019** a firm must state that it is the issuer or approver and must refer to its membership of SFA. The detailed contents requirements for specific investment advertisements described above do not apply. Instead, the provision has its own separate contents requirements.

Owing to the fact that there is no direct personal contact between the firm and the investor before the investor is committed to the agreement, the Core Rule element (Rule 5–10(1)) requires that the information given is adequate and fair having regard to the type of investors to whom the advertisement is directed and the regulatory protections available. Account can be taken, not just of United Kingdom protections, but also of any applicable overseas protections. At the third tier (Rule 5–10(3)) SFA requires a firm to take reasonable steps to ensure that the advertisement includes sufficient information upon which the investor can base his investment decision. In other words, the investor must be able to make an informed decision about the suitability for him of the investment or investment service which is the subject of the advertisement.

In addition, SFA requires the advertisement to contain, where **12–020** applicable to the investment or investment service being advertised, information set out in four tables. These tables refer, respectively, to regulated collective investment schemes, life policies, BES investments and execution-only dealing services. Effectively, the tables contain the matters which SFA regards as the minimum which a firm needs to cover if it is to give an investor sufficient information upon which to make an informed investment decision.

1. *Unit trusts*

For example, in the case of a regulated collective investment scheme, the information which is required includes: the minimum amount which can be invested; the scheme's investment objectives; the issue price or the basis for determining it; the nature or basis of the charges payable by the investor; the expected annual gross yield; how income will be reinvested; details on valuations, the redemption of units and withdrawal facilities; the intervals at which valuation statements will be sent; and how scheme particulars may be obtained.

2. *Life policies*

In the case of a life policy, the matters required include: the minimum amount which can be invested; where full details of the contract may be obtained; details of linked benefits; the nature and times at which valuations will be sent; the appropriate product particulars; and details of any cancellation rights.

3. *BES investments*

For BES schemes, the information required includes: the BES scheme particulars; a copy of a prospectus or statement of prescribed information relating to each company in which the manager has or intends to acquire an interest for the scheme; and a statement that applications can only be made and accepted subject to the conditions of the scheme particulars. A BES scheme is a pooled arrangement or fund, or a managed portfolio, invested mainly in BES shares. A BES share is a share in a company the beneficial owner of which may qualify for the relevant BES tax relief. The March 1992 budget proposed the removal of the tax relief by the end of 1993.

For a private offer of BES shares, the advertisement must contain a statement of prescribed information. This means including all such information as an investor or his investment adviser would reasonably require or expect for the purpose of making an informed decision as to whether or not to invest in the shares of the particular company.

4. *Execution dealing services*

In respect of execution-only dealing services, the advertisement must: state the basis or amount of charges payable by the customer; refer to any delay in executing orders; and explain that orders may be aggregated, with aggregation sometimes operating to the disadvantage of customers.

5. *Other investments or services*

Where the advertisement relates to other investments or services, there are no special contents requirements. It is merely necessary that the advertisement includes sufficient information for an investor to make an informed investment decision. Notice that this applies not merely to equities and debt securities, but also to advertisements relating to unregulated investment schemes.

12–021 The old rules prevented direct offer advertisements being issued other than in connection with insurance contracts, units in regulated collective investment schemes, PEPs or BES investments. The only restrictions now on the types of investment or investment services for which direct offer advertisements can be issued relate to derivatives and warrants. The SIB Core Rule states that direct offer advertisements relating to derivatives or warrants can only be made where the firm itself issues the advertisement (it cannot approve it for someone else), and where it does so only to customers for whom it believes on reasonable grounds that the relevant investment or investment services are suitable. However, SFA has decided that it is never appropriate to issue direct offer advertisements in respect of these types of investments to private customers and, therefore, has banned such advertisements, even if the firm could satisfy the suitability requirement (Rule 5–10(2)).

Under the old rules direct offer advertisements could only relate to investment agreements to be entered into between the investor and the firm issuing the advertisement. There was no facility for a firm to issue such an advertisement on behalf of an unauthorised person. Such advertisements now advertise investment agreements to be entered into by the recipient with someone other than the firm, and so be approved by firms for unauthorised persons. However, if the entering into the investment agreement will be outside the scope of the rules, then the advertisement may need to contain the prescribed disclosure (see paragraphs 4–020 *et seq.* above); and, if it has been approved by the firm on behalf of an overseas investment business, the firm will have to have no reason to doubt the honesty and reliability of this person (Rule 5–12 and see paragraph 12–023 below).

Unregulated Collective Investment Schemes (Rule 5–9(3))

Section 57 deals with both issuing and approving investment **12–022** advertisements. However, section 76, which is concerned with the promotion of collective investment schemes, refers only to issuing. Basically, it prevents an authorised person from issuing or causing to be issued in the United Kingdom any advertisement inviting persons to become participants in an unregulated collective investment scheme, unless the promotion is done in accordance with SIB's Promotion of Unregulated Schemes Regulations 1991. This means that the restrictions on the promotion of unregulated collective investment schemes do not apply, in terms of the FSA 1986, to the issue of advertisements by unauthorised persons, provided the advertisements have been approved by an authorised person in accordance with section 57, because the restriction in section 76 does not apply where an authorised person only approves rather than issues an advertisement relating to such a scheme.

To close this loophole a rule has been introduced that a firm cannot approve a specific investment advertisement if it relates to units in an unregulated collective investment scheme (Rule 5–9(3)). This is a Core Rule provision which, because it applies to all members of SROs, attempts to deal with this inconsistency in the FSA 1986 drafting between sections 57 and 76. The loophole is not entirely closed because members of RPBs who have a certificate to do investment business are not subject to the Core Rules, but will be authorised persons able to approve investment advertisements. Hopefully, all of the RPBs will include a similar provision in their rules.

Where a firm is issuing an advertisement promoting an unregulated scheme, then the main category of persons to whom it can be promoted are:

(i)   existing participants in the scheme promoted or a substantially similar scheme;

(ii)   persons who, within the last 30 months, have been participants in the scheme being promoted or a substantially similar scheme;

(iii)   customers with whom the firm or another group company has an existing customer relationship, or a newly accepted customer of either whose business has not been obtained in contravention of section 76 or a Conduct of Business Rule, provided, in both cases, that the firm believes that the scheme is suitable for the customer having regard to his circumstances and investment objectives;

(iv)   non-private customers, including persons who are treated as expert investors;

(v)   persons who are included on a mailing list as willing to receive details of unregulated schemes with underlying property similar to the assets within the scheme which is being promoted.

There is a reasonable belief test. So a firm satisfies the regulations where it believes on reasonable grounds that the person falls within one of the above categories. Also, note that in respect of category (iv), non-private customers, there is no restriction on the type of scheme which may be promoted. The list given above is not exhaustive. Other minor categories are included in the regulations. Also, under section 76(2) such schemes may be promoted to any authorised person or a person whose ordinary business involves the acquisition and disposal of the type of property to which the scheme relates.

As already discussed, a firm cannot approve an advertisement for an unregulated scheme, even if it is only intended to issue it to the persons listed within SIB's regulations. Obviously, the approver cannot be sure that the advertisement's issue will properly be restricted to these persons. Therefore, where an unauthorised person wants to promote an unregulated collective investment scheme in the United Kingdom, he will have to arrange for an authorised firm to issue it itself. As we have seen in connection with direct offer advertisements, there is nothing now to prevent a firm issuing an advertisement under its own name which recommends the entering into of an investment agreement with a third party.

Overseas Person Advertisements (Rule 5–12)

As we have seen in paragraph 4–004 above, an unauthorised overseas **12–023** investment business may attract customers in the United Kingdom by issuing in the United Kingdom investment advertisements relating to its business, provided the advertisements have been approved by authorised persons. As long as the relevant advertisement has been so approved, then the overseas investment business will not need to be authorised under the FSA 1986, even though it is dealing with customers in the United Kingdom. As section 57 says nothing about the factors which must be taken into account by an authorised person in approving such an investment advertisement, there is a potentially wide provision in the FSA 1986 enabling business to be done with United Kingdom customers offshore outside the scope of the United Kingdom regulatory system.

Therefore, a Core Rule has been written imposing obligations on firms which issue or approve specific investment advertisements which are calculated to lead directly or indirectly to an overseas person carrying on investment business which will not be regulated business with or for private customers in the United Kingdom. In issuing or approving the advertisement, the firm must ensure that it contains the prescribed disclosure, warning about the loss of protection under the United Kingdom regulatory scheme. In addition, the firm must not have any reason to doubt that the overseas person will deal with investors in the United Kingdom in an honest and reliable way. The firm does not have to vet positively the overseas person, but it must not issue or approve the advertisement if it is aware, from whatever means, of any matter which throws doubt on the person's honesty and reliability.

As it is a specific investment advertisement, the firm will have to comply with the contents requirements described above. In other words, it will have to identify itself as the issuer or approver, identify itself as a member of SFA, and ensure that, where applicable, the detailed contents requirements of the three tables are included.

---

[1] Responsibilities for financial services regulation are being transferred from the Department of Trade and Industry to the Treasury following the April 1992 General Election.

[2] Only a few exceptions to the contents requirements for specific investment advertisements are set out in Rule 5–9(6). There is, however, effectively, another one because the contents requirements for specific investment advertisements do not apply to advertisements issued in the course of corporate finance business (see paragraph 4–038 above), even those issued to private customers. A question has been raised at the time of writing as to whether a firm undertaking corporate finance business with a customer may approve a specific investment advertisement for him without being responsible for ensuring that the detailed contents requirements for specific investment advertisements are included: in other words, the firm would be relying on the lighter advertising regime for corporate finance business. If the approval is a necessary part of the corporate finance investment services which the firm is providing to the customer at the time, only Rules 5–9(1) to (3) and 5–12 will apply. If, however, the approval is not so connected, then the

corporate finance special regime will no longer apply and the firm must comply with all of the advertising rules. Of course, having said that the detailed contents requirements may not apply, a firm may, nevertheless, need to ensure that some similar disclosures are included, depending on the circumstances, if the basic obligation is to be satisfied: namely that the advertisement is fair and not misleading.

Chapter 13

Unsolicited Calls

Meaning

An unsolicited call means a personal visit or oral communication **13–001** made without express invitation (section 56(8) of the FSA 1986). Unsolicited mail-shots are not included, however personalised the written communication is in respect of the recipient; nor are unsolicited messages sent by facsimile or from one computer terminal to another. Such messages do not amount to oral communications or personal visits.

"Personal visit" suggests that the caller must have actually left his usual place of business and that the investor is visited at some place with which he has an association, such as his home or place of work. Stopping passers-by in the street to hand out leaflets would not amount to personal visits. Such confrontations are only caught where they include oral communications. Owing to the fact that an unsolicited call includes either a personal visit or an oral communication, does the definition include personal visits where there is no oral communication? It is suggested that only personal visits made for the purpose of oral communication are caught. So the definition would not apply to an unsolicited personal visit to someone's house merely to deliver a leaflet or letter, however personalised the document.

Any oral communication is caught. This will include communication on a face-to-face basis as a result of a personal visit or an encounter in the street. It will also include any oral communication by telephone, even if the call is made by a machine playing a pre-recorded message. If there is no oral quality to the communication, then it is not within the definition. However, an oral communication does not have to be personal, in the sense that an oral communication made once, but to several people at the same time, would be included.

For the call to be an unsolicited one, it must have been made without the express invitation of the person called. A call made without express invitation does not become a solicited call merely because the recipient gives his consent to the call at the time that it is made. The mere giving by a person of his name and telephone number does not amount to an express invitation (Rule 5–18(6)). Likewise, if the investor merely fills out a coupon asking for further information, this does not suggest that he has expressly invited personal visits or oral communications. Instead, he may only intend that he should be sent fuller details in the post. It has even been suggested that an unsolicited call can be made upon someone whilst he is on the caller's business premises. For example, if a person has only attended his bank for the purposes of withdrawing or depositing money, he cannot be assumed to have expressly invited an employee of the bank to approach him about investment business (see paragraph 4, SIB Guidance Release No. 8/88). Similarly, a firm cannot assume that it has express permission to make a personal visit or oral communication on an investor merely because he has attended a financial seminar run by the firm.

If the investor has expressly invited a personal visit or oral communication about investment business, however, then the call does not become unsolicited merely because it strays to other investment areas besides the particular one for which the customer initially invited the call. Likewise, if a customer visits a firm's place of business to discuss a particular investment matter, the firm would not be making an unsolicited call on him if it went on to discuss other investment business matters at the same meeting.

Section 56

13–002 Except so far as permitted by regulations made by SIB, no person may, in the course of, or in consequence of, an unsolicited call, enter into an investment agreement with the person called, or procure or endeavour to procure him to enter into such an agreement (section 56(1)). This provision only applies where the call is made by way of business. It covers calls made on any person in the United Kingdom and calls made from the United Kingdom on any person overseas. Investment agreement means any agreement the making or performance of which by either party constitutes an activity which falls within Part II, Schedule 1 to the FSA 1986, or which would do so apart from the exceptions in Parts III and IV. The restriction does not merely relate to investment agreements entered into in the course of the call, but also to any agreements entered into in consequence of the call. Therefore, any further investment business will be tainted to the extent that it stems from an initial relationship which arose from an unsolicited call. The restriction applies to the entering into investment agreements with any person; it is not limited to agreements made with the person making the call, or his firm.

It is not a criminal offence to make an unsolicited call, but any investment agreement which is entered into in the course of, or in consequence of, such a call is unenforceable against the person on whom the call was made. Also, the person called is entitled to repudiate any such agreement and claim compensation for any loss suffered.

The relevant SIB regulations are the Common Unsolicited Calls Regulations. They partially came into force on September 1, 1991, and have been fully in force since January 1, 1992. Any investment agreement entered into as a result of an unsolicited call made in accordance with one of the permissions in SIB's regulations will be enforceable by the caller. The regulations do not change the meaning of an unsolicited call. They merely explain the circumstances when it is acceptable to make such a call.

SIB's regulations

SIB's Common Unsolicited Calls Regulations apply to anyone **13–003** making, by way of business, an unsolicited call which relates to an investment agreement, whether or not the person is authorised to do investment business under the FSA 1986, except when the call is made in the course of investment business for which the caller is subject to the rules of an RPB. In other words, there is a similar exception to these regulations for RPB members, as there is to the other designated Core Rules made by SIB.

Before examining the permissions, there are some general points to keep in mind. The regulations refer to the marketing restriction. This means the restriction in section 56(1) relating to unsolicited calls whose purpose is to procure or endeavour to procure the person called to enter into an investment agreement. They also refer to the dealing restriction. This is the restriction on entering into an investment agreement in the course of, or in consequence of, an unsolicited call.

The regulations provide a reasonable belief qualification. Whether a person is making a permitted unsolicited call in the circumstances is determined, not against absolute criteria, but against the reasonable belief on the part of the caller that the circumstances relating to the relevant permission were met at the time. If questioned, it will be for the caller to demonstrate that he had reasonable grounds upon which to form his belief.

In many cases firms will be dealing with customers with whom they entered into an initial investment agreement or relationship as a result of an unsolicited call made before the new SIB regulations came into force. In this case, that agreement and any subsequent agreements entered into in consequence of the original unsolicited call are not tainted, provided the call was one which would have been permitted under the new regulations. This should not cause a problem because the new permissions are more extensive than the old ones.

Overseas investment businesses

An overseas person is defined as someone who carries on investment **13–004** business, but who does not do so from a permanent place maintained by him in the United Kingdom. As we have seen in paragraph 4–004 above, such a person does not need to be authorised in respect of investment business which he carries on in the United Kingdom if that business is done: with or through authorised persons or exempted persons (acting in the course of their exemption); with persons whose business has not been solicited by the overseas person; or with persons who have been legitimately solicited. Legitimate solicitation means that the overseas person has not solicited the business in a way which has contravened sections 56 or 57 of the FSA 1986. These are the provisions relating to unsolicited calls and advertising. Therefore, if an overseas person is doing business with someone in the United Kingdom which has resulted from an unsolicited call permitted by SIB's regulations, it will not be regarded as doing investment business in the United Kingdom for which it needs authorisation.

Owing to the fact that an overseas person can engage in investment business with persons in the United Kingdom without authorisation, SIB has provided a more restrictive regime as regards the permissions available to unauthorised overseas persons to make unsolicited calls, as opposed to those available to authorised persons.

An overseas person, of course, may be authorised under the FSA 1986, even though he does not have a permanent place of business in the United Kingdom. The regulations do not want to penalise authorised overseas persons with respect to authorised United Kingdom persons. Therefore, the concept of an overseas person call has been introduced. This means a call made by or on behalf of an unauthorised overseas person, with a view to the provision by him of investment services to a person in the United Kingdom.

This distinction between calls by authorised and unauthorised overseas persons through the concept of an overseas person call has an interesting consequence in respect of overseas branches of authorised firms. As explained in paragraph 4–006 above, under the definition of regulated business an overseas branch of an SFA firm is effectively treated as if it is a separate legal entity. Therefore, it is not subject to the Conduct of Business Rules to the extent that it is dealing with investors in the United Kingdom whom it has legitimately solicited: namely, it has solicited them without contravening sections 56 or 57. In this context, it should be remembered that SFA has applied to overseas branches, for the purposes of determining whether there has been legitimate solicitation, its third tier rules on advertising and unsolicited calls (see paragraph 4–017 above). However, as the branch is part of an authorised person, it will not be making an overseas person call as defined. Therefore, it will not be subject to the same restrictions on unsolicited calls as unauthorised overseas persons. The overseas branch of an SFA firm can take advantage of the more generous permissions applying to authorised persons and has more opportunity, in terms of making unsolicited calls, of remaining within the foreign business carve-out to the Conduct of Business Rules than an unauthorised overseas person has of remaining within the exemptions to authorisable investment business within Part IV, Schedule 1. In other words, there is an "unlevel playing field" between overseas branches of authorised firms and unauthorised overseas investment businesses, weighted in favour of the overseas branches.

The more limited permissions for overseas person calls are discussed below in paragraph 13–010.

Permissions for SFA firms

As explained in the previous section, these permissions apply to all **13–005** SFA firms, including the overseas branch of an SFA firm and an SFA firm which does not have a permanent place of business in the United Kingdom. The following unsolicited calls are permitted:

(i) *Any calls to non-private investors.* Unsolicited calls may be made without restriction on non-private investors. A non-private investor is wider than the definition of non-private customer. It includes any person other than an individual (provided he is not acting in the course of carrying on investment business). In other words, small businesses which are run as partnerships or bodies corporate are not private investors, even though they are private customers.

Persons who would normally fall to be private customers may be treated under the Conduct of Business Rules as non-private customers if they are classified as expert investors (Rule 5–5). However, an individual who is classified as an expert remains a private investor for the Unsolicited Calls Regulations, unless he is acting in the course of carrying on investment business. It is unfortunate that there are not common definitions which operate between the Conduct of Business Rules, the Unsolicited Calls Regulations and the restriction of the section 62 right of action to private investors. It should be noted that the definition of private investor for the Unsolicited Calls Regulations is not as wide as that for section 62, because it leaves out the second part of that definition, which includes any person who is not an individual, otherwise than when he is acting in the course of carrying on business of any kind.

The remaining permissions apply to unsolicited calls on private investors.

(ii) *Calls relating to the sale of generally marketable non-geared packaged products.* There are definitions in the rulebook (Chapter 9) explaining what are generally marketable non-geared packaged products. (In addition, it will be necessary to look at the Financial Services (Regulated Schemes) Regulations 1991.) Basically, they are the life policies and regulated collective investment schemes which do not have any of the gearing factors associated with the newer types of warrant funds, geared futures and options funds and geared securities funds, including funds of funds and umbrella funds which invest in any of these geared funds.

Under the "new settlement" rulebooks, investment trust savings schemes have been brought within the definition of packaged product; and there is a definition of a geared investment trust savings scheme which is one investing in an investment trust whose borrowing exceeds 50 per cent. of the market value of shares held by the trust at the mid-value share price.

13–006   (iii) *Calls relating to the supply of callable investment services.* In this case, the permission only applies to authorised or exempted persons. "Callable investment services" means investment services where the only investments involved are either generally marketable non-geared packaged products (explained in (ii) above) or readily realisable securities (except warrants). "Readily realisable securities" are: government and public securities denominated in the currency of the issuer; and other securities which are either admitted to official listing on an exchange in an EC member state, or regularly traded on such an exchange or a recognised investment exchange.[1] In other words, it is similar to the definition of a readily realisable investment (described with reference to a non-readily realisable investment in paragraph 7–004 above) except that it does not include derivatives or securities traded frequently on a designated investment exchange. Investment services means activities undertaken in the course of carrying on investment business.

There is an important restriction on this permission. Basically, it only applies where the firm offers cancellation rights or a delayed entry procedure. The provision says that the agreement must be subject to (or exempted from) a cancellation or delayed entry procedure under the regulatory system; or the services must be provided under a cancellable customer agreement. In the case of a cancellable customer agreement, the firm must make clear, either in the agreement or in any accompanying letter or promotional material, that the investor has a seven-day cooling-off period.

A cancellable customer agreement is a written one (which may be a one-way document not signed by the investor) under which the investment services may only be provided after the expiry of seven days from the date on which the customer can reasonably be expected to have received a copy; and he must be able to cancel during this period without cost. For a further discussion on cancellation see paragraphs 14–009 *et seq.* below.

13–007   (iv) *Calls to existing customers.* A firm has permission to make an unsolicited call where there is a legitimately established existing customer relationship with the caller (the firm), the dealer, or an associate of either, and the customer relationship is such that the investor envisages unsolicited calls of the kind concerned. It should be noted that, unlike the old rules, there is no longer a requirement to have the permission contained in a written customer document. This is because it is possible to do a fair degree of investment business with a private customer without any kind of written documentation (for example, advisory services in readily realisable securities). The relationship does not have to have been formed with the caller, as long as it was made with the dealer, or an associate of the caller or dealer. "Legitimately established" merely means that the relationship was not formed as a result of a non permitted unsolicited call or in breach of any Conduct of Business Rules concerning customer relationships.

This provision does not give a general permission to make unsolicited calls on any matter. The call must be of the kind which the investor envisaged from the relationship. Obviously, the best way of ensuring what the investor actually envisaged is by setting out details in a customer document, even if it is only a one-way terms of business letter sent to the customer.

Interestingly, SFA has not included a clause on making unsolicited calls as part of its formal guidance on model clauses for customer documentation (see Appendix 7 below). Also this is not a provision which is required under the contents requirements for two-way customer agreements (Rule 5–23(4)). However, SFA has included a restriction similar to the old rules as to when calls may be made (Rule 5–18(2)). Calls may not be made on a private investor before 8.00 a.m. and after 9.00 p.m. (as measured in the locality of the recipient), unless he has specifically agreed to calls being made at other times.

There are some further qualifications to this permission. Unsolicited calls on existing customers which relate to geared packaged products may only be made by the customer's investment manager (for a discussion on this definition, see paragraphs 9–008 *et seq.* above). Where the firm is required to have a two-way customer agreement (investment services involving contingent liability transactions or discretionary management—Rule 5–23(2)), then an unsolicited call relating to such investment services may only be made where the investor has indicated in writing before the call (which will normally be in the customer agreement) that he envisages receiving such calls.

(v) *Calls by the acquirer of an investment business.* This is a new **13–008** requirement and enables a person who acquires the whole or part of a business to make unsolicited calls on the customers of that business solely for the purpose of finding out whether they are willing to establish a customer relationship with him. However, there is a restriction. The new relationship must not envisage unsolicited calls of any kind not envisaged by the investor under his relationship with the person disposing of the business.

(vi) *Calls relating to public takeovers.* Under the new regulations, there are more generous provisions relating to unsolicited calls in a corporate finance context (see also (vii) below). An unsolicited call may be made by, or under the supervision of, an authorised person where it is in connection with, or for the purposes of, a takeover or substantial acquisition of shares which is subject to the United Kingdom City Code on Takeovers and Mergers or the Rules Governing Substantial Acquisitions of Shares (published by the Panel on Takeovers and Mergers), or requirements in another EC member state which afford equivalent protection.[2] This means, for example, that firms acting for an offeror can make unsolicited calls on shareholders of the target company. Likewise, advisers to the offeree company may make unsolicited calls on its shareholders.

(vii) *Calls in respect of corporate acquisitions.*[3] The marketing restriction is lifted to the extent that the call is made on an employee for the purpose of arranging a management buy-out of the whole or part of the business of his employer (or one or more other undertakings in the same group), or a management buy-in relating to a business in which he would fulfil management functions. It is also lifted where the call is in connection with, or for the purpose of, a corporate acquisition or disposal within paragraph 21, Schedule 1 to the FSA 1986. This is one of the exceptions to the definition of investment business and is concerned with an acquisition or disposal where the acquirer ends up with 75 per cent. or more of the voting rights of a company.

The dealing restriction is similarly lifted provided the investor has been provided with a written statement giving sufficient information to enable him to make an informed investment decision and he has been given an adequate opportunity to seek independent advice.

13–009 (viii) *Calls between connected individuals.* Unsolicted calls are permitted:
  (a) between business partners, fellow directors and close relatives;
  (b) between the settler of a trust (other than a unit trust), its trustees, beneficiaries, and the agents of any of them—provided the call only relates to the settlement, management or distribution of the trust fund; and
  (c) between personal representatives, beneficiaries under a will or intestacy, and the agents of any of them—but only to the extent that the call relates to the management or distribution of the estate.

A close relative (referred to in (a) above) is defined as a person's spouse, children and step-children, parents and step-parents, brothers and sisters, and step-brothers and step-sisters.

(ix) *Calls in connection with employee share schemes.* Unsolicited calls can be made with respect to employee share schemes where the call is made by, or on behalf of, a body corporate, an undertaking in the same group, or the trustee of an employee share scheme. However, the purpose of the call must be to enable or facilitate transactions in shares, debentures and warrants in an undertaking in the group for the benefit of existing or former employees and their close relatives.

(x) *Calls in respect of the management of occupational pension schemes.* This permission enables a firm to call in order to seek a contract to manage the assets of an occupational pension scheme.

(xi) *Calls made in a non-commercial context.* A person may make an unsolicited call where he is not acting by way of business and has been provided with no incentive to make the call.

(xii) *Calls made in the course of a profession or other non-investment business.* Unsolicited calls relating to investment services may be made by a person carrying on any profession or business which does not constitute investment business, provided the call is a necessary part of other advice or services which the caller gives as part of carrying on his profession or business. The call is not deemed to have this character if the investment service is separately remunerated. It is suggested that there is no separate remuneration within the meaning of this provision if the investment service fees are charged in the same manner as the non-investment fees: namely, on time spent.

(xiii) *Calls by exempted persons.* Unsolicited calls may be made by exempted persons if the calls relate to investment business covered by their exemption. However, this permission does not apply to appointed representatives. They will only be able to call in accordance with the permissions stated above; and note that calls in respect of public takeover offers (permission (vi) above) may only be made by, or under the supervision of, an authorised person.

Permissions for overseas person calls

As indicated above, the permissions for an overseas person call are more restrictive. They are as follows: **13–010**

(i) *Any calls to non-private customers.* An overseas person call may be made on a non-private customer, rather than a non-private investor. The use of "customer" rather than "investor" would

237

suggest that there has to be a pre-existing customer relationship, making this permission more restrictive than the corresponding provision for authorised persons. However, this may not be so in practice, because "customer" includes a potential customer. Presumably, any unsolicited call on a person who is not an existing customer is made with the intention that he should become a customer.

Permitting calls on non-private customers could, therefore, appear a wider permission than that which relates to non-private investors. This is because, unlike the latter definition, the definition of non-private customer includes individuals who have been classified as experts. This is not the case, however, because unauthorised overseas persons do not have the ability, not being authorised persons, to classify investors who would prima facie be private customers as experts; and once an overseas person is authorised, he is subject to the permissions discussed in paragraphs 13–005 to 13–009 above.

The remaining permissions relate to calls on investors who are not private customers.

(ii) *Calls relating to the sale of non-geared packaged products.* The call cannot be made directly by the unauthorised overseas person. It has to be done through an authorised or exempted person.

(iii) *Calls to existing customers.* The permission here is as described under permission (iv) in paragraph 13–007 above for SFA firms, except that it only applies where the customer relationship was established whilst the investor was resident outside the United Kingdom. In addition, the investor must have been given the prescribed disclosure (explained in paragraph 4–020 above).

Where the call relates to a contingent liability transaction or discretionary management, then the customer must have given his written permission for such calls, even though the overseas person, as an unauthorised person, will not be subject to the two-way customer agreement requirements.

(iv) *Calls relating to public takeovers.* Any call in respect of a public takeover can only be made by, or under the supervision of, an authorised person (see permission (vi) in paragraph 13–008 above for SFA firms).

(v) *Other calls.* No other unsolicited calls may be made by an unauthorised overseas person, unless the call is made through an authorised or exempted person.

Compliance procedures for unsolicited calls (Rule 5–17)

In support of SIB's Common Unsolicited Calls Regulations, SFA has **13–011** written two third tier support rules. The first one deals with compliance procedures and the second with standards of conduct during unsolicited calls.

Under the first rule, a firm must establish and maintain compliance procedures and arrangements designed to ensure that all its employees and agents comply with the provisions of SIB's regulations and the supporting SFA rules.

Where a firm intends to make unsolicited calls on private investors in respect of geared packaged products, or any other futures and options funds, or property funds, it must, at least seven days before, inform SFA of its intention to make such calls. This enables SFA to determine whether it is appropriate for the firm to make such calls. In informing SFA, the firm must provide evidence of the compliance and supervision procedures which it has in place, and identify the relevant employees and agents who will be making such calls.

As already mentioned, unsolicited calls in respect of geared packaged products may only be made by the investor's investment manager. If requested, the firm must be able to show that this is in fact the case.

If SFA is unhappy about the firm's arrangements, then it will refuse permission to make unsolicited calls in respect of geared packaged products, other futures and options funds, and property funds; or it will impose such conditions as it considers appropriate. SFA has written guidance suggesting that, if a firm is to satisfy SFA that it has appropriate arrangements, its procedures should include the tape-recording of all such calls and the regular monitoring of the tapes. SFA will also need to be satisfied that the firm is properly complying with the suitability and best advice requirements when making any recommendations.

Standards of conduct (Rule 5–18)

This rule requires the individual making the call to terminate it as **13–012** soon as the investor makes it clear that he does not wish the call to continue. Calls must be confined to the hours between 8.00 a.m. and 9.00 p.m., unless the investor has given specific permission to calls being made outside these times. The caller should take reasonable steps to ensure that the investor understands the purpose of the call and the kind of investment and investment services which are to be discussed. In fact, the caller must not attempt to disguise in any way the purpose of the call or the nature of any investment agreement involved.

It is important to stress that, even though a firm has permission to make unsolicited calls, any recommendations made must comply with the suitability requirement. This means that a firm will need to obtain sufficient information about the customer's investment objectives and circumstances. Also, where there are risks involved, then a firm must take reasonable steps to ensure that the customer properly understands the nature of those risks. Firms should note the written risk warning requirements for derivatives and warrants and the oral warning requirement for non-readily realisable investments (Rule 5–30).

[1] It is not clear from the drafting whether the references to listing on an EC exchange and to trading on such an exchange or a recognised investment exchange also qualify government and public securities. It is suggested that they were intended to.

[2] Note that the calls do not have to be made by an authorised person: it is only necessary that the caller is supervised by an authorised person. Where such a call is made by an unauthorised person, however, the caller may find that he is carrying on an investment business activity which requires authorisation under the FSA 1986.

[3] Unlike permission (vi), this permission is not restricted to callers who are authorised persons or who are supervised by such persons. Beware, however, of the potential problem referred to in the previous note that the making of such calls may be an authorisable investment business activity.

Chapter 14

Retail Products

Definition of packaged products

The new rules introduced the term "packaged product", which is **14–001** defined to include a life policy, a unit in a regulated collective investment scheme and an investment trust savings scheme.

A life policy is an investment falling within paragraph 10, Schedule 1 to the FSA 1986. This is long term insurance business, including endowment policies, unit-linked policies, personal pension policies (if they amount to contracts of insurance on human life), other annuities on human life, the management of pension funds, and even certain permanent health insurance contracts (Schedule 1 to the Insurance Companies Act 1982). It does not include ordinary term assurance where there is no surrender value, or where there is a single premium policy with a surrender value no greater than the premium. For such a policy, however, to be exempt under paragraph 10, it must pay benefits only on death or incapacity; and where benefit is payable on a non-accidental death, it must be payable within 10 years of the date on which the person's life was first insured under the contract, or before he reaches a specified age not exceeding 70 years. Any such term assurance policy which is convertible into a policy not satisfying these conditions will be an investment within paragraph 10.

The definition of packaged product includes all regulated collective investment schemes. It also includes investment trust savings schemes, but not shares in investment trusts which are acquired otherwise than through such a savings scheme. An investment trust savings scheme is defined as a dealing service dedicated to the securities of a particular investment trust or of investment trusts within a particular marketing group, and includes the securities acquired through such a scheme.

The term packaged product does not include personal equity plans (PEPs). A PEP is a vehicle through which securities are held, but is not an investment in its own right. Also, Business expansion schemes (BES) and shares are not included; nor are broker funds. For convenience sake, however, the holding of investments through PEPs, BES schemes and broker funds, and the purchase of BES shares, will be dealt with in this chapter. Their selling and promotion is often regarded in a comparable light to the regime applying to packaged products, and they are seen as being investments or investment vehicles which are mainly aimed at the retail, private investor market.

Regulated collective investment schemes

14-002   Regulated collective investment schemes consist of both authorised unit trust schemes and recognised schemes. Authorised schemes are those which are authorised by SIB under section 78 of the FSA 1986. Recognised schemes are those overseas schemes which are recognised under sections 86, 87 and 88. Such overseas schemes are recognised because they are subject to similar regulation, or afford similar protection, to the schemes authorised by SIB. Recognised schemes include those constituted in another E.C. member state which satisfy the requirements under the UCITS Directive 85/611 (Undertakings for Collective Investment in Transferable Securities) for marketing throughout the European Community.

Regulated collective schemes may be marketed and sold generally to the public. The restrictions on the marketing of unregulated schemes have already been set out in paragraph 2–022 above.

Investment trust savings schemes

Although investment trust savings schemes have been brought within the definition of packaged product, there is a transitional provision deleting them from this definition until further notice, other than in the context of the Unsolicited Calls Regulations and SFA's supporting rule on compliance procedures for unsolicited calls (Rule 5–17). In other words, the permission to make unsolicited calls in respect of non-geared packaged products includes an investment trusts savings scheme, provided it is not a geared scheme (which is a scheme investing in an investment trust whose borrowings exceed 50 per cent. of the market value of shares held by the trust at the mid-value share price).

Investment trust savings schemes will be brought within the usual provisions for packaged products at the time when SIB is in a position to introduce the new disclosure requirement for packaged products proposed in its Retail Regulation Review Consultative Paper 60, dated March 1992.

Pensions

The categories of investments listed in Part I, Schedule 1 to the FSA 1986 do not specifically include pensions. Therefore, the extent to which a pension contract is caught depends upon its relationship to the other categories of investments. In other words, do the rights in a pension contract include rights in the categories of investments listed in Part I, Schedule 1? If the underlying investments are exclusively life policies, regulated unit trust schemes and investment trust savings schemes, the pension contract will be a packaged product.

It should be noted that occupational pension schemes are specifically excluded from the definition of collective investment scheme (section 75(6)(*k*) of the FSA 1986). An occupational pension scheme is defined as a scheme which has effect in relation to descriptions or categories of employment so as to provide benefits payable on termination of service, death or retirement to, or in respect of, earners with qualifying service in the relevant description or category of employment (section 207(1) of the FSA 1986). It should be noted that this definition does not include personal pension policies or free-standing additional voluntary contribution schemes. An employee's interest in an occupational pension scheme is not regarded as an investment (paragraph 11, note (1), Schedule 1 to the FSA 1986).

Polarisation

Polarisation is a concept which was introduced into the original **14–003** rulebooks. The basic obligation is that, where a firm advises private customers on packaged products, it must do so either as a member of a marketing group or as an independent intermediary (Rule 5–19(1)).

A marketing group means a group of persons who are allied together, whether formally or informally, for the purpose of marketing packaged products of the group. This means that at least one of the group is a product provider: namely, the life assurance company issuing the life policy; or the operator of the relevant regulated collective investment scheme or investment trust savings scheme. Polarisation is an all or nothing test. A firm which is within a marketing group may not advise on any packaged products which are provided by a company outside the group. Independent intermediaries must act in a truly independent capacity, not being affiliated in any way to a particular product provider.

Concerns have been raised in the past about the anti-competitive nature of polarisation, and whether the concept is in the best interests of investors and causes a "tied" firm to breach its fiduciary law obligations (see paragraph 15–001 below). Many investors do not appreciate, despite explanations, that their investment adviser may only recommend to them products from one particular marketing group. An investor's choice is limited when he is dealing with a smaller marketing group, which does not have a wide range of products available. The investor will not necessarily want to "shop around" between other marketing groups. He may, therefore, end up by taking out a policy which, although it appears to be the best for him from those available from the marketing group to which his adviser belongs, is not as suitable for him as some of the products available from other marketing groups.

Questions have been raised as to the capability of some independent intermediaries to survey the whole market in determining what is the best product available for an investor. In reality, many intermediaries will only deal with a limited number of product providers, because they cannot know in detail the products available from every product provider within the market.

Despite these concerns, however, SIB, in Consultative Paper 60, dated March 1992, has reaffirmed its commitment to the concept of polarisation. It thinks that it serves consumer interests best. Also, SIB has not been persuaded by the arguments to permit "multi-tying" or "badging". "Multi-tying" means that an adviser could be a member of more than one marketing group. "Badging" is a more restrictive form of multi-tying. In this case, the adviser could fill gaps in the product range of its marketing group by branding the products of another company or marketing group. Badging would allow a marketing group to complete its product range in a vertical manner; whilst multi-tying means extending the products which it can advise on in a horizontal fashion, being able to sell similar products from more than one marketing group.

SIB has also rejected the arguments for depolarising unit trust schemes. A strong case was put forward that unit trusts should be treated like shares, rather than life policies. This was not accepted, however, on the basis that there is a substantial degree of similarity between unit trusts and some life assurance products, such as unit-linked bonds, and SIB considered that they are generally sold in the same way and are linked in the public's perception.

Private customer

14-004   It should be noted that the polarisation regime and the consequent restrictions on selling packaged products only apply where a firm is dealing with private customers.

Investment manager

There is an important exception to the polarisation regime. This is where a firm is acting as the customer's investment manager. In this case, a firm which is a member of a marketing group is not restricted to advising on products from the group, but may advise its customer on any packaged product. The concept of investment manager has already been discussed in paragraphs 9–008 *et seq.* above. The more restrictive a firm's approach to regarding itself as a customer's investment manager for the purposes of the suitability obligation (Rule 5–31) and the periodic information requirements (Rule 5–35), the less it will be able to rely upon the exception to polarisation.

The narrowing of the exception to the concept of investment manager is much more restrictive than the old TSA "stockbrokers' carve-out".

Under this, a firm was not caught by the polarisation restrictions where it was acting as the customer's investment adviser or portfolio manager.

Buyer's Guide

Where a firm is advising a private customer (other than in its investment manager capacity) to buy a packaged product, it must take, or have taken, reasonable steps to ensure that the customer is aware of the firm's polarisation status, the buying process and any limits on the packaged products on which it can advise (Rule 5–21(1)). It should be noted that this requirement applies to all firms advising on packaged products, whether they are polarised or independent intermediaries.

SFA has produced two model Buyer's Guides (Appendix 10). The first one is for use by firms which are tied to a marketing group; the second is for independent intermediaries. There is formal guidance to Rule 5–21(1) to the effect that a firm will be regarded as having complied with this rule where it has given to the customer a copy of the relevant Buyer's Guide.

The Buyer's Guide should only be amended by the firm in the following circumstances. If there are limits on the kinds of packaged products on which the firm can advise, then it should omit the reference to those products in which it does not conduct business. Similarly, if it is only able to advise on certain types of regulated collective investment schemes, it should make it clear which these schemes are.

In SFA's view, the information contained in the model Buyer's Guides is sufficient to comply with the requirement in Rule 5–21(1) to give adequate information about the buying process. On this point, the Buyer's Guides state the requirements which are placed on the adviser to explain the features and risks of the product being recommended, and whether there are any cancellation rights. The Guides also explain that more detailed information will be provided to the customer direct by the product provider.

Standards of advice (Rule 5–20)

A firm must ensure that any person acting on its behalf, including its employees, other agents and appointed representatives, are fully informed about the products which they are able to sell. In the case of a firm which is a member of a marketing group, this means surveying all the packaged products which are available from the marketing group. In the case of a firm which is an independent intermediary, this means being aware of all packaged products which are generally available on the market, provided they are the kinds of products on which the firm is authorised to advise under its SFA approved business profile. For example, an independent intermediary which is not

14–005

authorised to advise on life policies only needs to survey the market in regulated collective schemes and, when they are finally included within the packaged product regime, investment trust savings schemes.

Marketing group member

Where the firm is a member of a marketing group, it must not advise a private customer to deal, or deal in the exercise of discretion for him, if there is another product available from the marketing group which would meet his needs better (Rule 5–20(2)). This is a suitability requirement, but it is only judged in terms of deciding which are the best available products for the customer from the packaged products available from the group. Due to the fact that the marketing group member has to survey all products available within the group, it must be authorised by SFA to advise on and arrange deals in all such products. If the group provides life policies and unit trusts, the member cannot be restricted in his SFA authorised business profile only to advising on unit trusts.

Although where a marketing group member is advising on a packaged product it only has to find a packaged product which is suitable for the customer from the range of products provided by the marketing group, it will still be subject to the general suitability rule (Rule 5–30(1)). Under this requirement, a firm should not advise a customer to buy one of the marketing group's packaged products if a non-packaged product investment would be more appropriate for the customer in respect of his investment objectives and circumstances. There is a fuller discussion on the suitability requirement in Chapter 9 above.

Independent intermediary

Where a firm is an independent intermediary, then it should not advise a private customer to buy, or deal as a discretionary manager for him in, a particular packaged product if there is another product generally available which would meet his needs better (Rule 5–20(3)). The intermediary, therefore, needs to carry out a more extensive survey than a firm which is a marketing group member. He must look at the whole market, or at least a reasonably wide selection of products and product providers. As discussed in the previous paragraph, the general suitability requirement will also apply, so that the firm would also have to be satisfied that it was suitable for the customer to invest in a packaged product, rather than another kind of investment.

Best advice

14–006   In practice, it is difficult for a regulator to test a firm's observance with this "best advice" requirement that there is no other product from either the marketing group (if the firm is tied) or from the market generally (if it is independent) which would meet the customer's needs better. It should be noted that the firm does not have to find the product which is absolutely the best. The requirement accepts that there may be a number of products which would, more or less, be equally suitable. Instead, the restriction is that the firm should not advise or deal if there is another product which is clearly better for the customer in the circumstances. SFA could only take disciplinary action if there was a clear case of the product falling well short of other products which were available to the firm to satisfy the customer's needs. In judging whether a firm has complied with the best advice test, the regulator must look at the information which was actually available at the time that the advice was given or the transaction made, rather than looking at subsequent events concerning the relevant product's performance.

Better than best

There is an additional requirement on an independent intermediary in the sense that he should only advise a private customer to buy an "in-house" product where he is satisfied that this product meets the customer's needs better than any other product available on the market. This is sometimes referred to as the "better than best" requirement. In other words, if there is no difference in reality between the qualities of an "in-house" product and an "out-of-house" product, the firm must advise the customer to buy the latter product. This test effectively prevents a firm from acting as an independent intermediary and selling in-house products because of the difficulty of establishing that the in-house product is absolutely the best one. The only circumstances in which this better than best provision does not apply is where the firm is acting as the customer's investment manager.

The reference to "in-house" products extends to products provided by the firm itself, any company within the same group, or members within the same marketing group as another group company. Therefore, a firm will not be able to recommend, unless it can satisfy this better than best requirement, a product provided by a non-group company if it is within a marketing group to which a company within the firm's group is tied (polarised).

Marketing group member as investment manager

Although, as stated earlier, there is a general exception to the polarisation and packaged product provisions for firms when they are acting as investment managers, this has a slightly perverse result in the case of a firm which is a member of a marketing group. Where a marketing group member is acting as an investment manager, it may still, if it wishes, restrict itself to advising on and dealing in products from within its marketing group. However, if it strays outside its marketing group (as it is entitled to do when acting as an investment manager) by recommending or dealing in a non-group product, then it must be satisfied, before making the recommendation or deal, that there is no other product generally available which meets the customer's needs better (Rule 5–20(4)); in other words, the marketing group member becomes subject to the same best advice requirement as an independent intermediary (Rule 5–20(3)).

Fact find disclosure

14–007   Interestingly, SIB is proposing, in its Consultative Paper 60, dated March 1992, that the standards of advice requirements should be "beefed-up". It has argued that a firm should ask a new customer to sign a copy of the "fact find" which is normally used by advisers in complying with the "know your customer" obligation. This signature requirement is intended to make the customer concentrate on the information which has been recorded by the adviser and confirm that it is accurate and comprehensive. The mere signing of a document, however, does not always mean that an investor has properly read its contents; and often, when required to sign something in the presence of another person, there is a tendency not to read the contents carefully.

Written explanation of recommendation

In addition, SIB wants to add an extension to the suitability Core Rule to the effect that, where a firm recommends a long term or illiquid commitment, it should explain in writing to the customer the reasons why it believes the commitment is suitable for him. A long term commitment means a regular premium life policy, an annuity, or a Business Expansion Scheme or Enterprise Zone investment. An illiquid commitment is basically defined as a property unit trust security which is not a readily realisable security (the latter term is discussed in paragraph 13–006 above) or an off-exchange transaction in derivatives (unless it is closing out an earlier derivatives transaction).[1] Of course, off-exchange derivatives transactions cannot normally be entered into for private customers (Rule 5–44), as explained in paragraph 11–025 above.

Product information (Rule 5–22)

Before or when making a personal recommendation to a private customer to buy a packaged product, the firm must give him information about the product which is adequate to enable him to make an informed investment decision (Rule 5–22(1)). It should be noted that this provision applies wherever a firm is making a personal recommendation, even if the firm is acting as an advisory investment manager. It does not apply in the case of execution-only business or in respect of discretionary transactions.

The wording about enabling the customer to make an informed investment decision is similar to that used in Principle 5 (Information for Customers). It could be asked whether this provision adds anything to the existing suitability requirement. Where a firm is making a recommendation to a private customer about an investment, it must take reasonable steps to ensure that the recommendation is suitable for him (Rule 5–31(1)).

Before or as soon as practicable after the customer buys a packaged product in a transaction recommended, effected or arranged by the firm or another authorised person, the firm must provide him with the appropriate written product particulars (Rule 5–22(2)); unless, as before, the firm is acting as a discretionary manager or dealing with the customer on an execution-only basis.

The firm does not need to provide the product particulars itself if it believes on reasonable grounds that they will be supplied direct by the product provider (see Rule 5–2(3)), which will usually be the case. If the firm is able to provide the customer with the product particulars at the time when it makes the personal recommendation to buy the product, then this should be enough also to satisfy the requirement in Rule 5–22(1) to give before, or when making the recommendation, information about the product which is adequate to enable the customer to make an informed investment decision.

The product particulars must be prepared in accordance with the rules of the SRO which is responsible for regulating the relevant life office, or the relevant unit trust or investment trust savings scheme operator. These will, therefore, usually be the product particulars prepared by the life office in accordance with LAUTRO'S rules or the scheme particulars prepared by an authorised unit trust manager in accordance with SIB's regulations. Some product providers will not be subject to these rules or regulations. For example, overseas life offices and operators of collective investment schemes constituted in another EC member state and recognised under section 86. In the case of their products, the product particulars must include, where applicable, the matters set out in Appendix 11 to SFA's rules, which are based on the similar LAUTRO and SIB requirements. As the life office or scheme operator will not be subject to SFA's rules, it will be for the SFA firm which recommended, effected, or arranged the transaction to prepare the product particulars.

New product disclosure regime

In its Retail Regulation Review Consultative Paper 60, dated March **14–008** 1992, SIB has put forward an amended version of the requirements discussed above on information (SFA Rule 5–22, SIB Core Rule 12). The reason for redrafting the rule is to facilitate the introduction of a three-tier disclosure requirement. However, the new draft only deals with the first two tiers of disclosure.

The first-tier obligation would be similar to that described above in connection with Rule 5–22(1). Before or when making the recommendation, the firm must give adequate information about the product to enable the customer to make an informed investment decision. The draft rule goes on to say, however, that this information must include a general written statement setting out the key features of the product. The key features are: a simple description of the nature of the product, including payments to be made, benefits and the main risks; a clear indication of the financial consequences of stopping payments in the early years, with a reference to surrender values in these years; an indication of how much of the investor's money is working for him, and how much is taken up in charges and expenses; and an explanation of how further, more detailed information may be obtained.

The reason for requiring a short written statement highlighting the key features of the product before or at the time when the investor makes his decision is that many investors do not read the product particulars, which are sometimes quite lengthy. Even if they read them, investors have difficulty in picking out the most salient features. SIB considers that the existing advertising and communication rules incorporating the "fair and not misleading" test (Rules 5–9(1) and 5–15(1)) are not sufficient in this respect. Also, the particulars are often sent after the investor has entered into the investment contract.

The second-tier disclosure requirement would be similar to the requirement in Rule 5–22(2) to provide product particulars. The draft rule requires appropriate written particulars of the customer's specific purchase to be supplied before or as soon as practicable after he buys the product. SIB indicates that these particulars should be given no later than the start of the cooling-off period.

As with the existing Rule 5–22, there are exceptions to both the first and second-tier disclosure obligations where the firm is acting as a discretionary manager or dealing for a customer on an execution-only basis.

The third-tier disclosure is not referred to in the suggested redraft of the Core Rule, but, in SIB's Paper, refers to any further information about the product provider and the product which will be made available to the customer on request: for example, the with-profits guide.

Cancellation

14–009   Section 51 of the FSA 1986 enables regulations to be made dealing with the circumstances in which investors may cancel investment agreements into which they have entered. The current regulations are SIB's Cancellation Rules 1989. It is likely that these rules will be revised in late 1992 or early 1993. The revisions, however, are unlikely to make too many substantive changes. Instead, SIB will write the rules in a simpler, shorter style, consistent with the "new settlement" rulebooks and link them to the new Core Conduct of Business Rules and relevant definitions. Also, it is proposed to include, within the Cancellation Rules, the separate SIB and SRO rules concerned with delayed entry.

The Cancellation Rules apply directly to all authorised persons, including RPB members. In other words, they are a form of designated rules (see paragraphs 1–008 *et seq.* above). They deal with the purchase of life policies and units in regulated collective investment schemes. They do not, however, apply to purchases by non-private customers and to private customers dealing on an execution-only basis or, except in the case of regular premium life policies, purchasing through direct offer advertisements. In other words, cancellation rights only apply where there is a personal recommendation to a private customer of the relevant product.

It should be noted that, at the moment, cancellation rights do not apply with respect to recommendations of investment trust savings schemes. It is likely that, when the Cancellation Rules are rewritten, they will apply to such recommendations because of the intention to treat investment trust savings schemes in a similar way to life policies and unit trusts.

The reason for providing cancellation rights is that packaged products are often sold to unsophisticated investors by hard selling techniques. The information about how they work is often quite complex. A significant part of the money expended by the investor at the outset of entering into the agreement, or in the initial period of the life of the product, may be taken up in charges, rather than being invested for his benefit. For all of these reasons, it was felt appropriate to give the investor an opportunity to unwind the agreement. The important thing to remember about cancellation is that the investor is cancelling an existing investment agreement, rather than being subject to a delay before he can enter into the agreement. In the case of delayed entry mechanisms, the investor's money is not invested until the necessary cooling-off period has expired.

Cancellation rights are owed by the product provider, not by the firm **14–010** advising on or arranging the purchase. The notice must be sent out within seven days after the date on which the customer enters into the investment agreement where, if he exercises his right to cancel, he will be liable to pay any shortfall. In any other case, the notice must be sent out within 14 days after the date on which the investor enters into the investment agreement.

The investor then has up to 14 days from the date on which he receives the cancellation notice to exercise his cancellation rights. All that is necessary is that he completes and sends off the notice to cancel within the 14 day period, rather than that it must be received by the product provider within this time limit.

If the investor is not sent a cancellation notice in accordance with the rules, then he may cancel the agreement at any time within two years of entering into it. In this case, he does not have to suffer the loss of any shortfall.

Where an investor cancels his agreement within the 14 days period, then he must have returned to him any money which he paid under the agreement, unless he made a lump sum investment or he entered into a periodic payment agreement which required an initial payment greater than the subsequent payments. In the latter two cases, the product provider can recover from the investor the shortfall between the purchase price which he paid and the current purchase price on the date on which the product provider becomes aware of the investor's cancellation. The shortfall must be calculated on an offer-to-offer basis, rather than an offer-to-bid basis. Also, the investor must have returned to him any charges which he paid in entering into the agreement, such as commission, front-end loading, or an initial management charge.

There is an important qualification. Cancellation does not have to be offered, except in the case of regular premium life policies, where the packaged product is purchased pursuant to a customer agreement or during negotiations intended to lead to a customer agreement.

14–011   What is a customer agreement for these purposes? When this provision was originally introduced, SIB and SRO rules generally required two-way customer agreements to be signed by private customers. Then, in 1989, provision was made for one-way (not signed and returned by the investor) customer agreements with private advisory customers, provided the services were to be limited to readily realisable securities. It is suggested that, in terms of the new rules, for a firm to continue to rely on this exception to the cancellation provisions, it will at least need to have sent, or intend to send, a one-way customer agreement.

Although a firm which is only an adviser on a packaged product, rather than the product provider, does not have to send the cancellation notice, it must still give the customer, when making its recommendation, information about cancellation (Rule 5–22(5)). If no cancellation rights apply, then the customer must be advised of this fact. If cancellation rights apply, the firm must tell the customer that he has such rights and of the length of the cancellation period which will be available to him. The firm must also advise the customer, if relevant, that he will have to suffer the shortfall in the value of the investment between purchasing it and cancelling it. If the product is one of the new generation of geared funds, then the firm must also advise the customer that the shortfall on cancellation may be substantial.

Where a firm is sending product particulars itself, rather than relying upon the product provider, then, if cancellation rights apply, the firm must ensure that the product particulars are sent to the customer no later than the date on which the cancellation notice is sent (Rule 5–20(4)). It is possible for an SFA firm to be a product provider itself. SFA has scope to authorise the operators of futures and option funds, warrant funds and property funds, and also the operators of investment trust savings schemes.

Delayed entry

The difference between cancellation and delayed entry is that, in the case of cancellation, a person cancels an agreement into which he has already entered; whilst in the case of delayed entry, the investor is prevented from entering into the agreement until a number of days have passed, normally seven days. Cancellation rights normally apply in respect of packaged products, whilst delayed entry mechanisms are relevant in the context of the other retail products (which are non-packaged products) discussed later in this chapter.

14–012

One form of delayed entry mechanism is the requirement for two-way customer agreements (as discussed in paragraph 6–003 above). A private customer cannot enter into a contingent liability transaction unless he has entered into a two-way customer agreement. Similarly, the firm cannot provide discretionary services to any customer unless such an agreement has been entered into. A two-way customer agreement is one which the customer has signed and returned to the firm after having had a proper opportunity to consider its terms.

It would be wrong for a firm to avoid the delayed entry mechanism procedures by asking the customer to sign a pre-dated form; that is, the form being dated seven days before. The intention of delayed entry is that the customer should have the ability to change his mind before he is committed to the agreement.

Owing to the fact that the agreement does not become effective until the delayed entry period has expired, any money which the firm receives from the investor in connection with the agreement before the expiry of the relevant period must be treated as client money. It will not be due and payable to the firm until the delayed entry period has expired. Also, note that, for the purposes of the Client Money Regulations, money is defined to include money in the form of cheques and other payable orders. The protection arises at the point at which the money is received, even if it is not banked until the expiry of the delayed entry period. The Client Money Regulations make no special provision for post-dated cheques. (See Chapter 18 below.)

Commission disclosures

In recommending or dealing in packaged products, a firm does not have to disclose the amount of the commission which it receives from the product provider. Before providing the service, it merely has to disclose the nature of the remuneration (Rule 5–33(2) and see paragraphs 9–013 *et seq.* above). After executing a transaction in a packaged product, other than a life policy, a firm must provide a

14–013

contract note. The contract note has to show any front-end loading in respect of the purchase of a unit in a collective investment scheme. It must also record the basis of any remuneration which the firm is receiving from the product provider, unless either the contract note or another written document sent to the customer explains that this information will be available to him on request (see paragraph 10–005 above). If the customer does request the information, then the firm is only obliged under SFA's rules to disclose the basis on which commission has been paid to it by the product provider, rather than disclosing the actual amount. SIB is not proposing in Consultative Paper 60 any change to the existing commission disclosure regimes for packaged products.

Forecasts and illustrations

A firm must not publish or provide any forecast or illustration of realisable value or benefits relating to one of the new generation of geared funds (Rule 5–22(9)). In the case of any other life policy or regulated collective investment scheme, a firm may only publish or provide to private customers forecasts and illustrations of realisable value or benefits which comply with the requirements in Appendix 13. These requirements link into SIB's tables concerning the methods of calculation which must be used. The tables require illustrations to be based on standard cost assumptions, which have been prescribed by LAUTRO, and standard rates of return.

Personal equity plans

14–014   PEPs as such are not packaged products. A PEP is merely a tax efficient way of holding certain investments. It is not itself a category of investment within Part I, Schedule 1 to the FSA 1986. Therefore, in the main, the extent to which the rules apply to a PEP depends upon the kinds of investments held within it. In other words, the packaged product rules will apply to the unit trust element of a PEP, but not the ordinary equity element. In this connection, remember that an investment trust share which is not held through an investment trust savings scheme is not a packaged product.

If unit trusts are held within a PEP, then the provisions discussed above on standards of advice and information will apply. The plan manager will be able to take advantage of the exceptions from the polarisation regime for investment managers if he is acting as a discretionary manager or an ongoing advisory manager (within the scope of the second Limb to the definition discussed in paragraphs 9–008 *et seq.* above).

SIB wrote an additional requirement for PEPs under the standards of advice Core Rule for packaged products (Rule 5–20(6)). This requires that, where a firm is advising on a packaged product which is to be held as a plan investment of a PEP, it must, in assessing the merits of the investment, take into account the characteristics of the PEP, as well as the product. In other words, in meeting the best advice requirement or the better than best test, the firm must examine the suitability of holding the packaged product as part of a PEP, rather than just looking at the packaged product in isolation. The firm should take into account the added cost of investing in the packaged product through the medium of a PEP, with its associated management charges, compared with direct investment in the product.

Although a PEP is not a packaged product itself, there are moves afoot to make all PEPs, including those only holding equity investments, subject to the packaged product regime. In its Retail Regulation Review Consultative Paper 60, dated March 1992, SIB has redrafted the information requirement for packaged products to include all PEPs (Rule 5–22). If this goes ahead, the new disclosure regime (described in paragraph 14–008 above), with its three tiers of information, will apply to all PEPs. This will mean that, before or when making a personal recommendation to buy a PEP, a firm will have to give the general written information sheet about the key features of the PEP (tier 1).

As regards the cancellation and cooling-off provisions which relate to **14–015** PEPs, the position is quite complicated and cooling-off applies in some situations where investments within the plan are not packaged products. The Cancellation Rules apply to type A PEPs, which are PEPs which only invest in authorised unit trust schemes. They also apply to new issue PEPs. A new issue PEP is defined as one under which the plan investor's initial subscription, that is his subscription during the period for which cancellation applies, consists of shares which he has transferred into the plan. Although, in the case of a Type A PEP or a new issue PEP, there is the standard exception which is that cancellation does not apply where the agreement is entered into pursuant to a customer agreement. See the discussion in paragraph 14–009 *et seq.* above.

Under TSA's rules, the only time where a firm had to provide a delayed entry mechanism (cooling-off) in respect of a PEP was where the PEP was being advertised off-the-page. Under the new rules, cancellation rights and delayed entry mechanisms do not apply with respect to direct offer advertisements (the new name for off-the-page and off-the-screen advertisements). SFA, however, at its third tier has introduced a delayed entry mechanism where a private customer invests in a PEP as a result of a personal recommendation by the firm or another authorised person (Rule 5–22(6)). The rule says that the firm must give the customer the right to withdraw from the PEP during the seven days following the receipt by the firm of the customer's offer. The firm must also provide the customer with a means of communicating his right to withdraw; in other words, sending him a cancellation document.

Although SFA's wording does not make it clear, it is suggested that the delayed entry mechanism only applies to the packaged product element within the PEP which is recommended; or, possibly, to any PEP containing a packaged product investment, even if some of the other investments within the PEP are equities. It seems wrong that an investor should benefit from delayed entry just because he has entered into an equity investment through the medium of a PEP, which is merely a tax efficient vehicle through which to hold his investments.

In reality, few investors cancel agreements or exercise their cooling-off rights. It is almost irrelevant to grant an investor cooling-off rights with respect to an equity-only PEP because he will be able to sell his investments at any time anyway. The only advantages of providing some sort of cancellation or cooling-off rights for PEPs is that the investor will be able to recover any initial charges which were payable on entering into the agreement and he will be free to enter into another PEP within the same tax year. Under the Inland Revenue's PEP Regulations, an investor is only entitled to hold one PEP in any tax year. If he cancels the plan during the relevant cancellation or delayed entry period, he will not be regarded as having held that plan at all.

14–016   Anyway, there are exceptions to offering delayed entry rights to PEPs (Rule 5–22(7)). A firm does not have to offer cooling-off where:

(i)   it is acting as the customer's investment manager;

(ii) the customer is entering into a PEP on substantially the same terms as a PEP already held by him (this covers the situation where a customer is taking out another PEP in the following tax year); or

(iii) the PEP is being transferred from another PEP plan manager.

It should be noted that these exceptions only apply to the requirement to offer a delayed entry procedure under SFA's rules. They are not exceptions for the purposes of offering cancellation rights under SIB's Cancellation Rules for Type A PEPs or new issue PEPs.

Due to the fact that the cancellation rules specifically refer to Type A PEPs and new issue PEPs, it is suggested that cancellation does not apply to a recommendation of a packaged product within a mixed PEP; in other words, a plan which is invested in equities as well. In this case, however, delayed entry applies unless one of the exceptions in Rule 5–22(7) is relevant.

SFA's rules do not lay down any specific customer agreement requirements for PEPs. Therefore, the usual rules will apply. If it is a discretionary PEP, then a two-way customer agreement will be required. Warrants can be included within a PEP provided they are attached to an equity. The investor will not have to sign a Warrant

Risk Warning Notice because that is only required where an investor is purchasing an unattached warrant (see Rule 5–30(4) and paragraph 7–003 above).

Business expansion schemes

BES investments[2] fall into three categories:

14–017

(i) direct ownership of shares in an individual BES qualifying company (BES shares);

(ii) a discretionary individual portfolio which is invested wholly or mainly in the shares of BES qualifying companies (BES managed portfolios); and

(iii) pooled funds which are invested in the eligible shares of BES qualifying companies (BES funds).

BES funds are arrangements which would be collective investment schemes except that an investor is regarded as the owner of part of the property and is able to take it out at any time. He does not merely have rights in a collectively owned pool (see section 75(5) of the FSA 1986).

BES investments, although regarded as retail products, are not packaged products. Therefore, they are subject to the general rule requirements, especially suitability (Rule 5–31) and understanding risk (Rule 5–30). In respect of the latter rule, it will be necessary for a firm recommending such an investment to provide the warning for non-readily realisable investments (Rule 5–30(5) and see paragraph 7–004 above).

Under the previous rules, BES investments could only be advertised to the public in general through a two-stage process. The first stage consisted of a trailer advertisement containing basic factual information about the investment on offer. If the investor liked what he read, then he had to apply for the full product information before he could enter into the investment. The only exception to this two-stage disclosure regime for general marketing to the public was in respect of a private offer of BES shares, provided the advertisement gave full information to enable the investor and his investment adviser to make an informed investment decision as to whether or not to invest in the shares.

These advertising restrictions have now been removed. BES advertisements are subject to the general advertising rules, already discussed in Chapter 12 above. There are, however, some specific advertising provisions for BES investments which apply in addition to the general advertising requirements.

The contents requirements for direct offer advertisements with BES investments have already been discussed in paragraphs 12–018 *et seq.* above. An additional advertising rule prevents a firm from issuing or approving a specific investment advertisement relating to a BES fund unless its terms provide that not more than 27.5 per cent. of the investors' subscriptions will be invested in any one company (Rule 5–11(1)).

14–018   As under the previous rules, firms must not issue, approve, reissue or distribute any forecasts or illustrations of realisable value relating to BES investments (Rule 5–11(2)). This provision extends to any forecast, projection or estimate of realisable value or return; and to any figures or statements which could lead to the calculation by the investor of realisable value or return on any particular assumption. It extends to statements expressed as an annual percentage yield or as a cash uplift on the original investment. In the past, some waivers to this prohibition have been granted, but only after careful consideration and where the forecast or illustration forms part of a prospectus or scheme memorandum.

The requirements on referring to guarantees in advertisements have already been dealt with in paragraph 12–016 above. An advertisement should not describe a return as guaranteed unless there is a legally enforceable arrangement with a third party. If they are to pass the fair and not misleading obligation, therefore, advertisements with BES investments should avoid the use of terms such as "guaranteed", "fixed", "certain" or "assured" unless the investor has a right of action against an independent third party of good standing to recover the difference between the stated return and an actual lower return.

There is a general requirement, similar to that for packaged products, that before or when making a personal recommendation to a private customer to buy a BES investment, a firm must give him adequate information about the investment to enable him to make an informed investment decision (Rule 5–32(1)). BES investments are not subject to the Cancellation Rules. Delayed entry, however, applies wherever a private customer invests in a BES fund or managed portfolio (not BES shares direct) as a result of a personal recommendation. The customer must be given seven days in which to withdraw following the firm's receipt of his offer to invest; and, also, the firm must provide the means through which the customer may communicate his withdrawal (Rule 5–32(3)).

It should be noted that there are no specific exceptions to the requirement to offer seven days cooling-off, unlike in the case of PEPs. However, because delayed entry only has to be offered where a firm is making a personal recommendation, it does not have to be provided in the case of discretionary investment management (rather than advisory investment management); or with respect to execution-only transactions.

Finally, there is a further restriction with respect to BES investments on the customer borrowing requirement. In paragraphs 8–001 *et seq.* above, it has already been explained that firms may only lend money or extend credit to private customers with their prior written consent

(Rule 5–27). This general proviso still applies, but, in respect of BES investments, credit facilities cannot be extended or arranged by the firm to enable a private customer to invest unless he has specifically sought such credit without any prior solicitation from the firm or any other person involved in the credit arrangements (Rule 5–32(2)).

Broker funds

A broker fund adviser is a firm or its associate which has the **14–019** following type of arrangement with either a life office (namely, a regulated insurance company, a regulated friendly society, an overseas life office authorised in a country designated under section 130(3) of the FSA 1986) or an operator of a regulated collective investment scheme. The arrangement must be one under which it is expected that the relevant life office or scheme operator will take into account the advice of the firm or its associate in determining:

(i) in the case of a life office, matters likely to influence the performance of any fund of, or investment issued by, the life office into which cash contributions of private customers of the firm have been made; or

(ii) in the case of a scheme operator, the composition of the property of any scheme into which cash contributions of private customers of the firm have been made.

In other words, a broker fund adviser is a firm, or its associate, which has a direct influence on the way in which a life office or scheme operator manages its funds or schemes in which the firm's private customers have interests.

A firm is not a broker fund adviser merely because it gives investment advice or carries on investment management activities for a life office or scheme operator. Nor is a firm a broker fund adviser where it has no direct relationship with a life office or scheme operator, but acts solely as an investment manager for another broker fund adviser. For the relationship of a broker fund adviser to be created, there has to be, effectively, a three-way relationship between the life office or scheme operator, the broker fund adviser and his private customer. The customer's investments are with the life office or scheme operator, but the way in which they are managed by the life office or scheme operator is directly influenced by the broker fund adviser. Therefore, a broker fund is a fund of a life office or other investment issued by a life office into which cash contributions of private customers of the broker fund adviser have been made; or a fund of a regulated collective investment scheme into which cash contributions of private customers of the broker fund adviser have been made.

As a broker fund consists of an investment in a packaged product, the rules discussed above on packaged products apply with respect to any personal recommendation made by the broker fund adviser to his customer to buy the relevant life policy or unit trusts. The broker fund adviser will either be tied to a marketing group or an independent intermediary. He will have to comply with the best advice requirement (or, if he is independent and recommending an in-house product, the better than best test). He must comply with the information requirements on the products which he is recommending.

The broker fund adviser must also be satisfied that it is suitable for his customer to invest in a life policy or unit trust through the medium of a broker fund. This assessment should be necessary under the general suitability rule (Rule 5–31(1)), but there is a specific provision on this point, like that for PEPs (Rule 5–20(8)).

14–020   This states that the firm must take into account the characteristics of the broker fund, including the charging arrangements, when assessing the merits of the investment. The firm must be satisfied that, by investing in a life policy or unit trust scheme through the medium of a broker fund, an investor will obtain a better investment return. The increase in return over straight investment in the life policy or scheme should at least equal, if not better, the increased costs involved in investing through a broker fund. There are increased costs because the broker earns a fee or commission for acting as the adviser to the life office or scheme operator in relation to the broker fund.

In fact, firms should only be advising customers to invest in broker funds if they really believe that there is no other comparable investment product suitable for the customer. Also, a broker fund adviser should make it clear to its customer that it has a dual role and acts as adviser to the life office or scheme operator (see paragraphs 15–007 *et seq.* below). Also, the firm will need to disclose the nature or amount of any remuneration which it is receiving from the life office or scheme operator (Rule 5–33(2)).

In addition, SFA requires a broker fund adviser to review on an annual basis whether the broker fund arrangement continues to be in the customer's best interests and satisfies the best advice requirement (or, if relevant, the better than best test). If the arrangement does not continue to meet these criteria, the firm must give the customer a suitable alternative recommendation. Before a significant change in the investment strategy of the fund is implemented, the customer must be advised of this change. At the same time, the firm must either confirm that the arrangement continues to be in his best interests or provide him with a suitable alternative recommendation (Rule 5–20(7)).

As a broker fund is invested in packaged products, product particulars will be required. A broker fund adviser, however, is not required to prepare or send product particulars in respect of a broker fund managed for a single customer (Rule 5–22(10)). A broker fund adviser must also regularly publish, or cause to be published (perhaps by the life office or scheme operator), the prices of each of the funds for which it is a broker fund adviser (Rule 5–22(11)). As with product particulars, however, there is an exception for single customer funds.

It is important that an investor in a broker fund receives regular **14–021** information concerning the performance of the fund. There is a requirement, therefore, to send him a valuation statement at six-monthly intervals (Rule 5–35(10)). There is a table of the matters which should be included in the statement. These include the aggregate value of commissions, benefits and other remuneration received by the firm or paid to a third party; and, unless the fund is managed on behalf of a single customer, comparisons with managed funds of the life office which are not broker funds and comparisons with published index or sector averages. Where the broker fund has a life policy linked to it, the customer must be provided annually with information about the units in the fund allocated to the life policy (Rule 5–35(11)). However, a firm does not have to provide the six monthly valuation statement or the annual information about the linked life policy where it believes on reasonable grounds that the life office or scheme operator will provide the same information direct to the customer, which will often be the case.

There are no special cancellation or delayed entry rights for broker funds. The usual cancellation rights for recommendations concerning packaged products will apply because the investment is in a life policy or a unit trust scheme. See paragraphs 14–009 *et seq.* above.

---

[1] This extension to the suitability Core Rule would not be limited to packaged products because the concept of an illiquid investment includes non-readily realisable securities. Since SIB's Consultative Paper 60, it has been suggested that the requirement to give a written explanation relating to the suitability of the recommendation should be extended to a recommendation to relinquish an existing long-term commitment.

[2] The March 1992 Budget proposed removing the tax relief for BES investments by the end of 1993.

Chapter 15

Conflicts of Interest

Background

Firms which carry on investment business with customers will owe **15–001** equitable fiduciary duties. Fiduciary obligations have been developed under the Common Law system over the centuries by judges under the general branch of law known as Equity.

The basic rule is that a firm acting in a fiduciary capacity must always put its customer's interests above the firm's own interests and must treat all customers fairly, not preferring one customer against the interests of another.

Owing to the fact that the law on fiduciary duties has been developed by the courts over many years, the extent of the law is uncertain in places and some of the duties which have been developed overlap with each other. The fact that the law may be uncertain in some cases is not necessarily a disadvantage. One of the advantages of the English Common law system is that the judges have been able to adapt the law to fit new business methods and operations, different commercial relationships, and changing mores and attitudes.

The four main obligations which a fiduciary has may be summarised as:

(i) *No conflict*—a fiduciary must not put himself in a position where his own interests conflict with those of his customer.

(ii) *No profit*—the fiduciary must not obtain any profit whilst acting as a fiduciary at the expense of his customer. If he does make such a profit, he must remit it to the customer.

(iii) *Undivided loyalty*—the fiduciary must always act in the interests of his customer. He must not put himself in a position where his duty to one customer conflicts with the duty which owes to another customer. He must use for the benefit of the customer all of his skill and expertise, including any information which he has acquired and which is relevant to the service which he is providing to the customer.

(iv) *Confidentiality*—the fiduciary must not use for his own benefit or for the benefit of any other person (including other customers) information which he has acquired in confidence whilst acting as a fiduciary for the customer.

A fiduciary relationship arises wherever a firm has a customer relationship, rather than a market counterparty relationship. It is not right to assume that fiduciary obligations are merely owed where a firm is dealing with private customers or dealing in an agency capacity. At least, this is the best way to approach the situation: a firm owes fiduciary obligations to all customers. The mere fact that a person is a customer suggests that he is relying on the professional skill and expertise of the firm to provide a service, and that this very relationship creates in law a fiduciary relationship, even where the firm deals as a principal with a sophisticated investor. A fiduciary relationship would only not arise where the parties are dealing with each other as commercial equals, which is really the market counterparty relationship situation.

15–002   Certainly, it is easy to see why a firm has fiduciary obligations where it is acting as a discretionary manager, a trustee or an agent. It is because of concerns that a fiduciary should obtain proper protection for his customer when dealing with another firm that the Core Rule definition of market counterparty does not apply where the agent identifies his principal. Where a person identifies his principal, he is clearly showing that he is acting as an agent with fiduciary obligations. Therefore, the argument is: he should be protected as a customer so that customer obligations flow through to his customer (the agent's principal). In fact, as soon as the agent (not being a market counterparty) identifies his principal, then the identified principal becomes an indirect customer; and, as we have already seen in paragraphs 5–041 *et seq.* above, an indirect customer is for most purposes under the rules treated as if he was in a direct customer relationship with the firm dealing with the agent. In other words, where a firm has an indirect customer, it has to look past the agent to provide customer protections direct to the agent's principal.

Of course, the newer types of options and futures markets work on a riskless principal-to-principal transaction basis. For example, a customer places a purchase order with a broker. The broker then goes into the market and purchases himself from another dealer a contract which represents the customer's order. The broker then sells on this contract to the customer. In this situation, although the broker is dealing on a principal basis with his customer, his obligations are similar to those arising in an agency market, like the London Stock Exchange, where the broker does not himself deal with the customer, but arranges for another dealer on the exchange, namely a market maker, to sell the stock direct to the customer to satisfy the customer's purchase order.

It was to reflect the fact that a broker dealing as a principal with a customer has fiduciary obligations that the Core Rule definition of order, which is relevant in respect of the best execution rule (Rule 5–39), includes the reference to an order to a firm from a customer to effect a transaction in circumstances giving rise to similar duties as those arising on an order to effect a transaction as agent.

Financial conglomerates

Before the major changes to the London Stock Exchange in 1985 and **15–003** 1986, which are commonly referred to as "Big Bang", the situation in respect of fiduciary obligations was fairly straightforward. Brokers who dealt with customers could only act as agents. They did not deal as principals, but arranged transactions on the customer's behalf with jobbers. The agent's duty was to obtain the best price possible for the customer and he was remunerated by commission charged for arranging the transaction. The basis on which he charged commission had to be disclosed before arranging the deal. The agent arranged the deal with a jobber who had no direct contact with customers. The jobber's function was to buy and sell stock, only dealing through Stock Exchange agents. The jobber's remuneration came from the principal's turn or mark-up between the bid and offer prices (the price at which he bought stock and the price at which he sold stock). This form of dealing was known as single capacity.

In addition, brokers and jobbers were partnerships, privately owned and run by the partners of the business. The partners were only able to run one business; for example, they were either agents or jobbers, they could not act as both.

The changes involved with "Big Bang" allowed the Stock Exchange partnerships to become incorporated companies and to be owned and controlled by non-Stock Exchange businesses, including businesses incorporated or controlled from outside the United Kingdom. The changes also ended single capacity, so that a broker did not always have to deal with his customer as agent, but could deal with him as a principal by selling stock from his own book.

These "Big Bang" changes effectively turned fiduciary law on its head, because it created the possibility for many conflicts of interest and breaches of the four basic obligations described above.

FSA 1986 regulation

The regulatory scheme under the FSA 1986 has acknowledged that **15–004** firms will be doing business where they have conflicts of interest. If the strict obligations under fiduciary law were enforced by the regulators, no multi-function financial services conglomerate would be able to operate. However, the rules have attempted to ensure that the basic principles underlying fiduciary law are conformed with: namely, that firms should treat their customers fairly, putting customers' interests above those of the firm and not obviously preferring one customer to the disadvantage of another. Also, the rules require disclosure to, or consent from, a customer in most cases where the course of action taken by a firm could amount to a breach of a fiduciary obligation.

The rules under the FSA 1986 are designed to ensure that firms manage conflicts of interest properly, rather than preventing them from acting where they have such conflicts. The problem which this has thrown up is the extent to which a firm may still be liable for a breach of a legal obligation under fiduciary law where it has conformed with the requirements on managing conflicts of interest laid down by its regulator. Ideally, firms would like comfort from knowing that, provided they are complying with the requirements of their regulator, they will not be in jeopardy of their beneficiaries, namely their customers, bringing actions in the civil courts for breaches of the firms' fiduciary obligations.

It was due to this concern that the Law Commission was asked by the Minister for Corporate Affairs to consider the relationship between, on the one hand, fiduciary and analogous duties owed by professionals and businesses subject to public law regulation and, on the other, the duties imposed by statutory and self-regulatory rules.

This is a difficult task because of the difficulty in the first place of establishing the scope of fiduciary obligations, and the uncertainty at law concerning the extent to which statutory and self-regulatory rules replace or override obligations arising under Common Law and Equity where no express provision has been made by statute.

The Law Commission process is taking three stages. An initial questionnaire was issued in November 1990, asking for replies by the end of January 1991. The second stage has been the preparation of a consultation paper analysing the nature of the problem, taking account of the answers to the initial questionnaire and setting out possible options for reform of the law. This second-stage consultation paper will be issued towards the middle of 1992. The third stage will be the formulation of policy arising from this consultation process and the publication of a final report. That final report may or may not suggest that legislative amendment is required. If this should be the case, there would be a further delay whilst the necessary Bill was drafted and then proceeded through Parliament.

15–005   It is unfortunate, but understandable, that this review process by the Law Commission is taking so long and was not complete at the time that the "new settlement" rulebooks were devised and introduced, with the Principles, Core Conduct of Business Rules and SRO third-tier supporting requirements. It would be in the interests of both firms and the regulators to know that compliance with the SFA scheme of regulation was a sufficient "safe harbour" in terms of complying with fiduciary obligations.

The continuing uncertainty is fueled by the fact that the precedents on fiduciary law were developed in respect of old business practices; certainly, before the "Big Bang" changes. Also, recent cases have dealt with conflicts in non-financial services areas, such as the organisation of a solicitor's practice.

This book is a commentary on the Principles, Core Rules and SFA's third tier. It concentrates on the obligations which a firm owes under these rules, rather than under fiduciary law. It is outside the book's scope to cover in detail a firm's fiduciary obligations. When a firm is conducting investment business, however, it should have an eye to any additional obligations which it may owe under fiduciary law beyond the strict requirements of the SFA Rulebook.

Having said this, many of the rules are really a restatement of the obligations which a firm owes in the circumstances as a fiduciary. Also, certain of the disclosures and consents which are required in the context of the rules are necessary anyway if a firm wishes to modify or avoid a fiduciary duty with a customer. The problem which arises is that, under fiduciary law, it may not be possible under any circumstances to avoid a duty, even where there has been detailed, prior disclosure to the customer. In addition, in some cases, fiduciary law may require a stricter disclosure before a firm can act with a conflict of interest than is required under SFA's rules. It is not always easy, because of the way that fiduciary law has developed and the lack of recent authority, to set out in exactly what cases the test under fiduciary law is higher than that under the FSA 1986 regulatory rules.

Until the results of the Law Commission's work are known, the writer suggests the following approach. In most cases, a firm should be able to take comfort from the fact that it has complied with SFA Rules. If a firm is not quite sure whether a particular course of action is legitimate or not within the terms of a particular rule, it should err on the side of caution. It should either not proceed with the matter contemplated, or do it in another way which it is confident is within the scope of the rule. The same cautious approach should be taken where a firm is unsure whether or not a particular action satisfies its fiduciary obligations, even if it is confident that the course contemplated is within the rules. The rules are expected to be read in a business-like and practical manner, and a firm must have regard to the spirit as well as the letter of a rule (Rule 1–3). It is suggested that a similar practice should be adopted in respect of compliance with fiduciary obligations.

If an action is brought in the civil courts for breach of a fiduciary duty in a financial services context, the court will want to hear evidence of how a firm was complying with a regulator's rules and what action was required under those rules. It may be that, even if the court is not prepared to accept that the rules have amended fiduciary law, at least the requirements under the rules may go some way to establishing what obligations are owed under fiduciary law in a modern day context in respect of the type of business involved. In other words, compliance with the rules will not necessarily be sufficient for a firm safely to ignore any additional obligations it may have under fiduciary law, but a firm which acts responsibly and cautiously in terms of its rule obligations is less likely to find itself liable for a breach of a fiduciary duty.

A breach of a fiduciary duty will not itself give rise to disciplinary action by SFA unless the duty is incorporated into one of the rules, including the Principles. The same applies to whether or not an investor has a claim under section 62. If a fiduciary duty is not reflected in one of the rules, then the only other circumstance in which it would become relevant is in determining whether the firm is fit and proper; and the fact that a firm broke a legal obligation which it owed to a customer would be relevant in this context: at least, if it was a significant breach.

Principles

15–006   Remember that the Principles (see Appendix 1 below) are written in wide terms and are overriding. It is suggested that the Principles enunciate ordinary fiduciary obligations. For example, Principle 1 requires a firm to observe high standards of integrity and fair dealing; whilst Principle 2 requires a firm to act with due skill, care and diligence. Principle 3 talks about a firm observing high standards of market conduct. Then there is a specific principle (Principle 6) on conflicts of interest which requires a firm to ensure fair treatment to all its customers by disclosure, internal rules of confidentiality, declining to act, or otherwise. Note that this Principle accepts that the conflict may be so great that a firm should not act in the circumstances; but there may be other areas where the conflict is merely technical in nature and does not prevent the firm acting because, in practice, it will be treating all its customers fairly.

The other Principles also emphasise obligations which a firm has while it is acting as a fiduciary. Principle 4 requires a firm to obtain sufficient information about a customer to enable it to fulfil its responsibilities. Principle 5 obliges a firm to give customers enough information to enable them to make balanced and informed decisions. Principle 7 requires a firm with responsibilities for a customer's assets to ensure proper protection of them. Principle 9 requires a firm to control its internal affairs in a responsible manner, to have well defined compliance procedures and to ensure that its staff are properly trained and supervised.

Disclosure

15–007   The best way of dealing with any potential breach or conflict with a firm's fiduciary duties to a customer is by making full and prior disclosure before the potential breach or conflict arises. In other words, where relevant, it should be explained to the customer that the deal will be executed with him as a principal, the firm making a profit on the difference between the price at which the stock was bought and the price at which it is sold on to him. It should be pointed out that the customer's order will be crossed with that from another customer, and that commission will be received by the firm from the other customer in respect of the same transaction. It should be disclosed that the firm has a long position in the stock which is being sold to the customer; or that the firm has assisted the company whose shares it is recommending the customer to buy. It should be spelt out that there is only one market maker in the shares (the firm) and that there are no independent criteria against which to assess the bid and offer prices which are being quoted. The firm should disclose that, where it is acting as an agent, it will receive back from the firm dealing for the customer a share of the commission charged or any other profit made by the dealer. It should be explained that the deal will be executed by a connected company, or that there is some other interest which a connected company has in the transaction which has been recommended.

Fiduciary law prevents a fiduciary acting where he has a conflict, even if he is not in fact prejudicing the customer. The important point is that there should be no risk of prejudice to the customer, rather than an actual disadvantage to him. A firm may only avoid these strict consequences if there has been a full and frank disclosure of all of the relevant details giving rise to the potential conflict, and if the customer does not object to the firm acting for him in the circumstances. The firm, however, still has a duty to act in the interests of the particular customer. The disclosure of the conflict merely enables the firm to continue to act for the customer. It must still put the individual customer's interests first, unless the customer has properly appreciated the consequences of his interests being subordinated to those either of another customer or of the firm.

There may be cases where it is impossible to make a sufficiently frank and full disclosure of the conflict for the customer to be regarded as having consented to the firm continuing to act for him. Also, despite making the disclosure, it may be impossible for the firm to act in the circumstances without being affected by the conflict against the interests of the customer. It will be a matter of judgment in the particular case. This is why it was stated above that a firm which has any doubt as to whether or not a course of action is permitted by the rules, or under fiduciary law, should not act in the manner contemplated.

A number of SFA's rules deal with disclosure where there could be a **15–008** potential conflict. However, some of the disclosures required by the rules are very general. It may be that the rule does not require the type of specific disclosure which is necessary for the purposes of avoiding the strict requirements of fiduciary law. Take the following general disclosures in a customer agreement: the firm may sometimes deal with the customer as a principal; cross the customer's orders with orders from other customers; deal through connected companies; receive remuneration from other persons with whom the firm deals on the customer's behalf; deal where it has confidential information in another part of the firm which is not disclosed to the customer, but which is relevant to the deal. Are such disclosures sufficient to raise the presumption that the customer, by not objecting, has consented to the firm, in relation to a particular transaction, acting with one of these conflicts?

The disclosure in the customer agreement may have been several years ago. For example, some firms have not reissued or revised agreements which were sent out in 1987 and 1988. To what extent does disclosure there still bind a customer? Also, some of the relevant disclosures have been made in one-way written terms of business letters. It may be harder to argue that the customer has consented where he has not signed and returned the agreement to the firm.

Whether consent may be implied in a particular case on the basis of a general disclosure made in a one-way document which a customer received several years ago will depend upon the nature of the conflict in the circumstances. For example, is the conflict one which is regularly practised and understood in the market, or is it a fairly unusual conflict? Since "Big Bang" it is accepted that many firms will deal with customers off their own books as principals. It is also fairly standard for firms to withhold information obtained in one part of the firm from another part through the device of a Chinese Wall.

In such cases, a general disclosure in a customer agreement may be sufficient for the purpose of obtaining the customer's informed consent in relation to most cases where the firm deals as a principal or acts without disclosing information obtained by another part of the firm. The profits on a particular principal transaction, however, may be so excessive, or the nature of the information held so sensitive and relevant to the business done with the customer, that the general disclosure in an earlier customer agreement would not be regarded as sufficient to enable the firm to act in the particular circumstances with the conflict.

To protect itself under fiduciary law, a firm will be tempted to give as detailed a disclosure as possible about the potential conflict. On the other hand, this is against the approach of the rules which only require two-way customer agreements, with detailed contents, in the case of discretionary business for customers and contingent liability transactions for private customers. There are other rules which require some sort of written consent or disclosure, but without requiring a full blown customer agreement. The focus of the new rules is that any agreements with customers should be shorter. Certainly, the contents should be presented for private customers clearly and fairly (Rule 5–15(2)). (See Chapter 6 above.)

15–009   Examples of rules which do not require full details of the potential conflict are as follows. A firm only has to state that it will receive remuneration from another person in connection with a transaction and that details will be made available on request. This does not even have to be included on the contract note, if it has been disclosed in an earlier customer agreement (Rule 5–34(9)). The rule on prior disclosure of charges only applies to private customers, rather than all customers; and the disclosure only has to be about the basis of the firm's charges and the nature of any other remuneration which it may receive (Rule

5–33(2)). A firm does not even have to disclose before the deal the fact that it is receiving commission from another customer as a result of an agency cross or other simultaneous matching transaction (Rule 5–33(3)). The full amount of a firm's profit on a principal deal is not disclosable on a contract note: only the mark-up or mark-down, which is the difference between the transaction cost and the best execution price (see paragraphs 9–013 *et seq.* above).

Firms will have to make their own judgment as to whether or not they need to protect themselves at fiduciary law by making extensive disclosures of potential conflicts, even though such disclosures are either not required under the rules or only required after the firm has acted, rather than before. In respect of post event disclosures, such as those required on a contract note that a firm has acted as a principal, has received remuneration from another person or has executed the transaction through an associate, a customer could object to the transaction having been carried out in one of these ways. He could hold the firm in breach of its fiduciary obligations because the disclosure had not been made properly before the deal. A customer can give his consent after the event, however, so that, if he does not object to the disclosure on the contract note, the transaction stands. Also, the fact that the customer has not objected to the first transaction may be sufficient for the firm to imply that he will not object on any subsequent occasion where the firm deals having a similar potential conflict.

Principle 6 (Conflicts of Interest)

This Principle has already been mentioned briefly above. It states **15–010** that a firm should either avoid any conflict arising, or ensure fair treatment to all customers by disclosure, internal rules of confidentiality, declining to act, or otherwise. Ideally, where a firm is in a fiduciary position it should avoid a conflict arising, but, as we have already seen, this is impractical in terms of the financial services conglomerate.

Disclosure, as discussed above, is one way of acting with a conflict of interest without breaching a fiduciary obligation. Where a firm has made full disclosure of the conflict before acting and the customer does not object, then the firm can presume that it has the customer's consent to continue to act for him despite the conflict.

Another way of managing conflicts under this Principle is through internal rules of confidentiality. In other words, a firm can act where the conflict is localised so that it does not operate on that part of the firm's business which is servicing the customer. The most usual form of internal rules of confidentiality are procedures on Chinese Walls.

Where a firm is a single legal entity, such as a company, then any matter known by one part of the firm is presumed by law to be known by all the firm, even if, in fact, it is not generally known; whereas where one is concerned with a financial services group, which operates different aspects of its business through separate legal entities, then one company is not presumed to have in its possession information obtained by another group company.

A problem arises in respect of groups where individuals have positions within more than one of the group companies, such as some of the senior managers and directors. As a company acts through its officers and agents, to what extent is information acquired by a person in his capacity as a director of one company attributable as information known to the other company? The answer depends upon whether the director is under an obligation to disclose the information to the second company in discharging his obligations to that company. This would be the case where, for example, the second company was the holding company for the group and the director had group responsibilities. It is suggested that, in most cases, it will be hard to argue that knowledge obtained by an officer or agent working for one company is not attributable as knowledge held by the second company where the officer or agent carries on similar activities and has similar responsibilities for each company.

The effectiveness of internal rules of confidentiality are discussed further below in paragraphs 15–013 *et seq.* under Chinese Walls.

15–011 Another method of dealing with conflicts is by declining to act. As with disclosure, this is an acceptable form of complying with a firm's fiduciary obligations. In fact, once a firm has allowed a conflict to arise, the best way of managing it is by declining to act. As already discussed, disclosure will only be effective if it is full enough so that the customer can give his proper informed consent. It should be noted that internal rules of confidentiality are not an acceptable way, in terms of ordinary fiduciary law, of preventing a breach of fiduciary duty, unless a disclosure to the customer that a firm operates such rules to manage conflicts is sufficient for the purpose of obtaining the customer's informed consent. To be sufficient, it may be necessary, at the very least, for a firm to describe the conflicts which may arise in the course of its business and which will be managed through its internal rules of confidentiality.

The question arises as to whether a firm's declining to act can amount to a breach of a fiduciary obligation itself. Certainly, there will be no breach if a firm declines to take on a new customer because of a potential conflict between the interests of the new customer and those of an existing customer. The problem arises where a firm refuses to act in respect of a particular transaction or type of business for an existing customer because of conflicts between that customer and another customer or between that customer and the firm.

The following factors are relevant. Was the conflict forseeable before the customer was taken on? Is the firm refusing to act for an older, established customer because his interests conflict with those of a newer customer whom the firm wishes to prefer because his business is worth more to the firm in the longer term? Is the firm refusing to act for the customer because it deliberately wants to put its own interests first? It is suggested that a firm will not be in breach of a fiduciary duty where it declines to act for the newer customer because of a potential conflict between his interests and those of a longer established customer; especially if the conflict could not have been easily contemplated at the time when the new customer was taken on, or if there was a clear warning when the new customer was taken on that the firm would decline to act for him if a future conflict arose between his interests and those of another customer. On the other hand, the firm will be in breach of a fiduciary obligation if it prefers the newer customer to the longer established customer, unless it gave a sufficient explanation, at the beginning of the customer relationship, about situations when it would decline to act. It will be the same result if the firm declines to act because it wants to put its interests above those of its customers.

The Principle is concerned with avoiding the conflict arising or managing the conflict in the ways described above to ensure fair treatment to all the firm's customers. Interestingly, it does not make a distinction between the treatment of connected and unconnected customers. So, as long as it treats all customers fairly, a firm does not have to prefer unconnected customers as against connected customers, although this is required in respect of the fair allocation rule (Rule 5–42).

The Principle goes on to say that a firm should not unfairly place its interests above those of its customers. This suggests that there may be some circumstances in which a firm may prefer its own interests, especially if a sufficiently specific disclosure has been given to the customer beforehand and he has consented to the firm putting its interests first. Obviously, it would be better if the consent was express rather than implied, and if the extent to which the firm's interests would be preferred were properly set out. The Principle itself puts a qualification on a firm putting its own interests first because it states that, where a properly informed customer would reasonably expect that the firm would place his interests above its own, the firm should live up to that expectation. Situations in which it might be proper for a firm to put its interests first are: where a customer is taking advantage of the firm's trading for its own book in a "piggy-bank" arrangement, the customer wanting to take advantage of the firm's trading, but agreeing to be subordinate to the firm's interests; or where a firm is dealing for itself in order to fulfill anticipated customers' orders (see the exception to front running research, Rule 5–36(2)(d): paragraph 11–004 above).

Material interests

Principle 6 is complemented by the rule on material interests (Rule 5–29). The first part of this rule is a Core Rule provision which states that, where a firm has a material interest, or any relationship giving rise

15–012

to a conflict of interest, in relation to any transaction to be entered into with or for a customer, it must not advise or deal with discretion unless it takes reasonable steps to ensure fair treatment for the customer. This provision is more limited than Principle 6: it only applies where a firm is arranging or executing transactions, and is limited to a material interest or conflict of interest in relation to the transaction. Principle 6 referred to ensuring fair treatment for all customers, whereas this rule is concerned with ensuring fair treatment for the particular customer. Fair treatment for one customer, however, requires an analysis of the way in which a firm will be treating other customers and itself.

The rule requires the firm to take reasonable steps to provide fair treatment, without describing what steps are applicable. Obviously, the type of steps described under Principle 6 would be relevant: namely, disclosure, internal rules of confidentiality and declining to act. SFA has provided, at its third tier, that one form of reasonable steps to ensure fair treatment is to operate an independence policy. This is described in paragraph 15–020 below.

The definition of material interest is negative in the sense that it is described as not including disclosable commission, or goods or services provided under a soft commission agreement. The exception for soft commissions only applies if the goods and services provided under the agreement may reasonably be expected to assist in relation to the investment services provided to its customers by the recipient of the softed goods and services. Disclosable commission is defined as commission which the regulatory system requires to be disclosed to a customer and, therefore, relates to the rule on disclosing charges to private customers (Rule 5–33). As this rule only applies to private customers, and has an exception in respect of simultaneous matching transactions, it could be implied that, by their omission, any other commission, charges, profits or remuneration levied or received by a firm amount to material interests; although SFA's requirements on contract and confirmation notes and on periodic statements require disclosure, albeit after the event, of charges levied in respect of business for non-private customers (see further the discussion in paragraph 15–021 below). Even if all non-disclosable commissions are material interests, their receipt by the firm does not by itself signify that it has not ensured fair treatment for the customer.

There are two places in the Conduct of Business Rules where a disclosure of a material interest is specifically required. The first is in respect of the specific contents requirements for specific investment advertisements, already described in paragraph 12–016 above. A firm must make a general disclosure that either it or its associate has a position in the investment concerned, or in a related investment; or that either of them has provided within the previous 12 months significant advice or investment services in relation to the investment concerned, or a related investment (Rule 5–9(8)). The second applies where a firm is required to give the warning about an investment not being readily realisable. It must disclose any position held by it or its associate in the investment recommended or a related investment (Rule 5–30(5) and see paragraph 7–004 above).

Chinese Walls

Principle 6, as we have already discussed, contemplates a firm **15–013** managing conflicts of interest by the use of internal rules of confidentiality, namely Chinese Walls. A Chinese Wall is an established arrangement which requires information obtained by the firm in the course of carrying on one part of its business to be withheld from persons with whom it deals in the course of carrying on another part of its business (Rule 5–3(1)). It also applies to an established arrangement between different legal entities within the same group which requires information obtained by one group company to be withheld from persons with whom another group company carries on business (Rule 5–3(2)). This is the only description which the rules contain. Therefore, the term covers any arrangement which is intended to have the effect that information should be withheld between different parts of a business or between different businesses.

Where a firm maintains a Chinese Wall between different parts of its business operations, then, for the purpose of the rules, information obtained by one part will not be imputed to one of the other parts. Employees in the first part will be able to keep confidential from the other parts of the business information which they acquire. The only condition for being able to withhold information is that either the part of the business acquiring the information or any part of the business from which the information is withheld carries on investment business (rather than regulated business) or associated business (see Chapter 4 above). This provision that information obtained by one part of a firm is not automatically imputed to the rest of the firm is contrary to the general legal presumption that information obtained by any part of a firm will be regarded as within the knowledge of the firm as a whole.

As already mentioned, a Chinese Wall arrangement can be imposed between different companies within the same group. Generally, information obtained by one legal entity is not attributable to another legal entity, unless both companies share the same employees. For the purpose of the Conduct of Business Rules, however, a firm often has to take account of an associate. For example, the restrictions in the dealing rules relating to own account orders include own account dealings by associates. Other rules require disclosures of positions or relationships held by associates (see the advertising and non-readily realisable investment recommendation requirements referred to in paragraph 15–012 above). In the case of Chinese Walls between group companies, it is provided that information may be withheld between different parts of the group, but only in respect of the requirements under the Conduct of Business Rules. In other words, the rule does not absolve one group company from having to comply with an obligation to transmit information to another group company outside the rules, such as under the Companies Acts or section 47 of the FSA 1986.

Some of the Conduct of Business Rules are specifically dependent upon a firm having knowledge: for example, the requirement to make a material interest disclosure on a specific investment advertisement (Rule 5–9(8)); the provision for extending credit to private customers (Rule 5–27); the material interest rule (Rule 5–29(1)); the requirement to disclose positions in respect of recommendations for non-readily realisable investments (Rule 5–30(5)); and the restriction on dealing ahead of publications (Rule 5–36(1)). Also, by implication, the other dealing rules (see Chapter 11 above) are dependent upon the knowledge of the individual employees responsible for receiving and executing the orders. Knowledge is also an ingredient in determining compliance with the rule on insider dealing (Rule 5–46 and see paragraphs 16–001 *et seq.* below). In all these cases which are dependent upon knowledge, a firm will not be regarded as having the information if it was properly withheld from the relevant part of the firm or from its associate through the mechanism of a Chinese Wall.

15–014   In fact, the rules go further than this. Rule 5–3(3) states that, where the Conduct of Business Rules apply only if a firm acts with knowledge, the firm will not be taken to have acted with knowledge if none of the relevant individuals involved on behalf of the firm has acted with knowledge. This suggests that, even if there is not a Chinese Wall in place, a firm will not be regarded as breaching one of these rules dependent upon knowledge if the particular employee acting for the firm was unaware of the relevant information. Obviously, it will be harder for a firm to satisfy SFA that the employee did not have the relevant knowledge if there was no Chinese Wall arrangement in place.

Interestingly, although SFA has placed the onus of proof on a firm to show that it had a reasonable belief or took reasonable steps (Rule 7–23(4)), there is no specific rule requirement on a firm to prove that, in the circumstances, the particular employee did not have the relevant information. In practice, however, it is suggested that, once SFA has proved that the firm itself had the information, the onus will naturally shift to the firm to prove that the employee concerned did not know.

It should be noted that this protection offered through the use of Chinese Walls only operates in terms of the application of the Conduct of Business Rules. It is not a device which is well recognised under fiduciary law as a way of managing conflicts of interest. As we have already seen, fiduciary law is concerned that a fiduciary should never put himself in a position which could conflict with his duties to his beneficiary, rather than looking at whether the beneficiary's interests have suffered in practice. Although SFA's rules do not require a firm to disclose specifically that it operates a Chinese Wall arrangement, a firm may wish to obtain its customers' consent to its reliance on such an arrangement in managing potential conflicts of interest. The more detailed and specific the disclosure is about potential conflicts and the way in which they will be managed, the more likely the firm is to be protected against committing a breach of a fiduciary obligation.

As already discussed, the rule on Chinese Walls (which is a SIB Core **15–015** Rule) only refers to an arrangement concerned with the withholding of information. It does not state what forms the arrangement must take. SFA, however, has made it clear that the Chinese Wall arrangement which a firm introduces must be "effective" in preventing the flow of information from one part of the firm to another or from one group company to another group company. This has been achieved by inserting the words "and effective" between the reference in the Core Rule to having an "established arrangement". SFA has accepted that, because of the entirely different organisational structures and kinds of business which SFA firms operate, it would be wrong to lay down standard procedures for Chinese Wall arrangements. Before a firm, however, can rely upon the protection of a Chinese Wall for the purposes of managing conflicts of interest, the arrangement which it puts in place must be effective, in terms of the particular firm, in controlling the passing on of information. In other words, a firm cannot rely upon the protection of Rule 5–3 merely by setting up an arrangement.

What is an effective arrangement? Obviously, the greater the physical barriers are between one part of the firm and another, or between one group company and another, the more likely it is that the arrangements will be effective in preventing the passage of information. For example, many firms restrict access to sensitive business areas, such as corporate finance, to the extent of even providing separate dining facilities. Physical barriers, by themselves, however, are not sufficient. Proper training and supervision of staff should be carried out regularly to enforce upon them the importance of maintaining the integrity of the Chinese Wall arrangement. This is an area which will require regular monitoring by the Compliance Officer.

Making sure that the arrangement is effective is important. Recently, the courts have shown a distrust for such arrangements, albeit that the two cases concerned conflicts of interest in merged solicitors' practices with respect to non-financial services client relationships (*Lee* v. *Coward Chance* [1991] Ch. 259 and *Re a Firm of Solicitors* [1991] N.L.J.R. 746). In both cases the courts were concerned about the potential for seepage or permeation of information through casual chatter and discussion; the passing on of some information which is not thought to be relevant, but which may prove to be the "missing link" in a chain of causation or reasoning. In the second case, it was doubted whether an impregnable Chinese Wall could ever be created.

In practice, it is difficult to prevent some seepage of information, and, anyway, there will always be some individuals within a firm or group who straddle a Chinese Wall arrangement. The Board of a firm has responsibility for the whole of the business; likewise, the Board of a holding company has overall responsibility for the business done by its subsidiaries. Ultimately, the responsibility for a firm's compliance with the rules rests with the Senior Executive Officer (see paragraph 3–008 above). He, therefore, together with the senior Compliance Officer, must be aware of all matters which are relevant to the firm's compliance with the rules.

If the integrity of the Chinese Wall arrangement is going to be preserved in terms of managing conflicts of interest, then it is important that those individuals within the firm who straddle a Chinese Wall are not directly involved with business done with customers or with trading for the firm's own account. If they are involved in such activities, then the use of a Chinese Wall arrangement to manage conflicts of interest could no longer be regarded as effective.

Sometimes, a firm will deliberately bring an employee from one part of its business across a Chinese Wall to the other part. A typical example is bringing an analyst from the sales or fund management side over the Wall to assist work being done by a corporate finance team. There may also be crossings of the Wall as a result of internal promotions and transfers. In such cases, firms will need to ensure that strict restrictions are imposed upon the activities of the individuals involved. They should not be put in situations where there will be conflict, in practice, between, on the one hand, information acquired and customers dealt with before they crossed the Wall and, on the other, customers with whom they will be having contact on the new side of the Wall.

Protection from section 47

15–016   Although, as has already been suggested, compliance with regulatory rules does not necessarily amount to full compliance with a firm's fiduciary obligations, there is one area in which a firm can take protection from a Chinese Wall arrangement. Section 48 of the FSA 1986 empowers the Secretary of State for Trade and Industry (until the functions are transferred to the Treasury) to make rules regulating the conduct of investment business by authorised persons. This power is one of those which was delegated to SIB. Under section 48(2)(h) it is specifically stated that the rules may make provision enabling or requiring information obtained by an authorised person in the course of carrying on one part of his business to be withheld by him from persons with whom he deals in the course of carrying on another part of his business. Section 48(6) states that nothing done in conformity with section 48(2)(h) shall be regarded as a contravention of section 47. Section 47 makes it a criminal offence:

(i)   to make, whether intentionally or recklessly, a misleading, false or deceptive statement, promise or forecast to induce another person to make a decision relating to investments;

(ii)   to conceal dishonestly any material facts for the same purpose; or

(iii) to engage in any conduct which creates a false or misleading impression as to the market in any investment.

Therefore, a firm will not be regarded as having committed an offence under section 47 merely because it withholds information in accordance with a provision made by SIB on Chinese Wall arrangements. The protection given under section 48(6), however, only applies to firms directly authorised by SIB, rather than to firms which are authorised as a result of their membership of an SRO or RPB (section 48(1)). It is for this reason that in SIB's Core Rule on Chinese Walls (and remember that the Core Conduct of Business Rules will be designated in due course to apply to all SRO members) there is an avoidance for doubt provision. This states that nothing done in conformity with Rule 5–3(1) will be regarded as a contravention of section 47 (Rule 5–3(4)). This provision only needs to refer to Rule 5–3(1), which is concerned with Chinese Wall arrangements within a firm, rather than to Rule 5–3(2), which is concerned with Chinese Wall arrangements between group companies, because the attribution of information presumption only applies within the same legal entity, rather than from one entity to another.

There is some uncertainty as to how effective Rule 5–3(4) is in terms of protecting SFA firms as they do not benefit from the same statutory provision as firms directly authorised by SIB. The mere fact that it is a SIB designated Core Rule does not extend the section 48(6) "safe harbour" to authorised firms which are not directly authorised by SIB. Nevertheless, it is suggested that the courts will recognise the close relationship between SRO and SIB rules and the public law nature of SRO rules in determining that the general legal presumption of imputing information to the whole legal entity has been modified by Rule 5–3(4). However, the further restriction placed by SFA's drafting should not be forgotten. To rely on this protection from section 47 liability a firm must not merely have an established Chinese Wall arrangement, but also an effective one.

Confidentiality

Fiduciary law imposes some additional problems for firms which have conflicts of interest. These are in terms of a firm's duty of confidentiality to its customer. When acting for a customer, a firm should keep confidential information which it obtains about that customer or on behalf of that customer. On the other hand, a firm, where it is a fiduciary, should use all its skill, care and diligence in acting on behalf of a customer, including using all the information available to it. A firm may have received confidential information from one customer which would be very relevant for the investment service

15–017

which it is providing to another customer. Its duty of confidentiality to the first customer conflicts with its duty to act in the best interests of the second customer by employing the information obtained from the first customer.

This may be the sort of situation where a firm, if it is properly to protect itself, should refuse to act for the second customer. A problem arises where a firm already has a relationship with both customers before the conflict occurs. This has already been discussed in paragraph 15–011 above.

Many firms deal with this potential difficulty by using the technique of a Chinese Wall, but serious problems can occur, especially where some individuals straddle Chinese Walls and other individuals are brought across Chinese Walls. The information obtained about a customer in one part of the firm could be extremely important to business being undertaken for customers in another part of the firm. For example, the corporate finance department could be acting for a company which is having severe financial problems. This company could be seeking help from the firm in terms of restructuring, raising new finance or finding a buyer. The information, if it became public, would severely depress the price of the company's stock. On the other hand, unaware of the parlous state of the company, the fund management or investment advice division could be actively promoting the company's stock as a good buy.

In such circumstances, employees who straddle or who have crossed the Chinese Wall are in an unenviable position. It would be difficult to argue that the duty of confidentiality to the corporate finance client is greater than the duty to act in the best interests of the fund management and advisory customers. There must be a tremendous temptation upon the employees who have crossed the wall to take some action to protect the interests of the advisory or fund management customers. It is for this reason that firms should be very careful as to whom they allow to cross the Chinese Wall.

Once an employee has such confidential information, it is hard for him not to be affected by it in practice. If, before he acquired the information about the corporate finance client, he was actively recommending that company's stock, he is likely, at the very least, to stop recommending it. If this is all he does, it is suggested that he will not be in breach of the firm's duty of confidentiality to the corporate finance client. Although, the very fact that he is no longer recommending the stock may be an indication to some of his customers that there is a problem with the company.

If, on the other hand, the employee recommends his customers to sell, he will be taking action which, although it is in the interests of his fund management or advisory customers, will be contrary to the interests of the corporate finance client, especially as a glut of sale orders will depress the price of the stock and may generate adverse rumours in the market. Also, the employee may well be guilty, in these circumstances, of an offence under the Company Securities (Insider Dealing) Act 1985, because he would be dealing on the basis of unpublished price sensitive information. Note that there would be no such offence where the employee changes from recommending purchases in the company's stock to making no recommendation at all about the company, as, in this case, there will be no dealing based upon the sensitive information.

Although this discussion has centred on the conflict between a firm's duty of confidentiality to one customer and its duty to act in the best interests of another customer, respect for a customer's confidentiality also applies in relation to the firm or the relevant employee dealing for its or his own account. In other words, the firm and its employee have a duty not to use confidential information acquired from a customer for their own benefit.

Public Law versus Private Law argument

Reference to the insider dealing legislation leads on to another point. **15–018** A firm's private law (fiduciary or contractual) obligations are not overriding in the sense that it or one of its employees should not breach a criminal provision in order to satisfy a fiduciary duty to a customer. Also, it is suggested that a firm will not be liable to a customer for not taking a course of action to comply with a fiduciary obligation if that action would have involved a breach of an SFA rule. This proposition rests on the assumption that rules made by FSA 1986 regulators have a public law element.

In practice, compliance with a fiduciary obligation should not mean that there will necessarily be a breach of an SFA rule. As we have already seen above, the disclosure and other management requirements under the rules in respect of conflicts of interest follow, but are less extensive than, the equivalent requirements under fiduciary law. Fiduciary law may require a firm to do more in the circumstances than SFA's rules, rather than involve a rule breach.

The extent to which regulatory rules override private law obligations becomes relevant in terms of a firm's duty to disclose information to its regulator. A firm will not be in breach of its duty of confidentiality where it discloses confidential information about a customer relating to a criminal or possible criminal offence committed by him or another person with whom he has contact. It is suggested that the same protection applies to a firm where it reports a matter which, whilst not concerning the commission of a possible criminal offence, is relevant in determining whether there has been a breach of one of SFA's rules or one of the authorisation requirements under the FSA 1986, or would be relevant in assessing the continuing fitness and properness of a firm or SFA registered person.

Restricted Lists

15–019   To assist the effectiveness of a Chinese Wall arrangement and to protect the confidentiality of customers, some firms rely upon Restricted Lists. These lists can take various forms. Some are "Stop Lists" which prevent employees of the firm dealing for customers, themselves or the firm in any of the investments included on the list. Others take the form of "Watch Lists" which do not have general circulation within a firm, but which are only seen by key individuals, such as departmental heads and compliance staff. Dealings in investments on such a list are not prevented, but they are closely monitored because of risks of potential conflicts of interest. There are other forms of Restricted Lists, some which allow dealings subject to various forms of approval.

The danger in producing such lists is that the inclusion of a particular company on the list may suggest that the firm holds some price sensitive information about it. There is, however, no indication as to whether the information is good or bad and, therefore, whether it is right to buy or sell the stock. In very sensitive cases, some firms have been known to leave certain corporate finance client companies off a Restricted List because the mere fact of their inclusion could cause too much speculation. Another technique is to include on the list a number of bogus entries in the sense that they relate to companies about which the firm has no confidential information which could lead to potential conflicts of interest. The inclusion of such names merely helps to protect the confidentiality of actual customers.

Another problem with Restricted Lists is that a firm is not able to act in the best interests of its customers. If, for example, a company has been included because it is a corporate finance client, then other customers of the firm could be prejudiced because their account managers and advisers will be limited in the range of stock in which they can deal. It may be that the stock of a company on the Restricted List would be a very good buy at the time. Also, a difficulty arises if the account executive cannot sell the stock for a customer, especially if an announcement is likely to be made through the corporate finance department which could adversely affect the stock's price. To this extent, it may be advisable for a firm which operates Restricted Lists to explain to its customers the purpose of these lists and the restrictions on dealing which result.

The same argument about Restricted Lists preventing a firm complying with its fiduciary duties could also be made about the concept of polarisation, with a firm tied to a marketing group only being able, under the rules, to survey products from the group. Of course, in this case there is the requirement to give the customer the Buyer's Guide which explains the effect of the firm's polarised status (see Chapter 14 above).

Independence Policy

Establishing a Chinese Wall arrangement is only effective in a large **15–020**
sized firm. Hence, SFA has provided an additional method by which a
firm may manage conflicts of interest. This is referred to as an
independence policy and is dealt with under the material interest rule
(Rule 5–29).

SFA provides that a firm may take reasonable steps to ensure fair
treatment for its customer in accordance with the material interest Core
Rule (Rule 5–29(1) and see paragraph 15–012 above) by relying on an
independence policy (Rule 5–29(2)). If a firm wishes to rely on an
independence policy, then the policy must require its employees, when
advising customers or dealing for them in the exercise of discretion, to
disregard any material interest or conflict. This includes conflicts of
interest between one customer and another customer and between the
interests of a customer and those of the firm. The policy must be set
out in writing, however small the firm. Under the old rules, a written
policy was only required where a firm had 20 or more employees. The
firm must also have drawn the policy to the attention of all employees
who will be dealing with or for customers. Where a firm is dealing with
a private customer, then it must have disclosed to him in writing that it
may be giving him advice or dealing for him where it has a material
interest or conflict, but that the relevant employee is required to put
the customer's interests first, disregarding the material interest or
conflict (Rule 5–29(3)).

An independence policy, therefore, does not absolve a firm from
ensuring fair treatment for its customer in accordance with Rule
5–29(1) or ensuring fair treatment for all customers in accordance with
Principle 6. A firm must still comply with its fiduciary obligations and
act in the best interests of each of its customers. All SFA is stating is
that, if a firm has a clearly laid down and understood policy that each
customer's interests must receive primacy in respect of the relevant
advice or deal, it is more likely that a firm will be ensuring fair
treatment for the relevant customer. Also, the rule enables a firm to
avoid making specific disclosures about every material interest or
conflict. No disclosure is required for non-private customers, whilst, in
the case of private customers, it is merely sufficient to give a general
disclosure at the beginning of the relationship that a firm may act in
some circumstances for the customer where it has a conflict of interest.

As already discussed in paragraphs 15–007 *et seq.* above, such a
disclosure, although satisfactory in terms of SFA's rules, may not be
sufficient to protect a firm under fiduciary law. Also, SFA has written
guidance to the rule warning a firm that, in order to ensure fair
treatment for customers, it may be necessary, in some cases, for the
firm to take other steps, such as specific disclosure of the material
interest or conflict.

Inducements

15–021   If a firm is to act in the best interests of its customers, it must not be unduly influenced by inducements from whatever source, including those offered by other investment businesses through whom it transacts business on behalf of its customers. The rule on inducements applies to both firms which offer inducements, as well as to firms which receive them (Rule 5–7). Not all inducements are caught. It is only inducements which are likely to conflict significantly with any duties of the recipient, or his employer, which are owed to customers in connection with regulated business. This, therefore, requires an assessment as to whether the inducement being offered or received, on an objective test, would be regarded as having a significant influence which would conflict with a duty owed to a customer. Although the rule only looks at conflicts arising in respect of regulated business, it catches any inducements offered, including those which are not provided in the course of regulated business. (For a discussion on regulated business, see paragraphs 4–005 *et seq.* above.)

The definition of an inducement is like that for a material interest, described in paragraph 15–012 above. It is similarly written in a negative sense, and excludes any disclosable commission, plus goods or services provided under a soft commission agreement. It should be noted that the reference to disclosable commission does not exclude all commissions which are in fact disclosed to the customer. The definition only excludes commissions which are required to be disclosed under the regulatory system.

This would, however, cover commissions disclosable after the relevant event, such as on contract notes and valuation statements, rather than just those required to be disclosed before, as is the case with private customers under Rule 5–33. It is wrong to suggest that, because the rule on prior disclosure of charges (Rule 5–33(2)) merely applies to private customers, only commission charged to a private customer is not caught by the inducements rule, whereas commission charged to a non-private customer is. Commissions disclosed under the rules on contract notes or valuations to non-private customers are "disclosable commissions".

In determining whether a commission is disclosable, however, it should be noted that sometimes under the rules a firm is not required to disclose the actual amount of commission charged or remuneration received. For example, under Rule 5–33(2) it only has to state the basis of its charges or the nature of other remuneration which it will receive. A similar position applies under Rule 5–34 in relation to contract and confirmation notes. A restrictive approach to the definition of disclosable commission would be that it only refers to commission charged by the firm, or another person through whom the firm transacts the business, and which is fully disclosed in terms either of the actual amount levied or of a percentage of the overall costs of the transaction. This is consistent with the approach to disclosure of conflicts under fiduciary law. Where the firm is merely giving a general description of the basis on which it makes its charges or only describing the nature of other remuneration which it will receive, it is suggested that this does not amount to disclosable commission within the definition.

Provided it is not regarded as disclosable commission, commission **15–022** rebates or shares of commission received from other firms to whom a firm has introduced business will be subject to Rule 5–7. Whereas SFA is not generally concerned about normal shared commission arrangements operating as unfair inducements, it would be so concerned about stepped commission arrangements or volume overriders. These are arrangements under which a firm receives a higher percentage of commission or a higher level rebate based upon the volume of business transacted. Such arrangements could significantly conflict with a firm's duty to its customers, encouraging it to put more business through another investment business which operates such arrangements, and tempting it to give unsuitable advice and churn accounts.

Another area of concern over inducements is with respect to broker funds. Obviously, a broker fund adviser is often earning extra income for acting as the adviser to the life office or scheme operator. A firm should disclose this remuneration under Rule 5–33(2). Also, as indicated in paragraph 14–021 above, a firm has to show the aggregate value of commission, benefits or other remuneration received by it on the six monthly valuation statement which it is required to send to the customer (Rule 5–35(10)). Because such remuneration is disclosed under the rules, it is arguable that it does not fall within the scope of the inducements rule. Any such potential loophole, however, is covered by Rule 5–20(8) which requires the firm to take account of the additional costs to the customer in investing through a broker fund.

The definition of inducements includes non-cash benefits, often referred to as indirect benefits, unless they are provided under a soft commission arrangement which complies with the rules. An indication of which type of indirect benefits will now be regarded as acceptable under Rule 5–7 can be found in the more flexible approach suggested in this area by LAUTRO (LAUTRO Consultative Bulletin no. 13, dated March 1992). For example, LAUTRO is proposing to permit its members, who will normally be the product companies, to participate in seminars held by independent intermediaries for bona fide business purposes as long as they do not contribute to the cost of the seminar. They will also be able to participate in seminars organised by third parties for independent intermediaries if the organiser does not provide any payment to the intermediaries for attending the seminar. LAUTRO members will be able to make available written technical information, such as regulatory reports and market up-dates, provided the material is freely available to independent intermediaries generally. Finally, they will be able to offer training facilities to independent intermediaries, provided any intermediary attending is charged at least £25 per day per person and does not receive any payment or contribution to either travelling or accommodation expenses. The other indirect benefits which a LAUTRO member can provide to an independent intermediary relate specifically to the products which it provides.

SFA does not propose to introduce such specific rules on what are acceptable indirect benefits in accordance with the inducements rule. It is probably right that there should be more specific control with respect to the relationship between the providers of packaged products and independent advisers. The LAUTRO proposals, however, give a good indication of the type of benefits which will not be regarded as giving rise to a significant conflict with the recipient's duties to his customers.

Soft Commissions

15–023   What is a soft commission arrangement? It applies where one firm, normally a fund manager, obtains goods or services paid for and arranged by another firm, a broker, through whom the fund manager transacts business on behalf of his customers, on the understanding that the fund manager will generate a particular level of business through the broker. In other words, the goods and services are provided free of charge by the broker to the fund manager on the understanding that the latter will guarantee the former a particular volume of business. The broker pays for the goods or services provided from the profits which he makes on the commission which he charges the fund manager. Sometimes the goods and services will be provided in-house by the broker. At other times, he will arrange for a third party to provide them and pay that third party's invoices.

Contrast this with traditional arrangements whereby the broker charges the fund manager an ordinary commission for business which the broker transacts for him. The broker may also provide free of charge certain goods and services, such as research. There may even be a tacit understanding that the fund manager will only receive certain goods and services provided he transacts sufficient business through the broker, but there is no specific agreement, as in the case of a soft commission arrangement, that the goods and services will only be supplied in return for a fixed level of commission business being put in the way of the broker.

Reference is made to a fund manager as the person in receipt of softed goods and services. Of course, the recipient does not always have to be acting in a fund management capacity, and, therefore, the reference here to fund manager should be taken to include any authorised firm which has customers and is the recipient of softed goods and services. The rules refer to a soft commission agreement which is defined as an agreement under which a broker provides goods and services to a firm which deals in securities on an advisory basis, or in the exercise of discretion, in return for an assurance that not less than a certain amount of business will be put through or in the way of the broker by the other firm. The agreement may be oral, rather than written. Under the Record Keeping Schedule (Appendix 18), however, a firm (whether the broker or fund manager) has to keep a copy of, or memorandum of the details of, any soft commission agreement to which it is a party.

It should be noted that the definition of soft commission agreement **15–024** only applies where the recipient of the goods or services is dealing in securities, rather than derivatives (options, futures and contracts for difference). This limitation was imposed because soft commission arrangements are mainly confined to the securities markets. If soft commission practices become more common in the derivatives markets, then it is possible that the soft commission rule (Rule 5–8) will be applied to all dealings in investments. It is already a common practice for introducing brokers in the derivatives markets to receive services in exchange for the amount of commission which they introduce to a broker-dealer. Although the receipt and offering of such services is not caught by the soft commission rule, it is still subject to the rule on inducements (Rule 5–7). Also, firms in the derivatives markets who are in receipt of goods and services from another firm in respect of the commission business which they introduce to it will, if they are acting in a fiduciary capacity, be under an obligation, at least, to disclose full details of the benefits which they are receiving to their customers.

As we have already seen in paragraphs 15–012 and 15–021 above, goods and services which can reasonably be expected to assist in the provision of investment services to the recipient's customers, and which are provided under a soft commission agreement, are not regarded as material interests or inducements. Effectively the soft commission rule operates as a qualification to those on inducements and material interests. A firm which, in accordance with Rule 5–8, is receiving softed goods and services and making the relevant disclosures will not be regarded as in breach of Rules 5–7 and 5–29.

In a soft commission context, reference is sometimes made to the practice of "soft for net". This is an arrangement under which the fund manager deals direct with a market maker or principal dealer, rather than using an agency broker. In this case, the agreement is not to generate a specific level of commission, but rather to generate transactions involving a certain volume of turnover for the market maker or principal dealer. The market maker or principal dealer pays for the provision of the softed goods and services out of the profit which he makes on his principal's spread or turn, the difference between his bid and offer prices or, if he is not quoting fixed prices, the difference between the price at which he buys and sells the same stock. As will be seen later, the rule on soft commissions attempts to ban the practice of soft for net.

Obviously, the operation of a soft commission agreement is in breach of the fiduciary duties owed to its customers by the firm which receives the softed goods and services. The obligation on the fund manager to transact a minimum level of business with the broker may cause a substantial conflict of interest. The fund manager may be tempted to deal with the broker from whom he receives the softed goods and services in respect of transactions which it could be in his customers' best interests to place with other brokers under traditional arrangements. Additionally, because he is being remunerated from another source, namely the broker, whilst acting as a fiduciary for his customer, the fund manager will be under a duty at fiduciary law to account to his customer for the full value of the goods and services received.

How do the rules attempt to deal with these conflicts? Rule 5–8(1) states that a firm which deals for a customer on an advisory basis, or in the exercise of discretion, may not deal through a broker pursuant to a soft commission agreement unless five conditions are satisfied. These conditions and the supporting SFA third-tier rules are explained below.

Condition 1

15–025 The only benefits to be provided under the agreement must be goods or services which can reasonably be expected to assist in the provision of investment services to the fund manager's customers. Also, the goods and services received must be used for the benefit of the firm's customers.

At the third tier, SFA states that the only goods or services which will be acceptable under this test are those which are used:

(i) to assist the fund manager in providing investment services to his customers by means of specific advice on investments, research and analysis on investments, or the use of computer and other information facilities;

(ii) to provide custodian services; or

(iii) to provide services relating to the valuation and performance measurement of portfolios.

SFA has provided two tables which, although not exhaustive, give indications as to the types of goods and services that will be acceptable. The first lists permitted goods and services, which include the provision of dedicated telephone lines between the fund manager and broker and the payment of relevant seminar fees for the fund manager. The second contains non-permitted goods and services, such as: travel, accommodation and entertainment expenses; general computer hardware or software which relates to the overall running of the fund manager's office, for example word processing and general accounting programmes; and payment of professional association membership fees and staff salaries.

The non-permitted table also includes direct money payments. Any hard cash payment made by a broker to a fund manager to attract his business will not be regarded as part of an acceptable soft commission agreement. Such payments will be subject to the normal rule on inducements (Rule 5–7); and it is suggested that they would never be acceptable under that rule.

Condition 2

The broker must have agreed to provide best execution to the fund manager. Under Rule 5–39(2) a firm must always provide best execution where it fulfills an order from a non-private customer, unless the customer has waived the requirement. A fund manager will normally be classified as a non-private customer. It is, therefore, important that he never agrees with the broker to any qualification of the best execution requirement. In fact, it is suggested that Condition 2 actually requires positive confirmation from the broker that he will always provide best execution. This then avoids any potential loophole in the best execution requirement if it is argued that the fund manager had not placed an order, but was merely dealing after making a request for the broker's price (see paragraphs 11–009 and 11–016 above).

This condition, therefore, is one way of trying to ensure that the fund manager acts in the best interests of his customers in entering into a soft commission agreement. Condition 3 is another safeguard in this respect.

Condition 3

The fund manager must be satisfied, on reasonable grounds, that the **15–026** terms of business and methods by which the relevant broking services will be supplied do not involve any potential for comparative price disadvantage to his customers. To a large extent, this echoes Condition 2 in the sense that the best way of ensuring that there is no potential for comparative price disadvantage is by ensuring that the broker must always provide best execution.

A fund manager will generally be placing very large orders in the market. He is likely to obtain keener prices from a broker if he deals with him frequently and in large volumes. For example, a fund manager will often be dealing in volumes greater than the normal market sizes for which fixed prices are shown on SEAQ (the London Stock Exchange's Automated Quotation System). In such cases, he should often be able to obtain a better price from the broker than the best bid and offer prices currently quoted on SEAQ for normal market sized transactions. Therefore, a fund manager should not always assume that he has obtained best execution, or that there is no potential for comparative price disadvantage, merely because the broker is willing to deal at the best SEAQ quoted prices. (See also paragraph 11–015 above.)

Also, in looking at comparative price disadvantage, the fund manager should bear in mind the commission which he is paying to the broker. The more frequently he deals and the greater the size in which he deals, the more likely it is that he should be able to negotiate reduced commission charges. If the broker is not prepared to offer these because of his concerns that the commission should cover the cost of the softed goods and services, then the fund manager may not be acting in the best interests of his customers. For example, it might be cheaper for him to deal with a broker under a traditional arrangement, paying himself in hard cash for the types of goods and services which are offered by the soft commission broker.

The fund manager should only rely on a soft commission arrangement because he believes that it is offering some added value to his customers. In other words, the soft commission broker is at least executing bargains at price levels which would be achieved by traditional brokers, and the fund manager is not paying more in commission than he would pay a traditional broker and is benefitting, in terms of the investment services which he provides to his customers, from the softed goods and services paid for by the broker.

SFA has written guidance as to how a fund manager can satisfy himself under Condition 3. One way is if he is able to monitor individual transaction prices and, therefore, can assure himself that the broker is complying at all times with the best execution obligation. Another is if the fund manager is not required to disclose to the broker, at the time of giving him the order, whether the commission generated by the transaction is to be allocated to the fund manager's softing account. In other words, he deals with the same broker on a traditional basis and under a soft commission arrangement, and, at the time when the broker receives the instructions, he does not know on which basis the business is being placed. In these circumstances, the broker will not be able to operate a different charging or execution policy for business done under the soft commission arrangement.

If neither of the two methods above can be satisfied, the fund manager should select the soft commission broker on the basis of the latter's ability to demonstrate independence of action within the market-place. This is unlikely to be the case where the broker deals exclusively with one market maker.

Condition 4

15–027   Where the broker acts as principal, he must not be remunerated by spread alone. This is the condition which effectively bans soft for net arrangements. The soft commission rules do not prevent a broker from dealing with the fund manager on a principal basis. In fact, "broker" is defined to include a broker-dealer and a market maker. Soft for net, however, is banned in the sense that the broker may not rely upon his spread alone in generating enough profit to pay for the softed goods and services. He must charge a commission element. The danger of allowing a broker to be remunerated by spread alone is that he will widen his spreads to accommodate his softing costs, and, especially if he is the only market maker or principal dealer in the stock, or one of a small number, it will be difficult for a fund manager to test that he is receiving best execution.

The softing brokers who only act on an agency basis would prefer to see a complete ban on soft commission brokers dealing as principals. They are concerned that the potential for comparative price disadvantage is greater where a fund manager is dealing with a principal dealer. In fact, the agency brokers have suggested that the word "alone" should be deleted so that a principal dealer could not receive any part of his remuneration from his principal's turn or spread.

SFA has written guidance to the effect that Condition 4 is not complied with where the broker is only partly remunerated by commission, unless the commission element constitutes the greater proportion of the remuneration. Also, SFA requires the commission to be disclosed. This really means being disclosed on the contract note. Although there is probably sufficient disclosure where the broker, at the outset of the soft commission arrangement, states that his commission element will be a fixed percentage of the transaction price on each bargain. In other words, the contract note will merely show a single price, but the fund manager will know that, for example, the top 1 per cent. of the price represents the broker's commission.

The fact that soft commission brokers are able to deal on a principal basis means that fund managers may enter into soft commission arrangements with the agency arm of a multi-function securities house which has a market making division. The fund manager deals with the agency arm in the knowledge that it will execute most orders through the in-house market maker. Some people argue that undertaking business in this way with an integrated house, even though the contact is between the fund manager and the agency arm rather than with the market making division direct, is so closely related to a soft for net relationship that it should be banned, or, alternatively, soft for net should be permitted. To deny an integrated house the possibility of dealing under a soft commission agreement, however, would be contrary to the "Big Bang" changes of 1986, already referred to in paragraph 15–003 above, which permitted dual capacity trading.

Where a fund manager is dealing under a soft commission arrangement with an integrated house, it must still ensure that Conditions 2 and 3 are satisfied. In other words, the agency arm should agree to ensure best execution and the fund manager should be satisfied that there is no potential for comparative price disadvantage. The agency arm may be able to satisfy the fund manager that it is able to obtain for him a good deal by dealing with the in-house market maker on the basis that the respective overheads of the agency arm and the market making division are lower by operating through an integrated house rather than as two completely separate entities. Economies of scale and shared overheads are ways of reducing costs within the integrated house.

15–028   The very fact of integration, however, causes some concerns. There is the potential for cross subsidies between the market making division and the agency arm. An integrated house could be tempted to allow its agency arm to offer soft commission services at a loss by setting its multiplier too low on the basis that the increased order-flow generated for the market making division will increase this division's profits, thus off-setting any loss made by the agency arm. It is not easy to prove that this type of cross subsidisation is happening because an integrated house may prepare its accounts on a consolidated basis, rather than for each of its divisions. Also, the agency arm may not separately identify, in cost terms, its share of the firm's overall overheads in determining whether or not its soft commission business is being run at a profit or loss.

It is for this reason that fund managers who deal with integrated houses should insist that the agency arm is, in practice, able to act in an independent way, not always transacting business through its in-house market maker. As already pointed out under Condition 3, it is less likely that there is no potential for comparative price disadvantage where the broker deals exclusively through one market maker. In addition, SFA has stated that a broker should set its multiplier at a level which it can demonstrate would generate sufficient commission income from softing transactions to cover all its costs, including the provision of the softed goods and services to the fund manager, the dealing and settling of the transactions undertaken for him, and the broker's administration in respect of operating the soft commission arrangement.

The multiplier relates to how much commission has to be paid to cover the cost of the softed goods and services. For example, a multiplier of 1.5 means that the fund manager has to pay £1.50 in commission for every £1 which the broker spends on a softed good or service. In practice, it is unlikely that a broker is able to make any profit at a multiplier set at less than 1.4. In respect of dealings in illiquid stocks or on overseas markets, the multiplier may well have to be much higher if the broker is not to make a loss.

Condition 5

The fund manager must make adequate prior and periodic disclosure to his customers of the details of any relevant soft commission arrangement. As we have already seen in paragraph 15–007 above, full disclosure of the relevant details of a conflict is one way of avoiding the strict consequences of fiduciary law and enabling the firm to continue to act for the customer. At the third tier, SFA has written detailed rules concerning the two types of disclosure, namely prior and periodic.

Prior disclosure. A firm receiving softed goods and services must **15–029** provide to those customers whose commissions are being used to pay for these goods and services a written statement detailing its policy in relation to soft commission agreements. The statement must be made either at the outset of the customer relationship or as soon as is reasonably practicable after the relevant soft commission agreement is entered into. Wherever there is any material change in a firm's soft commission policy, then it should, promptly after the change, provide details of the change to any of those customers for whom the change is relevant. In describing its policy, a firm should explain why it thinks that it is beneficial to the customers to take advantage of a soft commission arrangement.

Periodic disclosure. The firm must then provide annually to customers whose commissions are used for soft commission purposes information about how the soft commission arrangements have operated during the last 12 months. This information should include: the percentage of total commission paid by the firm under its soft commission agreements; the total value, on a cost price basis, of the goods and services received under the agreements expressed as a percentage of the total commissions paid by the firm, including those not paid as part of a soft commission arrangement; a summary of the goods and services received under the agreements; a list of the soft commission brokers with whom the firm deals; and a statement confirming the firm's policy on soft commission arrangements, or a statement that its policy has not changed since its initial written statement to the customer. A firm should make it clear as to whether or not any of its soft commission business is directed through an associate. Remember, "associate" includes, besides companies within the same group, any person whose relationship, whether business or domestic, with any of the group companies, or their appointed representatives, might reasonably be expected to give rise to a community of interest which could involve a conflict of interest in dealings with third parties.

The periodic disclosure statement can be produced as a standard document sent to all customers whose commissions are used for softing purposes. The disclosure does not have to quantify the exact commissions used in respect of any one customer for softing purposes or the extent to which the softed goods and services have been utilised in respect of the services provided by the fund manager to the particular customer.

Where the goods and services received from the soft commission broker do not all satisfy the requirements in Condition 1 above, then the firm must allocate the costs and commissions between those goods and services which are permitted by the rules and those which are not. It should only disclose details about the permitted goods and services on the periodic statement. In respect of the non-permitted items, it should not be paying for these under the soft commission agreement. If it is not paying for their provision in hard cash terms, then the firm should only be receiving them if it is satisfied that it is not thereby breaching the inducements rule (Rule 5–7), and, as previously discussed in paragraphs 15–007 *et seq.*, the firm may need to make a specific disclosure to its customers.

15–030   There are some important exceptions to providing the periodic report. It is not required in the case of beneficiaries of funds under the firm's management, such as unit holders within a collective investment scheme. Nor is it required in the case of private customers who are individuals, rather than small business investors, provided the firm included in its initial written policy statement an estimate of the percentage of the total commission paid by the firm which it expects will be used for the purpose of soft commission agreements and a statement that full details will be made available on request. This second exception was inserted because it was questioned how relevant a periodic statement would be for a stockbroker's ordinary customers, where only a small amount of the total commission generated would be used for soft business. Also, there was an argument that the costs of providing such periodic statements outweighed the benefits to investors.

Finally, there is an exception from the periodic disclosure requirement for overseas customers whom the firm believes on reasonable grounds do not wish to receive such information. This is similar to the standard customer documentation exception already referred to in paragraphs 5–033, 6–003 and 7–003 above. Note that, at the moment, there is no such exception for overseas customers in respect of the provision of the initial written policy statement.

It should be appreciated that the prior and periodic disclosures required by SFA's rules are not necessarily specific and detailed enough to protect a firm properly at fiduciary law. For fiduciary law purposes, it may be necessary to give a much fuller description of exactly what a soft commission is and how it works. A firm may also need to give an exact break-down, for each individual customer, as to what part of his commissions have been used for softing purposes and of the actual goods and services received by the firm in respect of his commissions.

Obligation on Fund Manager

15–031   As can be seen from the five conditions described above, the obligations under the soft commission rule are on the fund manager, namely the recipient of the softed goods and services. It is his responsibility to ensure that these conditions are satisfied. A soft commission broker will not be in breach of the rule because he provides non-permitted goods or services, is remunerated by spread alone, or does not set his multiple at a level to generate sufficient commission income to pay for all of the costs involved in the soft commission arrangement. To the extent that he is providing non-permitted goods and services, however, he will be subject to Rule 5–7 on inducements which applies to providers as well as recipients of inducements.

Chapter 16

Market Integrity

Insider dealing

Insider dealing is a criminal offence, prohibited by the Companies **16–001** Securities (Insider Dealing) Act 1985. The offence is basically dealing in, whether buying or selling, securities on the basis of unpublished price sensitive information. A decision not to deal on the basis of inside information is not caught. The dealings must be through a recognised investment exchange[1] or a regular off-market dealer.[2] Private transactions are excluded. The offence concerns dealings in the securities of a company. Securities are defined to include any share, any debenture, or any right to subscribe for, call for or make delivery of a share or debenture. In other words, warrants, options and futures contracts concerned with rights to subscribe for, purchase or deliver shares or debentures are included, but not government or local and public authority investments. Also contracts for difference related to share indices are included.

It is only an offence to deal on the basis of unpublished price sensitive information. This is information which relates to specific matters relating, or of concern, to the company in whose securities the dealings take place. It does not extend to information of a general nature. The information must not be generally known to persons who are accustomed to deal in the company's securities, and it must be information which, if it were generally known to them, would be likely to affect materially the price of the securities.

The offence is committed by individuals who are insiders. These are people who are knowingly connected with the relevant company or have knowingly obtained the information from another person who is so connected. Insiders are also civil servants, and employees of SROs and of investment exchanges and clearing houses which are recognised under the FSA 1986, to the extent that they are holding information which they know is unpublished price sensitive information. An individual commits an offence under the Act where he does not himself deal, but counsels or procures another person to deal, or passes on the information to another person if he has reasonable cause to believe that that or some other person will deal, or counsel or procure another person to deal.

The insider dealing legislation only creates a criminal offence in respect of individuals. Rule 5–46(1), however, puts an obligation on a firm not to effect, whether in the United Kingdom or overseas, an own account transaction when it knows that an associate, or an employee of either the firm or its associate, would be prevented from effecting the transaction under the insider dealing legislation. In other words, SFA can discipline a firm for entering into a transaction which is prohibited under the insider dealing legislation. Also, a breach of this rule would give an investor who suffers any consequential loss a right to claim damages under section 62 of the FSA 1986. There is no right for a person to claim compensation under the insider dealing legislation, but under section 62 an investor can seek compensation where he suffers a loss as a result of a breach by an authorised firm of a regulatory rule to which it is subject. This right of action has generally been limited to private investors, but a breach of this rule on insider dealing is one of the three exceptions to this restriction (see paragraph 1–004 above). It should also be remembered that SFA has power to award compensation in disciplinary proceedings (Rule 7–31).

16–002   Rule 5–46(1) applies even though the own account transaction is executed outside the United Kingdom, including a transaction executed by a firm's overseas branch: the firm cannot rely, in this instance, on the usual foreign business carve-out to the application of the rules (see paragraphs 4–005 *et seq.* above). An own account transaction is one effected or arranged by the firm in the course of carrying on either investment business (rather than merely regulated business) or associated business on the firm's own account or for the own account of an associate. As has already been pointed out in earlier Chapters, "associate" includes not merely other companies within the same group, but persons who have a community of interest, in terms of their business or domestic relationship, with the firm.

Although the rule is addressed to the firm, the firm is only in breach where it acts with knowledge that its associate, or an employee of either it or its associate, is prohibited from dealing. As we have already seen in paragraph 15–014 above, a firm is not presumed to have knowledge where the individual responsible for executing the transaction on its behalf did not have the relevant information (Rule 5–3(3)).

Rule 5–46(2) then provides that a firm must use its best endeavours to ensure that it does not knowingly effect in the course of any of its business a transaction for a customer which it knows is one prohibited under the insider dealing legislation. This is a lighter requirement than the earlier provision where a firm deals for its own account. The obligation is not an absolute one, in the sense that a firm has to use its best endeavours to avoid effecting a prohibited transaction. Also, there are two tests of knowledge which have to be proved before the firm breaches this rule. First, the firm must know that the customer is prevented from dealing under the insider dealing legislation and, second, the firm itself must knowingly effect such a transaction. In other words, even if the firm knows that the customer is prevented from dealing, if the deal is arranged through the firm without the firm realising that it is being done for or on behalf of the customer, then the firm will not be liable. Oddly, the rule only applies where a customer is prohibited from dealing; not where a non-customer, such as a market counterparty, is prohibited. As with the earlier provision, however, the scope of this rule extends beyond regulated business, to any business which the firm transacts.

Rule 5–46(3) provides three exceptions to the above two rules: **16–003**

(i) A firm is not prevented from dealing where the only price sensitive information is knowledge in the market of the firm's own intentions. In other words, the price of the relevant securities is likely to be affected materially only because the market has knowledge that the firm is about to deal for itself or for a customer.

(ii) A firm may, nevertheless, deal where it is a recognised market maker with an obligation to deal in the investment. This mirrors a similar exception in the insider dealing legislation. Under section 3(1)(d) of the 1985 Act a person is not prevented from dealing in relation to any particular securities if the price sensitive information was obtained by him in the course of his business as a market maker in those securities and was of a description which it would be reasonable to expect him to obtain in the ordinary course of that business, provided he deals in good faith in the course of that business. A recognised market maker is defined in the rules in a similar way to the definition of market maker in the 1985 Act. It is a person who holds himself out at all times in compliance with the rules of a recognised investment exchange[3] as willing to buy and sell securities at prices specified by him, and who is recognised as doing so by the relevant exchange. It should be noted that this exception only applies where the firm is a market maker in the relevant investment which is subject to the deal, rather than being a general exception for deals in any investments.

(iii) The firm will also not be in breach where it is a trustee or personal representative acting on the advice of a third party who appears to the firm to be an appropriate adviser and who is not himself subject to any restriction under the insider dealing legislation. Again, this effectively repeats a similar exception in the 1985 Act (section 7). To rely on this exception, the firm should be entirely reliant on the advice of the third party and have no reason to doubt his integrity and reliability.

Stabilisation

Stabilisation is basically a price support mechanism employed to **16–004** prevent the price of newly issued securities falling in the initial period after their issue. It is a form of market manipulation which would prima facie give rise to an offence under section 47(2) of the FSA 1986. This section provides that any person who does any act, or who engages in any conduct, which creates a false or misleading impression as to the market in, or the price or value of, any investments is guilty of an offence. A statutory "safe harbour", however, is provided where a firm engages in stabilisation in accordance with SIB's Stabilisation Rules (section 48(7)).

Hence, Rule 5–47 requires a firm which takes action for the purpose of stabilising the price of securities to comply with SIB's Stabilisation Rules. As with the rules on insider dealing discussed above, the scope of this rule is not limited to the definition of regulated business. It applies to any stabilisation done within the course of any business which the firm undertakes. This is necessary to ensure that the firm obtains the benefit of the statutory safe harbour, because section 47(2) applies where the false or misleading impression is created in the United Kingdom, even if the relevant act or course of conduct is engaged in overseas (section 47(5)).

The reason for permitting stabilisation in controlled circumstances is that it is seen as a protection for investors. When a new issue floods onto the market, there is the danger that, when dealings first open, prices may be depressed because of the volume of stock available. This would be to the disadvantage of investors who had subscribed for the stock at the initial issue price before dealings commenced and for investors holding associated securities whose price could be affected by the price of the newly issued securities. Allowing the stabilising manager to support the price for an initial period provides a degree of stability to the market, avoiding sudden sharp falls in the price of the relevant and associated securities.

Stabilisation Rules. These permit the stabilising manager to purchase, agree to purchase, or offer to purchase any relevant or associated securities, provided his action is taken with a view to stabilising or maintaining the market price of the relevant securities. He may only carry out such stabilisation if: the stabilising period is still running; he has taken the necessary preliminary steps; and he does not exceed the rules as to the maximum price at which stabilising action may be taken. All of these terms need explaining.

Stabilising Manager. This is such one of the managers as has been agreed between them to be the sole stabilising manager in relation to an issue. There can, however, be a separate stabilising manager for each country abroad where stabilisation of the issue takes place outside the United Kingdom. It is only the stabilising manager who has the benefit of the safe harbour to section 47(2). Any other managers involved in the issue who engage in stabilising activities could, therefore, find themselves committing a criminal offence.

Relevant Securities. These are investments falling within paragraphs 1 to 5 inclusive of Schedule 1 to the FSA 1986 and are basically shares, debentures, gilts, warrants and depositary receipts. There are some restrictions, however: the investments must be ones which are not being issued in connection with a takeover offer; and they must be dealt in on one of the listed exchanges, or an application for such dealing should have been made. The listed exchanges are: the American Stock Exchange; the International Securities Market Association (formerly AIBD); the London Stock Exchange; the National Association of Securities Dealers; the New York Stock Exchange; the Pacific Stock Exchange; the Paris Stock Exchange; the Tokyo Stock Exchange; and the Toronto Stock Exchange. On the face of it, this definition of relevant securities is fairly limited. Reliance is placed, however, on London Stock Exchange Rule 535.2, which is effectively that exchange's over-the-counter (OTC) market permitting dealings between exchange members in securities which are not listed or quoted on the exchange. It should be noted that units in collective investments schemes, options, futures and contracts for difference cannot be stabilised.

Although the relevant securities which can be stabilised are defined by reference to dealings on the exchanges listed above, stabilisation of them may be carried out on any exchange, and even off-exchange, because the reference to permitted stabilisation only being carried out on a specified exchange has been deleted until at least the end of 1992 under SIB's Transitional Rules.

Associated securities. These are securities: **16–005**

(i)   which are in all respects uniform with the relevant securities;

(ii) for which the relevant securities may be exchanged, or into which they may be converted;

(iii) which the holders of the relevant securities have rights to acquire or subscribe for by virtue of their holdings of the relevant securities;

(iv) which are issued or guaranteed by the issuer of the relevant securities and whose market price is likely to have a material influence on the market price of the relevant securities; or

(v)   which are depositary receipts in respect of the relevant securities.

Associated securities also include associated call options; namely options to acquire particular amounts of the relevant securities or of any of the associated securities listed above.

Stabilising period. This means the period beginning with the date on which the earliest public announcement of the issue is made, and ending with the earlier of:

(i)   the thirtieth day after the closing date; or

(ii) the sixtieth day after the date of allotment.

The earliest public announcement which starts the stabilisation period running is the first one to state the issue price, unless the investments are debentures or government and public securities where the total offer is for less than £15 million or the equivalent in foreign currency; in which case, it is the earliest public announcement of the issue. The closing date is the date on which the issuer receives the proceeds of the issue or the first instalment payment, or, in the case of an offer for sale, the last date for acceptance of the offer. The date of allotment is the date on which the securities are allotted to subscribers or purchasers.

Preliminary steps. The stabilising manager must take certain preliminary steps before he can take stabilising action. He must take proper steps to make it known that stabilisation is possible. He must be reasonably sure that the price is not already false. He must have set up proper systems for recording what he does. From the beginning of the introductory period, any screen-based statement, press announcement, invitation telex, offering document, or prospectus referring to the issue, issued by or on behalf of the issuer or the stabilising manager, must contain a disclosure that stabilisation may take place. No warning has to be included, however, on allotment telexes, pricing telexes, contract notes or short form image advertisements. The introductory period means the period from the first public announcement from which it could reasonably be deduced that the issue was intended to take place until the beginning of the stabilising period.

If there are already associated securities in existence in the market the price of which may have been inflated as a result of a contravention of section 47(2) of the FSA 1986, the stabilising manager must be satisfied that the issue price of the relevant securities to be stabilised is no higher than it would have been had there been no such contravention. He must not stabilise shares or certificates associated to bonds, loans or debentures if one is to be converted into the other, unless the terms of the conversion have been announced.

16–006   *Maximum price.* The provisions are as follows:

(i)   The initial stabilising price (price x) must not exceed the issue price (price y).

(ii) Subsequent stabilisation must be equal to or below price x, the initial stabilising price.

(iii) If there are no sales and purchases independent of the stabilising manager on the principal exchange above price x, he can operate at prices below price x, moving up or down as he wishes. ("Principal exchange" means the investment exchange which the stabilising manager reasonably believes to be the principal investment exchange on which the relevant securities are dealt in at the time of the transaction.)

(iv) If an independent buyer and seller do a deal on the principal exchange at a price (price z) between price x and price y, the stabilising manager has a new maximum price (price z) instead of price x.

Ancillary activities. As well as purchasing, agreeing to purchase or offering to purchase relevant securities or associated securities, the stabilising manager may also carry out the following ancillary activities:

(i) With a view to effecting stabilising transactions in relevant or associated securities, he may:

(a) make allotments of a greater number of the relevant securities than will be issued; or
(b) sell, or offer to sell, relevant or associated securities so as to establish a short position in them.

(ii) He may purchase, or offer to purchase, relevant or associated securities in order to close out or liquidate any positions established under (i). In this case, the maximum price limits do not apply.

(iii) He may sell, or offer to sell, relevant or associated securities in order to close out or liquidate any positions established by stabilising transactions.

Warning. The Stabilisation Rules apply to the stabilising manager. However, firms which recommend to private customers purchases of securities which may be subject to stabilisation should give them a warning that the securities are subject to stabilisation and that, therefore, the price may not be a true indication of market interest in the issue. Such a warning is required if a firm is to comply with the general obligation on understanding risk in Rule 5–30(1) (see paragraph 7–008 above). The detailed warning requirements under the old rules have been deleted. It is no longer necessary to give a detailed explanation about stabilisation in a customer agreement. SFA, however, has produced a suitable model clause (see Appendix 7 below); but, as the note at the end of that clause makes clear, merely relying on such a written clause may not be sufficient for the purpose of ensuring, in accordance with Rule 5–30(1), that the customer understands the risks involved.

Support of Takeover Panel

16–007   The United Kingdom Panel on Takeovers and Mergers is a non-statutory body; and, because it is not responsible for authorising securities firms, it does not have the sanctions of the SROs available to it, such as fining, or suspending or removing an authorised person's licence to do investment business. The Panel hopes to persuade people to comply with its rules and directions by voluntary agreement. Where such agreement cannot be obtained, then the Panel relies on other regulators, such as the SROs, to take action in support of the Panel against their recalcitrant members, and encourages the recognised investment exchanges to deny their facilities to the persons concerned.

As already indicated in paragraph 1–009 above, it is intended to endorse under Principle 3 (Market Practice) the Panel's City Code on Takeovers and Mergers and the Panel's Rules Governing Substantial Acquisitions of Shares Rules (SARs). This will mean that a firm will have to comply with the provisions of the City Code and the SARs as if they were additions to the 10 Principles. In other words, SFA may take disciplinary action against a firm for breaching one of these provisions, but the firm will not be liable to civil action under section 62 of the FSA 1986.

By endorsing the City Code and the SARs under Principle 3, however, there is no intention that SFA should act against a member firm without prior consultation with the Panel. The Panel will retain the prime responsibility to enforce the Code and SARs by general consensus and obtaining the agreement to its rulings from the persons concerned. In fact, SFA has specifically provided that, where a firm fails to comply with a code of practice endorsed under Principle 3, SFA may only take disciplinary action, or exercise its powers of intervention, in respect of the breach at the request of the body issuing the code (Rule 7–2).

SFA requires that a firm should provide to the Panel such information, documents and records as the Panel requests in performing its functions in respect of the Code and SARs. Also, a firm must render all such assistance as it is reasonably able to provide to enable the Panel to perform its functions (Rule 5–48(2)).

A firm must not act or continue to act for a person who has been named in a notice published by the Panel as a person with whom SFA firms should not deal until such time as the Panel withdraws the notice (Rule 5–48(1)). This restriction on acting for such a person only applies to matters done in connection with a takeover, a substantial acquisition of shares or dealings during an offer period which are subject to the announcement requirements of Rule 8 of the Code; and it does not apply if the firm obtains the specific consent of the Panel to deal in the circumstances.

Trade reporting

One of the best methods available to a regulator in checking what **16–008** business a firm is doing, what customers it is dealing with and how it is carrying on its business is by requiring reports on all the transactions which the firm executes. From such reports, SFA is able to monitor the extent to which a firm is complying with the dealing obligations (as discussed in Chapter 11 above) and the restrictions on insider dealing (see paragraphs 16–001 *et seq.* above). It also means that SFA is able to carry out much of its monitoring work without visiting firms. Programmes can be run to analyse the trade reporting information which comes in, looking for inconsistencies of various types.

Trade reporting is also a good exercise for a firm in the sense that it encourages it to maintain good compliance records and procedures, properly recording all relevant details about the business which it is doing. If it knows that it is reporting the essential details of a transaction to its regulator, it is more likely to take care over whether the execution of that transaction complies with the normal Conduct of Business Rules.

As we have already seen in paragraphs 4–014 and 4–015 above, for the purposes of the trade reporting requirement a firm must report transactions in investments which are exempt under paragraphs 17 and 18 of Schedule 1 to the FSA 1986 from the meaning of investment business in terms of the FSA 1986 authorisation requirements. In determining whether or not a firm is treating its customers fairly, it is important to know what transactions it is carrying out for its own account and for an associate's own account, and what transactions are being entered into between it and other group companies. The transaction reporting requirements, however, do not extend to all principal transactions and inter-group transactions. A firm only has to report such transactions to the extent that they would be regulated business but for the fact that they are exempt from the definition of investment business (Rule 5–1 (1) (d) and (e)). In other words, it only has to report transactions which are subject to the normal application of the Conduct of Business Rules through the definition of regulated business. Transactions done by its overseas branches within the usual foreign business carve-out are exempt.

Under Rule 5–49 SFA requires transactions (whether on- or off-exchange) in all kinds of investments to be reported to it, except for the following:

(i) Transactions in public municipal debt issued or guaranteed by the governments or government agencies of Japan or the United States. This exception may be extended, in due course, to public or municipal debt issued in some other countries.

(ii) Transactions in wholesale money market instruments of the kinds referred to in paragraph 2 (2) of Schedule 5 to the FSA 1986. This exemption applies even where the normal wholesale counterparty limits are not satisfied and where the transaction is executed by a firm which is not a section 43 listed money market institution. It extends to Euro commercial paper and Euro certificates of deposit.

(iii) Transactions in units in collective investment schemes, whether or not regulated. This exemption extends to transactions in the shares of open-ended investment companies. Transactions in the shares of closed-ended investment companies, such as investment trusts, however, must be reported.

(iv) Transactions in currencies.

(v) Transactions in any commodity, whether a soft commodity or a metal, including bullion.

(vi) Transactions in options and futures contracts based on any of the above. Commodity options and futures are excluded; this will be reviewed in the future.

(vii) Transactions in contracts for difference, unless they are equity index options and futures. Therefore, options and futures on the FT-SE 100 Index must be reported; as must interest-rate swaps and caps (unless excluded under (ii) above) and equity swaps.

(viii) Transactions in life policies.

16–009 (ix) Issuing market allotments and syndication. This exemption is intended to exclude all primary market activities where the stock is issued direct to the investor. It is quite wide and covers the situation where sub-underwriters are involved if they enter into a direct obligation with the issuing company to subscribe at the issue price for securities not taken up in the initial offer. The transactions would only have to be reported where the main underwriter initially takes up the securities and then transfers them to the sub-underwriters. Where a shareholder fails to take up his allocation in a rights issue, there is not necessarily a reportable transaction where the rights are transferred by the issuing company cancelling the original allocation and then creating a new right to subscribe in favour of the underwriter or sub-underwriter. In the case of a takeover where the offeror offers to acquire the whole of the issued share capital of the offeree in exchange for an issue of new securities, it is suggested that the exemption extends to the selling of the new securities to the issuing company's adviser by shareholders of the offeree who have accepted a separate cash offer. The exemption should also apply to a similar transfer of shares between the issuing company, vendors and placees in a vendor placing. Although there are technically two transfers, the transaction can be looked at as a single one: the second transaction should be viewed as a primary market activity because it is organised as part of the first transaction.

(x) Transactions involving repurchase or reverse repurchase agreements, and any stock lending or borrowing. This exemption extends to two individual trades arranged together as a sale and buy back or a buy and sell back, whether or not undertaken on a single ticket. Two tickets are sometimes made out with the same trade date, but with different settlement dates. These tickets, even if not cross-referenced, may indicate a normal repurchase or reverse repurchase agreement.

(xi) Any asset trading, to the extent that it amounts to investment business.

(xii) Any transactions which are already notifiable under Rule 2–49. This is the rule which requires a firm to notify SFA of the acquisition, disposal or dissolution of a subsidiary; or the acquisition of a firm by a holding company; or the acquisition by a firm which is not a body corporate of a holding of more than 50 per cent. of the equity share capital of a company.

Reports must be made no later than the end of the business day **16–010** following the date of the transaction, unless the transaction is in a new instrument. In this case, the report can be made on the later of the day after the date of allotment or the day after the date on which the issue price is fixed.

SFA may announce extended deadlines where there is a prolonged central failure of an approved reporting system on which firms are relying. If it is the firm's own system or that of its reporting agent which fails, the firm should immediately inform SFA, which may specify an alternative means of reporting. If the failure is outside the firm's control, then it may be able to rely anyway on the *force majeure* requirement (Rule 1–6 and see paragraph 2–007 above).

A firm may appoint a transaction reporting agent to make reports on its behalf. The firm, however, will still retain full responsibility for compliance with the trade reporting requirements and must ensure that its agent uses the firm's identifying code for each transaction which is reported on its behalf.

A firm may report as a single trade a series of transactions executed within a 24 hour period which constitutes an exact replica of an index (a "basket trade"). This provision extends to basket trades for the following indices: the Standard and Poors 500; the Dow Jones 30; the Nikkei 225; the LSE/Nikkei 50; the Hang Seng; the CAC 40; and the DAX 30.

A single report is only required where a firm has executed an aggregated transaction for its discretionary funds (such as PEPs) where allocation at the transaction price is made in a fixed ratio which has been previously notified to SFA. Similarly, unless it is also reporting them as separate trades, a firm may report as a single transaction any transactions for which it is issuing a single contract note showing an averaged price in accordance with Rule 5–34 (13) and (14) (see paragraph 10–011 above). These are the contract and confirmation note provisions allowing a firm to issue a contract note recording as a single transaction a number of transactions executed to achieve one investment decision or objective within a 24-hour period for a private customer or a five-day period for a non-private customer. The firm must still keep records of the underlying separate transactions (Rule 5–34 (15)).

The transaction report must show the price at which the bargain was transacted, excluding any charges which are separately disclosed on the contract or confirmation note. In reporting the transaction, the firm must also ensure that the following information is given: the firm's identifying code; the investment's identifying code; the date and time of the transaction; the transaction size, price and currency; whether it is a purchase or sale; whether the firm dealt as principal or agent; the settlement date; and the transaction's reference number. If any of these details can properly be implied, they do not have to be given by the firm: for example, where the firm may only be able to deal in the particular market as a principal or if the reporting system which it uses generates information such as the time and date of the trade. The firm should also give any other information which is required by the reporting system used and should, if the system permits, show the counterparty's identifying code. There is no requirement at the moment to show a customer identifying code; although a firm must be able to make this information available to SFA through its own records.

16–011 Instead of having to make its report direct to SFA, a firm may report the transaction through an approved reporting system. These are systems to which SFA's surveillance monitoring system is linked. They are: the London Stock Exchange's SEQUAL system and CHECKING system; the International Securities Market Association's TRAX system; the Euro-clear EUCLID system operated by Morgan Guaranty; and CEDEL's CEDCOM system. If a firm is not connected to one of these systems, then it may manually report the transaction on a form produced for this purpose by SFA; but a firm must seek SFA's permission before making manual reports. SFA is also willing to receive, with its prior agreement, reports by other means, such as a computer disk.

The reason for encouraging firms to report through approved reporting systems is to reduce costs. Obviously, the more standardised the reporting systems are, the easier it is for SFA to capture and monitor the information. It is also cheaper for firms only to use one system. It is possible for firms to report under the approved reporting systems transactions in investments which are not currently traded on the respective markets which the systems principally serve.

Whenever a firm is a party to a reportable transaction, it must report it, even if the transaction will also be reported by the counterparty. This applies even where the firm is executing an own account transaction.

A firm does not, however, have to report the transaction if it, or another person who is sending the contract or confirmation note to the firm's customer, has reported the transaction to a qualifying exchange; or the transaction is a traded option, a future, or an index option or future (contract for difference) which has been executed on, and reported to, a qualifying exchange by a member of that exchange. A list of qualifying exchanges is given in Appendix 7.

The relaxation where the report is being made by one party to a qualifying exchange is based on the fact that SFA is less concerned about on-exchange transactions which are being properly reported to the relevant exchange. The qualifying exchanges are willing to co-operate with SFA in supplying information to assist SFA's monitoring work. The list only includes United Kingdom recognised investment exchanges and the overseas exchanges designated by SIB. In all these cases, the exchanges have proper arrangements for recording transactions effected on them, and have effective arrangements for enforcing compliance with their rules and investigating complaints related to business transacted by means of their facilities (see the requirements in Schedule 4 to the FSA 1986 for recognised investment exchanges).

[1] The London Stock Exchange, the London International Financial Futures and Options Exchange (LIFFE), NASDAQ International (National Association of Securities Dealers) and OM London (the United Kingdom exchange set up by the Stockholm Options Market) are recognised investment exchanges for the purposes of the 1985 Act.
[2] The reference to off-market dealer in the 1985 Act only includes persons who are authorised under the FSA 1986.
[3] "Recognised investment exchange" under the 1985 Act is a narrower concept than a recognised investment exchange under the FSA 1986. See n. 1 above.

Chapter 17

Safe Custody

Merely having safe custody responsibilities for a customer's investments **17–001** is not an investment business activity under the FSA 1986. Safe custody is, however, a facility which is often operated by investment business firms as an integral part of dealing in, arranging deals in, advising on and managing investments. As a result, SFA is concerned to regulate any safe custody responsibilities undertaken by its members because of the inter-relationship between these responsibilities and the investment business activities for which a firm needs authorisation under SFA.

In fact, where the safe custody service involves more than the physical safe-keeping of the customer's stock, then a firm may well find that it is in fact doing investment business within the meaning of Part II, Schedule 1 to the FSA 1986. For example, a firm which arranges for a customer to subscribe for shares in a rights issue or arranges for the customer to sell his nil-paid rights may be carrying on the activity of arranging deals (paragraph 13). A firm may find that it is carrying on discretionary management (paragraph 14) if it has discretion as to whether to elect, on the customer's behalf, to receive a scrip dividend rather than a cash dividend, take up the customer's rights allocation, take an exchange of stock as part of a capital reorganisation or accept a takeover offer. In these cases, the firm would be carrying out discretion-ary management for which it would need a two-way customer agreement under Rule 5–23 (2). Even if the firm is only advising the customer as to what he should do in these situations, it will be giving investment advice (paragraph 15). Therefore, a firm which only provides safe custody facilities may find that it carries on activities in support of those facilities which amount to investment business for which it must be authorised under the FSA 1986.

It is important to be aware of the fact that a firm may be dealing in, advising on or managing investments in the course of its safe custody activities. Where it is carrying on one of these activities, then the firm will be subject to the normal Conduct of Business Rules to the extent that the activities are performed in the course of the firm's regulated business.

Safekeeping Rules (Rules 4–1 to 4–12)

Application

The rules concerned with safe custody apply where a firm has **17–002** custody of a customer's investments in connection with, or with a view to, regulated business. In other words, they do not apply to firms which are authorised institutions under the Banking Act 1987 in respect of property not held in connection with any investment business which the firm carries on for a customer, as long as the safe custody facilities do not themselves involve investment business activities, as explained above.

Also the Safekeeping Rules do not apply to safe custody facilities provided in connection with investment business done within the foreign business carve-out (see paragraphs 4–005 *et seq.* above), even if the safe custody facilities are provided in the United Kingdom.

Notification (Rule 4–2)

Before a firm provides safe custody facilities to, or receives collateral from, a customer, it must notify the customer in writing (which may be in a one-way document) of the obligations it will have in relation to registering the investments if they are not to be registered in the customer's own name, and, if applicable:

(i)   claiming and receiving dividends, interest payments and other rights accruing to the customer;

(ii) exercising conversion and subscription rights;

(iii) dealing with takeovers, other offers or capital reorganisations; and

(iv) exercising voting rights.

The firm must also point out the extent to which it will be liable in the event of a default by another custodian which it is employing. The written notification is required for both private and non-private customers. It is not necessary, however, where the firm is only holding the securities temporarily whilst awaiting valid settlement instructions.

Safe custody investments

The Safekeeping Rules apply where the firm holds safe custody investments. These are investments, except for collateral, falling within paragraphs 1 to 6 inclusive, Schedule 1 to the FSA 1986. In other words, they do not include options, futures, contracts for difference, and life policies. Before a firm is subject to the rules, the investments must have been paid for in full by the customer and not be the beneficial property of the firm. The rules apply whatever form the investments are held in, whether as registered or bearer certificates, or electronically recorded. If the safe custody investments are registered in the names of both the customer and that of an associate of the firm, they should be treated, for the purpose of the rules, as registered in the customer's name, except that the customer should be told under Rule 4–2 about the dual registration.

A firm is no longer subject to the Safekeeping Rules once a valid **17–003** instruction to effect disposal of the relevant investments has been issued. A valid disposal will encompass gifting, selling and inheritance. The rules do not apply to investments held as collateral, except for Rule 4–2 on the notification of the firm's responsibilities (as discussed above) and Rules 4–11 and 4–12 on reconciliations and statements (discussed in paragraph 17–005 below). Rule 4–13, however, contains separate provisions on handling collateral which largely mirror the Safekeeping Rules, (see paragraph 17–006 below).

Registration

Generally, safe custody investments should be registered in the customer's name, unless he has been notified in advance to the contrary. If not registered in his name, then they must be registered in the name of an eligible nominee, an eligible custodian or, with the prior consent of SFA, the firm itself. SFA would only permit the investments to be registered in the firm's name where overseas laws or market practices prevent the other forms of registration. An example might be where marking names are commonly used; for example, in the Japanese market when permission may be granted to treat such securities as bearer.

Eligible nominee

An eligible nominee is:

(i) an individual nominated by the customer who is not an associate of the firm;

(ii) a nominee company controlled by either the firm or an affiliated company (any body corporate controlled by the firm, the firm's parent company, or any body corporate controlled by the latter);

(iii) a nominee company owned by a recognised or designated investment exchange provided the investments are held in a safe custody account controlled by the firm; or

(iv)   a nominee company controlled by an eligible custodian.

A nominee company is any body corporate whose business consists solely of acting as a nominee holder of investments or other property.

Eligible custodian

An eligible custodian is:

(i)   An approved bank. This means, in respect of an account opened at a branch in the United Kingdom, the Bank of England, a central bank of another EC member state, an authorised institution under the Banking Act 1987, or a Building Society registered under the Building Societies Act 1986 which offers unrestricted money transmission services.

Where the account is opened outside the United Kingdom, it includes any of the above bodies, plus a bank which is the subsidiary or parent of such a body, or a credit institution established in an EC member state (other than the United Kingdom) and duly authorised by the relevant supervisory authority in that state.

SFA has made additions in Appendix 6 to this list of approved banks where money is held outside the United Kingdom. Included are banks supervised by the central banks of member states of the Organisation for Economic Co-operation and Development, institutions licensed under the Isle of Man Banking Act 1975, banks regulated by the New York State Banking Department, banks supervised by the South African Reserve Bank and some Channel Island banks and Canadian trust companies.

(ii)   Approved depositories. These are listed in Appendix 6. Although this list includes CEDEL, it does not include the Euro-clear system operated by Morgan Guaranty because Morgan Guaranty is already an authorised institution under the Banking Act 1987. Similarly, the Central Gilts Office and the Central Moneymarkets Office are not referred to because these are covered by the reference to the Bank of England under (i) above.

(iii)   An FSA 1986 authorised person which is a clearing firm.

(iv)   Any member of a recognised or designated investment exchange.

(v) A person specifically approved by SFA as an eligible custodian. This list is included in Appendix 6.

In the case of a non-private customer who is an ordinary business investor, rather than an expert, an eligible custodian may also be any person whom the firm reasonably believes to be a person whose business includes the provision of investment custodial services, even if that person does not fall within the above list.

Segregation

A firm must effectively segregate its own investments, and **17–004** investments belonging to its directors or partners, where they are registered in the same name as the customer's investments. This segregation must be done either by registering the customer's investments in a designated account different from that designated for the firm's, or its directors' or partners' investments, or by holding separate certificates evidencing title to the customer's investments. Such segregation need not necessarily be done at the level of the register. It should be noted that the segregation of customers' investments from the firm's, or its directors' or partners', does not extend to those of associates, such as other group companies, employees, or the close family or business partners of the directors or partners. Apart from this provision, there is no difference in the application of the rules to the firm's directors' and partners' investments and to those of other customers.

How held

The firm must hold investments which are in registered or bearer form in the firm's physical possession; or with an eligible custodian,[1] either in a fungible account in the firm's name designated for customers' investments, or in a safe custody account designated for customers' investments. A fungible account is one in which identical investments are commingled, without any specific investment being attributable to any particular sub-account or customer. Where the investments are commingled, then at least those belonging to the firm's customers should be kept in a separately designated account in the firm's name (account client). They should not be commingled with investments of customers of other firms who are using the same custodian.

A firm must not lodge customers' investments with an eligible custodian in a fungible account unless the custodian has confirmed in writing to the firm that:

(i) the account is designated to show that the investments do not belong to the firm or an affiliated company;

(ii)   the custodian is not to permit withdrawal otherwise than to the firm or on the firm's instructions;

(iii) the custodian will, at the firm's request, deliver a statement showing the description and amounts of all investments credited to the account and send the statement within one month of it being requested; and

(iv)   the custodian will not claim any lien, or right of retention or sale, over the investments within the account, except in relation to its administrative charges for the safe custody service.

Where the custodian is not keeping the investments in a fungible account, then he must still confirm the above matters, except that, in respect of the stock check statement (item (iii) above), he must identify, in relation to registered stock, the amount registered in each customer's name.

Nominee's records

Where the investments are registered in the name of a nominee company controlled by the firm or an affiliated company, the firm must ensure that the nominee maintains accounting records in accordance with SFA's Financial Rules (see Chapter 19 below).

Reconciliations (Rule 4–11)

17–005   A firm must reconcile its books and records relating to its safekeeping activities at least every six months by either the Total Count Method or the Rolling Stock Method, and promptly correct any discrepancies which are revealed from the reconciliation. Where the stock is held by a nominee company controlled by the firm or an affiliated company, it is the firm's responsibility to ensure that the nominee company carries out such a reconciliation. It should be noted that the reconciliations should include reconciling customers' beneficial positions, that is trade date positions, to the actual physical positions by taking into account unsettled bargains.

Total count

The Total Count Method is the physical counting and inspection of all customers' safe custody investments, together with any other property (such as collateral and cash) belonging to the customers, which are physically held by the firm. If any of the investments or property are held by custodians, the firm must obtain written confirmation from them as to what they hold.

Rolling stock check

Under the Rolling Stock Method all kinds of investments and other property held must be inspected and physically counted on a rolling basis every six months. This method may only be used with SFA's prior consent; and SFA will first require written confirmation from the firm's auditors that they have examined the firm's systems of internal control for the safe custody, identification and keeping of documents and records, and that, in their opinion, the systems are sufficient to enable the firm properly to comply with the Rolling Stock Check Method. Rolling stock checks may now be operated on a customer-by-customer basis, rather than only a stock basis. However, SFA will wish to satisfy itself that teeming and lading fraud cannot be carried on, and will, therefore, insist on more rigid and complete internal controls.

Statements (Rule 4–12)

At least once a year, a firm must provide all customers with a statement listing the investments and other property (including collateral) legally or beneficially owned by each customer for which the firm is accountable. The statements may be issued on a rolling basis provided each customer receives at least one in every 12 month period. No statement is required, however, in respect of a customer for whom the firm did not actually have a custody responsibility for any of his investments or other property at any time during the preceding 12 months. The statements should explain in what form of custody the investments and other property are held, lodged or deposited. They do not need to detail the names of custodians used or the registration details, except to distinguish between those registered in the customer's name and those registered in another name. Investments and property being used as collateral, or pledged to third parties, must be separately identified; and the market value of the collateral, as at the statement date, must be given.

Trade date

The statements for private customers should be based on trade date information as regards cash balances and investments. For example, investments which have been purchased should be included on the statement even if the bargains have not yet been settled, whilst sold investments should be excluded as at the trade date. Client money balances do not have to be included to the extent that they have been separately notified to the customer within one month of the date to which the statement has been prepared. Where a contract note has been issued regarding a customer's purchase of securities within the previous three months and there is no intention to offer a custodial service in relation to those securities, they need not be included on any statement.

Collateral (Rule 4–13)[2]

17–006   We have already seen that Rules 4–2, 4–11 and 4–12 apply to a customer's stock which is used as collateral. Collateral is defined, similarly to safe custody investments, to include investments falling within paragraphs 1 to 6, Schedule 1 to the FSA 1986. It also includes commodity warrants, but not cash, bullion or other property. It must have been paid for in full by the customer; and held or controlled by the firm other than by way of ordinary safe custody: in other words, as security against any obligation owed by the customer in respect of an investment transaction.

A firm is required to take reasonable steps to ensure that any collateral from a customer for which it is responsible is properly safeguarded. It must be able to identify at all times each customer who has provided collateral and must ensure that that customers' collateral is separately identifiable from the firm's own assets. Where the firm suspects that the collateral will not be properly utilised or safeguarded by a third person with whom it is deposited or pledged, it should withdraw it unless the customer agrees otherwise in writing.

A firm should not deposit (unless it is by way of safe custody), pledge or charge a customer's collateral to a third party unless it has the customer's written consent and has properly considered the credit risk to him. It should have notified him, if applicable, that the collateral will not be registered in his name. In the case of a customer receiving client money protection, it should also have warned him that that part of the proceeds from the sale of his collateral which exceeds the amount owed by him to the firm will be pooled with other customers' assets in the event of the firm's default. The firm must have obtained the customer's written consent if it wishes: to return to him collateral which is not the identical collateral originally deposited (except where the firm returns a cash equivalent in respect of an investment which has matured); to substitute or provide collateral from one customer to satisfy collateral obligations owed by another person; and to use a customer's collateral as collateral for its own obligations. Instead of obtaining written consent one-way written notification of the matters referred to in this paragraph will be sufficient in the case of a non-private customer. All of the disclosures and consents may be dealt with in a normal customer agreement, terms of business letter or document creating a legal charge.

Similarly to safe custody, where a firm deposits, pledges or charges collateral to a third party, the firm must notify that person that:

(i)   the collateral does not belong to the firm; and

(ii)   he (the third party) must not hold any lien, or right of retention or sale, over the collateral except to cover the obligations owed by the customer for which the collateral has been provided or to cover the third party's charges in administering his safekeeping of the collateral.

[1] A firm which uses a custodian is not required to ensure that the latter uses sub-custodians who are themselves eligible custodians, as defined.

[2] Paragraph 17–006 contains the amendments to the collateral rule (Rule 4–13) which it is proposed will be implemented following the consultation exercise undertaken through SFA Board Notice 67, dated February 7, 1992.

Chapter 18

Client Money

Introduction

New Client Money Regulations made by SIB under section 55 of the **18–001** FSA 1986 came into force on January 1, 1992. These regulations create a statutory trust. Client money held under them by an authorised person is held on trust for the benefit of the firm's clients in accordance with their respective shares in it.

Reform of the previous regulations was prompted by a series of financial services company failures in 1989 and 1990. There are two sets of regulations. The main set (The Financial Services (Client Money) Regulations 1991) are designated as Core Rules to apply to all firms authorised to do investment business by SROs. They, therefore, apply directly to all SFA firms and cannot be amended unilaterally by SFA; although waivers can be granted to individual firms on application (see paragraph 2–005 above). The supplementary set (The Financial Services (Client Money) (Supplementary) Regulations 1991) apply to settlement and margined transaction bank accounts. They are not designated for SFA firms. SFA has adopted them, however, as its third tier rules, together with some additional regulations. The advantage of this non-designation is that SFA will be able to grant general waivers of them, or amend them without SIB having to issue a separate derogation instrument.

SIB issued Consultative Paper 61, dated March 1992, suggesting amendments to both sets of regulations. These amendments are likely to be effective from July 1992. For the purpose of this chapter, it is assumed that the proposed amendments will be made.

In this chapter, any reference to the CMRs includes both SIB's main and supplementary regulations, together with SFA's supporting rules.

Application

The CMRs only apply where a firm is carrying on investment business **18–002** which is regulated business. In other words, overseas branches of SFA firms may take advantage of the foreign business carve-out as described in paragraph 4–005 *et seq.* above.

For the purpose of the CMRs, investment business is defined to include activities which would normally be exempt under Parts III and IV of Schedule 1 to the FSA 1986 from the authorisation requirements. It is suggested, however, that this extension of the definition of investment business only applies to the reference to investment business in the regulations themselves, rather than to the use of the same term in the definition of regulated business. Otherwise, the effect of the foreign business carve-out for overseas branches would be completely lost because they would not be able to rely upon the exemptions referred to in Part IV, Schedule 1: namely, dealing in the United Kingdom with or through authorised persons, or with customers who have been solicited without any breach of either the section 57(1) advertising provision or the unsolicited calls permissions. The reason for extending the definition of investment business is that, once a firm is doing regulated business, it must provide client money protection wherever it holds money received in the course of investment business, even if that business would not normally require authorisation because it is an exempted activity under Parts III or IV.

The CMRs do not apply to an SFA firm which is an approved bank (as explained in paragraph 17–003 above in relation to eligible custodians) in so far as it is holding the money in an account with itself. Where the firm deposits a client's money, however, in the course of investment business with another approved bank, it may have to comply with the CMRs. The general criterion used is whether the firm has an agreement with its client to make such a deposit. If it is merely receiving money into its correspondent nostro accounts, this will not generally be caught by the CMRs.

The CMRs do not apply either to exempted persons, such as appointed representatives, or to SFA firms in the course of conducting business for which they are exempt from the FSA 1986 authorisation requirements: for example, where they are acting as listed money market institutions under section 43 of the FSA 1986. Although they do not apply to appointed representatives, it should be noted that firms which have appointed representatives are responsible, to the same extent as if they had expressly authorised it, for anything said, done or omitted by their representatives in carrying on investment business for which the firms have accepted responsibility (section 44(6) of the FSA 1986). Therefore, firms are responsible for ensuring that any money from clients which is received by their appointed representatives is protected properly in accordance with the CMRs.

Finally, the CMRs do not generally apply to oil market participants (see paragraphs 4–025 et seq. above).

What is Client Money?

18–003　The CMRs apply where a firm is holding client money as defined until such time as the firm has discharged the fiduciary duties which it owes to the relevant client in respect of the money.

Included

Client money is money of any currency which a firm holds in respect of any investment agreement with or for a client which is not immediately due and payable to the firm. An investment agreement means any agreement where one of the parties has entered into it in the course of dealing in, arranging deals in, managing or advising on investments, or establishing or operating a collective investment scheme (section 44(9) of the FSA 1986). The exemptions in Parts III and IV of Schedule 1 are disregarded in this context.

Money becomes client money at the point of receipt by the firm, rather than at the point at which it is banked. Therefore, it includes cheques, except cheques made payable to persons other than the firm which the firm merely forwards to them. It includes interest payable by the firm to the client, any settlement moneys which have become payable from the due settlement date in respect of securities acquired by the firm as principal from the client, and margined money. A firm does not need to segregate money when it does not know that it has been received, but it must have adequate arrangements to be promptly notified of receipt by banks and overseas agents.

Client money also includes: money received during a cooling-off period before a firm is able to enter into an investment agreement for the client; liquid funds held by an investment manager which were previously in the form of investments; money received by an operator of a collective investment scheme until such time as he has allocated units to the client; and money held by a firm acting as an intermediary or agent, except to the extent that it represents fees and commissions which can be properly claimed by the firm.

Excluded

Client money does not include precious coins owned for their intrinsic value, rather than as legal tender; although care needs to be taken in some case, such as krugerands, where the coins may be held either for their intrinsic value or as legal tender. Client money also does not include money from connected customers or group companies and money held in connection with cash against delivery or similar same day delivery transactions, apart from the qualifications mentioned below.

Connected customer

A connected customer is:

(i)   a partner, director, company secretary, controller or appointed representative of the firm; or

(ii) the spouse, minor child or step-child of any of the above; or

(iii) a trustee of a trust under which at least one of the beneficiaries is any of those described in (i) and (ii) above.

A connected customer is also any client of the firm with whom the firm has an agreement that it will have an interest of 25 per cent. or more in any transaction undertaken by the firm with or for the client.

There are two circumstances, however, in which money from connected customers is client money. The first is where the connected customer is acting as trustee for a trust in which no beneficiary is a connected customer. The second is where the money is held or received in respect of a PEP in the name of a connected customer. In all other cases, although the money of the connected customers is not protected as client money under the CRMs, there is no reason why a firm cannot hold it in a separate designated account, holding it in a bare trust for the benefit of the connected customers; however, practical difficulties may preclude this.

Group companies

18–004   Money from group companies is not client money unless the other company is an authorised person or a client at arm's length from the firm.[1] It is also client money where the group company is a manager of an occupational pension scheme or a non-United Kingdom company, and, in either case, the money is given to the firm in order to carry on investment business for or on behalf of clients for whom the group company has requested client money protections.

Delivery versus payment window

Where a firm receives money in respect of a delivery versus payment or cash against delivery transaction, it does not have to treat it as client money (although it may), provided delivery of the investments occurs by the close of business on the third business day following the firm's receipt of the money. Where the firm receives the money, however, in its capacity as the operator of a regulated collective investment scheme, it must have determined the price of the units by close of business on the day following the date of receipt of the money. A business day is any day which is not Saturday, Sunday or a United Kingdom public holiday, and, in respect of overseas settlement or any part of the settlement occurring overseas, a day reasonably believed to be a non-business day in the relevant overseas country. Once the relevant three- or one-day period has passed, then the firm must treat the money as client money.

Discharge of fiduciary duty

Money which was client money loses this character as soon as it is paid to the client, to a third party on his instructions, or into an account solely in the name of the client which is not also regarded as an account belonging to the firm. Where the payment is made to the client by cheque, then the cheque must be dispatched within one business day of it being drawn. Where the payment is made from an account other than a client bank account, an equivalent sum of money from the client bank account will not become due and payable to the firm until the client has received cleared funds.

Fees and commissions

Money is not regarded as immediately due and payable to a firm in respect of fees and commissions claimed by it unless one of three conditions has been satisfied:

(i) The fees have been accurately calculated in accordance with a formula or basis previously disclosed to the client. This applies to all clients, not merely clients who are private customers. Therefore, a firm may need to give prior disclosure of the basis of its charges to non-private customers, even though this is not required under the relevant Conduct of Business Rule, which is limited to private customers (Rule 5–33(2)).

(ii) Five business days have elapsed since the firm delivered to the client a statement detailing its fees, provided the firm has no reason to believe the client questions the sums involved.

(iii) The precise amount of the fees has been agreed by the client.

Who is Protected?

Client rather than customer

The CMRs apply where the money is held for a client. A client is **18–005** defined differently from a customer. It means any person with or for whom the firm has entered into or intends to enter into an investment agreement. Therefore, it includes persons who are exempted from the definition of customer, such as market counterparties, trust beneficiaries and third parties in respect to corporate finance business (see paragraphs 5–003 *et seq.* above).

It should be noted, however, that an overseas branch of an authorised person only has to provide client money protection to customers rather than clients. This is because the definition of regulated business in respect of business carried on in the United Kingdom from an overseas location only applies where the branch is carrying on business with, or for, customers. Therefore, the overseas branch may take advantage of the exceptions to the definition of customer.

Private customers and experts

The basic principle is that client money protection applies to all private customers. It also applies to expert investors (the second category of non-private customer described in paragraphs 5–026 *et seq.* above), unless the expert has consented in writing to waive the protection after having had a proper opportunity to consider a clear written warning from the firm that it will not provide CMR protection and that, as a consequence, the expert's money will not be segregated from that of the firm and may be used by the firm in the course of its business. This warning is additional to the general warning required under Rule 5–5 for the purpose of treating this person as an expert investor under the Conduct of Business Rules (see paragraphs 5–030 *et seq.* above). The client money warning, however, can be provided in the same document, provided the expert separately signs to confirm that he is willing to forgo this protection. A suitable model is set out as Appendix 5 below. Use of this document amounts to formal guidance for the purpose of Rule 1–4(1). Also the warning does not have to be signed by an expert to whom the firm was not giving CMR protection under the old regulations, provided it was sent to him by July 1, 1992. It should be noted that there is no exception from the written consent requirement under the CMRs for overseas experts as there is under the Conduct of Business Rules.

Ordinary business investors except authorised persons

18–006   A firm does not have to provide client money protection to an ordinary business investor (the other type of non-private customer) provided it has sent it a similar written warning about the loss of CMR protection to that mentioned above for experts; but, in this case, there is no need to obtain written consent from the investor to the loss of protection. This exception does not apply, however, where the ordinary business investor is another authorised person. Additionally, the written warning has to be sent out as a separate notice, not included in any other written communication; although it may be included in the same envelope as another document. In the case of a partnership, the notice must be addressed to one of the partners. In the case of a body corporate, it should be sent to an executive director. If the ordinary business investor rejects the notice (and an oral rejection is sufficient), the firm must, as soon as possible after the rejection, either write to the investor stating that its money will now be protected as client money or return the person's money.

Authorised persons

Where a firm receives money from another authorised person (whether a market counterparty or an ordinary business investor, including a RPB member certificated to carry on investment business), it must provide client money protection unless the authorised person has consented in writing that the money should not receive this protection. Consent in this context is expected to be obtained in a two-way signed agreement. The agreement should only be entered into by the authorised person in respect of money which it is not itself holding as client money; and, in practice, few such persons have agreed to sign such an exclusion. Where the authorised person is holding client money, it should not allow the other firm to whom the money is passed to treat it other than as client money. It should be noted that, if there is no agreement between a firm and any other authorised persons with whom it deals, any money which it receives from those authorised persons which is not immediately due and payable to the firm must be treated as client money, whether or not it had that quality in the hands of the other persons.

Overseas branches of authorised persons

Money which is received from overseas branches of authorised persons can be removed from client money protection in the same way as money received from non-authorised ordinary business investors. In other words, the firm merely has to send a one-way notice warning about the loss of protection and does not have to receive an indication from the branch that it wants the benefit of the CMRs.

Subsequent request for protection

Where a person who is not receiving client money protection subsequently changes his mind and requests it, then the firm has 10 business days after receiving the request either to treat his money as client money or to return it to him.

Segregation

18–007 Where a firm holds client money it must ensure that it is held in a client bank account with an approved bank (see the explanation in paragraph 17–003 above in relation to eligible custodians). Where the approved bank is another group company, this fact must be disclosed in writing to the client.

Overseas accounts

A firm may not hold client money belonging to a client who is a private customer in a free money bank account (explained in paragraph 8–010 below) outside the United Kingdom unless the firm has informed the client in writing:

(i) of the country or territory in which the account will be held; and

(ii) that the bank has acknowledged that money in the account will be properly segregated and protected as client money.

The acknowledgment under (ii) must be to the effect that: money standing to the credit of the account is held by the firm as trustee; the bank is not entitled to combine the account with any other account; it is not entitled to exercise any right of set-off or counterclaim against money in that account in respect of any sum owed to it on any of the firm's other accounts; interest earned on the account will be credited to it or another account of the same type; and the account's title sufficiently distinguishes it from any account containing money belonging to the firm. If the bank is not prepared to give such a written acknowledgment, then the firm must inform the private client in writing that, by holding his money in such an account, it will not be protected as effectively as if it were held in a free money bank account in the United Kingdom. The firm may then only hold the money in the overseas account provided the client has given his written consent after having had a proper opportunity to consider all the written information referred to in this paragraph which the firm is required to give.

Once the firm has placed client money in a free money bank account outside the United Kingdom, then, if the firm has any reason to believe (other than not receiving the acknowledgment referred to in (ii) above) that the money will not be protected as effectively as if it had been held in the United Kingdom, it must not continue to hold client money in that account unless:

(i) it has informed the relevant clients that their money may not be protected as effectively as if held in a similar account in the United Kingdom; and

(ii) obtained their written consent to it remaining in the overseas account.

It should be noted that this requirement applies to all clients, not just private clients.

There is an exception to obtaining both the initial and subsequent written consents (but not to the obligations to send the information) where the firm is dealing with a client ordinarily resident outside the United Kingdom, if it believes on reasonable grounds that he does not wish to enter into a written agreement. This is a similar exception to that provided under the Conduct of Business Rules in respect of customer agreement requirements (see paragraph 6–003 above, under "overseas customers"). **18–008**

All these warning and consent requirements for money held in free money bank accounts outside the United Kingdom apply even where the money is held in the overseas branch of a United Kingdom incorporated bank. They also apply to money held in the Channel Islands and Isle of Man as these territories are not within the United Kingdom. Also the written acknowledgment which is required from the bank that the client money will be properly segregated and protected is required in respect of all non-free money client bank accounts (namely, dividend claims, settlement and margined transaction accounts).

United Kingdom accounts

Where any client money is held in a United Kingdom bank account (whether or not a free money account), the firm must still obtain an acknowledgment from the bank that the money will be segregated and protected in a way similar to that required above in the case of overseas accounts. Unlike with overseas accounts, the money can be paid into a United Kingdom account before the acknowledgment is received. If it is not received within 20 days of being requested, however, the firm must withdraw all money standing to the credit of the account, close the account and deposit it with another approved bank.

Next day payment

The general rule is that a firm must pay money which it receives or begins to hold as client money (for example, it becomes liable to pay money to a client) into a client bank account by the close of business on the following business day;[2] or it must pay it out in such a way that it is no longer regarded as client money (as discussed in paragraph 8–004 above, under "discharge of fiduciary duty"). A problem arises with post-dated cheques. They are client money unless promptly returned to the clients. This is not really a practical option for many firms, but they will not be immediately accepted by the banking clearing system. Probably the best way of dealing with them is to hand them over to an approved bank, requiring the bank to keep them in safe custody until they become current, at which stage they can be processed through the normal clearing system. Until the value date is reached, they would comprise a non-valid negotiable instrument and as such should be included as "other property" for the purpose of the safe custody reconciliations and statements referred to in paragraph 17–005 above.

Automated transfer

18–009   Where the money is received by automated transfer into a firm's own account, it must be transferred into a client bank account by the close of business on the following business day after the transfer.

Mixed remittance

Where a firm receives a mixed remittance consisting only in part of client money, it must pay the full amount into a client bank account, and then transfer the non-client money out of the account by the close of business on the day after which the remittance would normally be cleared. Where a firm receives a single payment representing different types of client money, it may pay the money into any client bank account, splitting and transferring it on the business day following the day on which it becomes cleared funds.

Receipt by field representative

Where the money is received by a firm's field representative, he must have remitted the money to a specified business address for the firm at the latest by the last posting time for first class post (if available) on the following business day after receipt, or otherwise deal with it in such a way that it arrives at the relevant address by the close of business on the next business day following receipt.

Overseas dividend receipts

Where a firm receives dividends payable overseas on behalf of its clients, it must see that the money is distributed to its clients or paid into a free money bank account within five business days of receipt. Up to that time, it can be banked into any account operated by the firm.

Keep separate

Until the client money has been banked, the firm must keep it separately identifiable from any other money. Thereafter, it must ensure that the money remains separate from the firm's own money. The only non-client money which a firm may keep in a free money bank account is any minimum sum required to open the account and keep it in being, any money which was received under a mixed remittance, or interest credited to the account which exceeds the interest due to clients.

Associates

A firm must not pay client money to or for the account of an associate who is not an authorised person unless the money actually belongs to the associate. This does not restrict a firm using accounts at an approved bank which is an associate, because the money is only held with the bank, rather than paid to it.

Types of Account

Client money can be held in six types of account: **18–010**

   (i)   general client bank accounts;

  (ii)   designated client bank accounts;

 (iii)   designated client fund accounts;

 (iv)   dividend claims accounts;

  (v)   settlement bank accounts;

 (vi)   margined transaction bank accounts.

The first three accounts are "free money bank accounts".

Titles

A firm must ensure that each client bank account is described by the approved bank in such a way as to make it clear that the money does not belong to the firm.

General client bank accounts

A general client bank account is one which holds the money of one or more clients. A firm may open more than one of these accounts. Where the account is in the United Kingdom, then, in the event of a default by the bank, the account is pooled with all other client bank accounts of the firm, except for designated accounts ((ii) and (iii) above).

Designated client bank accounts

A designated client bank account holds the money of an individual client only. The only exception is where all the clients whose money is held in the account have been informed of the identity of the other joint participants. This enables such an account to include the money of persons, such as husband and wife, who hold their investments jointly. The account must include the word "designated" in its title. The clients must have consented in writing to the use of the bank where the account is held. In the event of the bank's default, the account is not pooled with any other account.

Designated client fund accounts

A designated client fund account is one which holds at least part of the designated fund of one or more clients. The clients whose money is in the account must all have consented in writing to their money being held in that account and all the other designated client fund accounts which may be pooled with it: namely, they must have consented to the use of the same approved banks for the holding of their money. The account must include in its title the words "designated fund". In the event of a default of a bank in which part of a designated fund is held, then all designated client fund accounts held with the defaulting bank form a pool with any designated client fund accounts held at other banks containing part of the same designated funds. In other words, all the money from the designated fund is pooled, even if some of that money is held in designated client fund accounts at non-defaulting banks.

Dividend claims accounts

A dividend claims account is one which is used only for the receipt, holding and distribution of dividends on securities or of interest on loan stock received by the firm pending proper distribution. It may hold dividends and interest payments due to non-clients. The account cannot be overdrawn and the firm must take reasonable steps to ensure that money paid into it which is client money is distributed within 10 business days of its receipt by either being paid into a free money account or being paid out in such a manner that it no longer remains client money. On a default by the bank, the amount is pooled with all other client bank accounts except designated ones.

Settlement and margined accounts

Settlement bank accounts and margined transaction bank accounts are described in paragraphs 18–016 *et seq.* below. Designated client bank accounts and designated client fund accounts may not be used as settlement bank accounts or margined transaction bank accounts. General client bank accounts may be used for settlement as long as the firm does not net off one customer's liabilities against another's assets.

Pre-1992 accounts not designated accounts

No client bank account existing before January 1, 1992 may constitute a designated account. In other words, a firm must set up new accounts following the procedures outlined above if it wishes to create designated client or designated client fund accounts.[3]

Overdrawn

A firm must not allow a client's balance in one free money bank account to go overdrawn unless he has a credit in another free money bank account which cancels out the relevant debit. In other words, the client's overall net position must not result in a debit balance.

Interest

A firm must pay interest on free money bank accounts and dividend claims accounts, but interest is not payable in respect of money in a dividend claims account which is not due to clients.   **18–011**

The interest rate which is payable is a rate which is not less than the minimum deposit rate offered by the relevant bank with which the money is deposited. (In fact, the regulation is worded so that it would be possible to pay the lowest deposit rate on offer from the banks taken as a whole with which the firm deposits client money, rather than the minimum rate of the bank where the particular account is held.) The interest should be paid or credited to the client at least once every six months. Obviously, the interest is only payable to the extent that money is standing to the credit of the client. The firm may either treat the money as standing to the client's credit at the moment at which it is received (book balance basis) or at the moment when it becomes cleared funds (cleared funds basis). A firm must, however, use the same basis of assumption for both receipts and payments.

The firm may withdraw and retain any excess interest standing to the credit of the account after the interest to which each of the clients is entitled has been properly allocated. This should be done at least every five weeks, when the reconciliation is performed (see paragraph 18–015 below).

There are certain circumstances in which a firm either does not have to pay interest or may pay a lower rate of interest in respect of the respective client credit balances. These are as follows:

(i) where the firm has sent a one-way written notification to a non-private customer;

(ii) where the firm has obtained a private customer's written consent;

(iii) where the sum which would be payable is less than £20 for the relevant six-month period (or, where a shorter accounting period has been agreed with the client, the equivalent pro rata amount, for example £3.33 per month); or

(iv) where the client money is less than £10,000 and is held for less than 10 business days: if it is held for longer, then interest is payable from the first day on which it was held as client money.

Where a firm is paying interest at a lower rate than the relevant bank's minimum deposit rate, this fact must be given due prominence in the notification or agreement required under (i) or (ii) above.

Default

Pooling event

18–012 As we have already seen, a firm is under a duty to pay client money which it receives or holds into a client bank account with an approved bank. This obligation, however, is immediately interrupted on the occurrence of a pooling event. There are two main types of pooling event. The first occurs where there is either a default by the firm, a vesting order made under section 67(1)(b) of the FSA 1986 requiring assets of the firm's clients to be transferred to and held by a trustee appointed by SIB, or a direction made by SFA relating to all client money held by the firm. The second concerns a default by an approved bank with which client money has been deposited.

Default by firm

Where the pooling event is of the first type, basically a default by the firm, money held in all the firm's client bank accounts is pooled and must be used to meet its segregated clients' respective claims (that is the claims of clients who have not opted out of CMR protection). All segregated clients have equal precedence. No distinction is made between the different types of client bank account. Also the claims for clients whose money should have been held in the accounts are treated *pari passu* with those for clients whose money was actually held in the accounts at the time. Where a cheque has been paid into an account before the pooling event but has not cleared, then the amount credited in the bank's records in respect of the uncleared cheque is pooled until or unless it becomes clear that the cheque will not be cleared.

Overseas accounts

There is one qualification to the single pot on the default of a firm. If the amount of client money in all the client money bank accounts is insufficient, or is not immediately available, to satisfy the clients' respective claims, then, to the extent that the shortfall is attributable to a bank holding money overseas not recognising that the money is held in accordance with the CMRs, a separate pool is formed for all client money held with that bank (apparently, including accounts held at branches in the United Kingdom). This second pool is only to be used to satisfy the claims of clients whose money was held, or should have been held, in accounts with this bank. Such clients will only be able to claim from the main pool to the extent that a surplus remains after the claims of all other clients have been met.

Money received after pooling

Where a firm receives money from a client after a pooling event which is free money, it must pay that money into a newly opened free money bank account so that it is not subject to being pooled with client money held at the time of the pooling event, but non-free client money received after the pooling event is so pooled.

Default by approved bank

As soon as a firm becomes aware that a bank where it has deposited **18–013** client money has defaulted, it must immediately inform SFA. It must calculate the amounts of client money held for each client, distinguishing between money held for a client with the defaulting bank and money held for him with other banks. If a client demands repayment, then the firm must only repay to him that share of his money which the firm has calculated is due to him from accounts held at the non-defaulting bank (provided, presumably, that the accounts are not subject to being pooled with accounts at the defaulting bank); and the repayment must be from these accounts.

A client's claim is for money which should have been held in the accounts, as well as money actually there. Again, uncleared cheques credited in the bank's records before the default are included, unless and until it becomes clear that they will not be cleared. Any client money received after the default must not be pooled with money held with the bank at the time of the default.

On the bank's default, money held in all the firm's client bank accounts, except to the extent specified below, is pooled into a single pot, available to meet claims from the firm's clients. In other words, it is not merely the client money held at the defaulting bank which is subject to pooling.

As indicated, there are a number of exceptions to this single pool. A firm does not pool and may continue to operate normally:

(i) designated client bank accounts at banks other than the defaulting bank;

(ii) designated client fund accounts for clients who had not chosen the defaulting bank as one with which their money could be held: if they had chosen the defaulting bank, even if there was no money held there at the time, their designated client fund account would be caught by the default situation;

(iii) any of the other types of client bank accounts (general client, dividend claims, settlement and margined transaction bank accounts) to the extent that no account of the particular type is held at the defaulting bank: if a general client bank account was maintained at the defaulting bank, then all other general client bank accounts are brought into the pool.

Designated client bank accounts

Where a client has a designated client bank account at the defaulting bank, he has an exclusive claim against the money in that account, but is not able to claim against any other client bank account for any shortfall in his designated client account.

Designated client fund accounts

A separate pool is formed in respect of designated client fund accounts held at the defaulting bank and designated client fund accounts at other banks which contain part of the same designated fund. This pool is only available to satisfy claims of clients who consented to their fund being held at the defaulting bank. (If there was more than one designated fund involved, each fund would form a separate pool.) Similarly to a designated client account, the designated fund clients do not have a claim on any other client accounts in respect of any shortfall arising from their pool.

Money held overseas

Where client money was held overseas with the defaulting bank, a separate pool is formed of all the client money held overseas, except to the extent that this money was held in designated client bank accounts and designated client fund accounts. This pool is only for money held overseas with the defaulting bank: other client money held overseas is not included. The pool is then available to satisfy the claims of clients whose money was or should have been held in the relevant accounts. If there is any shortfall, they cannot claim against money held in any other client bank accounts until all other clients' claims have been met in full.

Distribution of surplus

Where, following distribution, a surplus remains in one or more of **18–014** the pools or accounts described above, then it is made available to satisfy, on a *pari passu* basis, the deficiencies arising in respect of all other client bank accounts, except those held outside the United Kingdom with the defaulting bank or with a bank which does not recognise CMR protection. The outstanding claims on these overseas accounts may only be settled after those on all other client bank accounts have been met in full.

Pooling of free and non-free money

Concern has been raised that on a default, whether by a firm or an approved bank, free money may be pooled with non-free money (dividend claims, settlement or margined transaction money). The reason for this single pooling is that it is administratively more efficient to operate and should lead to claims being settled more quickly; and, consequently earlier payments, where relevant, under the Investors Compensation Scheme. Of course, if a firm wants to protect fully its clients' money in respect of the firm's default, it should operate separate accounts for each client in his own name over which the firm has a mandate. Obviously, such a procedure still does not protect the individual client in the case of therelevant bank's default.

Records

A firm must keep daily records showing: all money paid into and out of its client bank accounts; all receipts and passing on of client money which is not banked; the balances on each client bank account; and, in respect of the free money bank accounts, the balances held in respect of each individual client. In respect of each deposit into or withdrawal from a client bank account, the firm must record, both on a bank account by bank account basis, and on a client by client basis: the name of the relevant client; the date; and the name of the person from whom or to whom the payment was made. The records should also include interest earned on each account, the date on which it is credited to the account, and the amount due to each client, showing when it is paid or credited to him.

The records may be kept in any form, as long as they are capable of reproduction in hard printed copy in English. Where all the documents relating to one client are not kept together, there must be cross-referencing to show how access can be had to the other records. The firm may rely on records supplied by a third party provided they are capable of being reconciled with the records created by the firm. In fact, a firm may delegate its record-keeping obligations to a third party: although the firm will still be responsible for ensuring that the records are kept accurately in accordance with the CMRs. They must be maintained in a way which enables a proper audit trail to be done and allows prompt access to any particular item recorded. They must be retained for six years; and during the first two years, they must be retrievable within 24 hours.

Reconciliations

18–015   Reconciliations must be performed at least every five weeks and they must be carried out within 10 business days of the date to which the reconciliation relates. Where any differences arise, they must be corrected as soon as possible unless they result solely from timing differences. There are two types of reconciliation. The first consists of reconciling the balance on each client bank account as recorded on the firm's ledgers with the balance shown on the relevant bank statement. The second concerns reconciling from the firm's records the balances for each free money bank account with the total of the credit balances for each client. Both reconciliations must be carried out in respect of the same date. Control totals should not be used unless separately reconciled.

In respect of the second reconciliation, the firm may reconcile different parts of its free money independently. In other words, it may reconcile the balance on each free money bank account with the total of the credit balances in respect of each client whose money is held in that account. These separate reconciliations, however, must still be performed in respect of the same date as the first reconciliation with the relevant bank statements.

A firm must inform SFA where it is unable to perform these reconciliations. Pending resolution of a difference which arises from a reconciliation, a firm should, for the time being, correct the difference in its clients' favour rather than to its own benefit.

Auditor's Report

The firm's client money records must be examined by its auditor, who must prepare a written report at least every 12 months on how the firm has complied with the CMRs. (Where a firm's accounting period is longer than 12 months, two reports would be required.) In fact, the auditor's report on CMR compliance must be for the same period in respect to which it is required to report on the firm's financial statements under SFA's Financial Rules. The report must be sent to SFA within three months of the end of the period to which it relates. (This is a tightening of SIB's requirement in the CMRs which is four months.) It should include any breaches (other than trivial ones) of the CMRs which have come to the auditor's attention during the period reported on, together with his views on whether the firm had adequate systems to comply with the CMRs and whether it was, at the end of the period, in compliance with the CMRs. Breaches at the year end date should be outlined in full, including trivial breaches.

Mandated Accounts

Where a firm has mandates over clients' bank and building society accounts, it must:

(i) maintain an up-to-date list of all its mandates, including the conditions placed upon their use by clients or the firm's management;

(ii) ensure that all transactions entered into under the mandates are recorded and are within the scope of the mandated authority;

(iii) ensure that pass books and similar documents are safeguarded in such a way as to minimise the risk of destruction, loss, theft, fraud or error.

Of course, pass books and similar documents of value are caught by the Safekeeping Rules. They must be physically counted and inspected every six months and accounted for on the annual statement sent to the customer (see paragraph 17–005 above).

Settlement Bank Accounts

18–016   Where a firm wishes to settle transactions by using client money of one client to discharge the liability of another client, it must open a settlement bank account. In fact, most firms will need a minimum of two settlement bank accounts: money relating to overseas settlement must be kept in a separate account from that relating to transactions settled within the United Kingdom. The reason for the two separate accounts was originally to protect United Kingdom settlement money from the higher risk of failures and delays prevalent in certain overseas markets. To some extent, with a single pot on default, this raison d'être has fallen away. In determining whether or not a transaction is a United Kingdom settled one, the location of the market or counterparty should be looked at, rather than that of the client. However, common sense should prevail: for example, a transaction between two United Kingdom counterparties settled in Euro-clear would be foreign settled.

Settlement money

Money which is specifically remitted by a client to settle a transaction should be paid into the relevant settlement bank account by the close of the next business day after receipt, no matter how early the client has paid it before the settlement date. Where the firm will be using free money from a free money client bank account, the money should be transferred into the settlement bank account on the trade date or, in respect of TALISMAN-settled transactions, after the last day of dealing for the relevant London Stock Exchange account in which the transaction was effected. As already mentioned above, where a firm receives a mixed remittance which consists of settlement money and free money, the firm may pay the full amount into any client bank account, as long as transfers are made to the appropriate client bank accounts within one business day of the day on which the remittance is cleared.

A firm should only withdraw money from the settlement bank account at the latest practical time to ensure timely settlement. Money received from third parties in respect of the settlement of client transactions should be paid into the relevant settlement bank account. Once settlement of a client transaction has been completed, the firm should ensure that any money due to him is paid by the close of business on the following business day after it becomes due to him, either to him, to a third party at his written direction, or into a free money bank account.

Non-segregated customers

A firm may use its United Kingdom settlement bank accounts in connection with the settlement of transactions for non-segregated customers (customers opted out of CMR protection), provided it has received SFA's consent to do so and the money required from the non-segregated customers to settle the transactions is paid into the account prior to the relevant transactions being settled.

Reconciliations: United Kingdom settlement

On every business day a firm must carry out a reconciliation of its **18–017** United Kingdom settlement bank accounts as at the close of business on that day or on the preceding business day. A firm must ensure that the total money held in each of these accounts is not less than:

(A) its liabilities to its clients, settlement agents or market counterparties in respect of transactions for segregated clients (namely, clients who are not opted out of CMR protection);

plus

(B) the contract value of investments sold by the firm as principal but not yet delivered, or delivered but not yet paid;

minus

(C) the amounts which its clients, settlement agents or market counterparties are liable to pay for transactions effected for segregated clients;

and minus

(D) the contract value of securities bought by the firm as principal from the clients, but not yet received and paid for.

In other words, the money available should not be less than (A) plus (B), minus (C) plus (D).

In respect of the liabilities of a firm's clients, settlement agents or market counterparties ((iii) above), the firm should disregard:

(i) to the extent that it has itself settled the corresponding amounts, debts known to be bad debts and other debts which have been outstanding for more than 30 days from the due settlement date; and

(ii) any amounts lent by the firm to its clients.

The firm must deposit its own money into the settlement account to cover any shortfall by the close of business on the day of the reconciliation. This money will then be treated as client money.

Foreign settlement bank accounts

Similar provisions apply to foreign settlement bank accounts as to United Kingdom ones, except that reconciliation is required once every five business days rather than daily; although the reconciliation may be performed more frequently. Between the reconciliations, the firm is allowed to settle foreign transactions out of its own accounts and to receive the proceeds of settlement into these accounts. The firm must not withdraw money from the foreign settlement accounts until it carries out the next reconciliation.

Reconciliation with settlement agent's records

Every five weeks a firm must reconcile the balance as shown on its ledgers for each transaction account for its clients held with a settlement agent with the balance shown on the agent's statement for the relevant account. The reconciliation must be carried out within 20 business days of the date to which it relates. Any difference must be corrected unless it arises solely from timing differences.

Margined Transaction Bank Accounts

18–018 Where a firm undertakes margined transactions with or for clients, it must open a margined transaction bank account unless it believes that it will be able to undertake such margined transactions without combining client money belonging to different clients. Settlement of margined transactions is required to be done through a different account from other settlement because of the greater risks involved in terms of client exposure.

A margined transaction is basically a transaction in a future, option or contract for difference under the terms of which a client may be liable to pay further amounts of cash or collateral over and above the amount initially paid to the firm. Settlement of single-premium option contracts may be done through a settlement bank account. At the election of the firm, however, single-premium option contracts may be settled through the margined transaction bank account. Settlement of forward foreign exchange contracts must be put through that account, whether settlement or margined transaction, through which the associated transaction is being settled.

Money must be paid into a margined transaction account in similar circumstances to those described for a settlement bank account. In other words, any money received in respect of a margined transaction is paid into the margined transaction bank account. Unlike with a settlement bank account, however, surplus margin does not have to be withdrawn from the account unless or until it is required for a non-margined transaction purpose: for example, settlement of a non-derivative transaction. Therefore, where a firm is solely dealing in margined transactions, it only has to open one type of client money account: namely, a margined transaction bank account.

On-exchange and off-exchange accounts

A firm has to have two types of margined transaction bank account. The first is for margined transactions undertaken for on-exchange transactions. The second is for all other margined transactions: namely, off-exchange transactions. The definition of an on-exchange transaction is the same as that for the Conduct of Business Rules referred to in paragraph 11–025 above. In other words, it includes transactions effected on a recognised or designated investment exchange, or under the rules of such an exchange, and a transaction which is both matched and identified with one of the above transactions (as long as it is not prohibited by the rules of the relevant exchange).

There are two qualifications to the requirement for separate accounts for on-exchange and off-exchange business. Where at January 1, 1992 a firm was using a single margined transaction bank account for its clients in respect of both on-exchange and off-exchange margined transactions, it may continue to use that single account: it is not required to open two separate accounts. Also, with the prior written consent of SFA, a firm may settle through its on-exchange margined transaction account off-exchange margined transactions entered into for private customers which are permitted under Rule 5–44 as hedges against currency risk involved in positions which the customers already hold (see paragraph 11–026 above).

Client transaction accounts

A firm must ensure that client money paid from its margined transaction accounts to exchanges, clearing houses, intermediate brokers or counterparties is received by them into a separate client transaction account for the firm. This will mean that client money paid over by the firm will be segregated from other money received from the firm and from client money received from other firms. Such segregation should ensure that, when excess margin is returned to the firm, it is clearly identified as client money due to be paid into the firm's margined transaction account.

341

In respect of the exchange, clearing house, intermediate broker or other counterparty, a firm must: instruct that any money received from it in respect of a margined transaction should be credited to the firm's client transaction account; and obtain confirmation that the firm's client transaction account is not to be combined with any other account, and that no right of set-off is to be exercised against money credited to the client transaction account in respect of any sum owed on any other account. Where an intermediate broker or counterparty does not provide this latter confirmation within 20 business days of it being requested, then the firm must cease using its client transaction account with that broker or counterparty, and arrange, as soon as possible, for the transfer or liquidation of any open positions and the repayment of the money in the account.

Intermediate brokers

18–019   An intermediate broker is any person through whom a firm undertakes a margined transaction. A firm should only use intermediate brokers who are: other authorised persons; overseas investment businesses who are subject, under their own regulatory system, to hold client money in segregated accounts; or overseas investment businesses who have agreed to hold client money received from the firm in a segregated bank account. In this latter case, the relevant clients must have given their written consent to the firm using the broker.[4]

Reconciliation: on-exchange transactions

A firm must carry out a reconciliation on each business day relating to the relevant positions at the close of business on the previous business day. Essentially, it must ensure that:

(i)   the balances on its on-exchange margined transaction bank accounts;

plus, if positive, or minus, if negative,

(ii)   the net aggregate of its equity balances on its client transaction accounts for on-exchange margined transactions with exchanges, clearing houses and intermediate brokers;

plus

(iii)   the current market value of approved collateral deposited with the firm;

are, when totalled, not less than the aggregate of all its clients' required contributions at the time. The clients' required contributions are the greater of either the total amount of their initial margin requirements, or the total of their equity balances and the current market value of their approved collateral deposited with the firm. In other words, the amount held in the margined transaction bank accounts should equal the difference between the equity held at the exchanges, clearing houses and intermediate brokers and the greater of either the clients' initial margin or the amounts actually due to them. This daily reconciliation is based on the information recorded in the firm's own records.

Initial margin and equity balances

A client's initial margin requirement is the total amount which is required to be deposited under the relevant exchange's or clearing house's rules by the firm or intermediate broker in respect of all the client's open positions in margined transactions at that time, ignoring any unrealised profit or loss on such positions. A firm's equity balance is the amount which it would be liable to pay to the exchange, clearing house or intermediate broker in respect of the firm's margined transactions if each of the open positions of the firm's clients was liquidated at the relevant exchange's published closing or settlement prices. A net aggregate equity balance is produced by deducting negative balances (the firm is liable to pay) from positive balances (payments due to the firm). A client's equity balance is the amount which he would be liable to pay the firm (negative balance) or the amount which he would be due from the firm (positive balance) in respect of his margined transactions if each of his open positions was liquidated at the relevant exchange's published closing or settlement prices.

Foreign currency receipts

As it is impossible to receive foreign currencies in cleared funds on the same day as the firm calls for their delivery from the client, a three-day window has been provided for the purpose of calculating the balance on the firm's on-exchange margined transaction bank accounts. A firm may regard foreign currency (that is any currency other than sterling and US dollars forwarded via London town clearing) as received in cleared funds at the close of business on the day on which the firm calls for the amount to be forwarded, provided the money is reasonably expected to be received in cleared funds by the close of business on the third business day after the call. If the money is not cleared by this time, then the firm must top up with its own money in respect of the uncleared amount.

Topping-up

A firm is required to top up from its own money its on-exchange margined transaction bank accounts to make up the shortfall in its clients' required contributions. The topped-up money becomes client money and may only be withdrawn by the firm when there is a sufficient surplus over the required contributions on a subsequent reconciliation.

Approved collateral

18–020 In respect of on-exchange margined transactions, approved collateral is any form of security which is acceptable, under the rules of the relevant exchange or clearing house, as an alternative to a deposit in cash in discharging any liability arising from an on-exchange margined transaction; but it does not include a guarantee. A firm may use its own collateral to top up any shortfall on the daily reconciliations which it carries out. Its collateral, however, must be held on trust, the trust must be evidenced in writing and the collateral must be clearly distinguishable from the firm's own property. The proceeds of any sale of such collateral must be paid into the on-exchanged margined transaction bank accounts.

Where a firm on-pledges a segregated customer's approved collateral to an exchange, clearing house or intermediate broker, it must notify them that it is under an obligation to keep customers' collateral separate from its own and instruct them that the current market value of the customers' collateral which has been passed on is to be credited to the firm's client transaction account. Sale proceeds of customers' approved collateral should be dealt with in accordance with the relevant exchange's or clearing house's rules. Where the collateral has been liquidated by an intermediate broker, the balance of the proceeds which are remitted by direct transfer should be paid into the firm's relevant client margined transaction bank account.

Reconciliations: off-exchange transactions

Ideally daily, but at least once every five weeks, a firm must ensure that, at the close of business on the previous business day, the aggregate of the balances on the firm's off-exchange margined transaction bank accounts, plus (or minus if negative) the net aggregate of its equity balances on transaction accounts for segregated clients with counterparties in respect of off-exchange margined transactions, were not less than the aggregate of the liquidating balances due to its segregated clients for off-exchange margined transactions. The liquidating balance consists of a client's account balance plus the open value of his positions. In working out the liquidating balances, a firm should use approximate market closing prices on the previous business day. It should be noted that, unlike for on-exchange reconciliations, no account is taken of clients' initial margin requirements and of any approved collateral which has been deposited. The firm must top up any shortfall, the topping-up becoming client money. As with on-exchange transactions, there is a three-day window allowing a firm to treat payments remitted in foreign currency as cleared funds for the next three business days after call.

[1] A firm will be regarded as dealing with a group company on an arm's length basis where it offers the group company similar terms and conditions of dealing and settlement as it provides to comparable non-group clients.

[2] A firm may segregate a sterling or other base currency equivalent amount of any foreign currency client money received, provided the equivalent amount is segregated on the same day as the foreign currency is received. The closing rate of exchange on the relevant day should be used both on initial segregation and thereafter to maintain the sterling or base currency equivalent.

[3] The existing accounts do not have to be physically closed and reopened. The firm must merely put in place the necessary arrangements described in paragraph 18–010 in relation to designated accounts.

[4] If a firm is unable to set up suitable arrangements for segregation with an overseas intermediate broker, it may segregate the funds in the United Kingdom and remit its own funds to the broker.

Chapter 19

Financial Supervision

A firm must maintain at all times financial resources of the type **19–001** required by SFA which are in excess of the firm's financial resources requirement under the rules in Chapter 3 of the SFA rulebook. This provision is to ensure that a firm only conducts investment business whilst it is solvent. It must always have sufficient capital to fund its trading activities. The financial resources requirement is related to the nature of a firm's operations, its past expenditure, its current investment holdings and the amount owed by its customers. The financial resources to meet this requirement must be maintained in cash or assets which are easily converted into cash.

Categories

For the purpose of the Financial Rules SFA firms are divided into various categories.

Broad scope firms

The main type of firm is termed a broad scope firm. This is any firm which is not an adviser, arranger, local or a traded options market maker.

Advisers

An adviser is a firm which only gives investment advice. It does *not*: hold or receive money or property belonging to other persons; have a mandate over any customer's bank account; carry on as its main business the activity of introducing persons to other investment businesses; or deal as a principal or agent in investments or physical commodities.

Arrangers

An arranger is a firm which, as well as giving investment advice, may deal in, arrange deals in or manage investments; but it must not hold or receive money or property belonging to others, and it must not have any mandates over customers' bank accounts.

Locals or traded options market makers

A local or traded options market maker is a firm which is recognised as such by a recognised or designated investment exchange and whose business is cleared through a clearing firm. A clearer is a firm which accepts the responsibility for settling transactions for the customers of locals or traded options market makers.

Financial Resources Requirement

19–002　The financial resources requirement is made up of three separate requirements: the primary requirement; the position risk requirement (PRR); and the counterparty risk requirement (CRR).

Primary requirement

The aim of the primary requirement is to ensure that a firm can survive difficult trading periods, with a sharp fall in its revenue. A firm's primary requirement is the sum of the following six elements:

(i) *Base Requirement.* This is the highest of:
  (a)　The absolute minimum requirement. This is £10,000 for an arranger. It is £50,000 for: an agency broker (that is a broad scope firm normally only dealing on an agency basis); a financial bookmaker; a firm handling clients' money and assets relating to margined transactions, provided it affords client money segregation to all its clients (no opting out); and a non-clearing member of a recognised investment exchange with floor trading rights who does not handle client money. For any other broad scope firm, it is £100,000.
  (b)　The expenditure requirement. This is 6/52 of the firm's relevant annual expenditure if it is:

(i) an investment manager or introducing broker, without, in either case, responsibility for settling its customers' transactions; or

(ii) a model A clearing firm.

A model A clearer is a firm which uses its own money for settlement, but which is reimbursed on a daily basis by the non-clearing firms for whom it carries out settlement. In the case of any other broad scope firm, it is a quarter of its relevant annual expenditure. Relevant annual expenditure is calculated from the firm's most recent audited annual financial statements submitted to SFA.

(c) The volume of business requirement. This is only relevant for firms which settle margined transactions under the rules of a recognised, designated or other SFA approved investment exchange, or under the rules of such an exchange's associated clearing house. It is 3.5 per cent. of the aggregate gross amounts of any initial margin requirements of the firm's counterparties at the relevant time. A counterparty is any person with or for whom the firm carries on regulated or associated business.

(ii) *Liquidity Adjustment.* Adjustments are made to the net book value of assets shown on the firm's balance sheet. As these adjustments are intended to reduce the net book value, they must be added to the firm's primary requirement.

(iii) Assets subject to a legal charge, or otherwise pledged as security for a liability.

(iv) Any contingent liability.

(v) Any deficiency in shareholders' funds in a subsidiary company of the firm.

(vi) A percentage calculation based on the risk assumed by a clearing firm which clears for a local or traded options market maker.

Position risk requirement

PRR is based on positions that the firm holds in any investment or **19–003** physical commodity. Its purpose is to enable the firm to fund safely any losses that it could suffer from falls in the value of the investment or commodity. Various methods are permitted for calculating PRR, depending upon the type of investment or commodity. A firm may, however, calculate its total PRR by multiplying any long or short position in an investment or commodity position by various percentages (position risk adjustments or PRAs) and totalling the results.[1]

Counterparty risk requirement

CRR covers the risk of the counterparty to any of the firm's transactions failing to fulfil his obligation. The calculation is complex and requires an allowance for overdue sums, with different time limits being specified for different types of transaction. It takes account of the difference between amounts due from the counterparty and the value of any securities or physical commodities not yet supplied to him.

Frequency of calculation

A firm should be able to monitor its capital resources requirements on an intra-day basis. For many firms, the primary requirement will be fairly static and, therefore, will not need constant recalculation. A PRR, however, should be calculated in a full and detailed manner before executing any trade which is likely to increase total PRR to such a level that the firm's current financial resources requirement might exceed its current financial resources. At any rate, total PRR should be calculated at least once every business day. Likewise, a firm should calculate its CRR at least once each business day using prices of investments and physical commodities as at the close of business on the previous business day.

Qualifying Financial Resources

19–004 The primary requirement, PRR and CRR together form the firm's total financial resources requirement. As we have already seen, this must be exceeded at all times by the firm's resources. A firm's qualifying financial resources are the sum of its tangible net worth and eligible capital substitutes.

Tangible net worth

Tangible net worth may include: ordinary share capital; preference share capital; the share premium account; the balance on the profit and loss account; other approved reserves; and partners' current and capital account balances. Intangible assets are deducted from the sum of the above to arrive at a firm's tangible net worth. Redeemable share capital may only be included with SFA's prior written approval and a firm must give SFA six months written notice of redemption. Other than retained profits, reserves also may only be included to the extent that SFA has given its prior written approval.

Eligible capital substitutes

Eligible capital substitutes are: subordinated loans; approved bank bonds; and approved undertakings. None of them may be regarded as an eligible capital substitute unless they are drawn up in accordance with SFA's relevant standard forms and signed by authorised signatories (see paragraph 19–008 below) of all the parties. Details of the approved lenders for subordinated loans, approved bank bonds and approved undertakings are contained in the Financial Rules and supporting definitions. For example, the lender of a subordinated loan must normally be the firm's controller, an approved bank, a registered person, or a regulated financial institution, as defined. Basically, an eligible capital substitute must be something which is immediately available on demand to the firm and under which the lender's rights are subordinated to the rights of all other creditors, apart from lenders of other eligible capital substitutes.

A firm must obtain SFA's prior written approval before repayment or termination of one of these capital substitutes if, after repayment or termination, the firm's financial resources will be no greater than 120 per cent. of its financial resources requirement. The amount of capital substitutes must not exceed four times the firm's tangible net worth. A subordinated loan which is repayable within three months is not normally acceptable. Approved bank bonds should not exceed 30 per cent. of the firm's base requirement and its CRR on exchange traded margined transactions. If the capital substitutes consist of both approved undertakings and approved bank bonds, then the total of both the undertakings and bonds must not exceed 30 per cent. of the firm's base requirement.

Qualifications

There are some qualifications to the financial resources requirements stated above:

   (i) *Corporate Finance Advisory Firms*. A firm which is only carrying on corporate finance business, as defined (see paragraphs 4–030 *et seq.* above), and which does not hold or receive money or property belonging to other persons, only has to maintain financial resources which meet the following: at all times its tangible net worth and its net current assets each exceed £10,000.

(ii) *Venture Capital Firms.* A venture capital firm is one whose only investment business is concerned with venture capital schemes. These are schemes for providing capital to any body corporate whose equity is not traded or listed on an exchange. Where such a firm holds money or property belonging to others, it will be a broad scope firm, but does not need to comply with the PRR and CRR requirements. Otherwise, it will fall within the definition of a corporate finance advisory firm.

(iii) *Advisers.* The capital requirements for an adviser are that, at all times, its tangible net worth and its net current assets must each be positive.

(iv) *Locals and Traded Options Market Makers.* They are required to ensure that, at all times, their tangible net worth is positive and they are able to meet their liabilities as they fall due.

Records

19–005 A firm must keep accounting records on a continual basis so that either its records are constantly up-dated or they may be brought up to date within a reasonable time. The records must show and explain the firm's transactions and commitments. In particular, they must: demonstrate whether the firm is complying with the financial resources requirement; enable it to prepare within a reasonable time any financial reporting statements required by SFA; and disclose with reasonable accuracy the financial position of the firm at any point in time over the preceding six years (or, if shorter, the period of its membership with SFA).

Contents

The records must show: daily entries for all money received and expended by the firm, including receipts and expenditure on behalf of others and the purpose for which the money was received or expended; all income and expenditure of the firm, including its nature; all assets and liabilities of the firm, including commitments and contingent liabilities; day-by-day entries of all purchases and sales of investments by the firm, distinguishing those made for its own account from those made by or on behalf of others; daily records for the receipt and despatch of documents of title in the firm's possession or control; and a record of all investments and documents of title in the firm's possession and control, identifying physical location, beneficial ownership, purpose for which held, and any applicable charges.

Accessibility

The records may be maintained in any form, as long as they are capable of prompt reproduction in hard printed form. Where records relating to one counterparty are not kept together, there should be pointers on each part indicating how access can be obtained to the other parts. Where a firm relies on records supplied by a third party, it should ensure that his records are reconcilable with the firm's. If not maintained in English, the records must be capable of being reproduced into English within a reasonably short time. They must be arranged in such a way that it is possible to have prompt access to any particular record. As with client money, they must be maintained for six years. Unlike the CMRs, however, it is only during the first year that it must be possible to produce the records within 24 hours of their being requested. Thereafter, the time limit is extended to 48 hours.

Internal controls

A firm must ensure that it has effective systems of internal financial control, taking into account: the size of its business; the diversity of its operations; the volume, size and frequency of transactions; the degree of risk associated with each part of its operations; the amount of daily control by senior management; and the degree of centralisation. Its records must be maintained in such a way that they are capable of disclosing, in a prompt and appropriate manner, financial and business information sufficient to enable a firm's management to:

(i) identify, quantify, control and manage the firm's risk exposures;

(ii) make timely and informed decisions;

(iii) monitor the performance of all aspects of the firm's business on an up-to-date basis;

(iv) monitor the quality of the firm's assets; and

(v) safeguard its assets, including those belonging to others for which the firm is responsible.

A firm's accounting records must enable actual exposures to be measured easily against its exposure limits and credit management policy. The firm should be able to monitor all its transactions and commitments, ensuring that they are within the scope of both the firm's authorisation from SFA and the individual's authority from the firm. There should be procedures to safeguard assets, including assets belonging to third parties for which the firm is accountable, and to control liabilities. Also, there should be measures to minimise the risk of losses to the business from irregularities, fraud and error; such matters being identified as they occur so that prompt remedial action can be taken. Financial records, working papers and documents of title in the firm's possession must be properly safeguarded to prevent loss, unauthorised access, alteration or destruction.

Reconciliations

19–006 At least every five weeks, a firm must reconcile each non-client bank or building society account balance as shown on the firm's records with the balance on the relevant statement issued by the bank or building society. (Similar reconciliations are required for client bank accounts under the CMRs; see paragraph 18–015 above). The firm must correct any differences immediately, unless they arise solely as a result of timing differences. It must also reconcile, at least once every five weeks, all balances and investment positions with exchanges, clearing houses and intermediate brokers (as recorded by the firm) with the balances or positions shown on the statement from the relevant party. Then, at least yearly, it must reconcile its recorded balances and securities (rather than derivatives) positions with each market counter-party[2] who is an exchange member to the balances or positions shown on the relevant statement from the market counterparty.

Reporting Returns

Firms must submit regular financial reporting statements to SFA. The type and frequency of reports depends upon the nature of a firm's business.

Advisers, locals and traded options market makers

Sole traders

To the extent that they are sole traders, these firms must submit a solvency statement. A solvency statement is one drawn up in a format required by SFA, prepared as at the firm's annual accounting reference date. It must have been reviewed and signed by the firm's SFA approved independent reporting accountant, who, in addition, must submit a report in the form required by SFA. Both the solvency statement and the accountant's report must be submitted within two months of the annual accounting reference date.

Partnerships and companies

Where the adviser, local or traded options market maker is a partnership or body corporate, then it must submit an auditor's report and audited annual financial statements within three months of the firm's annual accounting reference date. The audited annual financial statements must be drawn up in accordance with Schedule 4 to the Companies Act 1985. The auditor's report must be drawn up in the format required by SFA and must be prepared using the same audited figures and accounting reference date as the audited annual financial statements.

Subsidiaries

Such firms, whether sole traders, partnerships or companies, must also submit, within three months of their annual accounting reference date, the audited accounts of any of their subsidiaries.

Arrangers

Arrangers, as we have already noted, are firms which are not **19–007** authorised to hold or receive money or property belonging to other persons, and which do not have mandates over customers' bank accounts. Venture capital firms which do not hold client money and assets and corporate finance advisory firms are arrangers.

The required reporting statements are as follows:

(i) Quarterly reporting statements, which must be accompanied by PRR and CRR reporting statements prepared to the same date. All three statements must be submitted within 15 days from the date to which they are prepared. They must be prepared at three monthly intervals, with the fourth set of statements being prepared at the same date as the firm's annual accounting reference date. These statements have to be prepared in the format required by SFA, but corporate finance advisory firms and venture capital firms may dispense with the separate PRR and CRR reporting statements, and may omit the PRR and CRR reports in the quarterly reporting statements.[3]

(ii) Audited annual financial statements and an auditor's report, as described above in connection with partnerships and companies who are advisers, locals or traded options market makers. Also an annual reporting statement in the SFA format is required, using the same audited figures and accounting reference date. These reports must be submitted within three months of the firm's annual accounting reference date.

(iii) An internal control letter. This is a letter which must be prepared by the firm. It should state whether the firm has received a letter from its auditor commenting on its systems and internal controls as a result of his audit of the firm's most recent audited annual financial statements. The firm should point out whether the auditor made any recommendations about remedying weaknesses in the firm's systems and internal controls. If he did, the firm should explain how it is implementing these recommendations or give its reasons for not doing so. The letter must be submitted within five months of the firm's annual accounting reference date.

(iv) An annual reconciliation. This is a reconciliation and explanation of any differences:
(a) between the balance sheet figures on the audited annual financial statements and the annual reporting statement; and
(b) between the annual reporting statement and the last quarterly reporting statement for the financial year which will have been prepared to the same date as the annual reporting statement.
This annual reconciliation must be submitted within three months of the firm's annual accounting reference date.

(v) The firm must also submit, within three months of its annual accounting reference date, audited annual financial statements for any subsidiary.

Broad scope firms

19–008   Broad scope firms, including venture capital firms holding client money, must submit the following financial reports:

(i) Monthly reporting statements. These must be drawn up in the format required by SFA. The format contains a segregated accounts reporting schedule to be completed by firms holding client money and prepared at monthly intervals, the last one in any 12-month period being prepared as at the firm's annual accounting reference date. They must be submitted within 15 business days of the date at which they have been prepared.

(ii) The other reports are all those required for arrangers. However, the quarterly reporting statements are not required because of the monthly reporting statements; although the PRR and CRR reporting statements must be completed and submitted at three-monthly intervals, as for arrangers, except that any venture capital firm, including one holding client money, is not required to report its PRR and CRR.

(iii) The published accounts of any group of which the firm is a part must also be submitted to SFA as soon as they are published.

Authorised signatories

All financial reporting statements must be signed by two authorised signatories, except for those for sole traders where only one authorised signatory is necessary. Also, the auditor's report or reporting accountant's report should be signed by the firm's auditor or independent reporting accountant, rather than by the authorised signatories. Authorised signatories are directors, registered partners or, in the case of a sole trader, its proprietor.

Late reporting fines

SFA has a system for levying standard fines on firms for late reporting. The size of the fine is determined by a firm's financial resources requirement on its last submitted reporting statement and the number of days by which the reporting statement is overdue.

Optional additional reports

SFA may require its firms to provide, together with the relevant monthly, quarterly or annual financial reporting statements, additional statements: for example, on PRR, CRR and the primary requirement. In fact, SFA may ask for any additional financial information at any time to enable it to assess properly that a firm is maintaining at all times sufficient resources in excess of its financial resources requirement.

Notification

There are detailed notification requirements in the Financial Rules. **19–009** Basically, a firm must immediately inform SFA of any breach, suspected breach, or impending breach of the rules. It must notify deficiencies of net assets in subsidiaries; also any substantial financial contingencies and commitments. It should point out any material changes which have occurred since its last reporting statements which mean that those statements are now misleading in a material respect; also, any claim on a professional indemnity or similar insurance policy; and any systems failure.

Firms which are arrangers or broad scope firms must notify SFA immediately if their qualifying financial resources fall below 110 per cent. of their financial resources requirement. A broad scope firm must also promptly inform SFA when its tangible net worth falls by 10 per cent. from the figure shown on its most recent submitted financial statement. Prompt notification is required by an arranger or broad scope firm which has been informed by its auditor that he is likely to qualify his report on the firm's audited annual financial statements; or which believes that its liability to repay unsecured loans exceeds 10 times its tangible net worth (except where these loans are eligible capital substitutes or money borrowed to finance long positions). Such a firm must also inform SFA where it is unable to carry out reconciliations of safe custody investments, client money, and other third party assets for which it is responsible; or, if having done so, it is unable to rectify differences, other than timing differences, arising from the reconciliations.

Accounting Policies

19-010 In preparing the financial reporting statements, a firm must ensure that they are in agreement with its books and records. They must be prepared so as to give a true and fair view of the results for the period, and the firm's financial position and state of affairs. In general, no off-setting or netting is allowed, except in the case of balances either with customers who have agreed to their transactions being settled on a net basis or with market counterparties who have agreed that transactions for the same value date should be settled on a net basis. A firm must not consolidate the accounts of separately incorporated group companies into the figures on its financial reporting statements.

A firm must use trade date accounting. It must report in sterling, unless SFA agrees to the contrary. In translating assets and liabilities denominated in foreign currencies into sterling, the closing mid-market rate of exchange should be used, or the rate fixed under the terms of related or matching forward contracts executed for commercial purposes to hedge against currency risk.

A firm should follow the usual accounting principles and rules which would apply if it was drawing up financial statements under the Companies Act 1985: it should comply with the Statements of Standard Accounting Practice. The firm should ensure that items included in its statements reflect the substance, not merely the legal form, of underlying transactions and balances. It must record all accrued liabilities and make adequate provision for doubtful debts, and current and deferred taxation.

A firm must value its positions on a prudent and consistent basis. Generally, this means valuing investments at close-out prices: long positions at current bid prices and short positions at current offer prices.

Where a firm is lending stock, it should record the lent stock as part of its own positions. Likewise, a firm should record repurchase agreement transactions as secured borrowings and reverse repurchase agreements as secured lending. It must not net off repurchase liabilities against reverse repurchase assets; and, where it is a repurchaser, it must record investments securing the borrowing as its own position and account for interest on the borrowing as an accrued liability.

Auditors

All firms must appoint an auditor who has been approved by SFA. (In fact, firms who are not subject to the appointment of auditors requirements in the Companies Acts 1985 and 1989 must appoint an independent accountant; but the criteria for such an appointment are the same as those applying to an approved auditor.) To be an approved auditor, a person must usually be a registered auditor in accordance with the Companies Act 1989. Also, he must satisfy SFA that he has the necessary knowledge and experience to act as auditor for the firm concerned. He must be completely independent of the firm: therefore, he must not be an associate, within the meaning of that definition.

The auditor must have a right of access at all times to the firm's records. The firm must provide him with such information and explanations about its business as is necessary for him to perform his duties properly. His full duties and rights in respect of his appointment as the firm's auditor must be properly set out in an engagement letter. He is required to comment annually in writing to the firm on its internal financial controls, and he must submit a report to SFA within three months of each of the firm's annual accounting reference dates commenting on the matters specified in the table to Rule 3–53.

A firm must give 14 days' notice to SFA of the removal or resignation of an auditor. The firm may only change its auditor after prior written approval from SFA. Where the auditor resigns or is removed by the firm, the firm must provide a statement signed by the auditor specifying the circumstances connected with his resignation or removal which he considers should be brought to the attention of SFA.

In addition to approving a firm's auditor, SFA may appoint additional accountants to report on any matters relating to the firm's state of affairs and financial position which SFA considers necessary. The costs incurred by these accountants may be imposed on the firm.

[1] An additional PRR calculation is required in respect of currency risk exposure where a firm has any asset, liability or off-balance sheet contract denominated in a currency other than the currency of its books of account.

[2] This reference is to the Core Rule definition and SFA's third-tier extension (Rule 5–4) as explained in paragraphs 5–006 *et seq.* above.

[3] Other firms may apply to SFA for an exemption from reporting PRR and CRR when their activities or the levels of risk undertaken are limited.

Chapter 20

Compliance

Self Regulation

The FSA 1986 provided a statutory structure for a system of **20–001** practitioner-based regulation. Investment businesses need to be authorised under the Act to carry on investment business. They become authorised by becoming a member of an SRO or obtaining a certificate to do investment business from their RPB. The SROs and RPBs are controlled by Boards or Councils and supporting committees whose members are drawn from the investment business firms authorised by the SROs and RPBs. In other words, it is the industry which regulates itself within the framework of regulation provided by the FSA 1986.

Of course, the day-to-day inspection and enforcement work carried out under the direction of the Boards and Councils of the various regulators is undertaken by full-time staff, together with support from other agencies, such as legal and accountancy practices, brought in as and when necessary. An example of the latter is the power reserved by SFA to appoint additional reporting accountants to examine a firm's financial resources, controls and records (see paragraph 19–010 above under "auditors").

The concept of self regulation flows through into firms. Each firm is expected to have appropriate procedures for monitoring and ensuring compliance by the firm, its employees, agents and appointed representatives with the rules, including the Principles. In fact, as we have already seen in paragraph 3–008 above, each firm must separately appoint and register with SFA a Senior Executive Officer, Compliance Officer and Finance Officer. Compliance with the rules is ultimately the responsibility of the Senior Executive Officer. Under him, however, the Compliance Officer is responsible for compliance with all the rules, including those on client money and safe custody, except for the Financial Rules (Chapter 3 of SFA's rulebook), which are the responsibility of the Finance Officer. In smaller firms, the same individual may carry out two or all three of these functions. Whereas, in larger firms, it is quite likely that the Compliance and Finance Officers will need to have a number of assistants.

It is important that the individuals who hold these offices are able to take independent judgments on what is required to ensure compliance with the rules, without their judgments and decisions being overridden by the ordinary commercial and business interests of their firm. It is for this reason that there should be direct reporting links between the Compliance and Finance Officers to the Senior Executive Officer, and hence the Board or main Management Committee.

Internal organisation (Principle 9)

How successfully a firm complies with the rules is dependent upon its internal organisation. Principle 9 requires a firm to organise and control its internal affairs in a responsible manner, keeping proper records and having adequate arrangements to ensure that its employees, agents and appointed representatives are suitable for the task which they are required to do, adequately trained and properly supervised. The Principle also requires a firm to have well-defined compliance procedures. Records are dealt with in detail in paragraphs 20–009 and 20–010 below; and staff supervision is included in paragraph 20–004 and the restrictions on staff dealings we covered in paragraphs 20–005 to 20–007.

Compliance with the rules should become a "state of mind". All staff, however junior their role, should be aware of the importance of ensuring that they act in conformity, not merely with SFA's rules, but also with the general criminal and civil law. Obviously, a firm with a good compliance record will, in the long run, be the sort of firm which is more likely to succeed. Good compliance should not be seen as an inhibitor to business development, but as a quality to be promoted and relied upon in developing new products and new business operations. It should attract more business to the firm because of the greater confidence which it should engender in customers and counterparties.

It is for this reason that compliance should not be seen as an unnecessary financial burden, but rather as a factor which contributes to a business' growth and development. Obviously, it is difficult to quantify, in financial terms, the compliance factor in a business' profitability; but this does not mean that it is not a significant contributing factor. The importance of compliance means that a firm's Compliance Department (by which is meant any person responsible for compliance, including the Senior Executive Officer, Compliance and Finance Officers, and their supporting staffs) should know intimately how all the firm's business operations work and the characteristics of the various investment products in which the firm carries on business. The Compliance Department should be consulted in respect of all decisions made on developing new business areas and new investment products.

One of the most important tasks for the Compliance Department is to ensure that, in terms of the multi-function financial services conglomerate, the procedures for managing conflicts of interest operate properly. It must be aware of the obligations which a firm owes under fiduciary law (as discussed in Chapter 15 above). It should be closely involved where anybody crosses a Chinese wall and should regularly monitor the effectiveness of Chinese wall arrangements. In fact, the Compliance Department must, at all times, have access to any part of the firm's business operations and to all information held by the firm, in whatever means and however confidential.

As has already been mentioned, Principle 9 requires a firm to have well-defined compliance procedures. Unlike some of the other regulators, SFA does not require a firm to have a compliance manual as such. There are certain procedures which need to be in writing; for example, if a firm relies on an independence policy (Rule 5–29(2) and paragraph 15–020 above); if the firm operates an adequate credit management policy (see Rule 5–28(6) and paragraph 8–006 above); in respect of restrictions on personal dealings by staff (see paragraphs 20–005 *et seq.* below); and in relation to handling customer complaints (see paragraph 20–011 below).

Of course, many firms will find it easier to have a compliance manual, setting out all procedures and directions relating to compliance. It was, however, deliberately decided not to make it a rule requirement. SFA has a wide, diversified membership. Procedures which are suitable for one firm may not be appropriate for another. Also, the costs of producing such a manual may outweigh any benefit to investors in terms of a small firm, where there is strict day-to-day control and monitoring of all the firm's business operations by its senior directors or partners. In any case, the "new settlement" rulebooks are intended to be written in a shorter, simpler style, which means that they should be more accessible and understandable to a firm's employees.

Two important aspects of a firm's internal controls relate to financial supervision and protecting client money and other assets. These have already been discussed in Chapters 19 and 18 respectively above.

Relations with SFA

Principle 10 requires a firm to deal with SFA in an open and co-operative manner, and keep SFA promptly informed of anything concerning the firm which might reasonably be expected to be disclosed to it. It is important that firms have a regular two-way dialogue with SFA, especially with their appointed inspection team. SFA and its member firms have a common interest. Both want to ensure compliance with the rules; and both should be working together to ensure this compliance. SFA should not be seen as the overbearing schoolmaster who is only interested in finding out malefactors and handing down heavy punishments. Such an approach does not lead to compliance becoming a "state of mind". Obviously, SFA must root out rule breaches and take decisive action where there has been risk to investors, particularly private investors. SFA's main interest, however, 20–002 is to ensure, through close co-operation with its member firms, that all of them are encouraged to operate high standards of compliance. In other words, firms should feel free to approach SFA in an open manner: looking for interpretations and guidance of the new general rules in the context of their particular business operations; alerting SFA early to any potential problems; and owning-up fully and promptly to serious rule breaches.

It is in the interests of both member firms and SFA that there should be good compliance amongst all firms. If alerted to a problem early enough, SFA may be able to assist a firm in limiting the consequences of a compliance failure, in terms of risks to investors and damaged reputations. A failure on the part of one firm tarnishes not only the reputation of SFA as a regulatory body, but all its member firms. Open, regular dialogue between SFA and its members is more likely to achieve consistent compliance across the board which will be in the best interests of investors.

It is better to tell SFA too much, rather than too little. The specific notification requirements concerning client money and financial supervision have been noted already in Chapters 18 and 19. The main specific notification provisions appear in Chapter 2 of the SFA rulebook. As pointed out in Chapter 3 above, a firm must keep SFA informed of significant changes to any information which it was required to give as part of the application process in becoming a member. It must also give details about material changes relating to its employees who are individually registered with SFA.

The most significant notification requirement is in Rule 2–46. This requires a firm to inform SFA immediately of any transaction or event which has involved, or is likely to involve, either a significant contravention of a rule, or any other matter which would be material to a firm's or registered person's obligation to remain fit and proper. This notification requirement is an aspect of self regulation. A firm must be prepared to report upon itself to its regulator in respect of significant rule breaches. The consequences for a firm which does not report, but which is subsequently found out, are likely to be much more severe.

In reality, a firm's Compliance Department should be aware of any sort of rule breach. It should be noted that SFA does not require every minor rule breach to be reported, such as the failure to time stamp a dealing slip or send out a notice promptly, unless such a breach gives rise to some other, more important concerns: for example, it could lead to a dispute between a customer and the firm; indicate lack of staff training and supervision; suggest a deliberate cover-up of a more serious wrong; or be symptomatic of poor compliance procedures. If a trivial breach suggested any of these matters, it should be reported to SFA. Also, the Compliance Department should look into every trivial breach to satisfy itself that it is not indicative of a greater problem.

SFA needs to know about anything material in respect of the continuing "fit and proper" requirement (see paragraphs 3–005 *et seq.*

above). In this respect, a firm may need to report upon matters which are not directly connected with its investment business: for example, a matter arising in a non-investment business part of the firm; or something relating to a registered person outside his employment. SFA would need to know if an employee is suspected, even in relation to something occurring outside his employment, of being involved in a criminal offence (except a minor traffic offence) because of the bearing which this may have upon his integrity to carry out his duties as a registered person: for example, managing his firm, dealing with investors and committing his firm in market dealings. Likewise, it may be very relevant that a registered person is in severe financial difficulties, or is closely associated to another person who is in such difficulties, because of his increased susceptibility in these circumstances to do wrong.

If a firm is to co-operate in an open manner with SFA, it must promptly and frankly comply with any request from SFA for information about anything relating to its business operations or any of its employees, agents and appointed representatives. A firm should not try to hide things or put a misleading gloss on the information or explanation which it provides. It must give SFA inspectors open access to any part of its business and records which are relevant to its SFA authorised business and to the continuing fit and proper requirement for itself and its registered persons.

Compliance review

Each year a firm is expected to undertake a review of its business to enable it to determine the effectiveness of its compliance and monitoring procedures (Rule 5–53). It must then report to SFA the main conclusions of the review. This is another aspect of self regulation by the firm. A firm is expected to stand back and analyse how effective its compliance operation is. (SFA is expected to undertake a similar self-assessment process in relation to its continuing authorisation as an SRO by SIB.)   **20–003**

Rule 5–53 has a different focus than the previous TSA rule which it replaces. That rule required a firm to establish whether or not it had contravened any rules within the previous 12 months and report to TSA that a proper review of its investment business over this period had been carried out. Identifying individual rule breaches was not particularly helpful by itself. Such rule breaches should have been detected shortly after they occurred and, if they were significant, should have been reported immediately to TSA, now SFA, on discovery.

The purpose of the new rule is to give firms an opportunity to take an overview of their compliance arrangements. In a sense, the review is more important in firms which do not have a separate, full-time compliance staff. Where compliance is the responsibility of a manager involved in the ordinary revenue areas of the firm, it is more important that an assessment should be done to ensure that compliance is being given due weight and that there are proper procedures for monitoring the firm's compliance with the rules.

The rule talks about a firm carrying out a "review of its business". There is no obvious limitation to investment business or even regulated business. However, as this is a rule which appears in the Conduct of Business Rules Chapter, it is subject to the application rule at the beginning of that Chapter (Rule 5–1(1) and see Chapter 4 above). As a result, it is suggested that the review does not extend to business which is within the foreign business carve-out, but it does include activities which, although not investment business themselves, are carried on in connection with the firm's regulated business. The review should include the firm's non-investment business activities to the extent that they have an effect on its regulated business: for example, if they could affect the firm's compliance with the financial resources requirement or its continuing to satisfy the fit and proper requirement. As was noted under paragrpah 4–014 above, activities within paragraphs 17 and 18 of Schedule 1 to the FSA 1986 are regarded as investment business for the purpose of the application of SFA's rules on compliance (Rules 5–51 to 5–54).

Rule 5–53 requires the compliance review to be undertaken once a year, without stating a specific date. For many firms, it will be appropriate to carry out the review near the firm's annual accounting reference date; this is not necessary, however, as long as it is done on a regular 12-monthly basis.

SFA has deliberately avoided stating the procedures which must be followed in undertaking the review. This is because what may be appropriate in one firm will not be in another. Obviously, SFA inspectors will be interested to enquire from firms how they have conducted the review.

The firm must report the main conclusions of the review to SFA. This should be done fairly promptly after the review is completed. The report may be short. For example, if the firm is reasonably satisfied with its compliance procedures after carrying out its review, it may make a brief written statement to this effect, confirming that it is not carrying out any changes to its compliance arrangements. If it is carrying out any changes, then it should briefly describe these and the reasons for them.

Indemnities against rule contraventions

20–004   Rule 1–7 prevents a firm from entering into any contract or arrangement which is specifically intended to indemnify or compensate it against any liabilities or consequences which may arise from a breach of the rules, or from any action which SFA may take against the firm or any of its employees. This provision is not intended to prevent a firm from entering into a normal professional indemnity or similar insurance arrangement to protect it and its employees from claims arising from their negligence. It is aimed at preventing any insurance contract or similar arrangement which might encourage a firm or its employees to commit a rule breach; for example, by covering the cost of any fines levied by SFA. A bona fide arrangement, however, whose main purpose is to ensure that a firm will be able to pay its debts would be acceptable.

Compliance with statements

A number of the Conduct of Business Rules require a firm to make certain statements or disclosures to, and to obtain certain consents from, customers: for example, the advertising rules, the requirements on customer agreements, the rule on prior disclosure of charges, and the requirement to obtain a customer's prior written consent before he is given credit. Rule 5–52 provides that a firm will commit a rule breach where it fails to carry out a matter which it is required to state under the rules that it will do, or where it does something which it is required by the rules to state that it will not do.

Therefore, if a firm fails to comply with a statement which it is required by the rules, in the circumstances, to insert in an advertisement or in a customer agreement, it will be in breach of this rule. This rule is necessary because, by including the statement in the advertisement or customer agreement, it will not have broken the rule which required such a statement, and the statement may not specifically relate to a matter which is caught by an obligation owed in any of the other rules.

Staff supervision

As we have already seen, Principle 9 requires a firm to have adequate arrangements to ensure that its employees, agents and appointed representatives are suitable in respect of the investment business activities which they carry on, and that they are adequately trained and properly supervised. This requirement is supported by SFA's requirements on individual registration for directors, partners, managers, representatives and traders. It should also be remembered that firms' appointed representatives, and any of their staff carrying out the activities of a registered representative, must be individually registered with SFA. These individual registration requirements, supported by the appropriate examination passes or exemptions for the main categories of registered representative and trader, are an important way in which SFA can be assured that a firm is employing suitable staff who have the necessary qualifications for their positions. It should also be noted that, when submitting an individual registration application, a firm has to support it by confirming, on the basis of appropriate vetting, including the taking-up of satisfactory references, that the applicant is competent to conduct investment business on behalf of the firm and is a fit and proper person to be admitted to the particular register.

Firms will need to ensure that proper supervision is given to staff. Obviously, the level of supervision will depend upon the grade of staff and the type of activities carried on. Firms should have proper arrangements for providing continuous training and up-dating. They should keep staff aware of new business practices and developments so that the staff remain competent to carry out the functions for which they are employed and to provide the best service to their firms' customers. Further, firms should ensure that staff are regularly trained and up-dated on any aspects of the rules which relate to their employment functions. In fact, Rule 5–51(1) requires a firm to ensure that all its employees, including those of its appointed representatives, act in conformity with their own and their firm's relevant responsibilities under the regulatory system; with the statutory provisions against insider dealing; and with the firm's arrangements on personal dealings.

Staff dealings   Rule 5–51(2) to 5–51(11)

20–005   Staff who work in member firms may, through their employment, acquire information which may amount to inside information. If they deal, or arrange for someone else to deal, on the basis of it, they may commit a breach of the insider dealing legislation. Also, there may be temptations for staff to put their own interests first before those of the firm's customers: for example, by dealing for themselves ahead of customers' orders or dumping stock which they no longer want into customer accounts.

Personal Account Notice

To this extent, it is important that firms exercise careful control over personal dealings by staff. To support firms in this aspect, SFA requires that every employee should be given a written notice, called the Personal Account Notice, which sets out the firm's restrictions on staff dealings. The minimum restrictions which must be contained in the Notice are those set out in SFA's rules, but there is no reason why a firm should not impose more restrictive provisions than those required by the rules.

Employees

An employee is defined to include, not merely employees under a contract of service, but also persons employed as independent contractors under a contract for services, or under any other contract or arrangement whereby an individual is required to provide services to the firm, or is placed at the disposal and under the control of the firm. Therefore, the term includes employees of one company being seconded to an SFA firm for a particular job or to provide particular services. It also includes directors and partners, and, in relation to an unincorporated association, any member of its governing body, and its secretary and treasurer.

Summary of Insider Dealing Act

Where the firm's business involves securities or derivatives on securities, the Notice must contain a summary of the Company Securities (Insider Dealing) Act 1985. The restriction to securities and derivatives on securities is because these are the only investment instruments covered by the Act. It does not extend to derivatives on commodities. For a fuller discussion on the insider dealing legislation see Chapter 16 above.

Written undertaking

To emphasise the importance of the restrictions on personal dealings, SFA requires a firm to ensure that all its employees enter into a written undertaking with the firm to observe the requirements of the Notice, including, if the firm's business involves securities or derivatives on securities, the provisions of the insider dealing legislation. By entering into such a written undertaking, compliance with the restrictions in the Notice becomes an important condition of an employee's employment with his firm. A breach, therefore, could amount to a significant breach of his contract of employment, entitling his employer to dismiss him without notice. There is no need for the actual Notice to be signed if, instead, the employee has signed a contract of employment which specifically refers to the Notice, wherever it may be set out (such as in a compliance manual), as amended from time to time.

Act of misconduct

It should be noted that a failure to comply with any requirement of a Personal Account Notice amounts to an act of misconduct for which SFA may institute disciplinary proceedings against the firm, a registered person, or both (Rule 7–23(2)(f)).

Prior permission

The Notice must require that an employee cannot deal for his own account, without prior permission from his firm, in investments of any kind in which his firm carries on regulated business to any material extent, or in any investments related to such investments. It is important to note that the restriction only relates to investments of the type in which the firm carries on SFA authorised business, and related investments. If a firm deals in equities, related investments could be company debentures, options and futures contracts related to shares and debentures, or contracts for difference based on share indices.

The permission required from the firm does not have to be given separately for each transaction. A firm may give a general permission to all employees to deal in certain types of investments up to predetermined limits. For example, it could grant a general permission to deal in any shares within the FT-SE 100 Index (except for those included on any Restricted List issued by the firm from time to time) provided the transaction size does not exceed, say, £5000 in value.

Conflicts with customers

20–006 The Notice must prevent the employee from dealing for his own account with any of the firm's customers, unless they are other authorised persons, listed money market institutions or overseas investment businesses. He must not deal at a time, or in a manner, which he knows, or should know, is likely to have a direct adverse effect on the particular interests of any of the firm's customers; and he must also not deal if he knows or should know that his firm or its associate intends to publish written research material which could reasonably be expected to affect the price of the relevant investment. These restrictions enable a firm to control conflicts between the interests of its employees and those of its customers. To this extent, the Notice must also require that the employee does not accept any gift or inducement from another person which is likely to conflict with his duties to any customer of the firm. (Note that this is not restricted by a reference to "significantly" conflicting, as in the case of the similar restriction on firms: Rule 5–7 and paragraph 15–021 above.)

Reports

Once he deals, the employee must report promptly the details of the transaction to his firm, unless: either he has arranged for his firm to receive promptly a copy of the relevant contract or confirmation note; or he dealt through his firm or an associate of the firm which is an authorised person or listed money market institution. It should be noted that this reporting requirement applies even in cases where a general permission has been given to all employees in respect of the type of transaction involved.[1] Although separate confirmation is not required where the deal is done through the firm or an authorised associate, the firm will, nevertheless, need to make sure that it is able to monitor such deals properly. Of course, some firms find that the most appropriate way of controlling personal account dealings by staff is to ensure that all their dealings are done through the firm itself; and often solely on an execution-only basis.

Compliance Department control

The Notice must identify the Compliance Officer, or another employee designated by him, as the person responsible for granting permissions and receiving details of the relevant transactions. Personal dealings ought to be controlled by the Compliance Department, who, in most firms, will be in a position to make a more independent judgment about the dealing than a line manager in a normal revenue-earning area.

Separate account designation

A firm must designate its employees' own accounts, and any other accounts subject to the Notice requirements (as explained below), in a way which enables them to be distinguished from other customer accounts. It does not matter how this designation is done, as long as the accounts are clearly distinguishable. This will obviously enable firms to monitor more easily personal dealings, as well as making it simpler for SFA to inspect such transactions.

Control receipt of gifts

In addition, a firm must establish and maintain compliance procedures designed to ensure that no employee accepts any gift or inducement which is likely to conflict with his duties to any of the firm's customers. Obviously, one of these procedures will be the restriction in the Personal Account Notice referred to above. A firm may decide that it is necessary to draw up a list of, on the one hand, acceptable benefits, and, on the other, unacceptable inducements. It may be appropriate for the Compliance Officer to require reports from all employees of the main details of any gifts and other benefits which they receive.

Acting as trustee

The Personal Account Notice must extend its provisions to dealings **20–007** by the employee in his capacity as a personal representative of an estate, or as a trustee of a trust, where, in either case, he, his associate, or any company or partnership controlled by him or his associate, has a significant interest (even if an unconnected third party makes the day-to-day decisions). It must also extend to any other dealings by him as a personal representative or trustee (namely, the beneficiaries are unconnected), except where he is relying entirely on the advice of another person from whom it is appropriate to seek advice in the circumstances. In other words, the estate or trust has employed another person, acting in an independent capacity, to advise it or manage the investments for it.

Associates

The Notice must also prevent the employee dealing for the account of another person unless the dealing is done in the normal course of his employment. In other words, the restrictions should apply where the employee is dealing for the account of an associate of his, such as a business colleague or a member of his close family. "Associate" includes any person whose business or domestic relationship with the employee might reasonably be expected to give rise to a community interest between them which may involve a conflict of interest in dealings with third parties.

Procuring others to deal

Where the employee is prevented from entering into a transaction for his own account, the Notice must direct that, except in the proper course of his employment, he must not procure another person to enter into such a transaction, or pass on information to another person in circumstances where he has reason to believe that the other will deal, or counsel or procure another person to deal. This extension mirrors the scope on the restriction against insider dealing in the 1985 Act.

Packaged products and discretionary transactions

There are a number of qualifications. To begin with, the restrictions in the Notice do not apply in respect of transactions in packaged products: namely, units in regulated collective investment schemes, life policies and investment trust savings schemes (see Chapter 14 above). Also they do not apply to discretionary transactions entered into without prior communication with the employee, provided the discretionary account is not managed by his firm.

Temporary staff

The Notice is not required for temporary employees, provided they will not be involved to any material extent in the firm's regulated business. A temporary employee is not defined, except to the extent that it is an employee who is "not regularly employed by the firm". The term is really intended to cover an employee filling a position on a temporary basis from an employment agency, such as covering for holiday and sickness absences or whilst a permanent replacement is recruited. If the temporary employee will be involved significantly in the firm's investment business, then the exemption is lost. In other words, the Notice would be required for temporary dealers, but not for temporary secretaries, receptionists and administrative clerks.

Overseas employees

There is another exception for overseas employees provided they are not based in the United Kingdom for any period over 29 days in any 12-month period.

Non-executive directors

There is a new qualification relating to non-executive directors. The Notice restrictions only have to apply to them in respect of their dealings in the firm's securities or those of any other company within the same group, or in any investments related to such securities. In 1988 and 1989 there were some notable resignations from some TSA member firms by non-executive directors who were directors of a number of companies and who felt that obtaining prior permission for all their share dealings was too onerous and too much of an invasion of their privacy. Obviously, the extent to which personal dealings by its non-executive directors should be supervised by a firm depends upon the particular director's involvement in the firm's business. If he is quite active and will attend Board meetings where sensitive issues are discussed relating to the firm's corporate finance business, the firm may think that it is appropriate to treat its non-executive directors as any other employee for the purposes of restricting personal dealings.

Group monitoring

Finally, a firm may delegate the performance of all the above requirements on personal dealings by staff to another undertaking in the same group. This may be appropriate where there is a single group Compliance Department which supervises the compliance operation for all companies within the same group.

Criminal Law

Although the Personal Account Notice only refers to one specific **20–008** piece of criminal legislation, namely the Company Securities (Insider Dealing) Act 1985, a firm should, in training and supervising its staff, ensure that they comply with all aspects of the law. In particular, employees' attention should be drawn to the following:

(i) *Misrepresentations.* Any person who makes, whether intentionally or recklessly, a statement, promise or forecast which is misleading, false or deceptive is guilty of an offence if he makes it for the purpose of inducing, or is reckless as to whether it may induce, another person to enter into an investment agreement or otherwise make a decision relating to investments (section 47(1) of the FSA 1986).

(ii) *Misleading Practices.* Any person who engages in any conduct which creates a false or misleading impression as to the market in, or the price or value of, any investments commits an offence if he does so for the purpose of inducing another person to enter into an investment agreement or make any other decision relating to investments (section 47(2) of the FSA 1986).

(iii) *Money Laundering.* Any person who accepts funds or investments, or facilitates their retention or control by another, knowing or suspecting that they are the proceeds of drug trafficking or terrorism commits an offence (section 24 of the Drug Trafficking Offences Act 1986 and section 11 of the Prevention of Terrorism Act 1989). "Facilitates" includes concealment, removal from the jurisdiction of the United Kingdom courts, transfer to nominees, and, obviously, an exchange into another currency or investment. A person may be guilty of a money laundering offence even if he did not know that the funds or investments were the proceeds of drug trafficking or terrorism. It is only a defence if he can show that he did not know and had no reasonable cause to suspect that the funds or investments were related to such activities; or if he immediately discloses his suspicions to the police. Both Acts provide a statutory protection against a person's breach of a duty of confidentiality in making such disclosure. In fact, section 18 of the Prevention of Terrorism Act makes it an offence not to disclose information which is believed to be of material assistance in preventing an act of terrorism or in relation to identifying someone who has committed such an act.

Records

20–009   Rule 5–54(1) requires a firm to take reasonable steps, including the establishment and maintenance of procedures, to ensure that sufficient information is recorded and retained about its regulated business and compliance with the regulatory system. This relates to the requirement to keep proper records under Principle 9. The specific detailed requirements for records in respect to safe custody, client money and financial supervision have already been examined in Chapters 17, 18 and 19 above. This section deals with the records which are more appropriate to compliance with the Conduct of Business Rules. The point to be emphasised is that a firm may need to keep additional records to the details specifically referred to in the rulebook (whether relating to financial or conduct of business matters) to comply with the general obligation in Rule 5–54(1).

All records which are required to be maintained under the FSA 1986 regulatory system may be inspected by any person appointed for this purpose by SFA. They must be produced promptly to that person on request. They may be made and held in any form, as long as they are capable of prompt reproduction in hard printed form in English.[2] In terms of a firm's compliance with the Conduct of Business Rules, it must, at the minimum, maintain the records of events and matters specified in Appendix 18 to SFA's rulebook.

The records required in Appendix 18 must be retained for three years from the specified date. This is unlike the regulations and rules for client money and financial supervision, which require retention for six years. For the period during which a firm is required to keep the records under Appendix 18, it must make available on request, within a reasonable period, to any existing or former private customer or non-private discretionary customer those parts of any written material and records which relate to that customer and which the firm has sent to, or is required to send to, the customer under the Conduct of Business Rules. It must also make available to him any correspondence received from him relating to regulated business; in this respect, even if it related to a non-conduct of business matter, such as client money or safe custody. It should be noted that it is only those parts of the firm's records which relate to items sent to, or which should have been sent to, the customer and items received from him which have to be made available to him. A firm does not have to make available any other part of its records. Also, the rule is silent on the question of payment. Therefore, as long as a firm complies with Rule 5–33 (paragraphs 9–013 *et seq.* above), it would be able to charge a reasonable fee for providing copies of the records.

The records which are required under Appendix 18 are as follows:

(i) *Advertisements.* A firm should keep a copy of any specific investment advertisement which it issues and a copy of any investment advertisement which it approves. The reason for only requiring copies of specific investment advertisements in relation to advertisements issued by the firm is so that it need not maintain copies of every item of advertising information which it transmits electronically on a screen-based information system. It is only where such information amounts to the promotion of a specific investment or investment service that it has to be recorded. A firm must, however, keep a copy of every advertisement which it approves for an unauthorised person; recording the date of approval, and the name and address of the person for whom the advertisement has been approved. As discussed in paragraph 12–009 above, firms may wish to retain more detailed records on advertisements to enable them to prove, if challenged, that they applied appropriate expertise and believed on reasonable grounds that the particular advertisement was fair and not misleading.

20–010   (ii)   *Customers.* A firm must keep proper information about all its customers.[3] This extends to recording a customer's categorisation in accordance with the rules, together with the information relied upon by the firm in making the particular categorisation. If the customer is an overseas resident who does not want written documentation, the firm must record its evidence to support its belief that the customer does not want such documentation. As already explained in paragraph 6–003 above under "overseas customers", a memorandum of a telephone conversation would be sufficient.

Full information must be included about the customer's circumstances and investment objectives if he is a customer to whom the firm owes the suitability obligation (Rule 5–31). To encourage firms to keep this information up-to-date, the firm is required to include the date on which the information was last up-dated or checked.

A firm must record all the details provided on the contract, confirmation and similar notes required under Rule 5–34, plus all the information sent to customers on the portfolio or account valuations required under Rule 5–35. The firm does not have to keep physical copies of the contract notes and valuations, as long as it is able to reproduce, if requested, all the information which was included on a particular note or statement.

All written communications between the firm and its private customers and between the firm and its non-private discretionary customers must be maintained; and the firm must record all details relating to complaints from any customer.

The records must be kept for three years from the date after which the customer ceases to be an active customer of the firm, except that correspondence, contract notes and valuations only have to be retained for three years from the date of the relevant communication. Also, details concerning complaints only have to be kept for three years from the finalisation of the firm's handling of the complaint.

(iii)   *Employees.* Records are required with respect to the firm's controls on personal account dealing by its employees. They are also required in respect of any other directorships or partnerships, or stakes of 15 per cent. or more in another body corporate, held by the firm's registered directors or partners. An up-to-date list of all its individually registered staff must be maintained, including those who were registered within the previous three years.

(iv) *Group Details.* Records are required on the firm's subsidiaries, associates and controllers, as defined (see paragraph 3–006 above).

(v) *Transactions.* Details are required in respect of all customers' orders,[4] recording when received and when executed. The records should be able to identify the employee who received the order, the one who passed it on for execution and the one responsible for execution. Any special instructions given by the customer should be recorded. The purpose for requiring such detail is to enable both the firm and SFA to monitor the firm's proper compliance with the dealing rules (see Chapter 11 above). In respect of the requirement to identify employees involved in the receipt and execution of orders, the maximum number of employees who need to be identified is three. Not all employees through whom an order passes, such as runners on a trading floor, need to be identified. The reference to identifying the employee who passes on the order for execution is really intended to cover the situation where the firm passes an order to another firm for execution, rather than executing it itself.

(vi) *Soft Commission Agreements.* As pointed out in paragraph 15–023 above, a soft commission agreement may be oral, rather than written, but a firm must keep a copy or memorandum of the details of any such agreement. Details of the agreement are required for three years after it ceases to be in force.

Complaints

Each SRO, as a condition of its authorisation by SIB, must have **20–011** effective arrangements for the investigation of complaints against its member firms (paragraph 6(1) of Schedule 2 to the FSA 1986). Hence, SFA maintains a Complaints Bureau. As part of the system of self regulation, however, SFA expects each of its member firms to have proper procedures in place for the handling of complaints from its customers. These procedures must ensure that appropriate remedial action is readily taken by the firm; and, if the complaint is not promptly remedied, that the customer is advised of his right to refer his complaint to SFA's Complaints Bureau.

It is important to realise that, initially, it is up to the firm to handle a customer's complaint. Each firm, however small, must have procedures in writing which should be known to every employee who has contact with any of the firm's customers. The procedures must ensure that each complaint is investigated promptly and fully by a senior person in the firm who was not originally involved in the matter giving rise to the complaint. If there is no such individual because of the small size of the firm, then the complaint must be investigated by the most senior person in the firm. A firm is required to keep a copy of every written customer complaint, together with any response given or action taken by the firm.

It should be noted that the rule requirements (Rules 6–1 to 6–4) for handling complaints apply to all complaints, whether made orally or in writing, except that the record-keeping requirements only apply to written complaints. No definition is given of a complaint, but it is suggested that a complaint arises where a customer is dissatisfied in some way with the service provided by the firm. It is not a complaint where a person merely makes an enquiry as to why he has not yet received the proceeds of the sale of his investments or asks for further detail as to how the firm's charges have been calculated. Such an enquiry would become a complaint if the firm fails to answer the enquiry satisfactorily. The reason for restricting the record-keeping requirement to written complaints is to prevent bureaucratic procedures operating. If the complaint never passes the stage of an oral communication, it is more likely that it was, in reality, an enquiry, or that it has been settled promptly.

If the complaint is not remedied promptly, the customer must be advised of his right to complain to SFA; even if his complaint is only an oral one. A firm satisfies this requirement by sending him a copy of the explanatory booklet produced by SFA's Complaints Bureau which gives information about the investigation and conciliation services offered by SFA.

Each complainant to SFA is required to set out his complaint in writing. The Complaints Bureau will investigate the matter provided that: the complaint relates to any business for which the firm was subject to SFA authorisation; the firm has had a reasonable opportunity to investigate the complaint; and the complaint is not already subject to another form of dispute resolution, such as civil proceedings or arbitration. The other point to note is that SFA will only investigate complaints relating to events or omissions arising on or after April 29, 1988, the date on which the FSA 1986 authorisation requirements came into force. At present there is no time limit as to how soon the complaint must be made to the firm or referred to SFA after the matter complained about arose.

It is suggested that the reference to customer in the rules on complaints includes former customers and persons who are claiming that they should have been protected as customers by the firm. The old TSA rules made it clear that the reference to a customer included a former customer, and the current definition of customer includes a potential customer.

The complaints service offered by SFA is free of charge. (Likewise, even though there is no rule on the point, a firm should not charge a fee for handling a customer's complaint.) SFA will investigate the matter and try to conciliate between the parties if there is a genuine dispute. Many complaints arise from poor communication between a firm and its customers, giving rise to a misunderstanding on the part of the complainant. If SFA finds that there has been a rule breach, then it may instigate disciplinary proceedings against the firm. The firm is required to co-operate with any person appointed by SFA to investigate a complaint.

Arbitration

If SFA is unable to conciliate, the parties may take advantage of the **20-012** arbitration schemes offered by SFA. There are two schemes: the Consumer Arbitration Scheme and the Full Arbitration Scheme. The Consumer Arbitration Scheme is available to existing or former private customers of a firm where the value of the claim does not exceed £50,000. A person may use this scheme if his claim is that he should have been protected as a private customer: for example, if the firm denies that it owed him customer obligations, or if his claim is that he was wrongly categorised by the firm as an expert investor (a category of non-private customer: see paragraphs 5-026 *et seq.* above).

Once a private customer has elected to use the Consumer Arbitration Scheme, the firm must: submit itself to the scheme; not refer the claim for adjudication by any other tribunal (except to seek interlocutory relief to protect any assets); and co-operate fully and promptly in the conduct of the arbitration. It should be noted that, unlike in the case of complaints, the submission to arbitration must be made within two years of the act or omission giving rise to the dispute, or, if the dispute has been the subject of an attempt at reconciliation by SFA's Complaints Bureau, within six months from the Bureau certifying that the dispute could not be resolved by such means.

The purpose of the Consumer Arbitration Scheme is to provide a quick and inexpensive resolution of the dispute. A single arbitrator is appointed, who will normally decide the case on the basis of written submissions and documents. He may hold an oral hearing if he considers it necessary to dispose of the proceedings fairly. Neither party is allowed to be legally represented, save in exceptional circumstances and with the permission of the arbitrator.

All the costs of the arbitration are borne by SFA, except that the claimant is required to pay a non-returnable registration fee of £10. Neither party is entitled to recover their costs, unless one of them has acted scandalously, frivolously, or vexatiously. In this case, the arbitrator has the discretion to award costs, but these are limited to a maximum of £500 in the case of a claimant.

Any other dispute (namely, a dispute involving more than £25,000, or a dispute between a firm and a person other than a private customer, including a dispute with a market counterparty) may be settled under SFA's Full Arbitration Scheme. The procedures are similar to those under the Consumer Arbitration Scheme, except that, if both parties so request, it must be determined by a panel of three arbitrators. Also, the parties have a right to be legally represented at any stage of the proceedings. The award made by the arbitrator may include an award of costs, which shall include the fees of the arbitrator and any experts or advisers appointed by him to report to him on any specific issues.

Monitoring

20–013   Each SFA firm is assigned to an inspection team. This team will monitor the firm's compliance with the rules. Any member of the team (or, in fact, any person appointed by SFA for the purpose) may: enter a firm's business premises without notice; require the attendance, upon reasonable notice, of any employee at a time and place specified by SFA; require such an employee to answer questions and give explanations on any matter within his knowledge which SFA considers relevant to its monitoring function; require the production of any of the firm's documents or records relating to its SFA authorised business; require, on serving a written Requisition Notice, the production of any other documents or records (not relating to the firm's SFA authorised business) to the extent that the documents or records fall within the class specified in the notice. SFA may record any telephone conversations or interviews with any of the firm's employees.

Post-visit letters

Following an inspection visit, the inspection team will normally write a post-visit letter to the firm, highlighting any concerns relating to the firm's compliance with the rules and raising some questions to be answered by it. The letter is intended as helpful advice to the firm. It is not part of any disciplinary process. Any suggestions which are included are intended as pointers as to how the firm may improve its compliance arrangements.

Warnings

Where SFA considers that a firm or registered person has failed, or intends or is likely to fail, to comply with a rule, it may serve a Warning. This specifies the act or omission, and the rule in question. Failure to comply with a Warning is not itself an offence, but will be taken into account by SFA's Disciplinary Tribunal in determining an appropriate penalty.

Directions

In a more serious case of an actual or suspected rule breach, SFA may issue a Direction rather than a Warning. A Direction sets out the steps which SFA requires the recipient (whether a firm or registered person) to take to remedy or avoid the breach. It will contain a time limit by which the relevant steps must have been completed. Failure to comply with a Direction is a disciplinable offence in itself.

Investigations

Besides conducting its normal monitoring visits, SFA may launch a specific investigation. Its powers on serving a Notice of Investigation are similar to those in respect of its ordinary monitoring work, except that they now apply, as well, to former firms and registered persons (see Chapter 3 above). Also, SFA can require the production of any documents and records which appear to be relevant to the investigation without the need for issuing a Requisition Notice.

Intervention orders

Where SFA considers that it is necessary to take urgent action, it will issue an Intervention Order. This may require a firm or registered person either to take specified steps or to desist from acting in a particular way. For example, it may be used to restrict the type of business being carried on; to prevent the disposal of assets, or to direct how they should be disposed of; or to prevent contact with particular persons. It can be used where urgent action is required to protect assets belonging to customers. As with a Direction, a breach of an Intervention Order is a disciplinable offence.

Disciplinary powers

In Chapter 3 we saw how SFA may take action against former firms **20–014** and registered persons provided an investigation or other enforcement steps are started within 12 months from the withdrawal from membership or registration.

SFA may institute disciplinary proceedings for any breach of SFA's rules; any breach of the FSA 1986 or provisions made under it; and failure to comply with a Direction or Intervention Order. SFA may also discipline for an act or omission of a firm which causes another firm to be in breach of the rules or the FSA 1986 (including provisions made under it); or an act or omission of a registered person which causes a firm or another registered person to commit a similar breach. As was noted in paragraph 20–005 above, SFA may discipline for non-compliance with a provision in a Personal Account Notice. It is a disciplinable act of misconduct: to provide false, misleading or inaccurate information to SFA; to fail to produce documents and records; or not to attend for interview and answer questions, as required by SFA.

Similarly, it is an act of misconduct not to comply with: a condition on membership or registration; the terms of a Settlement; a penalty imposed by SFA; or an award or direction made in an SFA administered arbitration. Finally, disciplinary action may be taken for a failure to comply with the continuing requirement to remain fit and proper.

Penalties

SFA's Disciplinary Tribunal may impose any conditions on membership or registration which it considers appropriate; and it may impose the penalties, in ascending severity, of a reprimand, severe reprimand, fine, suspension, expulsion from membership (in the case of a firm) or removal from a register (in the case of a registered person). In the case of a former registered person, the Tribunal may determine, in addition to awarding one of the above penalties, that the person should not be considered fit and proper to be admitted to any of the individual registers in future. Such a determination would prevent the person from being employed again as a registered person by any SFA firm.

Compensation

In imposing a penalty, the Disciplinary Tribunal may also make an order requiring the defendant, whether a firm or registered person, to pay compensation to a customer. Compensation will only be awarded where the Tribunal is satisfied that the customer has suffered a readily determinable loss as a result of the defendant's misconduct. The maximum compensation which may be awarded against any one defendant is £50,000, irrespective of the number of customers who have suffered loss.

Settlements

Instead of letting a disciplinary case run its full course, a firm may agree with SFA to a Settlement. The terms of a Settlement shall include a statement of the facts admitted by the defendant, and the penalties and any other conditions imposed. Once it is ratified by SFA's Enforcement Committee, it becomes binding in the same way as a decision of the Disciplinary Tribunal.

Publicity

SFA will give such publicity as it considers appropriate to the making of an Intervention Order, the imposition of any penalty, the terms of any Settlement, the termination of a firm's membership or individual's registration, the imposition of any conditions, and the award of compensation and costs. Such publicity acts as a deterrent to other firms and registered persons from committing rule breaches, as well as identifying the miscreants involved and publicising SFA's enforcement role.

[1] Reports are not required, however, in respect of transactions in investments for which no permission is needed under the Personal Account Notice.

[2] Although Rule 5–54 does not state so specifically, it is the intention that a firm should be able to delegate its record-keeping obligations to a third party. The firm, however, still remains responsible for full compliance with the record-keeping requirements and must ensure that the records held by a third party are capable of being made available for inspection promptly: at least within 24 hours of any request. This is similar to the client money keeping record requirements already explained in paragraph 18–014 above.

[3] This includes indirect customers, but not market counterparties (see paragraph 5–002 above).

[4] The Record-Keeping Schedule (Appendix 18) only requires details on customers' orders, not non-customer orders, such as those relating to own account orders and orders for group companies and market counterparties; and, as explained in paragraphs 11–009 and 11–016 above, not every transaction will be entered into as a result of an "order". Nevertheless, it is good practice, and, in fact, may be necessary in order to comply with the general obligation about records in Rule 5–54 (1), for a firm to record the relevant details in respect of any instruction to deal (whether or not on "orders" and whether or not involving a customer). Also the requirement in the Schedule relating to recording details on the execution of a transaction apply to any transaction, including those for non-customers.

Appendix 1

The Principles

Integrity

1 A firm should observe high standards of integrity and fair dealing.

Skill Care and Diligence

2 A firm should act with due skill, care and diligence.

Market Practice

3 A firm should observe high standards of market conduct. It should also, to the extent endorsed for the purpose of this principle, comply with any code or standard as in force from time to time and as it applies to the firm either according to its terms or by rulings made under it.

Information about Customers

4 A firm should seek from customers it advises or for whom it exercises discretion any information about their circumstances and investment objectives which might reasonably be expected to be relevant in enabling it to fulfil its responsibilities to them.

Information for Customers

5 A firm should take reasonable steps to give a customer it advises, in a comprehensible and timely way, any information needed to enable him to make a balanced and informed decision. A firm should similarly be ready to provide a customer with a full and fair account of the fulfilment of its responsibilities to him.

Conflicts of Interest

6 A firm should either avoid any conflict of interest arising or, where conflicts arise, should ensure fair treatment to all its customers by disclosure, internal rules of confidentiality, declining to act, or otherwise. A firm should not unfairly place its interests above those of its customers and, where a properly informed customer would reasonably expect that the firm would place his interests above its own, the firm should live up to that expectation.

Customer Assets

7 Where a firm has control of or is otherwise responsible for assets belonging to a customer which it is required to safeguard, it should arrange proper protection for them, by way of segregation and identification of those assets or otherwise, in accordance with the responsibility it has accepted.

Financial Resources

8 A firm should ensure that it maintains adequate financial resources to meet its investment business commitments and to withstand the risks to which its business is subject.

Internal Organisation

9 A firm should organise and control its internal affairs in a responsible manner, keeping proper records, and, where the firm employs staff or is responsible for the conduct of investment business by others, should have adequate arrangements to ensure that they are suitable, adequately trained and properly supervised and that it has well-defined compliance procedures.

Relations with Regulators

10 A firm should deal with its regulator in an open and cooperative manner and keep the regulator promptly informed of anything concerning the firm which might reasonably be expected to be disclosed to it.

The Financial Supervision Core Rules

A. Financial resources. A firm must at all times have available the amount and type of financial resources required by the rules of its regulator.

B. Records and reporting. A firm must ensure that it maintains adequate accounting records and must prepare and submit such reports as are required by its regulator in a timely manner. A firm's records:

a. must be up to date and must disclose, with reasonable accuracy, at any time, the firm's financial position at that time;

b. must enable the firm to demonstrate its continuing compliance with its financial resources requirements, and

c. must provide the information:

(i) which the firm needs to prepare such financial statements and periodical reports as may be required by its regulator, and
(ii) which the firm's auditor (where the regulator requires one to be appointed) needs to form an opinion on any statements of the firm on which the auditor is required to report.

C. Internal controls and systems. A firm must, for the purpose of its compliance with rules on financial supervision, ensure that its internal controls and systems are adequate for the size, nature and complexity of its activities.

D. *Ad hoc* reporting. A firm must notify its regulator immediately it becomes aware that it is in breach of, or that it expects shortly to be in breach of, the core rules on financial resources (A), records and reporting (B) or internal controls and systems (C).

E. Auditors. A firm shall appoint an auditor where required to do so by its regulator. A firm shall make available to its auditor the information and explanations he needs to discharge his responsibilities as required by the firm's regulator.

Appendix 3

Application of Core Conduct of Business Rules to Customer Categories

Core Rule No.	Title	SFA Rule No.	Customers
1.	Inducements	(Rule 5–7)	All
2.	Material Interest	(Rule 5–29)	All
3.	Soft Commission	(Rule 5–8)	All
4.	Polarisation	(Rule 5–19)	Private
5.	5(1)–5(3) Advertisements	(Rule 5–9)	Not specifically related to customers
	5(4) Direct Offer Advertisements	(Rule 5–10)	Private
6.	Advertisements for Overseas Persons	(Rule 5–12)	Private
7.	Overseas Business for U.K. Customers	(Rule 5–13)	Private
8.	Overseas Business with Overseas Customers	(Rule 5–14)	Private
9.	9(1) Communications (not misleading)	(Rule 5–15(1))	All
	9(2) Communications (presented fairly and clearly)	(Rule 5–15(2))	Private
10.	Customers' Understanding	(Rule 5–30)	Private
11.	Information about Firm	(Rules 5–16 and 5–21)	Private
12.	Information about Packaged Products	(Rule 5–22)	Private
13.	Appointed Representatives	(Rules 2–32 and 2–36)	Not applicable
14.	Customer Agreements	(Rule 5–23)	Private (SFA extension to non-private discretionary)

Core Rule No.	Title	SFA Rule No.	Customers
15.	15(1) and 15(3) Customers' Rights	(Rule 5–24(1), (3))	All
	15(2) Customers' Rights (extension)	(Rule 5–24(2))	Private
16.	Suitability	(Rule 5–31)	Private (SFA extension to non-private discretionary)
17.	Advice on Packaged Products	(Rule 5–20)	Private
18.	Charges	(Rule 5–33)	Private
19.	Confirmations and Periodic Information	(Rules 5–34 and 5–35)	All
20.	Customer Order Priority	(Rule 5–37)	All
21.	Timely Execution	(Rule 5–38)	All
22.	Best Execution	(Rule 5–39)	All (any deal for private; fulfilling any order for non-private)
23.	Timely Allocation	(Rule 5–40)	Not applicable
24.	Fair Allocation	(Rule 5–42)	All
25.	Dealing Ahead of Publications	(Rule 5–36)	All
26.	26(1) Churning	(Rule 5–43(1))	All
	26(2) Switching (packaged products)	(Rule 5–43(2))	Private
27.	Derivatives Transactions on Exchange	(Rule 5–44)	Private
28.	Insider Dealing	(Rule 5–46)	All
29.	Stabilisation	(Rule 5–47)	Not applicable
30.	Off-Exchange Market Makers	(Rule 5–45)	Private
31.	Reportable Transactions	(Rule 5–49)	Not applicable
32.	Safe Custody	(Rule 4–1)	All
33.	Scope of Business	(Rule 2–19(2))	Not applicable
34.	Compliance	(Rules 5–51(1) and 5–54(1), (2))	Not applicable
35.	Complaints	(Rules 6–1 and 6–3)	All
36.	Chinese Walls	(Rule 5–3)	Not applicable
37.	37(1) Cessation of Business (by firm)	(Rule 2–21(1))	Private
	37(2) Cessation of Business (incapacity of individual with firm)	(Rule 2–21(2))	Private (SFA extension to all)

Core Rule No.	Title	SFA Rule No.	Customers
38.	Reliance on Others	(Rules 1–4 and 5–2)	Not applicable
39.	Classes of Customer	(Rule 5–5)	Private (being converted into non-private)
40.	Application	(Rule 5–1)	Not applicable

Total Core Conduct of Business Rules = 40

Total Core Rules applying to customers = 31

Total Core Rules applying to non-private customers = 15

Additional Core Rules applying only to private customers = 16

Appendix 4

Draft Model Prescribed Disclosure Statement

[In order to [execute [all] [the following types of] transactions on your behalf] [provide investment services to you [in types of investments specified by you]] we will introduce [you] [your business] to an overseas investment business who is not authorised to carry on investment business in the United Kingdom.]

[The investment services undertaken on your behalf (or provided to you) are not covered by the rules and regulations made for the protection of investors in the United Kingdom.]

This means that you will not have the benefit of rights designed to protect investors under the Financial Services Act 1986, and under the rules of the Securities and Investments Board (SIB) and the Securities and Futures Authority (SFA).

In particular you will [lose] [not benefit from] the following protections—

(i)   the right to claim through the Investors Compensation Scheme for losses resulting from a default of obligations owed under SIB's or SFA's rules;

(ii)   in the event of a dispute access to SFA's Complaints Bureau and arbitration scheme;

(iii)   protection of money held on your behalf under the SIB's Client Money Regulations;

(iv)   the obligation that your transaction must be executed at the best price available in the relevant market at the time;

(v)   the obligation that any charges levied on you must be disclosed in advance;

(vi)   the obligation that any advice or recommendations in respect of investments may only be made to you if they are considered to be suitable for you in accordance with your disclosed investment objectives and financial resources.

Firms may make reference here to any comparable protections provided in the jurisdiction within which the business is to be carried on.

Non-Private Customer Notice
(Re Rule 5–5)

On the information you have given us, we have categorised you as a non-private customer, by reason of your experience and understanding, in relation to [all investments] [the following kinds of investments] [all investments except those of the following kind].

As a consequence of this categorisation you will lose the protections afforded to private customers under the rules of the Securities and Futures Authority. In particular the protections in the following areas will not apply:

(a) Risk Warnings

We will not be obliged to warn you of the nature of any risks involved in any transactions we recommend for you, or provide you with written risk warnings in relation to transactions in derivatives and warrants.

(b) Customer Agreements

We will be under no obligations to set out in writing the basis on which the services are provided:

> This clause should be deleted in the case of a discretionary customer, when a two-way agreement will still be required.

(c) Prior Disclosure of Charges

The rules do not require us to inform you of the charges applicable in relation to the services we will be providing.

(d) Suitability

When making any recommendations to you, we will assume that you are in a position to judge the suitability of any advice given. The protections of the rule on giving suitable advice will not apply.

> This clause should be deleted in the case of a discretionary customer, when suitability will be owed.

(e) Packaged Products

We are not required to send you the detailed information which normally has to be made available to customers when dealing in unit trusts and life products.

> This clause may be deleted if the firm does not deal in packaged products, or they are not included in the service being provided to the customer.

(f) Client Money

As a result of you being treated as a non-private customer under the rules of SFA, any money received from you and held by us in respect of any investment agreement (called "client money") will not be subject to the protections conferred by the SIB's Client Money Regulations. As a consequence of this your money will not be segregated from our money, and may be used by us in the course of investment business.

Please sign below separately to consent to the treatment of your money outside the Client Money Regulations.

> This clause may be used in respect of the treatment of money held on behalf of non-private customers under paragraph 2 of Regulation 2.02 of the Client Money Regulations subject to paragraph 4 of Regulation 5.01 (Transitional provisions).

> Where a firm is voluntarily providing the protections in (a)–(f) above it may add a statement to this effect.

Please note that your rights to sue [the firm] for damages under section 62 of the Financial Services Act 1986 will be restricted as you will only be able to sue for breaches of obligations owed to you, which will *not* include the private customer protections outlined above.

You will also lose the right of access to the Consumer Arbitration Scheme of the Securities and Futures Authority.

If you have any queries on this notice or require any further information, please contact us.

NON-PRIVATE CUSTOMER NOTICE (RE RULE 5–5)

[name of firm]
_____

I/We have read and understood the notice and consent to be treated as a non-private customer.

Date

Signature of customer(s)
_____

I/We have read and understood the notice and consent to my/our money being treated outside the Client Money Regulations.

Date

Signature of customer(s)
_____

Conduct of Business/Client Money/Safe Custody Customer Disclosure and Consent Requirements

The following tables set out the various disclosure and consent requirements contained within the conduct of business rules and the client money and other assets rules in respect of regulated business carried on by firms for private and non-private customers including discretionary arrangements. These tables are offered as a guide to firms in determining the need for customer agreements in addition to the requirements contained in rule 5–23. The notification requirements in respect of market counterparties (rule 5–4) and indirect customers and agents (rule 5–6) have not been included.

Table I

Advisory Arrangements With Private Customers

Requirement (rule number)	One-Way Disclosure	Two-Way Consent	Comments
1. Written customer agreement for contingent liability transactions containing the relevant details in Table 5–23(4)(a) and (b) (5–23)(2)(a))		★	
2. Derivatives Risk Warnings (5–30)		★	Applicable whether advisory or execution-only.

Requirement (rule number)	One-Way Disclosure	Two-Way Consent	Comments
3. Warrants Risk Warning (5–30)		★	Applicable whether advisory or execution-only.
4. Prescribed disclosure when carrying on non-regulated business or introducing customers to a person who undertakes non-regulated business (including client money introductions) (5–13)	★		
5. Customer consenting to be treated as a non-private customer (5–5)		★	Subject to customer passing experience and understanding test and written warning of private customer protections lost.
6. Written warning to trade customer opting to be treated as ordinary business investor (5–5(4))	★		
7. Disclosure of basis or amount of charges (5–33(2))	★		Disclosure can be oral or written.
8. Disclosure of independence policy in respect of material interests (5–29(3))	★		Written disclosure where firm intends to rely on an independence policy.
9. Consent to underwriting commitments (5–25)		★	
10. Disclosure of rights to realise other assets in setting-off a default by a customer (5–26)	★		Written disclosure of default remedies or oral or written notice to customer of remedies to be exercised.
11. Borrowing for, or lending to, a customer (5–27)		★	
12. Notification of margin requirements (5–28(2))		★	Must form part of a two-way customer agreement.

Requirement (rule number)	One-Way Disclosure	Two-Way Consent	Comments
13. Granting unsecured loans for margining purposes subject to an adequate credit management policy (5–28(6))		★	
14. Notification of the maximum amount of any secured loan (5–28(6))		★	Must form part of a two-way customer agreement.
15. Disclosure that orders may be aggregated and that this may operate to customer's disadvantage (5–41)	★		Disclosure can be oral or written.
16. Statement of policy in relation to soft commission agreements (5–8(3))	★		
17. Periodic statement of transactions carried out under a soft commission agreement (5–8(4))	★		Applicable only to small business investors (subject to rule 5–8(4)(c))
18. Notification of obligations in respect of safe custody facilities (4–2)	★		
19. Notification that safe custody investments are to be registered in the name of an eligible nominee (4–1)	★		
20. Consent for depositing with, pledging or charging to a third party safe custody investments (4–8)		★	
21. Relevant risk warnings eg non-readily realisable investments, stabilisation, guaranteed stops, etc (5–30)	★		Oral at the time of making a recommendation.
22. Permission to cold call			Subject to SIB's Common Unsolicited Calls Regulations.

Requirement (rule number)	One-Way Disclosure	Two-Way Consent	Comments
23. Holding client money in trust in an overseas bank (CMR Reg 2.05(2))		★	
24. Customer opting out of receiving interest on client money (CMR Reg 4.02)		★	
25. Designated client bank accounts and designated client fund accounts (CMR Reg 2.07(5)(c) and (6)(c))		★	

Table II
Discretionary Arrangements With Private and Non-Private Customers

Unless otherwise stated, the requirements specified in this table apply to both private and non-private customers.

Requirement (rule number)	One-Way Disclosure	Two-Way Consent	Comments
1. Written customer agreement required setting out the relevant details contained in Table 5–23(4)(a) and (b) (5–23(2)(b))		★	
2. Derivatives Risk Warning (5–30)		★	Applicable only to private customers.
3. Warrants Risk Warning (5–30)		★	Applicable only to private customers.
4. Prescribed disclosure when carrying on regulated business or introducing customers to a person who undertakes non-regulated business (including client money introductions) (5–13)	★		Applicable only to private customers.

CUSTOMER DISCLOSURE AND CONSENT REQUIREMENTS

Requirement (rule number)	One-Way Disclosure	Two-Way Consent	Comments
5. Customer consenting to be treated as a non-private customer (5–5)		★	Applicable only to private customers and subject to experience and understanding test and written warning of private customer protections lost.
6. Written warning to trade customers opting to be treated as ordinary business investor (5–5(4))	★		Applicable only to private customers.
7. Disclosure of basis or amount of charges (5–33)	★		Applicable only to private customer and can be oral or written.
8. Disclosure of independence policy in respect of material interests (5–29(3))	★		Applicable only to private customers. Written disclosure where a firm intends to rely on an independence policy. Disclosure of actual material interest may be necessary in some circumstances (see guidance to rule 5–29).
9. Consent to underwriting commitments (5–25)		★	
10. Disclosure of rights to realise other assets in setting-off a default by a customer (5–26)	★		Applicable only to private customers.
11. Borrowing for, or lending to, the customer (5–27)		★	Applicable only to private customers.
12. Notification of margin requirements (5–28(2))		★	Must form part of a two-way customer agreement.
13. Granting unsecured loans for margin purposes subject to an adequate credit management policy (5–28(6))		★	

Requirement (rule number)	One-Way Disclosure	Two-Way Consent	Comments
14. Notification of the maximum amount of any secured loan (5–28(6))	★ (non-private)	★ (private)	For private customer must form part of a two-way customer agreement.
15. Disclosure that orders may be aggregated and that this may operate to customer's disadvantage (5–41)	★		Disclosure can be oral or written.
16. Statement of policy in relation to soft commission agreements (5–8(3))	★		
17. Periodic statement of transactions carried out under a soft commission agreement (5–8(4))	★		Applicable only to non-private customers and small business investors (subject to rule 5–8(4)(c))
18. Notification of obligations in respect of safe custody facilities (4–2)		★	Must form part of two-way customer agreement.
19. Notification that safe custody investments are to be registered in the name of an eligible nominee (4–1)		★	Must form part of two-way customer agreement.
20. Consent to deposit with, pledge or charge to, a third party safe custody investments (4–8)		★	Must form part of two-way customer agreement.
21. Relevant risk warnings concerning non-readily realisable investments, stabilisation, guaranteed stops (5–30)	★		Can be oral at the time of making recommendation or exercising discretion.
22. Permission to cold call			Subject to SIB's Common Unsolicited Calls Regulations.
23. Holding client money in trust in an overseas bank (CMR Reg 2.05(2))		★	

Requirement (rule number)	One-Way Disclosure	Two-Way Consent	Comments
24. Customer opting out of receiving interest on client money (CMR Reg 4.02)		★	
25. Disapplication of client money protections (CMR Reg 2.02(2))	★	★ (experts opting to be treated as non-private customers)	Applicable only to non-private customers and subject to written warnings.
26. Designated client bank accounts and designated client fund accounts (CMR Reg 2.05(5)(c) and (6)(c))		★	

Table III
Advisory Arrangements With Non-Private Customers

Requirement (rule number)	One-Way Disclosure	Two-Way Consent	Comments
1. Notification of margin requirements (5–28(2))	★		
2. Granting unsecured loans for margining purposes subject to an adequate credit management policy (5–28(6))	★		
3. Notification of the maximum amount of any secured loan (5–28(6))	★		
4. Disclosure that orders may aggregated and that this may operate to a customer's disadvantage	★		Disclosure can be oral or written
5. Statement of policy in relation to soft commission agreements (5–8(3))	★		

Requirement (rule number)	One-Way Disclosure	Two-Way Consent	Comments
6. Period statement of trans-actions carried out under a soft commission agreement (5–8(4))	★		
7. Notification of obligations in respect of safe custody facilities (4–2)	★		
8. Notification that safe custody investments are to be registered in the name of an eligible nominee (4–1)	★		
9. Notification of intention to deposit with, pledge or charge to, a third party safe custody investments (4–8)	★		
10. Holding client money in trust in an overseas bank (CMR Reg 2.05(2))		★	
11. Customer opting out of receiving interest on client money (CMR Reg 4.02)		★	
12. Disapplication of client money protections (CMR Reg 2.02(2))	★	★ (experts opting to be treated as non-private customers)	Subject to written warnings.
13. Designated client bank accounts and designated client fund accounts (CMR Reg 2.05(5)(c) and (6)(c))		★	

Appendix 7

Model Clauses
For Customer Agreements

- Model clauses for use as part of—

Two-way agreements with private advisory customers in respect of contingent liability transactions, or two-way agreements with private or non-private discretionary customers entered into in accordance with rule 5–23(2) (customer agreements).

Other agreements entered into with customers at firm's discretion to take account of the disclosure and consent requirements in the rules.

- Part 1 refers to clauses that may be used in both one-way and two-way customer agreements.

- Part 2 refers to clauses that may be used only in two-way customer agreements as the customer's written consent is required before the provision can be relied upon under SFA's rules.

Although model clauses have not been provided in respect of the following, firms may wish to include such clauses as part of their customer agreements—

- a warning to private customers that telephone calls may be recorded and used as evidence in the event of a dispute;
- arrangements for amending the terms of the agreement;
- arrangements for terminating the agreement;
- a statement as to the governing law relating to the agreement.

Part 1

(A) The Services We Will Provide

We will provide investment advisory and dealing services in the following investments, [together with related research, valuation and safe custody facilities]:–

407

*(i)   shares in British or foreign companies:

*(ii)   debenture stock, loan stock, bonds, notes, certificates of deposit, commercial paper or other debt instruments, including government, public agency, municipal and corporate issues;

*(iii)   warrants to subscribe for investments falling within (i) or (ii) above;

*(iv)   depositary receipts or other types of instruments relating to investments falling within (i), (ii) or (iii) above;

*(v)   unit trusts, mutual funds and similar schemes in the United Kingdom or elsewhere;

[*(vi)   options on investments falling within (i), (ii) or (iii) above provided the related transaction has no contingent liability;]

[**(vi)   options on investments falling within (i), (ii), or (iii) above, including options on an option;

**(vii)   futures on investments falling within (i), (ii) or (iii) above;

**(viii)   contracts for difference.]

[In respect of [all] [the following] investments] [deals executed on the following markets] we [will] [may] enter into transactions with you as a principal and not act on your behalf as agent. We will, nevertheless, continue to be subject to the rules and regulations of SFA, and the Principles of conduct requiring us to act in the best interests of our customers.] [If we act as a principal you will be notified at the time of dealing [and a statement will be included on the contract note].]

---

* One-way agreements can only be used to provide investment services in respect of these investments.

** The provision of investment services in respect of these investments can only be made under a two-way agreement.

In respect of the provision of investment services to private customers in warrants, options, futures and contracts for difference firms are reminded that the relevant risk warning notices must be signed. These may be incorporated into a customer agreement, subject to the customer being required to sign separately that he has read and understood the notice. Clause (N) referring to margining arrangements may also need to be considered.

(B) Execution-Only Arrangements

Please note that we will not advise you about the merits of a particular transaction if we reasonably believe that, when you give the order for that transaction, you are not expecting such advice and are dealing on an execution-only basis. In such circumstances, we will inform you at the time that we will execute your order on that basis.

(C) Your Investment Objectives

We are proceeding on the basis:–

(i) that your current investment objectives are [a balanced return from income and from capital growth] [primarily to maximise income] [primarily to maximise capital growth]; and

(ii) that you are prepared to accept a [low] [moderate] [high] level of risk, [subject to a [moderate] [high] level of risk in respect of [   ] per cent. of your investment in terms of acquisition cost].

If this is incorrect or you would like to discuss your investment objectives with us, it is important that you should contact us as soon as possible. We will confirm in writing any amendments to the above objectives.

Firms may rely on a separate letter completed by the customer or a separate document which the customer is asked to complete in order to establish his investment objectives, and may refer to that letter or document instead of using the above wording.

(D) Restrictions on Types of Investment

If you do not inform us of any investments or types of investments which you do not wish us to recommend to or purchase for you, we may recommend to you any investment which falls within any of the categories set out in (A) above. [However, under the rules of the Securities and Futures Authority, we may recommend to you only investments which we have reasonable grounds for believing are suitable for you.]

(E) Charges

Our charges will be in accordance with our published rate card in effect at the time the charges are incurred (a copy of our current rate card accompanies this letter).

Any alteration to these charges will be notified to you at or before the time of the change.

> Details of interest payable by the customer in respect of late payments should also be set out if not contained on the rate card.

We may share dealing charges with our associated companies or other third parties, or receive remuneration from them in respect of transactions carried out on your behalf. Details of any such remuneration or sharing arrangements will not be set out on the relevant contract note or confirmation note, [but can be made available to you on request] [but are set out below for your information].

> This paragraph is not mandatory but should be included if details are not to be set out on the contract note or confirmation note (rule 5–34(9)).

(F) Conflicts of Interest

> The following wording may only be used where the firm has a written independence policy and requires its employees to comply with that policy.

Your attention is drawn to the fact that when we give you investment advice, we, an associated company or some other person connected with us, may have an interest, relationship or arrangement that is material in relation to the investment, transaction or service concerned. However, our employees are required to comply with a policy of independence and disregard any such interest when making recommendations to you.

When we recommend a transaction to you or enter into a transaction for you, we [or one of our associated companies] could be—

(i)   dealing as principal for our [or its own] account by selling the investment concerned to you or buying it from you; or

(ii)   matching your transaction with that of another customer by acting on his behalf as well as yours;

(iii)   buying or selling units in a collective investment scheme where we are [or an associated company is] the trustee, operator (or an adviser of the trustee or operator] of the scheme;

(iv)   buying investments where we are [or an associated company is] involved in a new issue, rights issue, takeover or similar transaction concerning the investment.

(G) Aggregating Orders

We may combine your order with our own orders and orders of other customers. By combining your orders with those of other customers we must reasonably believe that we will obtain a more favourable price than if your order had been executed separately. However, on occasions aggregation may result in you obtaining a less favourable price.

(H) Default Remedies

In the event of your failure to make any payment or to deliver any securities due to us (or agents used by us) we reserve the right to retain any funds, securities or other assets due to you and to offset the liability against them.

> Firm to include full particulars of its proposed remedies in respect of transactons in which a customer has defaulted.

(I) Non-Readily Realisable Investments

We may enter into transactions on your behalf in non-readily realisable investments. These are investments in which the market is limited or could become so; they can be difficult to deal in and it can be difficult to assess what would be a proper market price for them. Please inform us if you do not wish to be advised in respect of such investments.

(J) Off-Exchange Transactions

We may deal for you in circumstances in which the relevant deal is not regulated by the rules of any stock exchange or investment exchange. Please inform us if you do not wish us to enter into such transactions for you.

> Firms should note that they are not permitted to effect off-exchange contingent liability transactions for private customers unless they are to hedge against currency risk (rule 5–44).

(K) Stabilisation

We may deal for you in investments that may have been the subject of stabilisation.

Stabilisation is a price supporting process that may take place in the context of new issues. The effect of stabilisation can be to make the market price of the new issue temporarily higher than it would otherwise be. The market price of investments of the same class already in issue and of other investments whose price is related to the price of the new issue may also be affected.

This process is undertaken in order to ensure that the issue of investments is introduced to the market in an orderly fashion, and that the issue price and/or the price of associated investments is not artificially depressed because of the increase in supply caused by the new issue.

Stabilisation may only take place for a limited period, and there are limits on the price at which shares, warrants and depositary receipts may be stabilised (although there are no limits in respect of loan stock and bonds).

Please inform us if you do not wish to be advised in respect of such investments, or you do not wish us to enter into transactions in such investments.

> Firms to note that notwithstanding this clause disclosures may be necessary at the time of dealing in order to fully comply with the provisions of rule 5–30(1).

(L) Custody of your Investments

All securities or unit trusts purchased through us will be registered (except for bearer stocks) in your name, or, subject to your agreement, in the name of an eligible nominee or eligible custodian in accordance with the rules of the Securities and Futures Authority.

> Firm to include here details of the registration of investments where they are to be registered in the name of an eligible nominee or eligible custodian.

We will account to you promptly for all dividends, interest payments and other rights accruing to you.

We will obtain your instructions before—

    (i)   exercising on your behalf conversion and subscription rights and voting rights regarding your holdings; and

    (ii)   proceeding on your behalf in takeover situations, other offers or capital re-organisations concerning your holdings.

In the event of a default by an eligible custodian used by us we [will] [will not] be liable to the extent of

> Firm to include details of the extent to which it will be liable for default by an eligible custodian.

Should you fail to provide instructions by the stated time once notification has been given, we cannot be held liable to you for the outcome of such situations.

Part 2

The following clauses may not be incorporated as part of a one-way customer agreement as the customer's written consent is required before the provision can be relied upon under SFA's rules.

(M) Customer Borrowing

Please tick the "Yes" box below if you wish us to have authority, without referring to you first, to borrow money for you [on the security of your investments] to pay for purchases of other investments (including taking up rights), and to sign or execute on your behalf any documents which we consider to be appropriate.

Please indicate below the maximum amount we may borrow for you [on security of your investments:]

£ ——————— (exclusive
of interest
and charges)

Please indicate whether or not we may, without prior reference to you, enter into a transaction on your behalf which will or may result in you having to borrow money.

Please indicate below the maximum amount we may borrow for you:

£ ——————— (exclusive
of interest
and charges)

(N) Margining Arrangements

Please indicate below whether or not you may wish to enter into transactions in the following types of investments which will result in you having to provide margin payments.

Transactions in options	Yes/No
Transactions in futures	Yes/No
Transactions in contracts for difference	Yes/No

Providing margin payments means that you will be required to make further variable payments against the purchase price of the investment, instead of paying (or receiving) the whole purchase (or sale) price immediately. The movement in the market price of your investment will affect the amount of margin payment you will be required to make.

Margin may be provided in the form of cash or acceptable collateral.

If after a period of [ ] business days you fail to meet a call for margin payments made on you, we will be entitled to close out the position and use any collateral or cash held by us for that purpose, including investments held on your behalf. The rules of SFA require us to close out the position in any event if you fail to meet a call for margin payment on five consecutive business days.

> Firm to include details of any other circumstances which may lead to the customer's position being closed out without prior reference to him.

If you have ticked any Yes box, please set out below any limits or restrictions which you wish to apply as regards providing margin.

(O) Underwriting/Sub-Underwriting Commitments

Please indicate whether or not we may enter into transactions for you which commit you to underwriting or similar obligations in connection with a new issue, rights issue, takeover or similar transaction.

YES/NO

If you have ticked the Yes box, please indicate whether or not we can commit you to underwriting or similar obligations in connection with an issue, takeover, or similar transaction in which we and/or an associated company have been involved as sponsor, financial adviser, underwriter, lending bank or in some other capacity.

YES/NO

Please set out below any limit or restriction that you wish to apply.

(P) Portfolio/Account Valuations

We shall prepare valuations of your [portfolio] [account] as at

> Firms should describe the basis of the valuation.

[The valuation will [not] include a measure of portfolio performance [which will be on the following basis].]

(Q) Extent of Discretion

We will manage for you on a discretionary basis your [portfolio] [account] of cash and investments. Subject to any instructions from you, we shall have full authority at our discretion, without prior reference to you, to enter into any kind of transaction or arrangement for your account. Under the rules of the Securities and Futures Authority we may only exercise discretion in accordance with your investment objectives and in a manner that we believe to be suitable for you.

The above is subject to any limits or restrictions which you specify.

Please set out below any limit or restriction that you wish to apply—

  (i)   on the type of investment in which we may enter into transactions on your behalf; or

  (ii) on the amount of the consideration which may be involved in any transaction on your behalf or in any class of transactions on your behalf; or

  (iii) on the value of any investments or any class of investments which may be held for you; or

  (iv) in relation to any similar matters.

(R) Money Held on Your Behalf (Client Money)

We are obliged to treat money held by us on your behalf in accordance with the Securities and Investments Board's Client Money Regulations. Among other things, this requires us to hold your money in a bank account at an approved bank.

Group Banks

The following paragraph is subject to paragraph 6 of Regulation 5.01 (Transitional Provisions).

[The approved bank at which your money is held may be [ourselves or] a company which is associated with us.]

Firm to insert here the name of the associated company concerned.

Overseas Banks

> The following paragraphs are only necessary where the firm intends to hold money at a bank outside the United Kingdom.

Please indicate below whether or not we may hold client money on your behalf in a client bank account in a branch of an approved bank situated outside the United Kingdom.

We will hold money at [a bank] [banks] situated in

> Firm to insert here the country or territory in which the approved bank[s] [is] [are] situated.

The bank[s] concerned [has] [have] [has not] [have not] acknowledged to us that—

   (i)   all money standing to the credit of the account is held by us as trustee [as agent] and that the bank is not entitled to combine the account with any other account or to exercise any right of set-off or counterclaim against money in that account in respect of any sum owed on any other account of ours;

   (ii) interest earned on the account will be credited to the account, or to an account of that type; and

   (iii) the title of the account sufficiently distinguishes the account from any account containing money that belongs to us, and is in the form requested by us.

         [As a consequence of the bank not acknowledging the above matters, client money held with that bank might not be protected as effectively as money held in a client bank account in the United Kingdom.]

         YES/NO

> The following clause should be used where a firm intends to hold client money in a client bank account outside the UK, and has grounds for believing (other than the absence of the acknowledgement referred to above) that client money held in that account will not be protected as effectively as if it were held in a client bank account in the UK.

Please indicate below whether or not we may hold client money on your behalf in a client bank account outside the United Kingdom, even though this may result in your money being protected less effectively than if it were held in a client bank account in the United Kingdom.

YES/NO

Designated client bank account

Please indicate below whether we may hold client money on your behalf in a client bank account designated solely to you at the bank stated below. Your account will be opened with

> Firm to insert here the name of the approved bank with which the client money is to be held.

YES/NO

Designated client fund account

Please indicate below whether we may hold client money on your behalf in a client fund account designated for a number of clients at the bank stated below.

The designated client fund account in which your money will be held will be opened with

> Firm to insert here the name of the approved banks with which the client money is to be held.

YES/NO

> Note that designated client bank accounts and designated client fund accounts are optional accounts which a firm may wish to offer to clients.

Interest payable to clients

> Firm to include any arrangements agreed with the client in respect of the payment of interest on money held for him.

> If, as a result of these arrangements, the interest payable is to be less than under Regulation 4.01 of the Client Money Regulations, that fact should be given prominence.

(S) Lending or Pledging Collateral

Please indicate below whether or not we may pledge or charge to a third party collateral deposited with us (other than for safe custody) for the third party to use as collateral for its own obligations. Such collateral registered with a third party [will] [will not] be in your name.

YES/NO

Please indicate below whether or not you agree to collateral being returned to you which is equivalent but not identical to collateral originally deposited with the firm.

YES/NO

Index

All references are to paragraph numbers

Accountants
as ordinary business investors,
5–023—5–024
indirect customer confirmation,
5–048
see also **Agents; Auditors;
Customers, indirect**
Accounting practices. *See* **Financial
resources requirement**
Adequacy test, 1–006—1–007
Core Rules, 1–014
Adequate Credit Management Policy,
8–006
Advertising
criminal liability for, 15–016, 20–008
investment advertisements,
authorised issue, 12–001
criminal liability for, 12–001
definition of, 12–001
exceptions and exemptions,
12–002—12–005
direct offers, 12–018—12–021
information requirement,
12–020
fair and clear communications rule,
12–008, 12–011
fair and not misleading test,
12–009—12–010
reissues of, 12–007—12–008
risk warnings, 12–017
SFA application rules,
12–006—12–007
Misleading Advertising Directive
(EC), 12–012
overseas business, 4–017, 12–023
prescribed disclosure, 4–021
retention of copy, 20–009
short form advertisements, 12–015
specific investment advertisements,
12–013—12–014

Advertising—*cont.*
specific investment advertisements—
cont.
contents requirements,
12–016—12–017
Adviser firms
definition of, 19–001
AFBD. *See* **Association of Futures
Brokers and Dealers Limited**
Agents
appointment to overseas customers,
5–044
as customers, 5–041
authority of, 5–043
independence of, 5–044
indirect customers. *See* **Customers,
indirect**
recipient of communications, 2–012
reliance on, 5–045, 9–001
requirement for authorised persons,
5–046
responsibilities for settlement, 5–048
TSA rules on intermediaries, 5–045
two-way agreements, 6–003
see also **Principals**
Aggregation rule. *See* **Customers'
orders**
Agreements, customer. *See* **Customer
agreements**
Allocation. *See* **Customers' orders**
Appointed representatives. *See*
Representatives
Arbitration schemes (SFA). *See*
Securities and Futures Authority
Arranger firms
definition of, 19–001
financial reporting requirements,
19–007
Associated business. *See* **Regulated
business**

419

Reporting of financial position. *See*
  Financial resources requirement
Representatives
  appointed, 3–014
    client money, 18–002
    identity and status, 6–009
    inability to register as trader,
      3–012
    relationship to customers,
      5–003
    restriction on unsolicited calls,
      13–009
  corporate finance, 3–009
  futures and options, definition of,
    3–009
  general, definition of, 3–009
  money market, 3–009—3–010
  registration with SFA, 3–009
  securities, definition of, 3–009
  see also **Traders**
Research. *See* **Front-running**
**Resignation of membership (SFA
  firms).** *See* **Securities and Futures
  Authority**
Restricted lists, 15–019
Return of financial reports. *See*
  Financial resources requirement
RIE. *See* **Recognised Investment
  Exchange**
Risk, Understanding of
  advertisements. *See* **Advertising**
  customers as underwriters,
    8–008
  private customers,
    additional warnings and
      explanations, 7–006—7–008
  Core Rule, 7–001
  discretionary business excepted,
    7–005
  in investment objectives, 9–007
  oral warnings, 7–004
  stabilisation. *See* **Stabilisation**
  written warnings, 7–002—7–003
  see also **Credit; Default; Margin;
    Underwriting**
Risk warnings. *See* **Derivatives Risk
  Warning Notice; Non-readily
  realisable investments; Risk,
  Understanding of; Warrants Risk
  Warning Notice**
RPB. *See* **Recognised Professional
  Bodies (RPB)**

**Rule guidance and interpretation
  (SFA).** *See* **Securities and Futures
  Authority (SFA)**

Safe custody, 17–001—17–006
  application of rules, 4–009
  client money. *See* **Client money**
  collateral, 17–006
  disclosure and consent requirement,
    Appendix 6
  reconciliations of books and records,
    17–005, 18–015, 19–006
  safe custody investments, 17–002
  Safekeeping Rules, 17–002
    definition of customer, 5–005
  segregation of investments, 17–004
  statements to customers, 17–005
Safekeeping Rules. *See* **Client money,
  safekeeping; Customers,
  Safekeeping Rules; Safe custody,
  Safekeeping Rules**
Scheme management
  application of SFA rules,
    4–042—4–043
Section 62 (FSA 1986)
  experts, 5–037
  limitation to private investors,
    1–004—1–005
  non-individuals, 5–039
  right of civil action under,
    1–002—1–005
  see also **Investors**
**Securities and Futures Authority
  (SFA)**
  application of the Principles to
    registered persons, 1–009
  arbitration schemes, 20–012
  authorisation powers, 3–001—3–014
  authorised business. *See* **Authorised
    business (SFA)**
  Complaints Bureau, 20–011
  compensation orders, 1–005,
    1–008, 20–014
  compliance regime. *See* **Compliance
    regime**
  conduct of business rules. *See*
    **Conduct of Business Rules
    (SFA)**
  Disciplinary Tribunal, 20–014
  fit and proper person test,
    3–005—3–006
  inspection teams, 20–013